RANDOM
HOUSE
LARGE
PRINT

The
Yankee
Years

The Yankee Years

JOE TORRE AND TOM VERDUCCI

RANDOM HOUSE
LARGE PRINT

Published in the United States of America by
Random House Large Print in association with
Doubleday, New York.
Distributed by Random House, Inc., New York.

Cover design by Greg Mollica
Front cover photograph © Reuters/Mike Segar
Back cover photograph © Al Tielemans/Sports
Illustrated/Getty Images

The Library of Congress has established a Cataloging-
in-Publication record for this title.

ISBN: 978-0-7393-2832-3

www.randomhouse.com/largeprint

FIRST LARGE PRINT EDITION

10 9 8 7 6 5 4 3 2 1

This Large Print edition published in accord with
the standards of the N.A.V.H.

Joe Torre

To my wife, Ali, for all of her love, encouragement and support during our magical years in New York, and to our daughter, Andrea, whose first 12 were the Yankee Years.
Love you!

Tom Verducci

For Kirsten, Adam and Ben, the joys of my life.

Contents

x **CONTENTS**

The
Yankee
Years

1.

Underdogs

J oe Torre was the fourth choice.

The veteran manager was out of work in October of 1995, four months removed from the third firing of his managerial career, when an old friend from his days with the Mets, Arthur Richman, a public relations official and special adviser to Yankees owner George Steinbrenner, called him with a question.

"Are you interested in managing the Yankees?"

Torre made his interest known without hesitation.

"Hell, yeah," he said.

Only 10 days earlier, Torre had interviewed for the general manager's job with the Yankees, but he had no interest in such an aggravation-filled job at its $350,000 salary, a $150,000 cut from what he had been earning as manager of the St. Louis Cardinals before they fired him in June. His brother Frank Torre did not think managing the Yankees was worth the hassle, either. After all, Steinbrenner had changed managers 21 times in his 23 seasons of ownership, adding Buck Showalter to the bloody casualty list by running him out of town after Showalter refused to acquiesce to a shakeup of his coaching staff. It didn't matter to Steinbrenner that the Yankees reached the playoffs for the first time in 14 years, even if it was as the first American League wild card team in a strike-shortened season. Showalter's crimes in Steinbrenner's book were blowing a two games to one lead in the best-of-five Division Series against the Seattle Mariners, and resisting the coaching changes.

"Why do you want **this** job?" Frank Torre asked his brother.

"It's a no-lose situation for me," Joe replied. "I need to find out if I can do this or not."

Richman also had recommended to Steinbrenner three managers with higher profiles and greater success than Torre: Sparky Anderson, Tony LaRussa and Davey Johnson. None of those choices panned out. Anderson retired, LaRussa took the managing job in St. Louis and Johnson, returning to his ballplaying roots, took the job in Baltimore. LaRussa and Johnson received far more lucrative contracts than what Steinbrenner wanted to pay his next manager.

"I've got to admit, I was the last choice," Torre said. "It didn't hurt my feelings, because it was an opportunity to work and find out if I can really manage. I certainly was going to have the lumber."

On Wednesday, November 1, Bob Watson, in his ninth day on the job as general manager after replacing Gene Michael, called Torre while Torre was driving to a golf course in Cincinnati. Watson summoned him to an interview in Tampa, Florida. That evening, Torre met with Steinbrenner, Watson, Michael, assistant general manager Brian Cashman and Joe Molloy, Steinbrenner's son-in-law and a partner with the team. The next morning, Torre was introduced as the manager of the Yankees at a news conference in the Stadium Club of Yankee Stadium, standing in the same spot where Showalter had stood twelve months earlier as the 1994 AL Manager of the Year.

It was an inauspicious hiring in most every way. Steinbrenner did not bother to attend the introductory event of his new manager. The press grilled Torre. Not only had Torre been fired three times, but also he was 55 years old and brought with him a losing record (894-1,003), not one postseason series victory, and the ignominy of having spent more games over a lifetime of playing and managing without ever getting to the World Series than any other man in history. Torre was a highly accomplished player, even a star player, for 18 seasons with the Braves, Cardinals and Mets. He was named to nine All-Star teams and won one Most Valuable Player Award, with the Cardinals in 1971. When he played his last game in 1977, Torre was one of only 29 players in baseball history to have amassed more than 2,300 hits and an OPS+ of 128 (a measurement of combined on-base and slugging percentages adjusted for league averages and ballpark effects, thus making era-to-era comparisons more equitable). His career profile, however, was dimmed by never having played in the postseason.

Torre's baseball acumen and leadership skills were so highly regarded that the Mets named him a player/manager at age 36 during the 1977 season. He ceased playing that same year, the first of his five years managing awful Mets teams. When the Mets fired him after the 1981 season, the Braves, owned by Ted Turner, quickly snapped him up. Torre immediately led the Braves to their first division title in 13 years. He lasted only two more seasons with Turner's Braves. Torre spent almost six years out of baseball, serving as a broadcaster with the California Angels, until the Cardinals hired him to replace the popular Whitey Herzog in 1990. Those five seasons were the only seasons in which Torre did not play or manage in the major leagues since he broke in as a 20-year-old catcher in 1960 with the Milwaukee Braves, a team that also included Hall of

Famers Hank Aaron, Eddie Mathews and Warren Spahn and Joe's brother Frank.

One of Torre's great strengths as a manager was that he understood what it was like to both star and struggle at the major league level. For instance, he hit .363 when he won the MVP Award in 1971, and 74 points lower the very next year. "And I tried just as hard both years," he said. One day in 1975 with the Mets, Torre became the first player in National League history to ground into four double plays, each of them following a single by second baseman Felix Millan. He reacted to such infamy with humor. "I'd like to thank Felix Millan for making all of this possible," he said.

At his introductory news conference, Torre displayed his cool demeanor and ease in front of a hostile media crowd. He answered questions with humor and optimism, and did not hesitate to talk about his lifetime goal of winning the World Series, something the Yankees had not done in 17 years, the longest drought for the franchise since it won its first in 1921. He knew Steinbrenner had grown restless.

"When you get married, do you think you're always going to be smiling?" Torre said at the news conference. "I try to think of the potential for good things happening. That's the World Series. I know here we'll have the ability to improve the team . . . To have that opportunity is worth all the negative sides."

All in all, Torre was not warmly received as the replacement for a popular young manager Steinbrenner had chased off after a playoff season. He was an admitted last choice for the job, and soon heard even after his hiring that Steinbrenner was working back channels to see if he could bring Showalter back. Critics regarded Torre as a recycled commodity without portfolio. Torre was in Cincinnati with in-laws on the day after his news conference when a friend from New York called him up.

"Uh, have you seen the back page of the **Daily News?**"

"No, why?"

The New York **Daily News** welcomed the hiring of Torre with a huge headline that said, "CLUE-LESS JOE." The subhead read, "Torre Has No Idea What He's Getting Himself Into." It referenced a column written by Ian O'Connor in which O'Connor said that Torre "came across as naïve at best, desperate at worst." Wrote O'Connor, "It's always a sad occasion when man becomes muppet." A last choice, a placeholder for Showalter, a man without a clue, a muppet . . . this is how Torre was welcomed as the new manager of the New York Yankees. None of it bothered him.

"It didn't matter to me," Torre said. "I was so tickled to have the opportunity that none of it mattered. I was a little nervous starting out with it.

Every time you get fired there is always something you think you can do better. I started thinking, maybe I have to do this different or that different. And then one day before spring training began, I was thumbing through a book by Bill Parcells, the football coach. He said something like, 'If you believe in something, stay with it.' And that was enough for me."

Under Torre's recommendation, with input from Torre's new bench coach, Don Zimmer, Watson's first major player move was to acquire a strong defensive catcher to replace Mike Stanley, who was popular with Yankees fans for his hitting but was never known for his defense. On November 20, Watson traded relief pitcher Mike DeJean to the Colorado Rockies for Joe Girardi. It was the start of a frantic, sometimes curious 40-day period in which Watson, with assistance from Michael and, of course, Steinbrenner, assembled nearly a third of the 1996 roster, getting Girardi, first baseman Tino Martinez, reliever Jeff Nelson and outfielder Tim Raines in shrewd trades, signing second baseman Mariano Duncan and pitcher Kenny Rogers as free agents, and re-signing third baseman Wade Boggs and David Cone, their own free agent.

———

Actually, Cone's signing had less to do with Watson but instead illustrated the sheer force and will Steinbrenner exerted over the baseball operations of the

Yankees, who were the richest club in baseball but had yet to grow into the financial behemoth that would put them so far ahead of the 29 other franchises. In 1995, Steinbrenner spent $58.1 million on payroll, the most in baseball, but a somewhat reasonable 19 percent more than the second-biggest spender, the Baltimore Orioles. The 1996 Yankees would draw 2.2 million fans to Yankee Stadium, ranking them seventh among the 14 American League teams.

Cone was set to re-sign with the Yankees until Watson called his agent, Steve Fehr, to suddenly reduce the terms of the deal. An angered Cone immediately entered into negotiations with the Orioles, negotiations that moved so quickly the Orioles began internal plans for an afternoon news conference to announce his signing. One small hangup remained, however.

"I probably would have signed if it wasn't for those guys in the front office haggling over deferred money at zero percent interest," Cone said. "I'm telling you, when I talked to my financial guys they said it may be a couple hundred grand they were haggling over at that point. Not to piss on a couple hundred grand, but in the grand scope of things, a couple hundred grand shouldn't hold things up."

While the Orioles were holding up the deal, Steinbrenner called Fehr from a pay phone at a hospital, where he was visiting an ill friend. He asked Fehr to put Cone on the line.

"I had been with the Yankees only since the middle of '95," Cone said, "and hadn't had much workings with George. I just heard stories about how tough he was to deal with. He told me, 'We need you. We want you.' He said all the right things and swayed me right back, because I was right on the fence. He said, 'Everything we offered you is back on the table.' He apologized, called it a misunderstanding. He kind of threw Bob Watson under the bus a little bit. He blamed him, which I think was Bob just doing his job. But my heart was in New York. I had an apartment in New York. It's what I wanted."

Cone agreed to a three-year contract worth $19.5 million. Steinbrenner completed the deal with a vision for the future.

"We want you not just for this deal," Steinbrenner told Cone, "but for the rest of your career. Before your career is over with the Yankees, you'll be pitching in a new ballpark on the West Side of Manhattan and I hope we're drawing three million people a year."

Even Steinbrenner had no idea just how big a brand the Yankees would become.

That Steinbrenner could cut a huge free-agent deal from a hospital pay phone at a moment's notice spoke to his impact on the entire organizational culture. If he wanted something done, it was done. There was no haggling over deferred money with zero interest. Steinbrenner was himself one of the best closers in baseball, especially when motivated by intense criticism that came about because of the breakup with Showalter, as well as whirlwind changes that swept out popular Yankees such as Stanley, Randy Velarde and Don Mattingly, who faded into retirement. Steinbrenner's last-minute call from the pay phone, stealing Cone out from under the Orioles, the Yankees' main competition in the AL East, was a key moment in the building of a dynasty. Cone would become the most respected leader of the Yankees' four world championship teams under Torre. Cone was the glue, if not the very spirit, of the dynasty. In addition to being a ferocious competitor, Cone was a skilled, willful tactician in handling the New York media. His rapport with the media allowed more quiet types, such as Bernie Williams and Paul O'Neill, the best hitters on the team, to play free of the media responsibilities that typically fall to front-line everyday players in New York.

"I kind of fell into that role in my career," Cone said, "by watching Keith Hernandez and some of the Mets the way they did it. I remember watching Frank Cashen, the Mets general manager, talking in the dugout to reporters and going, 'On background guys . . .' and then talking on the record. You watched how they handled it and you could develop a little closer relationship with the writers. Those were the days when you could go out and have a beer with the writers after a game. It was a different animal.

"I think I was at least somebody my teammates with the Yankees knew wasn't doing it for self-promoting purposes. That's what I was always worried about: would it come across as self-promoting? That was a balancing act. I think going through the 1994–95 strike and being a de facto spokesman on the players' side really helped a lot. I was trying to flip everything, reverse everything, and trying to be a stand-up guy. And going through the strike and finding myself on the Yankees the year after the strike, I knew all the writers at that point. I just kind of fell into it."

On the first day of the 1996 spring training camp, Torre gathered his team for a meeting. Many of the players didn't know him and he didn't know many of the players. He looked around the room. Among the group were the veterans new to the team, such as Raines, Martinez, Nelson, Girardi, Duncan and Rogers; a 21-year-old rookie shortstop named Derek Jeter; returning outfielders Bernie Williams and Paul O'Neill, a guy people in the front office had warned him had a "selfish" streak; veteran pitchers Cone, Jimmy Key and John Wetteland; and young pitchers Andy Pettitte and Mariano Rivera. Torre's coaches were Zimmer, Mel Stottlemyre, Willie Randolph, Chris Chambliss, Tony Cloninger and Jose Cardenal.

"All of my coaches have been to the World Series," Torre told his team. "That's what I want. But I don't want to win just one. I want to win three of them in a row. I want to establish something here that's special. I don't want to sacrifice principles and players to do it one time. I want to establish a foundation to be the kind of ballclub that is going to be able to repeat."

Dick Williams, the former big league manager who was working with the Yankees as a special adviser, pulled Torre aside after the meeting and told him, "That was a hell of a meeting, one of the best I've ever seen."

Said Cone, "I remember right off the bat that calming influence that he had, the way he conducted team meetings, the way he talked to people. You could sense that he was going to be a calming influence. He had a lot of experience. There was still a lot of speculation at the beginning of spring training about Showalter, a lot of talk about George trying to bring him back. Maybe they were going to bump Joe upstairs and bring Showalter back. I remember the first couple of meetings showed how even-keeled and level he was."

———

The Yankees were getting Torre at the perfect time in his life. It wasn't just that his three managerial firings made him the made-to-order unflappable foil to Steinbrenner. "What's the worst that can happen? I get fired **again?**" he would tell reporters. The timing was just right also because in between his hiring and the start of camp Torre unburdened himself of a dark family secret he had been carrying ever since he was a boy growing up in Brooklyn. Torre's father, Joe Sr., was a New York City police detective who filled the family home with fear because of the physical and emotional abuse he brought upon his wife, Margaret. Joe, the youngest of five children, never was the direct target of such domestic violence, though it shaped who he was. Torre hated confrontation and loathed loud voices and noises. He so feared his father that if Torre saw his father's car parked outside the house when he came home from school, Torre would simply keep walking.

Torre suppressed those feelings and never spoke about his father's domestic abuse. Then, in December of 1995, Torre's wife, Ali, talked him into joining her at a Life Success seminar, a program designed to foster personal growth. Ali saw a guarded, aloof side to her husband. Each time she would say "We need to talk," she saw how he would grow tense. Maybe, she thought, the seminar could be helpful. Torre figured he would go through the motions of showing up at some new-age, self-help lecture. By the time the seminar and activities were over, Torre had emotionally unburdened himself to total strangers about the abusive household of his childhood. As a big league manager, Torre always preferred operating at low decibels, without confronting people. His method was to trust people and communicate in even, measured tones. But now his calm methodology was boosted by an inner peace that came from letting go of the dark family secret and understanding himself better. His personal confidence soared. His demeanor and optimism were exactly right for the 1996 Yankees, whose players returning from 1995 were pained by having blown the series to Seattle. They also had played under the tightly wound Showalter, who had played, coached and managed so long in the Yankees organization, where Steinbrenner's divide-and-conquer style of leadership was designed to keep everyone uncomfortable, that trust did not come easily to him.

"They had a taste of the playoffs," Torre said, "and I think they were grown up enough to know somebody has to make the decisions. Whether you like me or believe me, you have to understand that. They were at the point where they knew in order to win we have to work together. And somebody has to point us in that direction."

Torre provided a complete contrast to Showalter's micro-management style. He gave his coaches and players a wide berth. One word kept coming up over and over again in the application of his management philosophy: **trust.**

"What I try to do is treat everybody fairly," Torre said. "It doesn't mean I treat everybody the same. But everybody deserves a fair shake. That's the only right thing to do. I'd rather be wrong trusting somebody than never trusting them.

"I'm of the belief that the game belongs to the players, and you have to facilitate that the best you can. I want them to use their natural ability. If they're doing something wrong, you tell them, but I'd like it to be instructive, rather than robotic. The only thing I want them all to think about is what our goal is and what the at-bats are supposed to represent. And that simply is this: 'What can I do to help us win a game?'"

Players quickly bought into Torre's management-by-trust style, and they did so because its abiding principle was honesty.

"Honesty is important to me. Where does it come from? I don't know, but even when I think back it was always something that was ingrained in me. Even now I may have trouble when I have to tell someone the truth if it's not a pleasant thing, but I won't lie to them. I can't do that. The only way you can get commitment is through trust, and you've got to try to earn that trust."

Torre applied the same principle to dealing with the media. His work as a broadcaster with the Angels and his gift for storytelling made him a naturally relaxed witness in front of the prosecutorial-leaning reporters and columnists in New York. He was informative without compromising his team. He was refreshingly honest.

"I may have misled the media, but I never know-ingly lied to the media," Torre said. "I may not have answered something directly or changed the subject and gone in a different direction, but I don't re-member purposefully lying to somebody.

"I thought it was an important part of the job, the media being such a big part of what goes on in New York. I thought it was my obligation to communicate with them so they would have the in-formation right from me. So I thought it was some-thing that there was no time limit on.

"My one point to the players was they were never going to read something that they haven't heard from me, at least something significant. And that's part of the trust I try to create."

———

Before the 1996 spring training camp even be-gan, Torre showed his trust in Cone by naming him his Opening Day pitcher. Jimmy Key, Andy Pettitte, Dwight Gooden and Kenny Rogers would take the spots behind him in the rotation. Unbe-knownst to Torre, however, Cone was suffering from a mysterious tingling in his fingers. It started when Cone reported early for spring training and simply was playing catch. The tingling grew so progressively worse that the fingernail on his right ring finger turned blue. Cone said nothing about it.

On Opening Day in Cleveland, Cone threw the kind of game that practically defined his Yankees career. It emphasized his flirtatious relationship with disaster, though somehow the two of them never actually met. He walked six Indians batters and none of them scored. In 38-degree weather, Cone threw seven shutout innings in a 7-1 win. As soon as he walked back into the clubhouse, he looked down at his right hand. It was ice cold and clammy, worse than it had been all spring. His entire right ring finger was blue. He approached trainer Gene Monahan and said, "Something's wrong with my hand."

The Yankees sent him to Columbia-Presbyterian Hospital in New York for an angiogram. The head vascular surgeon, Dr. George Todd, was on vacation at the time.

"They couldn't find anything," Cone said, "so they put me on blood thinners and ran me back out there to pitch again, which in hindsight was probably not the right thing to do."

The symptoms continued. When Todd returned from vacation and saw the angiogram, he feared something was wrong with Cone—probably an aneurysm, or a clot, somewhere in his circulatory system, a potentially deadly problem depending on where it was located—and they needed to bring him back in for another angiogram.

"I pitched a complete game against the White Sox," Cone said. "I was pitching great, leading the league in ERA. I couldn't figure it out. I was barely able to feel the ball. I guess I didn't try to overthrow. I was just painting with everything and getting away with it."

The angiogram was a grueling procedure. As Cone described it, it involved a catheter through the groin, massive painkillers and lying on his back on a steel table for hours. Cone, drugged, sore and tired, saw the doctors and nurses rush back into the room with smiles on their faces after studying the results of the angiogram. "We found the aneurysm!" they announced.

Said Cone, "I was like, 'Fuck you. Don't tell me that way!' They were so happy because they found it. 'You've got an aneurysm!' I was drugged up, but that's when I really got scared. I knew something was wrong. I just thought it was something in my hand. I didn't know it was up there."

The aneurysm was found in the upper area of the arm, in the shoulder region. On May 11, in a three-hour surgery, doctors cut two arteries, removed the aneurysm, and took a piece of a vein from his thigh to patch the connection and restore blood flow. The Yankees were 20-14, in first place, but without their ace and leader. No one could be sure when or if Cone would be back that season.

Cone had thrown 147 pitches in his final game of the 1995 season, the Yankees' Game 5 loss at the

Kingdome in Seattle against the Mariners. On his last pitch, he walked in the tying run. Cone was so tired and depressed after that game that he barely left his Manhattan apartment for days. His arm was so sore that even combing his hair was painful. Doctors could never draw a direct link between those 147 pitches and his aneurysm, but Cone was left to wonder about the possible connection.

"I don't think there's any way to know for sure because of the wear and tear," he said. "It's like a flat tire. When do you get it? But it had to have something to do with it, because I showed up the next spring and immediately had tingling in my fingers when I started throwing the ball again."

The 1996 Yankees, though, were an extraordinary team precisely because their fate did not rest with any one player. Nobody on the team hit 30 home runs, collected 200 hits or stole 20 bases. The offense was below average, ranking ninth in the 14-team league. The pitching was good, though not spectacularly so. It ranked fifth in ERA. The Yankees never won or lost more than five games in a row. Their strengths were their resourcefulness, the ability to find any crack or crevice in any game or any opponent and exploit it, and a lockdown bullpen that made winning on the margins not nearly as risky as it appeared to be. Rivera and Wetteland typically could be counted on for the final nine outs with little trouble. The Yankees made the most of a mediocre offense to win 92 games. They hit .293 with runners in scoring position. They were 25-16 in one-run games. They were 70-3 when they led after six innings.

Resourcefulness, however, was an art form not fully appreciated by Steinbrenner. An aficionado of football, military history and intimidation, Steinbrenner wanted to crush opponents, not just carve them up with singles and one-run wins. Even as the 1996 Yankees racked up many of those efficient victories, Steinbrenner would call up Torre to complain. Steinbrenner, however, could not bully this manager.

"I was so excited to be managing a club that had a chance to win that whatever he dealt out to me, I was in a great frame of mind with it," Torre said. "We'd be winning games and he'd be semi-embarrassed because we'd win on a squeeze bunt or a base hit. He wanted to mutilate people."

On Tuesday, June 18, Steinbrenner summoned Torre to his office at Yankee Stadium. The Yankees would win that day to improve their record to 39-28 and their first-place lead over the Orioles to 2½ games. Steinbrenner, though, remained uncomfortable, particularly with the Yankees, racked by injuries to their pitching staff, leaving for a four-game series against the hard-hitting Indians (a team that would lead the league in wins with 99). Steinbrenner was concerned that Torre planned to use two rookie emergency starters pulled from the bullpen, Brian Boehringer and Ramiro Mendoza, in a doubleheader. The rookies were followed by two starters from the back of the rotation, Rogers and Gooden. Steinbrenner wondered if there was somebody else, anybody with experience, who could pitch, even if it meant calling up someone from the minor leagues.

"I had no idea how we were going to win against Cleveland, with the pitchers we were sending to the mound," Torre said. "But I told him everything was going to work out."

Eventually Steinbrenner stopped roaring and said to Torre, "Fine, but it's your ass that's on the line."

It was a scenario that would be repeated many times over in Torre's years managing the Yankees. Steinbrenner was always nervous or anxious about something. Torre, banking on his optimism and his trust in his players, would soothe the restless, fearful Steinbrenner with some assurance that things would turn out just fine for his team. The calming influence that Cone and the players took note of from the first day of spring training was as vital a trait for Torre while dealing with Steinbrenner as it was while in the dugout and clubhouse dealing with his players. The lion would roar menacingly and Torre calmly would stick his head into the animal's mouth and come out smiling and unscathed. The Yankees won all four games in Cleveland, three of them by one or two runs.

"Well, you're doing it with mirrors!" Steinbrenner barked at Torre.

"We're playing solid baseball, Boss," Torre said. "We stay in the game and our bullpen wins it for us. That's the whole thing: we shorten the game. We turn it into a six-inning game with the guys we have coming out of the bullpen."

The Yankees built a lead over the Orioles that grew to as large as 12 games on July 28, only to shrink to 2½ games with 14 games to play after a 21-24 regression. The Yankees, though, held on with six wins in their next nine games while Baltimore stumbled. The winning pitcher in the clinching game was none other than Cone, who had come back in September from the aneurysm surgery.

——

The postseason became a 15-game version of their regular season. The Yankees capitalized on any opening and their bullpen was virtually unbeatable, losing only one game. The Texas Rangers had the Yankees six outs away from a two-games-to-none deficit in Game 2 of the best-of-five Division Series when the Yankees flashed their resourcefulness again. Bernie Williams began the eighth inning with a single, alertly moved to second on a deep fly ball, and scored on an opposite-field single by Cecil Fielder. They won in the 12th inning on a sacrifice bunt by Charlie Hayes, which third baseman Dean

Palmer threw away, allowing Jeter to score from second base.

It wasn't the kind of baseball Steinbrenner preferred, but it was smart, unselfish baseball and it was working. The Yankees' fortuitous play continued against Baltimore in the American League Championship Series, a series the Orioles might have led two games to none but for another strange eighth-inning comeback by the Yankees in Game 1. With the Yankees down to their last five outs, trailing 4-3, Jeter lofted a high fly ball to the right-field wall, where Orioles right fielder Tony Tarasco began to reach for it. Before the ball could come down into Tarasco's glove, however, a 12-year-old kid named Jeffrey Maier reached over the wall and deflected the baseball into the stands. Right-field umpire Rich Garcia ruled a home run. There could be no doubt about it now; the Yankees were getting help from above. The game was tied. The Yankees would win in the 11th inning on a home run by Williams. They also would win all three games in Baltimore, sending Torre to the first World Series in his life. Upon the final out, Torre broke down in tears in the dugout.

———

Disaster awaited Torre at the World Series. Playing for the first time in seven days, and against a red-hot and favored Atlanta Braves team, the Yankees were blown out in Game 1 at Yankee Stadium, 12-1. They were staring at Greg Maddux, the best pitcher in baseball, in Game 2 when Steinbrenner walked into Torre's office about 90 minutes before the game, fishing for some of that familiar Torre assurance.

"This is a must game," Steinbrenner said.

Torre barely looked up at him.

"You should be prepared for us to lose again tonight," he said nonchalantly. It was hardly the assurance Steinbrenner wanted. But then Torre continued: "But then we're going to Atlanta. Atlanta's my town. We'll take three games there and win it back here on Saturday."

Steinbrenner didn't know what to say. Here was Torre saying the Yankees would lose again, but then sweep four straight games from the Braves and their all-time great rotation that included Maddux, John Smoltz and Tom Glavine? It was crazy talk. Sure enough, the Yankees lost to Maddux, 4-0. They had been outscored 16-1, the worst combined beating in the first two games in World Series history.

Steinbrenner grew more fearful. He worried about getting swept and being "embarrassed," always one of his great worries. Steinbrenner was always talking about being "embarrassed." He called up Torre in his office before Game 3 in Atlanta. "Let's not get embarrassed," a nervous Steinbrenner said.

"We're fine," Torre told him.

Not everyone felt that way. Mike Borzello, the

bullpen catcher, remembers standing in the outfield during batting practice before Game 3 with Boggs and Martinez. All of them had the same thoughts as Steinbrenner.

"We were talking about how we just didn't want to get swept," Borzello said. "We were all saying, 'We've got to get one, because it will be embarrassing to go four and out. But this team is so much better than we are.' Really, that's how we felt until the tide turned."

Game 3, as well as the entire World Series, reached critical mass in the sixth inning when the Braves loaded the bases against Cone with one out, trailing the Yankees, 2-0. Fred McGriff, the Braves' lefthanded slugging first baseman, was due up. Graeme Lloyd, a lefthanded reliever, was throwing in the Yankees' bullpen. Torre walked to the mound, still not sure whether he would leave Cone in or replace him with Lloyd. The book move was to go lefty-on-lefty. Torre looked Cone squarely in the eye.

"This is very important," Torre said. "I need the truth from you. How do you feel?"

"I'm okay," Cone said. "I lost the feel for my slider a little bit there, but I'm okay. I'll get this guy for you."

But then Torre grabbed Cone and pulled him closer so that they were practically nose to nose.

"This game is very important," Torre said. "I've got to know the truth, so don't bullshit me."

Said Cone, "I had anticipated what the questions were going to be. Basically, 'Hey, are you okay?' 'Yeah, I'm fine.' 'Okay, how are we going to go after this guy?' He basically said, 'No, that's not good enough,' and turned me around nose to nose. He said, 'No, I need to know you're okay,' almost imploring me to tell the truth. He made eye contact with me and made me look him in the eye. He got closer and closer and grabbed me to pull me closer. He said two or three times, 'No, I need to know you're okay.'

"That's the first time I heard a manager do anything like that, saying it that way. I was fine, as good as I was going to be for a guy who rushed back to the team from surgery. I was not fully all the way back at that point. But I always thought I could make a pitch, a splitter or something. It's like playing golf where you think you can make a shot. Somehow, someway."

Cone convinced Torre to leave him in the game. He made a pitch to McGriff, who popped it up. Cone then walked Ryan Klesko, forcing in a run. "It was a borderline call," Cone said, "but if you make a mistake there he can juice one." Cone ended the inning by getting Javy Lopez on a pop-up, preserving a lead for the Yankees, who would go on to win, 5-2.

———

As important as Game 3 was, Game 4 would become the signature game for the 1996 Yankees. Down 6-0 in the sixth inning, Torre gathered his players in the dugout for an impromptu meeting and advised them, "Let's cut it in half right here. Take small bites. Do the little things to get one run at a time. Let's put a little pressure on them."

No Yankees team ever had won a World Series game by coming from that far behind. Only one team ever overcame a bigger deficit in the World Series, Connie Mack's 1929 Philadelphia Athletics. The Yankees immediately responded to Torre's advice. They scored three runs with their first four batters of the inning, stitching together three opposite-field singles and a walk for the quintessential '96 Yankees rally.

The game-tying rally was more bombastic: a three-run home run by Jimmy Leyritz off Atlanta closer Mark Wohlers with one out in the eighth, a blast made possible when Wohlers made the mistake of throwing a hanging slider because Leyritz looked as if he were timing his 99 mph fastballs by fouling them off. The Yankees won, 8-6, in the 10th inning with the tie-breaking run scoring on a pinch-hit walk by Wade Boggs, the last position player left on Torre's bench. Torre used seven pitchers, five pinch hitters and one pinch runner. He used every one of his players except three starting pitchers, Cone, Key and Pettitte. It was the fourth time in 13 postseason games that year that the Yankees won a game after staring at defeat from the close proximity of six or fewer outs away.

The series was tied at two games each, with the Yankees giving the ball to Pettitte in Game 5 and the Braves going to Smoltz. Torre had some difficult decisions to make with his lineup, the first of which he actually made immediately after Game 4. Torre told Leyritz he would catch Pettitte rather than Girardi, the defensive specialist.

"I said to Leyritz, 'You know what? I'm going to catch you with Pettitte tomorrow,'" Torre said. "'And the only reason you're catching Pettitte is because you hit a three-run homer. I wasn't going to catch you. So just make sure you do the right thing.' Because he always wanted to do things his way. He didn't want to follow the game plan of how we were going to pitch people. But that was his personality. 'The King.'"

Torre filled out the rest of his lineup when he arrived at the ballpark for Game 5. He chose to play Hayes instead of Boggs at third base—emphasizing the likelihood of groundballs there with the left-handed Pettitte pitching—the hot-hitting Fielder instead of Martinez at first base, despite facing a righthander; and Raines in the outfield instead of O'Neill, who was limited by a sore hamstring. Torre called Boggs, Martinez and O'Neill into his office one-by-one to break the news to them they would not be starting.

"Boggs was disappointed," Torre said, "Tino was the only one where you could see the anger, and Paulie just looked resigned. He was down. He walked out with his head down and his shoulders slouched."

As O'Neill left the office, Zimmer saw resignation on O'Neill's face. The danger with sitting O'Neill against Smoltz was that O'Neill would not be there mentally whenever Torre did have to go back to him. Zimmer thought about O'Neill's reaction.

"This guy has been playing on one leg all year," Zimmer said. "I think we really owe it to him."

Torre agreed. It gave him an idea: why not play Strawberry in left and O'Neill in right? He told Zimmer to bring O'Neill back into his office.

"Manager's prerogative," he told O'Neill. "I changed my mind. You're playing."

Meanwhile, Fielder, rising to the occasion, was walking around the clubhouse, telling anybody within earshot, "Just get on base! Somebody get on base, and Big Daddy's got you today! I'll get you in. Just give me somebody on base."

Sure enough, Fielder drove in the only run of the game with a double, one of his three hits. Torre's agonizing lineup decisions worked out well. Leyritz called a smart game. Pettitte threw shutout baseball one out into the ninth inning with the help of 14 groundball outs, three of them by way of Hayes. Torre even allowed Pettitte to bat in the top of the ninth inning with two outs and two on rather than use a pinch hitter and turn the game over to Wetteland.

"People were yelling from the stands, 'Are you guys crazy?'" Torre said. "Zimmer turned around and yelled back at them, 'Sit your ass down!'"

A few sections out of earshot, Pettitte's wife, Laura, was sitting next to Torre's wife, Ali.

"What's he doing?" Laura asked. "He's never done this before. Andy doesn't pitch the last inning!"

As Torre explained, "You had Chipper Jones leading off the ninth, who at the time wasn't as good a righthanded hitter. Freddie McGriff, who scared the shit out of me, was the second hitter. I know letting Andy hit in a 1-0 game probably wasn't the sanest thing to do. But I just wanted him to be the pitcher in the ninth inning.

"Of course, the first pitch Jones hits for a double down the leftfield line. Then McGriff hits a groundball to second base and the tying run is on third. I bring Wetteland in and Javy Lopez hits a one-hopper to third. I lucked out.

"Then I made another decision. I intentionally walked Ryan Klesko and pitched to Luis Polonia, even though Klesko was the winning run."

Now Torre's last major lineup decision—putting O'Neill back into the lineup—would come into play. Polonia kept fouling off pitches—five in a row—and coach Jose Cardenal kept trying to get

O'Neill to move toward center field because the lefthanded Polonia was not getting around on Wetteland's fastball.

O'Neill, as was his habit, was too busy working on his batting stroke, taking imaginary swings in right field. Cardenal tried waving a towel, and then two towels, and then three towels to get O'Neill's attention. Finally, just before Wetteland's seventh pitch to Polonia, O'Neill caught sight of the frantic Cardenal and moved a few steps to his right. Polonia hit the next pitch hard and to the right-center field gap. O'Neill hobbled after it and thrust his glove up as he neared the warning track.

If O'Neill caught the ball, the Yankees would be one win away from the world championship. If he did not catch it, both runners would score, the Yankees would lose the game, the Braves would be one win away from the title, and Torre would be roasted for letting Pettitte hit and start the ninth and for intentionally putting the winning run on base.

O'Neill caught the ball, and without one wobbly step to spare. He smacked his left hand against the outfield wall for emphasis, while limping to a stop. "To see the expression on his face when he caught that ball," Torre said, "that was special." The Yankees were going home with a chance to win the World Series.

To win Game 6, the Yankees would have to solve the magic tricks of Maddux. They did just that in the third inning. O'Neill—there for Torre when he needed him—doubled, Girardi tripled, Jeter singled and stole a base, and Williams singled. It added up to a 3-0 lead for Jimmy Key, who left in the sixth inning having given up only one run.

By the seventh, it was time for what Torre called The Formula: Rivera for two innings and Wetteland for one. Rivera took care of the first part of the plan. Wetteland turned his end of the plan into a bit of an adventure. Three singles cut the lead to 3-2 and left runners at first and second with two outs in the ninth. Braves second baseman Mark Lemke then worked the count full. On the seventh pitch of the at-bat, Lemke lofted a foul pop-up off third base. Hayes squeezed it, and the Yankees were at last world champions once more.

"Ninety-six was a lot of fun," Torre said, "because we were underdogs the whole time."

The next two hours were a blur of tears, laughs, hugs and champagne for Torre. It wasn't until 2 a.m. that a friend drove him home. When Torre arrived home he found his house packed with people, people who wanted the night to go on forever. It was quite a sight: Torre arriving at his own house party still was wearing his champagne-soaked Yankees uniform.

———

Days later, Torre found himself sharing a late breakfast with Steinbrenner at the Regency Hotel in New York. They were perfect for one another, what with

Steinbrenner giving Torre a fourth chance and with his best team yet, and Torre giving Steinbrenner his world championship that had eluded him through 17 years and 16 managerial changes. Torre reminded Steinbrenner that he was due to make $550,000 in 1997. LaRussa, he pointed out, made about three times as much money, and now Torre had won as many world championships as LaRussa, who had won with Oakland in 1989. Steinbrenner agreed Torre deserved better. He tore up the second year of the contract and the two of them negotiated a new deal: $3.75 million over the next three seasons.

Privately, Ali Torre wished her husband, having fulfilled his dream of a World Series title, could walk away from managing. They had a baby girl, Andrea, at home. She also knew, however, that Torre had developed a special bond with this group of players. He couldn't leave them. He also wanted to make good on his spring training vision of winning multiple titles.

Torre and the Yankees would not win in 1997. Four outs from winning the Division Series against Cleveland, Rivera gave up a tying home run to Sandy Alomar. Rivera lost, 3-2, in the ninth on an infield single by Omar Vizquel. The Yankees lost another one-run game in the clincher, 4-3.

Torre came back after that season, too. And he came back after winning the World Series again in 1998 and he came back after winning it again in

1999 and he came back after winning it again in 2000 . . . 11 more seasons in all after that first year as Yankees manager fulfilled his dream. He went on because the 1996 world championship confirmed his belief in the power of trust. The championship was a validation. It changed him as a manager, even as a person, and he liked what he had become.

"I finally started getting self-esteem as far as the work I did," Torre said when explaining why he stayed with the job. "I finally discovered what I did worked. You always think you're doing the right thing, but there was always a reason why it didn't pan out. It came back to you got fired for one reason: you didn't get the job done.

"When we did it in '96, it was such a high for me, realizing that we won, and I felt very much in control of the situations where these players who had been there before I was there respected what I was doing. You never get enough of that. And that's why. That's why.

"And then the Yankee thing. You know eventually you're going to wear out your welcome. But the core of players that was still there, I wasn't ready to walk away from them. And the money was good. And the challenge. Every single year was different, even though the team was the same, the name of the team, there's always another ingredient introduced to what you're doing. I feel like I can look at a team and try to put the puzzle together."

Something else very unusual happened in that 1996 season, something unusual, that is, besides a recovering drug addict, Doc Gooden, throwing a no-hitter, a guy coming back from an aneurysm winning the division-clinching game and the pivotal game of the World Series, Dean Palmer throwing a bunt away, a 12-year-old kid turning an out into a home run, Mark Wohlers throwing a slider, the greatest World Series comeback in Yankees history, an 8-0 record on the road in the postseason and a recycled manager welcomed as "Clueless Joe" winning the World Series in his first year as Yankees manager, succeeding immediately where the 11 men before him had failed over the previous 17 years, some of them given multiple chances. What also was unusual was that a team so well stocked with savvy veterans such as Bernie Williams, Paul O'Neill, Wade Boggs, Tino Martinez, Joe Girardi, Jimmy Key and David Cone turned for on-field leadership and the reassurance of a clutch play to a 21-year-old kid who the previous season made 29 errors and hit just two home runs in Columbus, Ohio, for the Yankees' Triple-A affiliate. Derek Jeter was magic from the start.

"It was toward the middle of the season when the older players, the veterans, were looking to him to do something," Torre said. "That was something that was very unusual for me. I had never seen anything like that in the game. They were counting on him."

Sometimes the randomness of the match between a player and an organization, which is complicated by draft order and the arcs of franchise's rises and falls, comes out just about perfect, baseball's version of an online dating service spitting out from its complicated algorithms one true love. Boggs, for instance, grew up with a sweet inside-out lefthanded hitting stroke. In the 1976 draft he was passed over 165 times before the Boston Red Sox selected him. Boggs' stroke was a natural fit for Fenway Park, where for years he could slap balls off the Green Monster in left field as if he were playing handball. Boggs hit .369 at Fenway in his career, .306 everywhere else.

Jeter and the Yankees made for one of those perfect matches. A humble, hardworking kid from Kalamazoo, Michigan, raised by educators, he was the right guy at the right time for the right team. He was a superstar in training without the attention-hungry ego that typically comes standard with such a package. When he looked around the Yankees in 1995, with a spring training invitation and a late-season call-up, he saw the captain, Don Mattingly, playing with the kind of motivation that matched his own. What he saw in 1996, even with Mattingly gone, was an entire team of players that carried the same kind of ethic Jeter had learned from his parents. He saw a team built on hard work and the prioritizing of team success over individual goals. The kid fit right in.

"I picked it up from a lot of guys," Jeter said. "I don't know if there was just one. Guys like Coney— you saw the way Coney dealt with the media, in terms of being responsible and available to the media. I think how he handled that was great. There were different aspects from different guys. Tim Raines, how he enjoyed every day. He had a smile every single day. He just always made it fun. Gerald Williams, he was always so positive. He was just someone who always looked at the positives. Tino, he played hard and was intense. I took pieces from everyone.

"I think it was the perfect situation for me, especially playing in New York. All those things I talked about, you have to be understanding of those traits to be successful in New York. One, the media. Two, confidence. Three, having fun. And four, working hard and being intense. Those were the things I had always done. So it was almost like a reassurance when I got to the Yankees."

The 1995 Yankees used Tony Fernandez at shortstop, but when Torre was hired as manager the front office told him Jeter was going to be the short-stop and Fernandez would play second.

"I'd never seen him, never met him," Torre said. "Before spring training I happened to see Jeter on TV saying, 'I'm going to get an opportunity to win the job.' I said, 'You know what? He's put it in a better way than I did.' He took nothing for granted, not like he was inheriting the job.

"Basically, when you know this is what the organization wants—for Jeter to be the shortstop—and you have nothing to compare it to, you just let it fly. And he really didn't do much in spring training. He didn't swing the bat very well. Not that he had bad at-bats, but he didn't do anything extraordinary."

Near the end of spring training, Clyde King, one of Steinbrenner's many special advisers out of Tampa, recommended that the Yankees end the plan to start Jeter at shortstop and return him to Columbus for more seasoning. "He's not ready to play," King said.

"Not ready to play?" Torre said. "It's too late. We're already committed to him."

Said Torre, "I liked him by that time. We were going to bat him ninth and let him grow. And then Fernandez got hurt and Mariano Duncan, who we brought on board as a backup player, ends up being our second baseman."

"All of us," Cone said, "thought, If he could just hold his own defensively that would be enough. And really, from the Opening Day in Cleveland, it was sort of like, 'Wow!'"

On Opening Day, Jeter made a spectacular catch of a pop-up with his back to the infield, made a sweet backhand play in the hole in which he showed off a strong arm and smacked a fifth-inning home run off veteran pitcher Dennis Martinez to give the Yankees some breathing room in what was a 1-0 pitchers' duel at the time.

"And he didn't get excited like guys who hit their first big league home run," Torre said. "From there it was just a matter of progressing."

Said Cone, "He never looked back, really. We were all impressed. And he was real humble. That's the beauty of Derek. He handled himself the right way. It was hard to get on him. We'd always look for things—Straw, Raines and I would look at him and it was hard to find things to get on him about. He just carried himself so well.

"We had a veteran team that would have given him a rookie hazing if we thought he needed it. We couldn't find an opening anywhere. We were looking . . . the first six weeks, the first couple of months . . . looking for any opening to say, 'Hey, kid, you can't do that.' **Anything.** Anything on the field, anything on the bus, anything at the hotels, his wardrobe . . . Nothing.

"When you talk about great makeup, a great background, he had it. The whole time the way he carried himself, his demeanor, was so impressive. He was kind of quiet, kept to himself, and didn't say anything wrong or dumb like most rookies do to allow you to hammer him. Never happened."

Jeter wasn't above making rookie mistakes on the field, but even then he displayed such an easy way about himself that such mistakes never threw him off that placid equilibrium. On August 12, 1996, for instance, Jeter made the foolish mistake of trying to steal third base with two outs in the eighth inning of a tie game against the White Sox with Cecil Fielder batting. Jeter was already in scoring position with the potential go-ahead run. Third base was virtually inconsequential. He was thrown out. The Yankees would lose the game, 3-2, in 10 innings.

"I was pissed off," Torre said. "I was mad at myself, basically, for probably giving him too much credit, knowing what he should do there. And I was mad—more mad at myself. I said to Zim, 'I'm not going to talk to him until tomorrow. We've got the rest of the game to play.'

"What does Derek do? He comes in off the field and sits right between me and Zim. Just came right over to us. He knew what he did. I hit him on the back of the head and said, 'Get out of here.' And it was that way pretty much all year."

Jeter did not play well in his first postseason game. He left five runners on base in his first three times at bat, all hitless. He did manage a bases-empty single his last time up. The Yankees lost, 6-2.

Reporters asked Torre if he intended to talk to the rookie in an attempt to calm his nerves.

"I don't know," Torre said. "I'll get a feel for it and see."

After Jeter showered and dressed, he was walking past Torre's office on his way home when he poked his head inside the manager's doorway.

"Mr. T," the rookie shortstop called out to Torre, "tomorrow's the biggest game of your life. Make sure you get your rest."

Torre laughed and thought, Well, I guess I don't have to talk to him.

The next day Jeter had three hits, including a leadoff single in the 12th inning that led to him scoring the winning run. So was born his reputation as a clutch postseason player. From 1996 until the 2001 World Series, the Yankees played .746 baseball in the postseason, an outrageously great record over 71 games, playing against the best teams under the most pressure. They were 53-18 while winning 14 of 15 series. It ranks as one of the most astounding stretches ever of October greatness. Jeter batted .319 in that run and, like some comic book superhero, always seemed to show up at exactly the right time to save the day.

———

In the 2000 World Series, for instance, the Mets were at home in Game 4 after having acquired momentum in the series with an eighth-inning rally to win Game 3. They stood to tie the series at two games each if they sustained that momentum. In one pitch, however, it was gone. Torre batted Jeter leadoff that game, the third leadoff batter Torre used in four games. With one pitch, Jeter restored the Yankees to the commanding position in the series. With the usual World Series first-pitch flashbulbs firing all about him, Jeter ripped the first offering from Bobby Jones for a home run. The Yankees held the lead from the first pitch to the last, winning 3-2.

"A lot of times people think, First pitch, just let me lay it down the middle, just get ahead, especially in the World Series with everybody taking pictures," Jeter said. "No, I was aggressive. I was thinking, If he throws me a strike, I'm going to try to hit it."

One year later, in another World Series Game 4, this one against the Diamondbacks, Jeter hit the last pitch for a home run, a 10th-inning walkoff shot against sidewinding reliever Byung-Hyun Kim. The blast occurred in the first hour of November 1, bestowing upon him the unprecedented nickname of Mr. November.

"That was the first time I faced Kim," Jeter said. "It takes a while to pick up his release point. I had seen a lot of pitches. To be honest with you, I was just trying to get on base. He left a slider out over the plate. The only thing that could have made it better was if it was Game 7. Everyone dreams of playing in a World Series, of hitting a home run in a World Series. A walkoff home run in a World Series? It doesn't get any better, especially in New York, and after 9/11."

Jeter's definitive postseason moment, the one that best captured his deus ex machina dramatics, had occurred 18 days earlier in the third game of the Division Series against Oakland, an elimination game for the Yankees. The Yankees clung to a 1-0 lead with two outs in the seventh inning when Terrence Long pulled a pitch into the right-field corner off Mike Mussina with Jeremy Giambi running at first base. As right fielder Shane Spencer played the carom off the wall, second baseman Alfonso Soriano and first baseman Tino Martinez aligned themselves near the right-field line, Martinez behind Soriano, for a relay to home plate. If the throw sailed over Soriano, Martinez was there as a backup to catch the ball and relay it home. As Spencer caught the ball, turned and threw, Jeter instantly knew something was wrong. He could tell by how the ball came out of Spencer's hand that his throw was going to be too high for Soriano **and** Martinez to catch.

"So I reacted to that and then adjusted to the plate," Jeter said.

As the throw was in flight Jeter noticed it was also off line and ran to a spot where he calculated it would land.

"But I'm supposed to be in that area," he said. "I was where I was supposed to be. I'm the third cutoff man. If there was no play at the plate, I redirect it trying to get the runner going to third, because they just wave the other runner around and he keeps going. But in that situation, we still had a chance to get him at home."

How could Jeter know he still had a chance to get Giambi?

"You look," he said. "It was a reaction thing. If Spencer would have hit one of the first two cutoff men, Giambi would have been out by 10 feet."

Jeter made a play that only could have been made by a player with supreme alertness, the mental computing power to quickly crunch the advanced baseball calculus needed to process the trajectory and speed of Spencer's throw and the speed and location of a runner behind his back, and the athletic and improvisational skills to actually find a way to get the ball home on time and on target while running in a direction opposite to the plate. Jeter fielded the throw on a bounce and, like a hurried quarterback executing a shovel pass, flicked the ball backhanded to catcher Jorge Posada. The flip was perfectly placed. Posada caught it and reached for Giambi, who inexplicably failed to slide and ran into the tag a split second before his foot touched home plate. The 1-0 lead was preserved, as it would be for the remainder of the game. The Yankees also survived two more elimination games to win the series.

Great postseason moments become eponymous games that live on in posterity, especially when deciding home runs are involved. The Kirk Gibson Game. The Joe Carter Game. The Aaron Boone Game. Leave it to Jeter to put in baseball's time capsule a game defined by an impromptu seventh-inning defensive play: The Flip Game.

"I don't know if you can explain it," Jeter said of how he executed the play. "You always try to prepare. You always try to think of things in advance before they happen. And I think that's what slows the game down sometimes for you. It's not something that catches you off guard because in your mind you're thinking of different scenarios before they happen."

Said Torre, "He only improvised in the way that he did it. Ball down the right-field line, man on first base, the second baseman will go out and the first baseman will trail him. There's basically nobody between the first baseman and home plate. It's a sure double, so nobody needs to be at second base. The only thing the shortstop has to determine is, is the play going to be at third or is it going to be at home? So he's got to be between the mound and shortstop, on the grass, to see the play, watch the runner, and he has to make up his mind.

"That throw was so bad, in foul territory, because Spencer just got rid of it. And unless you're an athlete, you can't do something like that, like what Derek did. And I give Posada credit. He stayed home. He didn't say, 'Oh, shit, the ball is off line. I better go get it so this guy doesn't go all the way over to third.' But that was one of those plays of a lifetime—under that type of pressure: 1-0 game, seventh inning. I remember Moose was roaming around home plate and he gave one of those fist pumps when we got the out. Derek? He came in the dugout and it was, 'Okay, let's go.' He never gets excited about it."

———

What was it about Jeter that enabled him to succeed in clutch situations? He was comfortable with himself. There never were doubts about who he was or what the mission was all about.

"I'm an optimist by nature," Jeter said. "That's why when it comes to any negative stuff, I don't like to hear about it, I don't like to read about it, I don't like to know about it. I try to be positive. So I was always, in my mind, hopeful he would come back."

Such a strong belief in a positive outcome sustains Jeter, lifts him above any self-doubt or any awareness of the consequences of failure. It is a characteristic he brought to the 1996 Yankees as a 21-year-old rookie, not a vestige of the big league experience he gained. It is, as he said, his nature. Teammates tapped into that quality immediately. If you're looking for someone to follow, why not follow the one who is sure the outcome of the journey will be positive? Why not follow someone, even a kid in his first full year in the big leagues, who stays cool at all times, who is unfamiliar with worry and anxiety?

Said Mike Borzello, the bullpen catcher in those championship seasons, "Jeter's leadership comes from his confidence, and it started from Day One. I always look at guys when they fail to see if their confidence wavers. I've never seen Derek not look like he was going to win whatever battle he was going to be involved in. I've always said there are three or four guys in sports since I've been watching who are like that: Kobe Bryant, Tiger Woods and Derek Jeter. When Tiger's 10 shots behind, it looks the same. Kobe shoots 1-for-19 in a playoff series, and he's going to shoot again. Derek can be 0-for-4 with four strikeouts and he thinks he's going to beat you in the next at-bat.

"I think that's something so rare in sports. I mean, really rare, to see someone fail and still feel like, 'Give me one more shot. Let me get one more chance.' Some guys are like, 'I don't have it today. Hopefully it doesn't come down to me.' And Derek is not that guy. He is someone that when the game is on the line, he wants that ball hit to him. When the at-bat in the game is most important, he wants it, no matter what happened the past three or four at-bats. No matter if he just booted a ball in the eighth inning, he wants that ball hit to him in the ninth with two outs, the bases loaded, up by a run.

"That's what you feed off of with Derek Jeter. Just that he never wavers. You never see a chink in his armor. It's something that you really can't fully explain and you don't see very often."

Jeter's talent and confidence helped make him a great player right out of the box. It was his humility and desire to win above all else that made him a great teammate and a manager's dream.

"I remember one time Paul Quantrill, the relief pitcher, came up to me in Kansas City one game," Torre said, "and said, 'You know, you know Jeter is a good player, but you never realize **how** good until you play with him.' That's the highest compliment you can pay somebody, when you have someone just come up unsolicited and say something like that.

"There's a certain—**cold** is too strong a word—a business mentality with him. You earn your keep with Derek. He's never in all the years we were together asked to have a family member, his dad, anybody, come into the clubhouse or hang out in the dugout. One time, he said to me, 'Mr. T, there's this kid with cancer. Do you mind if I take him around the clubhouse?' That was the extent of it. One time."

It was a remarkable record of decorum: twelve years with Torre in New York, where he owned the town, and Jeter never parlayed his status into special privilege. Twelve years together and the manager never had a problem with him.

"No," Torre said. "Okay, maybe one thing. Every once in a while I'd catch him messing around at shortstop before a game, doing fancy stuff. You know, throwing the ball behind his back, things like that. I'd stop that because that's just creating bad habits. But that was it. That was the extent of any kind of stuff."

Twelve years and the biggest problem he created was flipping practice grounders behind his back? No wonder Jeter quickly became one of Torre's most reliable soldiers. Over the years Torre would use people like Girardi and Cone to deliver messages to teammates on a peer-to-peer basis. No one filled the role more than Jeter, especially once he was named captain in 2003. It was never Jeter's nature to be loud and extroverted. But if it meant speaking up for the good of the team, especially under the advisement of Torre, Jeter was all in.

"Jeter was such a big part of what we established," Torre said. "I filled him in on what we needed to have done. He would literally commit to it. I wouldn't say buy in. He would **commit** to do something. He trusted me to the point where he knew what was important.

"Jeter is unique. He's a gentleman, but there is a standoffish way about him. I've known him a long time and he doesn't show a lot of emotion. But the right things are important to him, the things a manager knows are important.

"I'd push him to speak up at team meetings. He'd do it, but when he spoke it was always 'we.' 'We're doing this . . .' After he became captain he got more into that. Sometimes I'd warn him, where I would tell him, 'I may want you to say something.' It wouldn't be rah-rah. He would be critical, like, 'We can't not run the ball out.' He may be aiming his comments at an individual but he would be critical in his remarks without naming any one person."

———

What also endeared Jeter to his Yankees teammates, but not the team's medical personnel, was his near maniacal desire to play, no matter how hurt he might be. Fact is, the Yankees medical people often didn't know the extent of Jeter's injuries because he would refuse to even admit he was hurt. Torre, for instance, learned quickly to stop asking Jeter if he needed a day off. Instead, Torre would have to ask, "Do you want this day off or that day off?" That way Jeter knew he was getting a day off and it was a matter of which one he chose.

Jeter, because he hits with a diving style that brings his arms and hands toward the plate, puts himself in harm's way of inside pitches. He frequently took fastballs off his hands and wrists. But the conversations were almost always the same with one of the trainers:

Trainer: "Let's get an X-ray on that."

Jeter: "No. Why do you want to do that?"

Trainer: "To see if it's broke."

Jeter: "What's the difference? I'm playing anyway. It doesn't matter what the doctor said."

"He is never good and he is never bad, he is always just ready to play," trainer Steve Donahue said. "Don Mattingly was like that, too. He never said he can't play. Never. He always goes, 'I'm playing.' Half the time he wouldn't even go see the doctor. He's had elbow, hand, wrist, shoulder, quad . . . every injury and he keeps playing. I love him. He had a really bad thumb against the Red Sox in the '04 playoffs, but he kept playing. He will never say, 'I need a day off.'

"I think the other guys on the team look at him and they see he's not a vocal leader, but **what** he does and the way he competes is what inspires guys. It's the way he carries himself, too. He doesn't say stupid things. He just wants to blend in and play. He wants everything to go smoothly. It's really a credit to his parents."

Said Torre, "He didn't care where the hell he hit in the lineup, he didn't have an issue with anything. He'd say, 'Whatever you want to do.' That one series he played, against Boston in 2004, he had a broken bone in that hand. They gave him a shot for pain, and he made them stop giving him the painkiller because he couldn't get a feel for things with his hand. He just played on.

"Even in 2007, in the playoffs, his body was beat up. As a manager, you think once the postseason comes around something is going to change, especially with him because he's been so good in the postseason. But that's when I said, 'He's trying, but he can't get it done.' He was frustrated, extremely frustrated. I think his body just wasn't able to keep the promises. The thing is, I can ask him right now if anything was hurting and he still wouldn't tell me, even if it was two years ago."

Another rare time when Torre saw Jeter frustrated was in April of 2004, when Jeter endured an 0-for-32 slump, the longest hitless streak by a Yankee in 27 years. It happened to be his first month playing with Alex Rodriguez, who had an 0-for-16 slide himself that month.

"There were people saying the slump was because Alex was there," Torre said. "You knew that wasn't the case, not if you were in the clubhouse and you knew the personalities. Of course, Alex came to me and said, 'I'm trying to help him.' I said, 'Good. That's important.'"

During the hitless streak Jeter fouled off a bunt attempt with a runner on second base and two outs, a concession to the slump rather than trying to drive in the runner. After the inning, Torre went up to Jeter and asked him, "What the hell are you doing?"

"Mr. T," Jeter said while laughing at himself, "I need a hit."

Said Torre, "He knew it was bad baseball. That streak got to him. But he wasn't about to be the kind of guy who was going to give in and take a day off. I presented it to him several times and he wanted no part of that. He could have been 0-for-100 and he was not going to give in and take a day off."

———

If there was any downside to Jeter, it was his range at shortstop, which statistical analysts annually derided as among the worst in baseball. When Jeter arrived in the big leagues, he had a habit of reaching for balls to his left with two hands, which effectively reduced his reach. Jeter worked to improve his technique, but according to the number crunchers who charted batted balls, he never conquered his difficulty ranging to his left. Part of the problem was that he often played through leg injuries without making it known publicly. If limited range was Jeter's Achilles' heel, Torre was more than willing to live with it because of everything else Jeter gave the Yankees. After all, the Yankees did win four World Series and six pennants with Jeter manning the shortstop position. Torre still wanted the ball hit to Jeter with the game on the line, as great a cut-to-the-chase test of a shortstop's value as anything.

"There were times he'd play more up the middle

than you'd want him," Torre said. "You'd move him, but then he'd keep creeping and you'd move him back. Then he'd make that play in the hole, the one with the jump throw, and there was nobody who could make a play like that. You knew his limitations as a shortstop, but when you looked at the whole package, it worked.

"I used to kid him about playing center field. He never wanted to move. What you love about him is that he doesn't make excuses, he doesn't showboat, he doesn't do any of that stuff. He just goes out and plays."

––––––

Fate brought Jeter to the right team, and it wasn't so much because it was the Yankees, the franchise he dreamed of playing for as a kid, as much as it was because of the band of brothers in those pinstriped uniforms. The way Jeter played baseball was the way all of them played baseball, and for their unselfishness they were blessed with four World Series titles. It was the only kind of baseball Jeter knew growing up and it was the only kind of baseball he knew as a major leaguer, until the Yankees began to change around him. It was foreign to him to see teammates concern themselves with individual statistics or to actually find comfort in the convenience of some sort of ailment as a means of taking off a day here or a week there. It became apparent to Jeter in 2002 that the gang he loved, the kind of baseball he loved, was gone. The Yankees lost the Division Series that year to the Anaheim Angels, and they did so without Paul O'Neill, Scott Brosius, Tino Martinez, Chuck Knoblauch, all of whom retired or were allowed to move on to other clubs. Jeter, uncharacteristically, bared his emotional wounds after the last game of the series, telling reporters who inquired about his surprise with the Yankees getting knocked out, "It's a different team."

Said Jeter, "It **was** a different team."

Torre knew it, too.

"It was just not an unselfish team," Torre said. "We were all spoiled. Derek, too. Derek comes up to the major leagues and all of a sudden you win four World Series in five years. When you look at the guys who were no longer there: O'Neill, Tino, Brosius, Knoblauch . . . You try to figure out why in 2002 that ferociousness wasn't there, the refuse-to-be-denied stuff. It wasn't there. The team wasn't tough enough.

"When you're in a clubhouse with people and you play alongside them, you know when you walk out on the field the other team is going to be in for a fight. You have to have that feeling. It's about trust. That guy on the mound might not get the batter out, but the game is not going to speed up for him. He knows how to channel his emotions. What changed was a number of players out there are trying to do the job to their own satisfaction, instead of getting the job done. A lot of those players are more concerned about what it looks like as opposed to getting dirty and just getting it done. Those other teams, they were ferocious."

Said pitcher Mike Mussina, who arrived in 2001, "I always thought the personality of the team fed off of Joe Torre. And Joe was never too emotional either way, up or down. He trusted his players and trusted them to be ready. One player may leave, but another player comes in. He's certainly capable of doing the same job the other guy did. The only question is, it's New York City. Can they do it in this atmosphere versus the atmosphere they were already doing it in?

"If you look at the group they put together that won four of five World Series, and if you're looking to put that group together again, well . . . It's like getting the best poker hand you can possibly get on the deal. That's how lucky you are to have it even once."

It never happened again. Jeter never won another World Series with Torre. Over time, the Old Guard Yankees and their unselfish ferocity dwindled to almost nothing, and the Yankees became something else entirely, no longer a perfect fit for Jeter. The clubhouse filled with quirky individuals and multitudes of agendas, and none of the interlopers were more complex than Rodriguez, who began riding an uncomfortable shotgun to Jeter in the Yankees infield in 2004. By the next spring

training, Rodriguez seemed so out of place in pinstripes that Torre was calling individual players into
his office to implore them to find some way, any
way, to help Rodriguez fit in. Sheffield, Giambi,
Posada, Jeter . . . Torre tapped all of them to help
with the maintenance of Rodriguez.

"My feeling is with every player," Torre said,
"you've got him on your team and you know what
his ability is, so now my job is do whatever I can to
get the most out of that ability. Every place he's
been, he's been the voice of the team. He's used to
more responsibility than he needed to take on with
the Yankees. So in this case I remember calling in
Sheff, Jeter, Giambi, Georgie, and just saying, 'He's
got to feel important. We need to do this, guys. He
can give us a lot, and we just need to make him feel
how much we rely on him and how important
he is.' "

Did Jeter get comfortable with performing that
kind of mental maintenance with Rodriguez? "Not
necessarily," Torre said. "But he did understand."

It was a long way from the culture Jeter knew as
a younger player. He looks back on those championships and it is not so much the titles that he
misses as much as it is the shared bond among people who all played the game the same way he did.

"I think everyone had the right mentality," Jeter
said. "The right frame of mind. Yeah, you have to
be talented in order to win, but you have to have
the right mindset. And that mindset is, do **what-**

ever it takes to win a game. It sounds simple, but we really didn't have anyone that cared more about putting up statistics, you know what I mean? I mean, if somebody had to hit a groundball to second base, they hit a groundball to second base. You don't get a stat for that. You actually get a negative stat for that. But that's how you win games.

"I never understood that part of baseball. You could have a guy at second base and no outs, all right? Guy hits a groundball to second base. That's good baseball, with nothing to show for it. The next guy hits a groundball to second base. Now he's an RBI machine. Then they say, 'Well, this guy doesn't hit with runners in scoring position.' He did exactly what he's supposed to do. And that's why this guy is an RBI guy? No. It depends on the situation.

"But you have some teams and some guys, they get a guy on second base with nobody out and they don't care about moving the guy over. If they get a hit that way, great, but they're trying to get a hit, as opposed to doing what they should be doing. And that's how you win.

"I think it was the character of the guys, but I think it was also that when we got used to winning, people understood that's what you have to do to win."

In his first eight full seasons in the major leagues, 1996–2003, Jeter played on Yankees teams that won 64 percent of their games, won 16 of 20 post-season series, played in six World Series, won four world championships and came within three games of winning six titles in eight years. It was and remains the greatest dynasty in modern baseball—that is, since the expansion era began in 1961 and in spite of free agency that began in 1975. It was a special dynasty because its trademark was more so the character of the players than it was their talent. The lasting impression is how those Yankees played collectively, not how they played individually. And when they were at their peak, at their optimum nexus of youth, know-how and fierce resolve, the Yankees were a thing of beauty that for one glorious year won more games than any collection of ballplayers ever assembled.

2.

A Desperation to Win

This may best capture the absurdist nature of what it could be like working for George Steinbrenner at the height of his obsessive, unforgiving, hands-on reign as commander in chief of the Yankees: Torre's job was on the line less than one week into managing the 1998 Yankees, the team that would win more games than any team in baseball history. With Mariano Rivera on the disabled list, the Yankees lost their first three games, in Anaheim and in Oakland, by a combined score of 21-6. Steinbrenner called his rookie general manager, Brian Cashman, the young former assistant who had replaced Bob Watson and was on the trip, and sent him home from the West Coast as punishment. The newspapers were full of speculation about who might replace Torre, such as Davey Johnson.

When the Yankees finally won a game, in the fourth game of the season in extra innings against the Athletics, Torre asked the staff and players to sign the lineup card and he sent it overnight to Cashman at his home, where, like a teenager, he had been grounded by The Boss. "Congratulations," Torre wrote. "The first of many." Little did Torre know the "many" that year would be a record 125 victories, postseason included.

First, however, came more pain and a full-blown crisis. The Yankees lost again the next night, a Monday night in Seattle, by getting blown out by the Mariners, 8-0. Not only did Seattle starter Jamie Moyer dominate the Yankees by striking out 11, but he also bullied them, dusting Paul O'Neill with a pitch without any retribution from the Yankees. The Mariners, under manager Lou Piniella, made a habit of throwing at O'Neill, who had played for Piniella in Cincinnati. Piniella knew he could throw the emotional O'Neill off his game with a strategically placed pitch or two.

"It got to be ridiculous," Torre said. "If Lou could have run him over at the hotel he would have done that. He knew what got Paulie's goat. That was about as obvious as it got, and it never went away."

After five games, the 1998 Yankees were 1-4, in last place, already 3½ games out of first, outscored 36-15, at risk of losing their manager and letting teams like the Mariners kick sand in their faces.

Torre was especially blue after the 8-0 defeat. Normally, he would grab a postgame dinner with Zimmer, his bench coach. That night he ate alone.

"It was an ugly game and I was down. Really down," Torre said. "I didn't ask anybody to go with me. Zim said, 'Do you want me to go?' I said, 'No.' I just went and had some dinner and some wine, and just sat there by myself."

The next day Torre called a team meeting, and before holding that meeting he reviewed his notes. On rare occasions, Torre held meetings immediately after a game. Those meetings usually were quick ones and allowed Torre to vent some anger. The full-blown ones required preparation. During games, if Torre saw something that needed to be addressed in a meeting, he would write notes to himself on the back of his lineup card. Whenever Zimmer would see Torre pull out the lineup card and flip it over, he would remark in a stage whisper, "Uh-oh." He knew what was coming. Sometimes Torre would ask Zimmer what he should do about addressing the team and Zimmer always would reply, "Wait 'til tomorrow. Wait 'til tomorrow." Torre took lots of notes during that 8-0 loss to Seattle. He decided this was a meeting that would wait until the next day.

"I was more down than angry at the time," Torre said. "And I wasn't about to have a meeting when I was down. I'd rather be angry. After I take notes I don't even refer to them at the meeting, but when I write them down it helps me remember them.

"That day when I spoke to them, I basically told them how I felt and how bad they were and how pissed I was. I told them what I did the night before. I retraced my steps. I told them I went out alone, didn't want to be with anyone. That's how bothered I was by how we were playing. I pretty much went through everything with them. We were playing horseshit, and it was especially bad coming out of spring training with such a bad feeling."

Said Cone, "It was one of his more forceful meetings. There was a lot of talk from people who said nobody had gone 1-5 to start the season and came back to win a World Series. There was some talk about that. I remember Joe started it off and he wasn't happy.

"Torre was good. He always got his point across and then he'd go around the room and a few guys spoke. Straw said something, Raines spoke . . . Joe would say, 'Anybody else got something to say? Bernie?' Bernie never had much to say. He'd go around the room and challenge guys to say something. He was real good at pointing out a veteran and asking, 'What do you think?'"

When Torre pointed to Cone, the veteran pitcher responded with an emotional speech. Cone started out by recognizing the potential impact of Steinbrenner's impatience. The Yankees knew what was at stake, even this early in the season. They knew the newspapers in New York were full of stories that Steinbrenner was thinking about getting rid of Torre.

"Guys, we've got to get going," Cone said. "We've got to get it together as a team. And we've got to do it now or this whole thing could be dismantled because the owner will react."

Like Torre, Cone was angered by what he saw the previous night. He watched Seattle designated hitter Edgar Martinez, batting in the eighth inning with an 4-0 lead, take a huge hack on a 3-and-0 pitch from reliever Mike Buddie—five innings after Moyer had dusted O'Neill with a pitch. Cone knew some position players were grumbling after the game that Pettitte, the Yankees starter, did not retaliate for Moyer's message pitch, a problem Cone calls "a brewing situation in the clubhouse between pitchers and hitters that can really cause divisiveness in the clubhouse—a hot button issue I've seen over the years." Martinez's brash swing with the game already in hand was another insult.

"It's the old-school mentality we have to have," Cone continued in front of his teammates. "You have to find something to hate about your opponent. Look across the way. These guys are real comfortable against us. Edgar is swinging from his heels on 3-and-0 when they're up by about 10 runs! Those guys are too comfortable. Our guys are getting knocked down.

"Listen, everybody knows Andy's a gamer, but

the hitters need to know we're going to protect them. We've got to get the emotion going here. We've got to look across the way and find something in our opponent we don't like. That team took us out in the '95 playoffs. I hate this place, the Kingdome. I left half my arm on that mound! I left a vein out on that mound in '95, and it pisses me off to see these guys walk all over us and us have no pride being the Yankees!"

Cone looked at Tino Martinez, the former Mariner who played on that '95 Seattle team that knocked off the Yankees.

"No offense, Tino," Cone said. "You're over here now, but I fucking hate those guys. I hate this place. If you want to find some motivation here, that's part of it. It's also Edgar swinging 3-and-0 trying to take us deep. They're sticking it in our face! And there's only one way to react to that."

It was classic Cone: emotional, honest and inspirational. He held the attention of all of his teammates. Starting pitchers rarely hold so much sway over a baseball team. They play only about 33 times a year, once every five days or so. Their skills are far more narrow than the position players; they have no need to field, hit or run with any great skill. They spend the majority of their time watching, not playing. As such, they tend to keep to their own group, as if a language or cultural barrier set them apart from the everyday players. But Cone was one of those rare specialists who crossed all lines and commanded the attention and respect of everyone in the clubhouse. They knew he had put himself on the front lines of the 1994–95 strike, survived turbulent times with the Mets, won a World Series with Toronto as a hired gun. He also took a great chunk of media responsibility in the clubhouse, even on days he wasn't pitching, which many of the more reserved players considered grunt work, like trench-digging, they were only too happy to see him shoulder. The entire package Cone gave the Yankees was made all the more meaningful by his competitiveness. They saw that he competed with the emotional attitude and edge of an everyday player.

Said trainer Steve Donahue, "He used to yell at me. We'd be in Baltimore in August. Hot as hell. His face would be cherry red. I'd come up to him with an ammonia towel, and he'd scream at me, 'I'll fucking let you know! Get the fuck away!' And he'd keep screaming at me. Happened every day game.

"Then he'd come in after the game and say, 'Sorry. Didn't mean to get on you.' Whether it was union issues or any controversial stuff going on, he was like the governor. He would take care of all of the media. And he was always great talking to the young kids. He was a huge influence."

While the championship Yankees looked to Jeter for his consistency and optimism, especially in the clutch, Cone was their fire and brimstone, the stuff that kept their furnace burning at peak capacity. He was a friend, a motivator, a mentor, a clubhouse policeman, a jokester . . . whatever he needed to be. No one on those championship Yankees teams occupied a more important dual role—on the field and in the clubhouse combined—than Cone, a truth made obvious when a worn-down Cone, his shoulder finally surrendering to all those pitches over all those years, was allowed to leave as a free agent after the 2000 season. The Yankees, despite replacing Cone with Mike Mussina, the top free agent pitcher then, would never win another World Series without Cone. On the day Cone left in 2000, Paul O'Neill, who would come back for one more year himself, said, "I said when I re-signed that I wanted to play out this run with this group of players. This shows that this run is coming to an end. The Yankees might keep on winning, but it'll be with a different group of players. In one sense, things continue because they brought in Mussina. But, in another sense, things are ending because Coney is gone."

The Yankees would give Mussina Cone's old locker, the one at the end of a row, near a hallway, and the closest to Torre's office, which was just around the corner in that hallway. Even Mussina, who never played with Cone, but as if aware of a ghost appendage, understood how important Cone was to the Yankees and their championships.

"When Coney left and I came in, that changed things," Mussina said, "because a lot of people really liked Coney. He had some great years, and he had some tough years, but everybody loved him. He just took the ball and said, 'I don't care. Just give me the ball. I'll go win.' Players respect that. Players respect other players' approach. If the results are good or bad, if your approach to playing the game is the right way, players respect that. If your approach is wrong, I don't care how good a player you are, other players don't look at you the same way."

Cone owned the total respect of his teammates, and so his words that night in Seattle resonated. The impact of the meeting was undeniable immediately. The Yankees suddenly were a different team. They were a historic team.

Chuck Knoblauch hit the first pitch of the game for a home run. Jeter doubled. O'Neill doubled. After a brief pause on a strikeout by Williams, Martinez singled. Darryl Strawberry hit a home run. After Tim Raines grounded out, Jorge Posada hit a home run. Eight batters into the game, the Yankees had five extra-base hits and a 6-0 lead. By the fourth inning it was 11-1, by the end it was 13-7 and by June the AL East effectively was over. The Yankees were that good.

They beat Seattle again after their breakout game to come home 3-4 on a two-game winning streak.

Steinbrenner's dark mood suddenly changed. After letting Torre's job status linger for public doubt, Steinbrenner greeted Torre at the team's annual Welcome Home dinner with a smile. "Ah, you're my guy," Steinbrenner told him. "You're my guy."

Beginning with that meeting in Seattle, the Yankees went 64-16, becoming the only Yankees team in history to play .800 baseball over 80 games. It was beautiful baseball to watch. They bludgeoned teams and they carved up teams—whatever means was necessary—and they were relentless no matter their methodology. There was, however, one problem: it was their counterculture lefthander David Wells.

———

On the night of May 6 in Texas, the Yankees gave Wells a 9-0 lead in the third inning. Wells, though, began to pitch carelessly, especially when he thought teammates were not making plays behind him. When he noticed relief pitchers warming up as he gave up hit after hit, Wells seemed to lose whatever little focus he had left. Wells gave up seven runs in a stretch of only eight batters before Torre pulled him from the game. The Yankees won the game, 15-13, but Torre was upset with Wells' effort, and made sure to tell reporters so after the game, going so far as to chastise Wells for being out of shape.

"When Boomer read it in the newspapers, he was livid," Cone said. "He was pissed at Joe. He was pissed at Mel. He was pissed at the world. He called me up and I told him, 'You call Joe and have a meeting and air him out. Get this thing out.' So he did. We both went to the ballpark early that day in Minnesota and Boomer went in and closed the door and he and Joe went at it pretty good, back and forth."

Wells told Torre he was pissed to read the comments in the newspaper.

"You've got a problem with me? Call me in," Wells said.

"You bring it on yourself," Torre said. "If you want to be here you better start acting like it."

Wells was also angry that Torre warmed up relief pitchers so quickly in a game, signaling a lack of confidence in Wells. Torre told Wells that he was pissed every time Wells threw his arms up in disdain if one of his fielders did not make a play behind him.

"I'll make you a deal," Torre told him. "I won't do that, I won't get relievers warmed up. But I can't have you out there throwing your arms up like, 'All these bad things. Why are they happening to me?' That doesn't work. Everybody out here is playing their ass off. Look at your infielders. After you go like that . . ."—Torre threw up his arms in mock disgust—"what do you want them to do? Everybody out there is trying to help you win."

The meeting ended in, at best, a cold truce. Both men were still angry. Cone saw Torre after the meeting finally ended.

"I told him to go talk to you, Joe," Cone said. "Better that way than what was going on."

"I know, I know," Torre said.

"Did you get it straightened out?"

Torre didn't give an answer. He just stared at Cone, the anger still evident.

"I'm working on him, Joe. I'm working on him," Cone said.

Wells' ERA stood at an unsightly 5.77 after that game in Texas. But after the meeting in Minnesota, he was a changed pitcher. The next time he took the ball he beat the Royals, 3-2, a game in which Torre gave him so much rope that Wells threw 136 pitches over eight innings. His start after that was simply perfect. Wells threw 120 pitches in a perfect game at Yankee Stadium against the Minnesota Twins, one of only 17 perfect games in history. He did not walk a batter and struck out 11 in the 4-0 win. Wells went from essentially quitting on the mound to throwing a perfect game with only one start in between. It was a 12-day snapshot that fairly captured the entire career of Wells, who could be as exasperating as he could be great.

"Wells would exert more energy to find a way not to be on the field for pregame practice than it would have taken to be out there," Torre said. "You have rules and the only way rules are effective is if everybody has to live by them. We had rules that you had to be on the field for however long it was, an hour of batting practice. I said, 'If you have to leave the field, you have to get permission from a coach or me.'

"I try to analyze it, try to be in somebody else's skin, but nobody needs that much work in the trainer's room that it can't wait 20 minutes. I think it could be a throwback to needing the attention. Whether it was positive or negative, he needed the attention. I think that was more a part of it.

"He can be an engaging personality, and then there are times as a manager where you could hate his guts. He'd go out there and I'd watch his body language, and I'd watch Jeff Weaver and I'd watch Sidney Ponson, those are two guys who gravitated toward him, and I saw the same things. 'Woe is me.' It drove you nuts.

"The players addressed that with him, too. Jeter or O'Neill said something. It was never any big deal. I told him everybody was trying to help him win and said, 'It's not fair to them.' He admitted it. But I think about his growing up without a male influence. Even though it doesn't stop you from being pissed at him, you try to understand it.

"But he could **pitch.** My favorite story was calling him in and telling him how much he weighed and saying, 'There's no way you can pitch effectively at that weight.' Of course, now he's going to go out there and pitch a gem because now he's going to prove it to me. He had an arm like Warren Spahn, blessed with a rubber arm. He could pitch any time for as long as you want him. There were other issues—back, gout, whatever—but there were never any arm problems."

After the blowout meeting with Torre in Minnesota, and including the postseason, Wells went 19-3 with a 2.91 ERA. The Yankees went 23-4 when he took the ball in that turnaround. Wells led the league in winning percentage, shutouts, strikeout-to-walk ratio, and fewest baserunners per inning.

"He needed somebody to push him, he really did," Cone said. "Once he got it going after that perfect game, he really changed. He was lights out for the rest of the year. It was a Cy Young type year. He did need to be pushed. I don't know if you can trace it back to his childhood and not having a father around or what, but after that meeting he was really good. Since he was pitching so well Joe and Mel eased up on him. I stayed on him. I told Joe and Mel, 'Hey, I'm on him. We're with him. We're building him up. We're going to stay on him.'

"That was the beauty of Torre. He knew he had guys in that clubhouse who could police themselves and he allowed it to happen. He allowed us to do that. So when he did call a meeting, which was rarely, it was effective. He always knew we were on top of it. That particular clubhouse, we were on top of everything."

———

By any measurement, the 1998 Yankees were the pinnacle of the dynasty. They led the league in runs (though no one hit more than 28 home runs), pitching and defensive efficiency (a measurement of how well a team turns batted balls into outs). The starting rotation—Cone, Wells, Pettitte, Orlando Hernandez and Hideki Irabu—combined for a 79-35 record. Mariano Rivera, with Mike Stanton, Graeme Lloyd and Jeff Nelson providing the setup relief, was 3-0 with a 1.91 ERA and 36 saves.

So deep was the lineup that Williams led the team in batting, O'Neill led in total bases, Martinez led in home runs, Jeter led in hits and Knoblauch led in walks. Scott Brosius, who hit .203 the previous season for Oakland, batted .300 and drove in 98 runs—while making all but three of his starts out of the eighth or ninth spots in the batting order. Posada and Joe Girardi helped give the Yankees 88 RBI out of the catching position. Five players combined to give them 74 RBI out of the left-field position: Chad Curtis, Strawberry, Raines, Ricky Ledee and Shane Spencer. Homer Bush was a pinch-running specialist who also happened to hit .380. The roster was so deep and productive that the players Torre brought off the bench produced a better on-base percentage (.370) than those who started (.364) that season.

"I give a lot of credit to Raines and Strawberry," Cone said. "They provided veteran leadership. They were real leaders, especially when we threw our secondary lineup out there with Straw, Raines and Homer Bush. We were almost better on those days. I think that set the tone. The depth of that roster really stands out for me. I was never on a team that was that deep. From one through 25, I don't think there was ever a better team."

Billy Beane, the general manager of the Oakland A's, watched in awe as the Yankees beat his club eight times in 11 games, outscoring Oakland 81-48.

"I've been in the game 30 years," Beane said. "That 1998 team was one of the greatest teams in the history of the game. The greatest teams I ever saw were the 1998 Yankees and the '75-'76 Reds. They had everything you'd a want a baseball team to have. To win one game against them was a big deal. I remember we had one game against them that was rained out, so we had to play a four-game series in three days. We didn't have a particularly great pitching staff. Well, the first game of the doubleheader, poor Mike Oquist was pitching. We knew we had three more games to play, so we had to leave him out there, otherwise we would have wound up throwing an infielder in the second game. We literally ran out of pitching in a four-game series.

"They wore you out. They pounded you. The impact they would have on your pitching staff when you were done playing them would carry over for another week. And one thing about getting beat by the Yankees: they did it with class. It was as if they beat you in rented tuxedos."

The roster was a near-perfect construct, of youth in the everyday positions, experience and wisdom off the bench, power and speed, lefthanded and righthanded pitching . . . the Yankees lacked nothing. They added to that talent with an insatiable desire to win. During the 1998 season Cone put his finger precisely on what made the Yankees great when he observed, "There is a **desperation** to win."

Martinez, for instance, was habitually hard on himself. The slightest slump, even a hitless game, would prompt the first baseman to grow angry with himself. Torre would have to call him into his office.

"Let me ask you a question," Torre told Martinez one time. "I know you don't want to hear this, but you're sitting here in this clubhouse and you're thinking you're letting everybody down. If Derek Jeter went 0-for-8, would you feel like he was letting you down?"

"No," Martinez said.

"Well, that's the way we feel about you."

———

The Yankees took it personally on those rare occasions when they did lose. Nobody took failure harder than O'Neill, the guy people in the front office had warned Torre back in 1996 was a bit "selfish." That reputation came about because of the regularity with which O'Neill would trash watercoolers, slam his bat to the ground or fail to run hard when he was mad at himself for hitting a routine pop-up or grounder.

"Paul O'Neill was just that guy who threw himself in there all the time," Torre said, "who never thought, What do I do if this doesn't work out? And he was a great soldier. Not selfish and not self-conscious. He didn't care what it looked like. He didn't care how ugly the swings were. His job was to get on base.

"His selfishness, if you want to call it that, came from the fact that he wanted to get a hit every time up. He didn't have a selfish bone in his body. He wanted to win above everything else. There was never an excuse in this guy. "

One time when O'Neill hit a routine grounder and, out of frustration, he failed to run hard, the fielder bobbled the ball. O'Neill still was thrown out at first. His lack of hustle prevented him from reaching base safely, and he knew it. After the game, O'Neill walked into Torre's office and threw a one-hundred-dollar bill on the manager's desk.

"You're not going to solve this thing by clearing your conscience," Torre told him. "You keep that hundred."

Said Torre, "What you had to understand was that **he needed to win.**"

Said Donahue, "When we lost a game, I don't care if it was in April or May, he'd come in the clubhouse and from halfway across the room he'd be firing bats into his locker. We'd be back in the trainer's room, hear the noise and know right away, 'Oh, shit. We lost.' He'd be so pissed. No pitcher was ever any good, either. When that guy they made the movie about, the science teacher for Tampa Bay, Jim Morris, got him out, O'Neill went crazy. 'Who are they going to bring in next to get me out? A gym teacher? A plumber?'

"He'd always say, 'That's it. I'm done. I can't hit.' And Zim would sit there and go, 'Hey, I got a buddy in Cincinnati who can get you a bricklayer's job . . .'

"He'd rarely come into the trainer's room. One time he broke a rib in Tampa right before the playoffs. He went into a wall and broke a rib. Didn't bother him. He used to say, 'The trainer's room is for pitchers.' In 1996 and 1998 he had a bad hamstring. He wouldn't even come in to get it wrapped. He was a bad patient."

"The thing about Paulie," Cone said, "was he was into his own routine, but it was not at all seen as selfish. I think people didn't realize how goofy Paulie was off the field. They saw he was intense, but after the game you could get all over him. Tino or I would say something to him and he was just so goofy. He was just very different from his on-field demeanor. The way he handled himself, he didn't take himself too seriously, even though it looked that way on the field. He was very self-deprecating, talking about how he stunk."

In the 1997 Division Series, O'Neill batted in the ninth inning of Game 5 with the Yankees down to their last out and down by one run against the Indians. He roped a hard line drive that smacked off the wall in right field. O'Neill dashed into second base, arriving with such an ugly, awkward slide that Torre ran to the field to check on him.

"I thought it was out!" O'Neill said.

Torre signaled for a pinch runner.

"I'm all right, Skip! I'm all right!" O'Neill protested.

"Paulie," Torre said, "I'm bringing in a pinch runner for you because the other guy is faster than you, not because you're hurt."

"I remember one time," Borzello said, "when we played in Detroit and I think he left nine men on base himself. And I remember him coming in and we lost the game by one or two runs. We came into the clubhouse, and I remember him saying, 'You left nine men on base! Nine fucking men on base!' When he had a bad game he had this glassy stare and he'd talk to himself. And then he picked up a chair and fired it. I just remember him feeling solely responsible.

"He wanted to get his hits, but his hits were important to him because of the success of the team. There are a lot of guys who want a hit every at-bat, but this guy, it was more about not letting the other 24 guys down. If he didn't do enough to help the team win the game, he felt like he let everyone down. And I think people fed off that, that his passion for success and how that translated to the team's success was what was important to him."

———

A desperation to win. That's what drove the 1998 Yankees to 114 victories—22 more than anybody else in the league. There was only one downside to being so much better than everyone else: the pressure to win the World Series was enormous. They were **supposed** to win it all, and it showed when they played Texas in the Division Series.

"We were very tight," Torre said, "as tight as I can remember. It was weird, though: even then, we just kept winning."

The Yankees didn't hit much; they scored nine runs in three games. They also were knocked back emotionally one day during the series when they learned that Strawberry had been diagnosed with colon cancer. But they swept the Rangers because they allowed Texas one run on 13 hits in the entire series. The Yankees used only six pitchers.

"They were a very professional group of guys," said former Rangers pitcher Rick Helling, who lost Game 2 when the Yankees forced him to throw 119 pitches in six innings. "I remember very well the way they worked the count and how unselfish they were as a team. They were not afraid to let the next guy do it. A lot of times a guy in position to get the big hit gets overanxious and wants to do it himself.

That team was not that way. It was a battle facing them. It was a great lineup, very unselfish for a bunch of star players."

———

The Yankees advanced to play the Indians, the team that knocked them out the previous year, in the American League Championship Series. After the Yankees rolled to a 7-2 victory in Game 1, they found themselves in a 1-1 tie in the 12th inning of Game 2 when Knoblauch committed an all-time infamous blunder. The second baseman stood arguing with the first-base umpire for an interference call—the baseball sitting in the infield dirt not more than a few steps away from him—while En-rique Wilson of the Indians was running all the way from first to home with the tie-breaking run. Nelson, Martinez and teammates in the dugout were yelling to Knoblauch to fetch the baseball, but the second baseman was too engrossed in his ill-timed argument. By the time he did get the ball and throw home, it was too late. The Indians went on to win, 4-1.

Knoblauch was a very strange case study in New York. He arrived with the Yankees in time for the 1998 season after a trade with the Twins, where he had established himself as a rugged leadoff hitter and fearless baserunner. But he often seemed jumpy and lacking in confidence with the Yankees. He wasn't the same threat on the bases. In 1997 with

Minnesota, for instance, Knoblauch attempted 72 steals. The next season with the Yankees he ran only 43 times, and never exceeded 47 attempts in his four years in pinstripes.

"I never realized how fragile he was," Torre said. "When we got him I thought it was a perfect fit. We could utilize his speed. But he never really exhibited it with us. He was afraid to run. He was afraid of getting thrown out. That fear of failure stuff. And you can't talk somebody into failing if they're afraid to fail.

"With Minnesota he was a tough, hard-nosed player. Certainly the son of a gun was a good hitter. But his mood swings certainly were a big contributor in his lack of consistency. I think New York got the best of him. He found more things to do, more trouble."

By 2000, Knoblauch's inner demons had coalesced into a mental block about fielding and throwing the ball to first base from second base. It was painful to watch. Then, on June 16, 2000, upon throwing away a baseball in that game for the third time in six innings, Knoblauch walked off the field, tapped Torre on the knee in the dugout, said, "I'm done," and kept right on walking up the runway and into the clubhouse. Torre followed him and reached him near his locker. Knoblauch was getting undressed. He told Torre he was quitting.

"You're going through a tough time," Torre told

him. "I can't let you just walk out on the spur of the moment and then you'll be sorry about it. Just go home for now and you think about it."

Said Torre, "I told Cash what had happened, and when Randy Levine got wind of what happened, he wanted to take his money away."

Knoblauch was back in the lineup the next day at second base, but he never fully regained his confidence there. The Yankees moved him to left field the following season.

"What happened in the championship series against Cleveland was sad," Torre said. "I just tried to get the team together after that. The players were mad at him. I was pissed with him at the time it was going on, but if you knew how fragile he was you couldn't stay angry. I talked to some players. Mariano, Bernie, O'Neill, Girardi, who was one of my soldiers. I said, 'It's done. It's behind us. The only way to get through this is to be there for him. We can't do anything about it but go on.'"

Said Cone, "Some of us talked to him, and he was almost in denial, blaming it on the umpire."

On the plane ride after the game to Cleveland, where the Yankees would have an off day before Game 3, it was Cone, of course, who provided the most important counseling to Knoblauch. He told him of a similar gaffe he had made in Atlanta as a pitcher with the Mets, arguing with an umpire while two Braves runners sped around the bases.

"You've got to take it," Cone told him. "You've

got to stand up for this one. Stand up and take it. Whether the umpire blew the call or not, you've got to get the ball. Whether the runner was out of the baseline or not is irrelevant. Now all you've got to do is take the blame and it will go away."

Said Cone, "He finally said, 'Okay,' and he did. He had his press conference and he said, 'I screwed up.' Finally. After being in denial for a while."

On that same flight to Cleveland Torre sensed that his team was uptight, and that it needed a complete day off, especially away from the media that he knew were going to milk another day's worth of stories out of the Knoblauch gaffe. He told his players not to come to the ballpark the next day.

"Guys, we're not going to work out tomorrow," he told them. "The best thing we can do is hide out from the media for a day. It'll probably serve us better."

A few minutes later, after Torre had returned to his seat near the front of the plane, a woman tapped him on the shoulder. It was Nevalee O'Neill, Paul's wife.

"Uh, Joe?" she said. "Do you mind if Paul goes in and hits tomorrow? He needs to hit."

Torre laughed. He changed his mind and offered the players an optional workout. The whole team showed up. Knoblauch held his news conference to admit his mistake.

———

The next day, before Game 3, Torre held a meeting in the Jacobs Field visiting clubhouse with his team. He sensed the weight of the 114-win season was bearing down on his players. He knew the Indians were not intimidated by the Yankees, as were most teams. During the season, for instance, Cone had noticed "certain situations in the middle of games when we start to mount a rally, and you can see pitchers panic a little bit. All of a sudden, we've got a big crooked number on the board, four or five runs." The Indians were not one of those teams to cave under to the Yankees' might.

"It was a tough matchup for us, especially tough against righthanded pitching, and the fact that they knocked us out the year before," Cone said. "They thought they could beat us. They didn't care how many games we won. They thought they were better, even though our pitching was clearly better."

Torre did not like the vibe he was getting from his team.

"Guys, you're uptight," Torre told them. "You aren't having enough fun. You've got to get back to having fun."

When the meeting was over and as players went back to preparing for the game, O'Neill called Torre aside.

"Ski-ip," O'Neill said in his high-pitched Cincinnati twang.

"Yeah, Paulie?"

"Fun? It's not fun unless you win, Ski-ip."

It was no fun that night for the Yankees. Cleveland righthander Bartolo Colon kept the Yankees' offense quiet and the Indians handily beat Pettitte, 6-1. Cleveland led the series, two games to one. The value of a 114-win regular season was in danger of becoming seriously diminished.

"Yeah, there was pressure," Cone said. "What we accomplished during the season would all go away if we lost. And in some ways, we were trying to validate '96, too. People pretty much viewed the Braves as better than us in '96 and we kind of stole one from them. Then we lost to Cleveland in '97, and then here's Cleveland going to knock us out again. So it was not only our record in '98 that was on the line, but the validation of '96, too. I don't know if a lot of guys felt that way. I did."

———

On the morning of Game 4, Torre went to the hotel coffee shop for breakfast. He thought the man with the shaved head busing tables and helping serve customers looked familiar. And he was: it was his Game 4 starting pitcher, Orlando Hernandez. "El Duque" had fled Cuba and his family on some sort of small craft—his raft version made for the most compelling and marketable one—to pursue his baseball career in the major leagues. He pitched with an outrageously high and limber leg kick and delighted in playing cat-and-mouse games with hitters. Raised in baseball-mad Cuba, where success in international tournaments can mean the difference betweeen a comfortable life or a strained one, Hernandez seemed oblivious to the drama of major league ball. The Yankees were so deep in starting pitching that they stashed him in Triple A, until, that is, Cone came to work one day with an odd bit of news for Torre: "My mother-in-law's Jack Russell terrier bit my finger. I can't pitch." The Yankees called up Hernandez. He made 21 starts for the Yankees and they won 16 of them. Because of the Division Series sweep and the resetting of the rotation for the ALCS, Hernandez had not pitched in 14 days when his turn finally came up in Game 4.

After breakfast, Torre got a message that Steinbrenner wanted to see him in his suite at the hotel. Torre walked into the suite and found Steinbrenner watching a college football game on television, a game between Ohio State and Illinois.

"Well, what do you think?" Steinbrenner asked.

Torre knew what he was after. This was another attempt by the perpetually uneasy Steinbrenner to have his calm manager assure him everything was going to be okay. So Torre decided to have some fun with him.

"What I think," Torre said, "is that Ohio State is going to win this game."

"No, no, no!" Steinbrenner barked. "I mean our team!"

Torre suppressed a laugh.

"I think we're in a good frame of mind," Torre

said, fulfilling his duty. "I know one thing: our starting pitcher won't be nervous. He's downstairs serving people in the coffee shop."

———

Said Torre, "I knew there was pressure. I talked to Bill Belichick, the Patriots coach, in 2007 about this. It's great being 15, 16, 17 and 0. But that means you **have to** win. It's enormous pressure, where you can't give the other team a chance no matter how bad or good they are. There was enormous pressure."

O'Neill hit a home run in the first inning, and even that small amount of support was all Hernandez needed. He was brilliant, throwing seven shutout innings in a 4-0 win. The series was tied, and the pressure eased on the 114-win Yankees. Wells, the Game 1 winner, started for the Yankees in Game 5. While Wells was warming in the bullpen, Indians fans, including children, made derisive comments to him about his late mother. Wells became so agitated and emotional about such hostility that he cut his session short after only about 25 pitches, half his normal warmup.

"You wouldn't believe the stuff they were saying about my mother," Wells told Torre in the dugout.

The Yankees gave Wells a 3-0 lead in the first inning, but, seemingly distracted and out of sorts, he immediately gave two back, eliciting a trip to the mound from Posada.

"You all right?" the catcher asked. "What's the problem?"

Wells told Posada about what the fans did during his warmup.

"Now you've got another reason," Posada said, "to shove it up their ass."

Posada, who turned 27 that year, was emerging as the team's most vocal everyday player and yet another fierce competitor as he gained more playing time over Girardi. Torre called Posada "Jeter's alter ego," because Posada and Jeter were such good friends and believed in the same unselfish baseball methodology and had no tolerance for anyone who thought otherwise. Unlike Jeter, however, Posada had no problem getting in the face of a teammate, including one time in 2002 when he and El Duque brawled in the trainer's room before a game. Posada and Hernandez, in fact, had a contentious, if odd relationship, almost like a vaudeville act, to get the best out of one another. One day they nearly came to blows in the dugout in Cleveland, and that same night Torre saw the two of them in a mall happily going off to dinner together.

"Georgie always wants to be a leader," Donahue said, "and sometimes he gets a little hot when he shouldn't. Georgie wants to win, and that's why he and Jeter are such good buddies."

Said Brian McNamee, the former Yankees strength trainer, "Luis Sojo and Posada would jump guys' asses for little things, like showing up late for stretching or messing up on the bases. They would keep it on an even keel so they could rag on guys, but Jorge was the guy. Jorge had a temper on him but he was always right. Jeet was laid back. He's on time all the time, he gets his work in, he's quiet, he handles the media well, but Jeter is not going to jump on somebody's ass."

Said Torre, "Georgie would get very frustrated with pitchers. I know Randy Johnson frustrated the hell out of him, even to the point where I decided to have John Flaherty catch him. And then Randy and Flaherty, old laid-back Flaherty, almost came to blows in Seattle. But Randy would get under Georgie's skin. Georgie was sure how he wanted him to pitch, and Randy would fight him, and Georgie would try to talk him out of it. It got to the point where in 2006 I said to Randy, 'Come post-season, Georgie is the catcher.' And he said, 'Why?' I said, 'He's my number one catcher.' Randy was trying to sort of change my mind on that one for the post-season."

Torre, of course, wasn't about to lose any confidence in Posada, especially in the postseason. Their relationship began poorly, when Posada in 1997 thought he deserved more than his 52 starts as Girardi's backup. But Torre soon came to trust Posada as much as any of his core players, especially in big spots and as someone he could use to deliver peer-to-peer messages to players.

"The thing I sensed about Georgie, once I got to

know him a little bit, was that he had a big heart," Torre said. "He cared a great deal and he played well under pressure. We didn't always agree on his catching philosophy, but I chalked that up to the fact that he just didn't do it his whole life. But under pressure, I trusted him as much as anybody, no matter the game situation.

"He could deliver messages to players for me, too. Sometimes his timing wasn't as good as Jeter's was. But if I needed to get a message across to someone and I thought Georgie could do it, I would mention it to Georgie. Or if I wanted to get a message to Georgie, I'd go to Jeter—if I felt coming from me he might have taken it differently. Georgie and I got along great. I felt like he was a son to me."

Posada struck exactly the right chord with a distracted Wells in that meeting on the mound in the first inning of Game 5. Wells immediately refocused and pitched a gem after that, allowing only one more run while striking out 11. The Yankees won, 5-3.

"David Wells was the key to the series," Cone said. "People don't realize that. Robbie Alomar and Omar Vizquel, you made them turn around and bat righthanded with a lefty. Plus, you neutralize Jim Thome. To me they were a different lineup against lefthanded pitching. Wells beat them twice."

The Yankees came home for Game 6 and the possible clincher. They walloped Cleveland starter Charles Nagy with two runs in the first, one in the second and three on a home run by Brosius in the third. It was 6-0 after three innings with Cone on the mound. What could go wrong? But Cone's fears about how the Indians attacked righthanded pitching were realized in the fifth inning. Cleveland loaded the bases on three consecutive singles. Then Cone walked in a run, prompting Torre to visit Cone with Manny Ramirez due up.

"I'll get this guy," Cone told him.

Said Torre, "So I went back to the dugout, and he did get him. He struck out Manny. But then I left him in and Jim Thome hit a grand slam. Killed it."

"It put a scare in us," Cone said. "We were up 6-1 and now it was 6-5. I hung a slider to Thome and bam, upper deck. It happened so quick. I threw two balls to the next guy. I was shaken up a bit. It was a pretty good scare."

Cone did get two fly-ball outs to end the inning without further trouble. Torre told him he was done for the game.

"I should have taken you at your word," Torre told Cone.

"What do you mean?"

"You said you'd get **this guy.** I should have taken you out after **this guy.**"

The Yankees simply summoned more offense, scoring three times in the sixth, two on a triple by

Jeter, to establish more breathing room. Mendoza gave them two scoreless innings in relief of Cone to get the game to Rivera, who closed out the 9-5 win with a nine-pitch ninth inning with his usual cleanliness.

———

All that stood between the 1998 Yankees and their appointment with history was a World Series meeting with the San Diego Padres. The Padres put up a fight for a while, even carrying a 5-2 lead into the seventh inning of Game 1. But the Yankees asserted their greatness suddenly. Knoblauch tied the game with a three-run home run and Martinez put the Yankees ahead 9-5 with an upper-deck grand slam off lefthander Mark Langston, one pitch after Langston barely missed the strike zone with his 2-and-2 pitch. The Yankees won, 9-6. They administered one of their more routine beatings the next day, 9-3, removing all doubt from the game with a 7-0 lead after three innings.

In Game 3, they returned to their comeback mode, wiping out a 3-0 Padres lead in the seventh inning to win, 5-4. Brosius, the World Series MVP, connected off San Diego closer Trevor Hoffman for a three-run homer in the eighth to put the Yankees ahead, but the methodology of the comeback was just as important as the final blow. The winning home run was set up by walks by O'Neill and Martinez.

The walk, especially one littered with annoying foul balls, was the signature play of the championship Yankees teams. It wasn't exactly a sexy image, especially not when the country was going ga-ga over Mark McGwire, Sammy Sosa and the longball in 1998. But it was an effective one. The walk symbolized not only the unselfishness of the Yankees, but also the trust they harbored in one another. There was no need to chase pitches if you believed the teammate hitting behind you was going to get the job done. The 1998 Yankees led the league in walks, drawing a whopping 187 more free passes than they gave out. From 1996 through 1999, the Yankees posted on-base percentages of .360 or better every year, the first time they had done so in four straight years since Joe McCarthy's four consecutive world championship teams from 1936 through 1939.

From a practical standpoint, the tactic of making opposing starters throw more pitches was made brilliant because of the weapon the Yankees possessed in Mariano Rivera. The Yankees strived not always to beat the opposing starter, though they did so on many occasions, but to wear him down. Once they drove the starting pitcher from a game because of a high pitch count, they reduced the game to a duel of bullpens, and Rivera gave them the edge over any team in baseball in such situations. The Yankees' bullpen was 28-9 in 1998.

"It was intimidating knowing he was at the end of the game," said Beane, the Athletics' general manager. "It gave you tremendous anxiety knowing that you had to beat the Yankees in seven innings, because with Rivera, you knew you couldn't beat them in nine. You knew going in, 'We're going to get seven innings to get a lead, and that's it.' It's Rivera after that."

Rivera, like Jeter, fit perfectly in the Yankees' clubhouse culture, another superstar characterized by quiet humility and confidence who defined himself by how many games the team won, not his individual statistics. Rivera arrived in the majors in 1995 without advance billing, having survived Tommy John surgery in 1992, being left unprotected in the 1992 expansion draft (the Marlins and Rockies passed on him) and a near trade to the Tigers in 1995 for Wells that Gene Michael killed once he heard Rivera's velocity suddenly jumped to 96 mph. Trained as a starter, Rivera had a breakout series out of the bullpen in the 1995 Division Series, throwing $5\frac{1}{3}$ scoreless innings. After his one-year apprenticeship under John Wetteland in 1996, Rivera became not only a reliable closer, but also a strategically unique one. Just as the game was further defining the closer into a super specialist limited to one inning, Rivera was Torre's ultimate weapon because he could begin closing games in the eighth inning. Rivera was brutally efficient, putting away hitters quickly because his cut fastball was so hard to hit and because he threw with such precision.

From 1997 through 2008, Rivera racked up more postseason saves of six outs or more (12) than the rest of baseball combined (11). In that same period, Rivera obtained at least four outs in 79 percent of his postseason saves, more than triple the incidence of such heavy lifting by all other closers combined (25 percent).

"I think what makes Mo special, first of all, is the size of his heart," Torre said. "But second of all, he's made some adjustments. Like there were times he'd throw one cutter after another to Darrin Erstad of the Angels and it was foul ball, foul ball, foul ball. You wish he had someplace else to go to. One time he wound up throwing him a changeup, unrehearsed, and he hit a fly ball. But Mel helped him with his grips. The two-seamer was a part of it. The four-seamer was a part of it. He had the front-door cutter. Then he added the back-door cutter. All of a sudden he had different looks.

"I think one of the best things about him was that even though he knew he had done something special, he never stopped trying to get better at what he was doing."

Rivera took care of closing the 1998 World Series, and of course, did so by going more than one inning. He entered Game 4 with a 3-0 lead and two

Padres on base, but locked down the final four outs without a run scoring. The '98 Yankees did what they were supposed to do ever since they roared far in front of the field way back in April: they won the world championship. The relief was apparent on the face of Steinbrenner in the clubhouse, where his trademark blue blazer dripped with champagne in the middle of the celebration. The Boss was weeping openly.

"This," he said, "is as good as any team I've ever had, and as good as any team I've ever seen. There's never been anyone better."

That night in San Diego was the height of the Yankees' dynasty under Torre. They won other championships, of course: as an underdog in 1996, as a clinically efficient follow-up act in 1999 and as a scrappy 87-win fighter in 2000. But it was never as good as it was in 1998, not with the near-perfect composition of the roster, the peak-age talent and the singular mindset of 25 grinders rolled into 125 victories. A **desperation to win.** That is what made them so historic.

"There was such a cohesiveness about that team," Torre said. "They really hung together. There really wasn't a lot of stuff for me to deal with. You'd go out and you'd see four guys at dinner together. Maybe three days later you'd see two of those guys with two others. They weren't always in the same clique. There were all interchangeable pieces, and that was pretty good.

"But there really was no talk about me, and if somebody had a special day it didn't detract from the game or the goal. It was always about the team. They were not going to be denied when they got to a certain point, when they said, 'We can win this game.' They certainly were playing more on the balls of their feet than the other team.

"When you get a chance to talk to players, you find out what's important. It's interesting. They were all leaders for different reasons. Bernie, I had to tell him he was a leader. He didn't know it. But he played every day and you relied on him. O'Neill never had to be reminded. That's the message that I tried to get across to my players, which I think is my strongest message: there's somebody else counting on you. It's one of your teammates. It's not what I want you to do.

"Between Tino and Jeter and Girardi, O'Neill, Bernie and Brosius, it was just a commitment these guys had. They were good and they knew it and they worked at it. They worked at it. They were a bunch of grinders. In spite of the maintenance of Wells, it was a machine. Mariano settled into the closer's role and was great. It was all about once you get a taste of winning and know how it feels and how satisfying it is, it doesn't go away. When you have a year where you put numbers up, people go, 'Okay.' But they pay attention to winners. They always pay attention to winners. That group felt a responsibility. You have to live up to yourself. There was a great deal inside those guys."

———

The Yankees' 1999 spring training camp was about to begin the next morning, February 18, when Joe Torre received a telephone call from general manager Brian Cashman. All was right in the Yankees' world. They had returned 24 of the 25 players who won the previous World Series and a record 125 games. Only the veteran Tim Raines did not return, pushed out by way of free agency because of the rise of young outfielders Ricky Ledee and Shane Spencer. The Yankees were about to sell 3.2 million tickets that year, the first time the franchise topped three million and the upper limit of the attendance dream Steinbrenner envisioned when he signed Cone in 1995. But Cashman brought news of a bombshell that would alter the look and feel of the seemingly perfect Yankees.

"We just made the deal for Roger," Cashman said.

The Yankees agreed to send pitcher David Wells, infielder Homer Bush and reliever Graeme Lloyd to the Toronto Blue Jays to obtain Roger Clemens, thus accommodating George Steinbrenner's long-standing wish to obtain his "warrior," as well as Clemens' desire to win himself a world championship ring. Steinbrenner had visited Clemens at his

Houston area home after the 1996 season in an attempt to convince Clemens, then estranged from his Boston Red Sox as a free agent, to pitch in the Bronx. Steinbrenner even lifted weights in Clemens' home gym during his recruiting visit. But Clemens took a four-year contract from Toronto instead. Two years into that deal, during which he earned the Cy Young Award each year, Clemens wanted out. Citing an agreement with Blue Jays president Paul Beeston upon his signing, Clemens demanded a trade based on his contention that Toronto was not spending enough money to build a contender around him. Clemens did not mention that at $10 million per year, his contract had become obsolete by those signed by Randy Johnson ($13.25 million per year) and Kevin Brown ($15 million per year).

Clemens was owed $16.1 million over the remaining two years of his contract. When Toronto attempted to trade Clemens to his hometown Houston Astros, Houston general manager Gerry Hunsicker ended the talks and excoriated Clemens publicly when Clemens asked for $27.4 million as a one-year sweetener to his existing contract. By February, with no other recourse to get out of Toronto, Clemens was ready to sign off on a deal to join the Yankees.

"The trade happened real quickly," Torre said. "There was really not a lot of conversation. Obviously, before he signed with Toronto we were trying to get him then. Back then I heard he didn't want to come to New York. Maybe it was the whole Boston thing, that he wanted to get away from all the craziness."

The Yankees held off on announcing the trade until the next morning so they first could inform Wells in person that he was traded. Wells was 39-14 for the Yankees over his two seasons with the team, including 5-0 in the postseason. He had thrown a perfect game in 1998 and established himself as a fan favorite, his lack of conditioning being excused, even weirdly appreciated, as long as he kept coming up big in the big games. If New York loved Wells, Wells loved New York right back, especially into the late hours of the night. As David Cone said upon hearing about the trade, "There are going to be a lot of bars going out of business in New York."

When Wells reported for the first day of the Yankees' 1999 spring training camp, he immediately was told that Torre wanted to see him. He broke the news to him that he was traded. Wells quickly left the complex in tears. "I'm a little emotional right now," he told reporters. "Give me a couple days. It's a little tough right now."

In Clemens, then 36, the Yankees were getting the best pitcher in baseball. Clemens had won the pitching triple crown in the previous two seasons, leading the American League in wins, ERA and strikeouts each year. The only problem Torre saw about getting Clemens was that the Yankees could not stand him. Clemens had a reputation for head-hunting, using brushback pitches as attempts to intimidate batters.

"Before I had Roger on my team he was someone you loved to hate," Torre said. "He loved to intimidate. But the thing you always admired about him was the fact that he always seemed to get that guy out when he needed to. With a man on third base and less than two outs, or guys in scoring position, I don't remember a pitcher who did a better job of getting that guy out when he needed that big out."

On the first day Clemens threw live batting practice to his new teammates, Derek Jeter and Chuck Knoblauch donned catcher's gear before stepping into the cage, an acknowledgment of Clemens' intimidation tactics, but done in the humorous vein of new teammates forced by circumstance to get along. The Yankees looked like a juggernaut again. If Torre's biggest worry was making sure his players welcomed the best pitcher in baseball into their fraternity, the season figured to be a breeze. But, in fact, Torre had something much more serious to worry about that spring. He was scared that he might have cancer.

———

Torre underwent his annual physical with his personal physician in New York during the previous winter. Everything checked out okay except for a PSA level that was slightly elevated. His physician informed him that several factors could temporarily cause a higher reading and that he shouldn't be alarmed, but he also should pay attention to the PSA reading when he took his annual spring training physical conducted by the Yankees. The Yankees had added PSA tests to the physicals only after outfielder Darryl Strawberry was diagnosed with colon cancer the previous year. When Torre took the spring training physical, the PSA level was still elevated. Now there was some concern among the doctors. They ordered another test to see if an infection was causing the spike in his PSA level, but that possibility was quickly ruled out. In early March doctors told Torre that they would have to do a biopsy to determine if he had prostate cancer.

"Age was something that never played a part in my day-to-day operation until I realized I was getting close to 60 years old," Torre said. "I was getting ready to turn 59 that year and for the first time I thought, 'Shit. I'm getting old.'

"So then they ran the biopsy test and they were going to get back to me with the results. When you go through something like that, you expect the worst. Because if you expect the best and you get the worst, you're going to free fall."

The Yankees were playing a spring training game in Kissimmee, Florida, against the Astros on the day Torre expected to hear the results of the biopsy. He left the game early and began driving back to Tampa at about the time he expected the call. Only later, however, would he learn that his cell phone was not receiving a signal as he drove on the highway. It was only when he stopped in Tampa to purchase a CD for his daughter that his phone rang. But it was not the doctors. It was Steinbrenner.

"Don't worry, Joe," Steinbrenner said. "You'll come through this fine and be all right."

Torre was stunned—and hurt. How did Steinbrenner know? Torre hadn't even heard from the doctors yet and here was Steinbrenner breaking the news to him that he had cancer.

"George called me and led me to believe that he knew the results, which pissed me off," Torre said. "So I stopped trusting, not so much George, but the people around him from that point. I heard from the doctors a little bit after the call from George. I then went back and told my wife what the diagnosis was. She was sort of in denial. It was a scary time."

How do you break the news to your team that you have cancer? The Yankees had split-squad games the next day, meaning half the team would be playing at home and the other half would be playing on the road. Logistically, it was difficult to pull everyone together. So Torre called Clemens and David Cone and told them he would like them to tell the players at the home game about his illness. Then he called Joe Girardi and asked him to perform the same duty on the road. He also called Don Zimmer, his bench coach, and asked him to manage the team while he was recovering from surgery.

It didn't take long for the Yankees to miss the way Torre calmly handled every crisis—often blunting them before they could blow up into a major issue—especially when it came to his expert lion-taming skills with Steinbrenner.

"I made the mistake of putting Zimmer in charge of the team," Torre said. "Emotionally, it was a ton for him. He was a mess. What I should have done was probably put Mel Stottlemyre in charge, and it might have been a little easier for everybody—to have Zim sit next to Mel, but have Mel answer for it with the media and George.

"At the end of that spring training is when George called Hideki Irabu 'a fat toad.' And then the team went out to Los Angeles to play an exhibition game and Zim wanted to start Ramiro Mendoza but George wanted to start Irabu. I called up Zim in L.A. and said, 'Zim, just let it go. When George said something you just say, "He's The Boss, blah, blah, blah," and do what you want to do. Just don't challenge it with George.' So when Zim just said, 'Okay, goodbye' and hung up, I knew he had no chance. He was going to challenge George. And it turned into a wildfire. So it started right there with Zim and George going at it."

Torre, meanwhile, underwent surgery March 19. Dr. William Catalona performed the two-and-a-half-hour procedure at Barnes-Jewish Hospital in St. Louis. Catalona assured Torre that the operation was successful and that he would be working again soon. It was a message that Torre wanted to deliver to his players personally.

"When I came back after my surgery I met the players and explained what was going on," Torre said. "I just wanted to keep them aware of it. It's the same way with any issues. If anything was whispered around the team, I'd always meet with them and be as honest as I can. If there was someone new around the team, for instance, I might say, 'I can't trust this security guy. I'm not telling you what to do. I'm just making you aware of what I'm aware of.' I'd like to think that honesty came through in the trust factor you need to have with your players."

Torre returned to manage the Yankees on May 18, almost two months to the day from his surgery, and just in time for a game in Boston against Pedro Martinez and the Red Sox. When Torre brought the lineup card to home plate before the game, the Fenway Park crowd rose and cheered for two minutes and the scoreboard passed along greetings of "Welcome Back."

"Sitting in the dugout after you know you've had cancer," Torre said, "you're thinking, 'This is a game we're playing, and how important is this?' I just didn't know if that same intense feeling was going to come back. And then when we got to Toronto on the next road trip I remember Bernie Williams was hitting with the bases loaded and I was willing to sell my soul for a hit. And Bernie hit a grand slam.

And that's when I knew I was all the way back. The bubbles were back.

"Every once in a while you have to step back and put things in perspective and where they belong. But the minute you start to minimize the importance of winning you're cheating everybody. You're cheating the players you're trying to lead. You're cheating the owners who are paying you.

"The cancer never really goes away. Cancer is there every day of your life. When I was diagnosed that spring, I said in jest, 'Now I know why all those balls were dropping in for us.' I never thought, 'Why me?' Instead, I thought, 'Why shouldn't it be me?' Why should it be that all things that happen to me are good things? Should this happen to somebody else who was struggling? So I never complained, 'Why me?' I've been very blessed."

———

The 1999 Yankees were not quite the machine that was the 1998 Yankees, but they were a reasonable facsimile—except for Clemens falling short of replacing Wells' excellence. They held first place for 131 days, including all of them after June 9. On July 18, two months into Torre being back on the job, and 14 months since Wells threw his perfect game, all about the Yankees was perfect again. It was a Sunday afternoon in which the Yankees honored Yogi Berra before an interleague game against the Montreal Expos. Don Larsen, the author of the only perfect game in World Series history, was there to throw the ceremonial first pitch to Berra, a nod to their collaboration in the 1956 perfecto. Larsen and Berra watched the game from Steinbrenner's suite-level box. They saw history repeat itself.

Cone, the Yankees' starting pitcher, dominated the heavily righthanded Expos, none of whom had faced him before, with fastballs and sliders that disappeared from their swing plane. After only five innings, the thought occurred to Cone that he might have a shot at throwing a perfect game. The Expos kept going down with amazing ease; Cone would throw only 20 balls to 27 batters. After almost every inning on the 98-degree day, Cone would return to the clubhouse to change one of the cutoff undershirts he wore beneath his jersey. By the time he retreated to the clubhouse in the eighth inning, the perfect game still intact, he noticed there was nobody in there. Nobody wanted to break the tradition of not talking to a pitcher when he has a no-hitter or perfect game in progress.

"It was a ghost town," Cone said. "Even the clubhouse attendants were gone."

Cone kept the perfect game going through the eighth, though to do so it took a backhand grab of a grounder and surprisingly true throw from the unpredictable Knoblauch at second base. Now Cone was only three outs away from baseball immortality. He walked back to the clubhouse. Again, the place was deserted. He changed undershirts again, then walked into the bathroom, stopping at one of the sinks in front of the large mirror. Alone, he looked at himself in the mirror and spoke aloud.

"What do we have to do to get this done?" he said. "This is the last chance you're ever going to have to do something like this."

He bent down, ran cold water from the faucet into his cupped hands and splashed the water over his face. He stared at himself in the mirror again.

"Holy shit," he said. "How am I going to do this?"

For a moment he was caught in a very awkward place between doubt and desire, trying to beat back one while encouraging the other in a battle inside his head.

Don't blow it, he thought to himself.

And then he shook his head.

No, don't think that way! That's negative.

But doubt crawled back.

Don't blow it.

No. No negative thoughts. Get it done!

But don't blow it.

Finally, he stopped the internal doubt for good. Still staring into the mirror, he thought to himself, **Screw the psychobabble! Go out there and get it done!**

Cone was 36 years old, a survivor of a scary aneurysm three years earlier, and well aware of his pitching mortality. He could not know it at the time, but this would be the last complete game he would ever throw, the last shutout, too. In fact, Cone would make 131 starts in his six seasons with the Yankees, and this would be his only shutout.

"I went out there for the ninth and—boom, boom, boom—struck out the first guy on three pitches," Cone said. "Then I got a humpback liner to left, which Ricky Ledee kind of lost in the seats or sun or whatever."

Ledee, though, caught the ball, however ungracefully. Cone needed one more out. The batter was Orlando Cabrera, a 24-year-old shortstop. Cabrera swung and missed at the first pitch and took the second one for a ball. On the next pitch, a slider, the 88th pitch of the game for Cone, Cabrera lifted a pop-up into foul ground near third base. Cone looked up and couldn't find the ball.

"I remember the sun was setting on that side of Yankee Stadium," Cone said. "As I looked up I got blinded by the sun, so I pointed, thinking Brosius might lose it in the sun. I just remember pointing at it, and Brosius was already camped under it at that point. I never saw the ball."

Brosius squeezed the pop-up in his glove. Cone was perfect. He dropped to his knees and reached for his head, in a sweet combination of disbelief and relief.

_____

Torre always believed championships began with starting pitching and 1999 was no different, even with Clemens underperforming. Torre's rotation was remarkably durable and reliable once again. Cone, Clemens, El Duque, Pettitte and Irabu made 152 of the teams' 162 starts, posting a 68-36 record. Steinbrenner, though, considered Pettitte a drag on the staff and wanted him gone, especially after Pettitte could not get out of the fourth inning of a game against the White Sox on July 28, 10 days after Cone's perfect game and three days before the trade deadline. Pettitte was 7-8 with a 5.65 ERA at that point. Steinbrenner had a deal in place to ship Pettitte to the Phillies.

While the Yankees were in Boston just hours away from the deadline, Steinbrenner conducted a conference call with Cashman, Torre and Stottlemyre. Steinbrenner said he was ready to trade Pettitte.

"I can't believe you would even consider doing it!" Stottlemyre said.

Torre and Cashman also spoke out against trading Pettitte. Finally, Steinbrenner gave in. He called off the deal.

"You better be right," he said to the three of them, "or you know what's going to happen."

Over the next 4½ years, or until Steinbrenner let Pettitte walk as a free agent, Pettitte went 75-35 for Steinbrenner's Yankees, a .682 winning percentage.

Over the rest of that 1999 season, Pettitte was 7-3 with a 3.46 ERA before tacking on a 2-0 postseason. Pettitte never truly engendered confidence from Steinbrenner, possibly because he carried himself with a sensitivity that belied his competitiveness.

Torre remembers one of the first big games Pettitte pitched for him, on September 18, 1996, against Baltimore. It was the first game of a huge three-game series at Yankee Stadium against the second-place Orioles, whom the Yankees led by three games with 13 games to play. Pettitte, 24, was pitching against veteran Baltimore righthander Scott Erickson. Torre walked into the trainer's room before the game and happened to find Pettitte there.

"He looked scared to death," Torre said. "He was just sitting there, staring."

Torre learned to interpret such a look from Pettitte as intense focus. Pettitte pitched magnificently against Baltimore, allowing the league's top home-run-hitting team just two runs over $8\frac{1}{3}$ innings. Pettitte did leave trailing, 2-1, but the Yankees rallied to tie the game in the ninth and win it in the 10th, 3-2.

"One thing I learned about Andy," Torre said, "is he thought you weren't allowed to be nervous. Jeter, as far as handling the pressure, is the best I've ever seen. But Andy, in spite of getting excited, managed to handle it the right way. The game never sped up for him.

"He's so honest, which is so refreshing, because not too many people own up to their shortcomings. He does. Whether it's a particular at-bat or pitch, he'll tell you. Andy is very honest.

"In fact, I remember when I talked to him about the possibility of coming back to the Yankees after he pitched those years in Houston. He said, 'I thought I had everything where I wanted it: coming home, being with family . . . I just didn't have fun playing. There was no fire. Just the thought of going back to New York has gotten me excited.' Probably the worst word in sports is being 'comfortable.' There's something about comfort that doesn't seem to fit with what you need to do. Andy missed New York. Andy was great. I think he taught Roger how to pitch in New York. And Roger taught Andy how to be stronger. Back then Andy was a little soft physically, but not mentally, that's for sure."

The trade for Clemens, meanwhile, did not turn out the way the Yankees expected. Clemens missed three weeks early in the season with a leg problem, and when he did pitch he looked nothing like the best pitcher in baseball as he had been in Toronto. He was 8-4 with an unseemly 4.98 ERA through the middle of July. He struck out 10 batters in a game only once. He looked far too ordinary.

"Roger struggled early on," Cone said. "He was getting booed at Yankee Stadium. Roger was always kind of aloof. He was kind of shy and insecure. People don't realize that about him. A lot of superstars are like that, surprisingly so. Roger was like that. He struggled to fit in. He struggled with New York. He was not pitching too well and in fact had trouble just hanging out. He would be disappearing before games. He was always hiding in the weight room or on the couch in the traveling secretary's office. Just kind of hiding out a lot. During the game he wasn't on the bench very much. He got better as he started to pitch better and got used to the guys."

One day in August, while the Yankees were in Seattle, Clemens asked Torre if he could use his office to call his mother. Torre said of course. A while later Torre stepped into the office to retrieve something and heard Clemens tell his mom, "I'm still just trying to fit in and be one of the guys."

When Clemens was done with the call Torre told him he wanted to speak to him.

" 'Fit in' my ass," Torre told him. "You be who you are. Be Roger Clemens."

"I know," Clemens said. "That's what my mom is always telling me."

"Listen," Torre said, "you're allowed to be selfish. We traded for you because we wanted the guy who was pitching in Toronto, not somebody different. Not somebody who is just trying to fit in. You're just trying to sort of blend in here and that's not what we want. That's not what we traded for. You're too tentative."

Clemens agreed with Torre's assessment and vowed to be more assertive, though the Yankees still didn't see the dominating version of Clemens. He pitched only marginally better over his final 11 starts, going 5-6 with a 4.34 ERA.

"The thing with Roger that I found was you loved him," Torre said. "There are all the bells and whistles that you get with Roger but his heart was always in the right place. He was a good teammate, and that sort of surprised me, because before he got to us he had this reputation about being able to go home and not be around the team. And I told him. 'You can't do that,' and it was never a problem.

"He was a cheerleader in between starts. And he reminded me of Bob Gibson when he did start. We wouldn't be scoring for Gibby and he'd go, 'You guys . . . you've got to be shittin' me.' And he'd go inside the clubhouse. Roger would do that. He was very outgoing, and yet it wasn't an act. If it was, he had himself convinced of that.

"He also had tremendous belief in himself and his pitching. If you don't believe that pitch is going to go exactly where you want it, then it's not going to go there. Roger believed every pitch was going where he wanted it to go."

———

Clemens did not come close to replacing Wells' production with the 1999 Yankees. He finished 14-10 with a 4.60 ERA, the worst ERA of his 24-year career. The Yankees still won the AL East with 98 wins, four more than second-place Boston. On the final weekend of the season, Torre sat down with Stottlemyre to map out their pitching plans for the playoffs when Torre decided to include Clemens in the discussion. Clemens, by reputation, was a pro-typical Game 1 starter, but in reality he had not been that kind of pitcher for the Yankees all year. Orlando "El Duque" Hernandez had led the staff that season with 17 wins. Torre decided he wanted Clemens to recognize that reality himself.

"Roger, who do you think should start Game 1?" Torre asked him.

"Duque," Clemens said.

Torre was a bit relieved to know he would not have to convince Clemens otherwise.

"What I like to do is see if people evaluate the same way I do," Torre said. "I figured, 'As much as he thinks of himself, let's see what he said.'"

If Clemens had said he deserved the ball for Game 1, Torre said, "we would have talked him out of it. We would have explained why that's not true. I always liked to believe that you could always try to make sense to people. I always try to make these guys understand there is another perspective other than theirs."

Clemens was Torre's number three starter, behind Hernandez and Andy Pettitte. The Yankees blew through the Texas Rangers in the Division Series again, allowing only one run in the three-game sweep. Torre used the same order of pitchers in the American League Championship Series against Boston, an arrangement that left Clemens returning to Fenway Park to pitch against Pedro Martinez in Game 3. The game was promoted in the manner of a heavyweight fight, a bout between Clemens, the expatriate Red Sox star, and Martinez, his replacement in Boston as the best pitcher in baseball and the soul of the franchise. The crowd arrived with the meanness and edginess of a mob. Indeed, before the day was done packs of fans would climb over themselves trying to claw down a canvas mural hung in one of the concourses in celebration of Clemens' two 20-strikeout games with Boston.

Clemens, a shell of himself all season, failed miserably amid the hostility. Torre removed him only one batter into the third inning with the score 4-0. Clemens walked off the mound and down the dugout steps gingerly, having something of a ready-made excuse because of some back stiffness. Clemens was charged with five runs in what became a 13-1 Boston victory, its only one of the ALCS. In the middle innings, with Clemens long gone and Martinez cutting apart the Yankees lineup, the crowd mocked Clemens by chanting, "Where is Roger?"

———

Part of what made Clemens great as a pitcher was his inflated sense of self, the same trait that prompted Torre to check with Clemens before aligning his postseason rotation. There is almost no concession in the man. He enjoyed not just being Roger Clemens, but also playing the role of Roger Clemens.

"He is needy, and he's got his own world he lives in. As far as competing, they're different people. Roger's always going to go out there and have that positive attitude. That's the way he has to think."

Said Brian McNamee, Clemens' former personal trainer, and the one who told baseball special investigator George Mitchell in 2007 that he injected Clemens with steroids, "The worst day was the day after Roger lost a game. Because he would blame everybody on the field. It was the umpire, it was the fielders, it was Jeter can't go to his left, it was the outfielders playing back too deep . . . it was always something. The ball. The ball's too slick. Oh, Posada? All the time. It was just a nightmare."

Torre never knew Clemens to look for excuses. He understood that Clemens' knack for ignoring reality at the cost of preserving his grand sense of self would not play well in the wake of his debacle in ALCS Game 3 in front of the Boston mob. Blaming his third-inning knockout on a stiff back, for instance, would invite his critics to diminish him further. Torre was concerned about what Clemens might say to reporters after the game.

As Torre took Clemens out of the game, he told him on the mound, "Just do yourself a favor. When they come in and talk to you, just tell them you were horseshit. Because I know you're hurting. You know you're hurting. But that won't play well."

After the game, first the reporters asked Torre if Clemens, by evidence of the pained look he gave leaving the mound, was diminished by an injury.

Said Torre, "I think the score was making him grimace."

Then the reporters approached Clemens. Would he blame the results on his back? Was the ball too slick? This time, thanks to Torre's intervention, he actually revealed some concession.

"I think the thing for me tonight was location," Clemens said. "I didn't have good command, I fell behind and they made me pay for it."

———

Pettitte, the man Steinbrenner wanted gone, immediately righted the Yankees in Game 4. With little room for error, he brought the ball and a 3-2 lead directly to Mariano Rivera. Pettitte allowed the Red Sox only two runs in 7⅓ innings. The Yankees broke open the close game with six runs in the ninth to win, 9-2. After the game Steinbrenner visited Torre in the tiny visiting manager's office at Fenway Park. Torre was happy for Pettitte, and he was also happy for Joe Girardi, the selfless catcher who had been Torre's first recommended acquisition when he was hired in 1995. Problem was, Steinbrenner knew Girardi was one of Torre's soldiers and he would criticize Girardi often.

"Did you see how well Andy pitched?" Torre said to Steinbrenner. "And he couldn't have done it without Girardi!"

Torre started breaking down. Tears were coming down his cheeks. Steinbrenner didn't know what the hell was going on.

Said Torre, "I was on hormones for my radiation treatment, and I was emotional. I remember George had been trying to dump Girardi from just about day one."

The next morning Steinbrenner called up Torre at the team's hotel.

"Do you want to have lunch?" Steinbrenner asked.

"No, Ali's here," Torre said.

"Well, bring Ali."

"No. We just want to be by ourselves here. I'm going to go work out and then we're going out to eat."

And then Torre hung up the phone.

Torre took the hotel elevator down to the floor with the fitness center. When the doors opened and he stepped out, he saw Steinbrenner standing there.

"You all right?" Steinbrenner asked.

"Yeah, I'm all right," Torre said. "Just emotional, that's all."

Said Torre, "That was the fun part about George. His bark was worse than his bite. He cared a lot."

That night Hernandez followed Pettitte's gem

with one of his own: he allowed one run on five hits over seven innings. The Yankees clinched the pennant so easily, 6-1, that Torre did not even have to use Rivera.

As with San Diego the previous season, the Yankees stormed through their National League opponent in the World Series, even if it was a Braves team with a renowned rotation of Greg Maddux, Tom Glavine, John Smoltz and Kevin Millwood. The Yankees outpitched the famous Braves' staff, permitting Atlanta nine runs in a four-game sweep. Maddux held a 1-0 lead in the eighth inning of Game 1 and Glavine held a 5-2 lead in the seventh inning of Game 3 and yet the Yankees came back against both pitching greats.

With a three games to none lead, the Yankees could comfortably give the ball to their new number four starter, Clemens, who had fallen in line behind Hernandez, Pettitte and Cone. That morning, Torre received a phone call with sad news: O'Neill's father had passed away at about 3 a.m. Charles O'Neill was 79 and had been suffering from heart disease. Torre immediately called Paul. O'Neill's wife, Nevalee, answered the phone.

"Paul's not home," she said. "Oh, Joe, I don't know how we're going to get him to the ballpark. But we've got to find a way to get him there. That's where he needs to be."

O'Neill did make it to Yankee Stadium for Game 4, and batted third in the lineup. He went

0-for-3, but his teammates picked him up by jumping on Smoltz in the third inning with another of those quintessential Yankee rallies: one walk, two infield singles and two opposite field singles. They added up to three runs.

The Yankees would win 299 regular season games and three consecutive world championships from 1998 to 2000 without ranking among the top three home-run-hitting teams in the league and with no player hitting more than 30 home runs. Every other team in baseball over those three years had someone hit more than 30 homers at least **twice.** Viewed another way, there were 113 times a player hit more than 30 homers in those three seasons—none of them were Yankees.

Buoyed by the 3-0 lead, Clemens brought the championship home from there. He pitched well two outs into the eighth inning, allowing the Braves only one run in the 4-1 clinching victory. The Yankees had their second straight world championship and their third in four years, and Clemens at last had his first. The Yankees streamed out to the mound after Rivera retired Keith Lockhart on a fly ball to Chad Curtis in left field. Across the crush of players, O'Neill found Torre and walked over to his manager. He threw his arms around Torre and hugged him, sobbing uncontrollably on his shoulder.

Clemens enjoyed the party as much as anyone. He was so excited by the title that he arranged for his teammates to receive a second world championship ring, this one he commissioned out of platinum. This is why he had asked Beeston to get him out of Toronto, to jump aboard the Yankees' championship train while it was still rolling. Including the postseason, the Yankees won 109 games in 1999. It wasn't the record of 125 wins from 1998, but it was staggering nonetheless, especially when you consider their postseason dominance. The 1999 Yankees were 11-1 in the postseason, allowing only 31 runs in those 12 games and coming within one start by Clemens at Fenway Park from running the table without a loss. The championship did fill a void in Clemens' prolific career.

"Roger was what he was coming out of high school," Torre said. "In a lot of ways, he's like Alex: they didn't let the advance notices down. Coming out of high school and college people expected big things and he delivered right away. He's a guy that doesn't know negative. Doesn't know failure. He paints a different picture of failure than a lot of people.

"Roger is a guy who, when I got to know him, I realized what a bulldog he was. Before, it looked like it was ability but the guy steering the ship wasn't a guy I'd put in the class of pitchers such as Koufax, Gibson, Drysdale and Ryan—until I got to know him. Now, in my mind, he belongs there."

3.

Getting an Edge

The 1998 baseball season was a party of epic proportions, the equivalent of an all-nighter with the music cranked and every care in the world, or at least the anger and bitterness of the 1994–95 players' strike, easily forgotten. The 1998 Yankees, the winningest team of all time, were just part of the fun for Bud Selig, whose caretaking role as interim commissioner finally ended in midsummer. Bud Selig, who had owned the Milwaukee Brewers, was the ultimate insider.

It was an expansion year, with the Tampa Bay Devil Rays and Arizona Diamondbacks adding two more television markets, $260 million in expansion fees, and another 324 games to the inventory of moneymaking possibilities. Attendance jumped 12 percent, with almost seven and a half million more people paying their way into ballparks. The per-game major league average improved by 4 percent to 29,054, the best it had been since before the strike hit. The ratings for games televised by Fox improved by 11 percent.

It was the year David Wells threw his perfect game, a rookie Cubs pitcher named Kerry Wood struck out a record-tying 20 batters and the age-defying Roger Clemens, while in the employ of the Toronto Blue Jays at that stage of his pitcher-for-hire phase, became the first pitcher to strike out 18 or more batters in a game for the third time.

Most of all, it was the year that belonged to hitters, who just happened to be growing cartoonishly large and hitting baseballs into parts of ballparks where no baseballs had gone before. It was a freak show and baseball loved it. It was the first season in history in which four players hit 50 home runs. Greg Vaughn and Ken Griffey Jr., half of the 50-plus bombers that year, were dwarfed in size, production and attention by Mark McGwire and Sammy Sosa. Both McGwire, with 70 home runs, and Sosa, with 66, blew away the record 61 home runs of Roger Maris that had stood as the standard for 37 years. America was captivated by the two huge men and the great home-run race. Senator Edward Kennedy, Democrat of Massachusetts, praised McGwire and Sosa as the "home-run kings for working families in America." McGwire, with fore-arms the size of a grown man's neck, 17 inches around, was a gate attraction unto himself, a modern wonder of the world. Ballparks opened their gates early and called in concession staffs to clock in early just to accommodate the thousands of fans who wanted to see him take batting practice. On September 9, Fox scrapped the season premieres of its prime-time Tuesday night shows to televise the game in which McGwire would hit his record-breaking 62nd home run. More than 43 million people watched.

Baseball was awash in goodwill, national attention and money like it had not seen in many years. The Los Angeles Dodgers garishly flaunted such largesse after that season by giving Kevin Brown, a pitcher soon to turn 34 years old, an age when players traditionally had neared retirement as their bodies gave out, a seven-year contract worth $105 million, sweetening the deal with private jet service back and forth from his Georgia home.

That same winter, with the party raging at full throttle, one man rose up and basically announced the whole damn thing was a fraud. Rick Helling, a 27-year-old righthanded pitcher and the players' representative for the Texas Rangers, stood up at the winter meeting of the Executive Board of the Major League Baseball Players Association and made an announcement. He told his fellow union leaders that steroid use by ballplayers had grown rampant and was corrupting the game.

"There is this problem with steroids," Helling

told them. "It's happening. It's real. And it's so prevalent that guys who aren't doing it are feeling pressure to do it because they're falling behind. It's not a level playing field. We've got to figure out a way to address it.

"It's a bigger deal than people think. It's noticeable enough that it's creating an uneven playing field. What really bothers me is that it's gotten so out of hand that guys are feeling pressure to do it. It's one thing to be a cheater, to be somebody who doesn't care whether it's right or wrong. But it's another thing when other guys feel like they have to do it just to keep up. And that's what's happening. And I don't feel like this is the right way to go."

What Helling had just done was the equivalent of turning up all the lights, clicking off the music and announcing the party was over. "He was the first guy," David Cone said, "who had the guts to stand up at a union meeting and say that in front of everybody and put pressure on it."

There was only one way for baseball to react to this kind of whistleblowing:

Crank the music back up and keep the party rolling.

The union was having too much fun and making too much money to pay much attention to Helling's warning. It was far easier and financially prudent to ignore the issue, to assume that Helling was an alarmist prone to exaggerating, and to make sure everyone involved knew as little as possible about players injecting hard-core steroids into their asses. Don't ask, don't tell and don't care was the unwritten code of the day.

"What really bothered me was there were plenty of good guys, good people, who were feeling the pressure to cheat because it had become so prevalent," Helling said. "I firmly believed at the time that it was an unlevel playing field. I was trying to find a way to do something about it. Make it as fair of a game as possible. Play it the right way.

"When you see guys coming into spring training camp thirty pounds heavier than they ended the previous season, or they had gained four or fives miles an hour on their fastball, I mean, those things are not normal. My whole career was played in the peak of the steroids era. I saw guys throwing 87 miles an hour one year and 95 the next. Unfortunately, a lot of people, the press, the owners, the players, they turned the other cheek. I was like, 'Are you serious? Can't you see what's going on? Are you seriously going to let these guys get away with it?'

"Unfortunately, it turned out just the way I thought it would. It blew up in our face."

———

The union's executive board paid little attention to Helling. The owners were of a similar mindset. In fact, within a matter of days of Helling sounding an alarm that went unheeded, baseball provided official proof that steroids were not considered an urgent problem. At those same 1998 winter baseball meetings in Nashville, baseball's two medical directors, Dr. Robert Millman, who was appointed by the owners, and Dr. Joel Solomon, the designee of the players, delivered a presentation to baseball executives and physicians about the **benefits** of using testosterone. Angels general manager Bill Stoneman was so surprised at the tone of the presentation—basically, the message he heard was that no evidence exists that steroids were harmful—that he wondered why Major League Baseball even had allowed it.

Also in attendance was Dr. William Wilder, the physician for the Cleveland Indians. Wilder was so disturbed by the presentation that he wrote a memorandum to Indians general manager John Hart that whether testosterone increased muscle strength and endurance "begs the question of whether it should be used in athletics." Wilder also endorsed sending information to players about the "known and unknown data about performance-enhancing substances."

Wilder also spoke directly with Gene Orza of the players association. Orza advised him to hold off on any education about supplements until more information was available. Wilder was incredulous. Of Orza's request to postone any action, the doctor wrote, "That will be never! Orza and the Players Association want to do further study . . . so nothing will be done."

Orza infamously revealed the players' position

on steroids more blatantly in 2004, even long after the lid blew off the steroid epidemic in baseball. Speaking as part of a panel discussion in a public forum, Orza said, "Let's assume that [steroids] are a very bad thing to take. I have no doubt that they are not worse than cigarettes. But I would never say to the clubs as an individual who represents the interests of players, 'Gee, I guess by not allowing baseball to suspend and fine players for smoking cigarettes, I am not protecting their health.'"

Well, there you had it. No wonder nobody wanted to listen to Helling. The owners and players didn't even want to acknowledge that something harmful was going on. A presentation on the **benefits** of testosterone? Not worse than cigarettes? Helling, though, didn't give up. Each year he would make the same speech at the players association board meeting . . . 1998, 1999, 2000, 2001 . . . and each year nothing would happen, except that more and more bodies grew unnaturally bigger and the game became twisted into a perversion, its nuances and subtleties blasted away by the naked obsession with power. Baseball was reduced to the lowest common denominator: to whack the ball farther or to heave it faster. Baseball's inability and unwillingness to act made silent partners of Selig and his traditional rivals at the union, leaders Don Fehr and Orza. Neither side had the smarts or the stomach to make steroids a front-burner public issue.

"Steve [Fehr] and Don came to me and said, 'Rick Helling is talking up steroids. Do you think there's a problem here?'" Cone said, referring to the Fehr brothers, including Steve, Cone's agent. "I said, 'Maybe we need to talk to guys, but I don't really see a problem.'"

The union, Helling said, did talk to some players about it, but the pitcher was wise enough not to expect anything to come of it.

"I understood their side of it, from a lawyer's side," Helling said. "Their thinking was, 'This isn't anything ownership has asked us for. It's never been an issue [in bargaining]. So why would we give them something without getting something in return. Why open this box?'

"I was active in the union. I know Don and Gene very well. Still to this day I talk to them. I understand. 'We don't want to go down that road if we don't have to.' Every year I brought it up. I'd say, 'This is more of a problem than you think.' Bud, Gene, Don . . . they had an idea of what was going on. They didn't realize how widespread it was. As players, we kind of did know. Whether it was 50 percent or whatever, I can't say. It was more than people thought. It was more than Don, Gene and Bud thought. So the thinking was more, 'If ownership didn't ask for it, why volunteer it? It's probably not that big a deal.'"

Helling said he never saw a player inject steroids, but he heard all the clubhouse talk about what players were doing, as they would euphemistically put it, to "get an edge." Helling himself had a very clear understanding of what was cheating and what was not. He was born in Devils Lake, North Dakota, and became one of only fifteen men born in that state to become a big leaguer. He attended Stanford University and made his major league debut with Texas only two years after the Rangers selected him with a second round pick in the 1992 draft. He pitched decently for both the Rangers and Marlins (he was once traded to Florida and back within 11 months) before committing himself to a strenuous conditioning and fitness program after the 1997 season. In 1998, his first full year as a starting pitcher, he won 20 games. He would pitch twelve seasons in the majors, compiling a record of 93-81 while earning more than $15 million.

"I can look back on my career, and whether it was good or bad, I know that everything I did, I did myself," Helling said. "I didn't do any form of cheating. It's unfortunate that there were a lot of people I knew who thought, 'I need to do something to keep up.' You hear the excuses of the guys who admitted it: 'I felt like I had to do it.' The way I looked at it, when I wasn't good enough to do it myself, it was time to move on. A lot of players didn't think like that. Guys always had an excuse of why they could do it.

"That's not what I was about. I can look back and know it was all me. That's the most important thing. I have my name and my reputation. Anybody who knows me knows there was no doubt that I played it the right way. And that's what I wanted to leave the game with. I couldn't care less if I made one million dollars or one hundred million dollars, whether I won one game or whether I won three hundred games. I was in it to be honest to myself and my teammates and to be a good father and husband. For me it was just the way I was brought up."

Rick Helling, by playing clean, was swimming against the tide.

The party that was 1998 was also the same year the Toronto Blue Jays hired a man named Brian McNamee to be their strength and conditioning trainer. McNamee was a Queens, New York, kid, the son of a detective, who had attended St. John's University, majoring in athletic administration and playing baseball. In 1990 he began working as a New York City police officer. Three years later McNamee met Tim McCleary, an assistant general manager for the Yankees. Like McNamee, McCleary was a St. John's guy. McCleary helped hire McNamee in 1993 to be a bullpen catcher for the Yankees. McNamee spent three seasons with the Yankees until he became a casualty of the managerial and staff changes after the 1995 season, when Torre replaced Buck Showalter. McCleary also moved on after that 1995 season. He quit the Yankees and quickly resurfaced with the Toronto Blue Jays in a similar capacity.

McNamee, meanwhile, reinvented himself as a strength and fitness trainer. He was out of baseball for three years before McCleary reached out to his friend in 1998 to come back not as a bullpen catcher but as a strength coach for the Jays. McNamee had been out of baseball for three years. What he found shocked him. Steroids and drugs were everywhere. What had been a rogue, underground, fringe culture of steroid and performance-enhancing drug use only three years ago had become an all-out pharmacological war by 1998.

"From '93 to '95 you didn't see any of it," McNamee said. "Supplements and some things here and there . . . Then in '98 . . . it was just . . . I couldn't believe it."

Drug use had become so prevalent by 1998 that ballplayers talked openly about it among themselves, including speculation about who was using what and what drugs provided the best benefit. McNamee was stunned by the prevalence of the drug use and openness with which players discussed it.

The physical stature, success and popularity of McGwire and Sosa obviously contributed to the rush for players to gain strength. According to the book **Game of Shadows,** by Mark Fainaru-Wada and Lance Williams, it was the adulation given McGwire and Sosa that pushed Barry Bonds into the world of performance-enhancing drugs. Bonds, then 33 years old and at his natural peak, was an enormously gifted and far better all-around player than either McGwire or Sosa. In 1998 Bonds batted .303 with 37 home runs, a career-high 44 doubles and 122 runs batted in while stealing 28 bases and winning a Gold Glove. It was an astonishingly great season. It also was completely ignored. Seventeen players hit more home runs than did Bonds. McGwire and Sosa eclipsed all of them. McGwire and Sosa redefined not only the home-run record but also what it meant to be a national baseball hero. They were largely one-dimensional players who could not run, field or throw like Bonds, but America loved them for their heft and their ability to hit a baseball a very long way. Bonds, the superior player who was ignored, was just one of many players who recognized in McGwire and Sosa that the rules of engagement had been changed.

Said Cone, "After that, after 1998, there was a little four- or five-year window there where things happened real quickly."

Nineteen ninety-eight didn't invent steroids in baseball; it only made them mainstream inside the game. Until then, steroid use occupied a dark corner of the game that was best left unspoken. Former Most Valuable Player Jose Canseco began shooting steroids thirteen years earlier, in 1985. One dealer, Curtis Wenzlaff, was supplying 20 to 25 ballplayers with steroids at the time of his conviction in 1992. Lenny Dykstra, the former Mets and Phillies outfielder, admitting to using steroids as far back as 1989, according to Kirk Radomski, the former Mets clubhouse attendant who became a key drug supplier to ballplayers. Radomski was busted by federal authorities in 2005 and forced to cooperate with the 2007 baseball investigation into steroids chaired by former senator George Mitchell.

"I think [baseball] guys were taking it in the '70s and early '80s, but they didn't work out," Mc-Namee said. "Working out became prevalent in the '80s, the mid- to late-'80s, so that's when you saw the bulk. That's when you saw the power. Because you just can't take it in high doses and see the bene-fit. You have to work out. And that's when the strength and conditioning era came into play, where they started to say, 'Well, it's not bad [to weight train]. It doesn't make you tight.'

"That's when they started hiring strength coaches, who were basically people's friends, but at least they monitored the weight room. They had guys lifting heavy. They were all ex-football guys, from college programs. Penn State. Florida State. They were hiring these assistant guys and they had football [training] programs. And everybody in college was taking steroids, so at least the knowledge was there.

"Guys that got big had success. Canseco was a sprinter in a big body. Dykstra was a short, little fast guy. Now, the bigger they got the more hurt they got. But they did put up some good numbers. Then the education got better, where the pitchers weren't getting bulky but they were getting better."

Radomski was the right guy at the right time. He turned his baseball connections and own experiences as a weight-lifting gym rat into a booming business. Radomski told Mitchell that first baseman David Segui admitted using steroids as far back as 1994, when Segui played for the Mets and Radomski still worked for the club as a clubhouse attendant for the team. Segui, Radomski said, took the steroid Deca-Durabolin "because it was safe, did not expire for three or four years and was thought to alleviate back pain."

———

Safe? Baseball, like other sports, had turned a significant corner in making steroid use acceptable. The health risks associated with steroids, including high-blood pressure, increased cancer risks and the shutdown of natural testosterone production by the body, had caused much of the taboo status associated with steroids. It used to be that an athlete had two hurdles between him and taking the plunge into steroid use: one was the severe health risk and the other was the moral issue of what was an illegal form of cheating. What happened in the 1990s was that ballplayers, with the help of trainers and drug "gurus," completely knocked down the first hurdle. (And the second? Well, it wasn't cheating if there were no rules, right? Down it, too, went.) The athletes learned, largely from the guinea pigs of the gym and bodybuilding cultures, how to use steroids "properly." Deca, for instance, might require one or two injections a week, perhaps in the range of 300 to 600 milligrams per week, for a cycle of about eight weeks. An anti-estrogen drug such as Clomid may be required at the end of the cycle.

The specter of Lyle Alzado no longer haunted them. Alzado was the former NFL lineman who told **Sports Illustrated** in 1991 that he had injected himself with steroids and human growth hormone almost constantly and, in his view, such chronic use was the reason why he was dying from a brain tumor. (Alzado died the following year at age 43.) The **Sports Illustrated** cover image of a gaunt, bald, dying Alzado was arresting. So were his words.

"Now look at me," said the once hirsute, brawny man. "My hair's gone. I wobble when I walk and have to hold on to someone for support, and I have trouble remembering things. My last wish? That no one else ever dies this way."

His warning had less shelf life than Deca. Almost immediately, and certainly within a year or two, baseball players had dismissed Alzado's death as an anomaly of another age that did not concern them. His problem, they reasoned, was that he had taken too many steroids for too long without properly educating himself. Ballplayers could go to their drug "gurus," or even one another, to learn how to use steroids. This was very good for the business of people such as Radomski, who quickly went from picking up sweaty socks and dirty jocks from the Mets clubhouse floor to helping change how baseball was played with his supply of drugs and the expertise with how to use them.

"Yeah, there were whispers about what was going on," Cone said, "but we really didn't know for sure. I was stunned about the oil-based steroids. I keep going back to Lyle Alzado. Stacking steroids? I never made the connection. I never understood that. I saw Lyle Alzado die because of that. I would never think about that. For what? So you can get big and blow up? Maybe I was naïve. Guys were getting big around the league here and there but who knew what they were taking. I made the connection to over-the-counter supplements rather than Lyle Alzado–type synthetic oil-based steroids. I was stunned to hear that later."

After the 1995 season, according to the Mitchell report, Mets catcher Todd Hundley asked his clubhouse buddy, Radomski, for some help. Hundley was 26 years old and by and large an average major league player. He had played six seasons in the big leagues and never had hit more than 16 home runs or earned a salary of more than $1 million. Radomski started him on cycles of Deca and testosterone. This stuff was so good, Radomski told him, that he would hit 40 home runs on it. In 1996, Todd

Hundley truly made Radomski look like a guru; he hit 41 home runs. He went on to make more than $47 million.

Radomski's business was taking off. It began with his personal connection to several Mets players or those he knew who came through the Mets' system, including Hundley, Segui, Fernando Vina, Chris Donnels, Josias Manzanillo and Mark Carreon. Business boomed through word-of-mouth referrals, and as those Mets players moved on to new teams to introduce whole new subsets of players to Radomski's magic. Segui, for instance, became Radomski's friend and one of his best salesmen, according to the Mitchell Report, sending customer after customer to Radomski as he bounced among six teams after leaving the Mets. The Mitchell Report alone names at least four players Segui introduced to Radomski: F. P. Santangelo, Mike Lansing, Larry Bigbie and Tim Laker.

All types of players flocked to Radomski. In 1995, for instance, Laker was a nondescript backup catcher for the Montreal Expos who was ready to jump the two hurdles of the health risk and the morality issue to get his hands on steroids. Segui was his connection, even though Segui had joined him as a teammate with the Expos only on June 8 of that same year. Segui put Laker in touch with his own steroids supplier, Radomski. Laker and Radomski met at the New York City hotel where the Expos stayed while in town for a series against the Mets.

Laker was 25 years old and owned a lifetime major league batting average of .205 with no home runs entering that 1995 season. He was the very definition of a fringe player, at risk at any time of being washed back to the minors and possibly even out of the game. He had trouble putting on weight, which he later blamed on a digestive disease for which he was diagnosed three years earlier.

The brass ring, however, was to hang around the big leagues long enough to make some money, provide for his family and maybe even qualify for one of those nice pensions for which the players association had bargained. What would you do for the brass ring? Work hard and eat right? Sure. But what if that wasn't enough? What if there was something else, even if it was illegal, that could bring the brass ring further into reach? And what if you knew there were no rules against it? And what if you knew guys in your clubhouse and guys across the field were taking it? Laker gladly took the leap over the two hurdles.

Radomski set him up with a doping regimen of Deca and testosterone. Laker would administer it himself. The catcher would inject himself in the buttocks once a week for 8 to 10 weeks, take some time off (in part so the body's natural testosterone production, fooled by the synthetic drugs, would not shut down entirely), and then crank up another cycle. When the Expos were home Laker would shoot up at his residence. When they were on the road he would shoot up in his hotel room, which presented something of a problem as far as how to dispose of the dirty syringes laced with an illegal drug. Laker decided he would wrap them up and transport them in his belongings out of the country and back to Montreal. He would dispose of them there.

Laker put on weight. The Montreal trainer complimented him on his improved physique. He kept doping for six years. Tim Laker did not transform into a star even with the help of performance-enhancing drugs. He never became an All-Star who hit 41 home runs in a season. He never set the home run record or made the cover of **Time** magazine or hit balls more than 500 feet or aroused suspicion from the media or fans. But he did carve out a major league career that included parts of 11 seasons and a .226 batting average. He was still in the big leagues at age 36. Tim Laker was nothing special. No, there were hundreds and hundreds of Tim Lakers out there in professional baseball.

"It's unfortunate," Helling said, "that I had a lot of people I knew say, 'I feel like I need to do something to keep up.' They'd say, 'I played with this guy for four or five years and suddenly he's hitting 30 home runs. We play the same position. I need to keep up.'

"You hear excuses from guys who have admitted [juicing]. 'I felt like I had to do it.' 'I did it to keep healthy.' The way I looked at it, when I wasn't good enough myself, it was time to move on. A lot of players didn't think that. When they lost velocity or they did not have enough power to hit home runs, guys always had an excuse for why they could do it."

Laker became yet another Radomski success story. The story might have been small scale, but it was a success story nonetheless. It was a story that was being repeated with growing frequency in every major league clubhouse, including that of the model franchise of major league baseball, the New York Yankees.

———

Nineteen ninety-eight was also the year Roger Clemens met Brian McNamee, Tim McCleary's St. John's buddy hired to be the Blue Jays strength coach. McNamee had earned his doctorate at something called Columbus University in Louisiana, which later would move to Mississippi after being shut down in Louisiana after it was found to be an online "diploma mill." Clemens and McNamee made a connection, not so much as personal friends but as devotees of training. Clemens loved to work, but he always needed company, almost in the manner of someone who needed an audience rather than a taskmaster. McNamee, quiet and perpetually somber, was not a gregarious audience. But he was loyal, industrious and serious almost to a fault about training. McNamee gained Clemens' trust. That was never more apparent than in June of that season, just months after they had met, when Clemens asked McNamee to stick a needle full of Winstrol in his buttocks, according to what McNamee told Mitchell in the presence of federal agents and later repeated in a sworn deposition to Congress. Clemens several times, including in front of a congressional committee, denied ever using steroids and filed a defamation lawsuit against McNamee.

"I knew nothing about it until Clemens came to me and asked me to stick him in the ass in '98," McNamee said. "Winstrol was stupid [good]. You get a guy throwing 82 [mph], he takes Winstrol he's throwing 92. It's a sprinter's drug. For fast-twitch muscle fiber. If I took Winstrol in college I would have thrown a hundred. Without a doubt. I don't know if it existed then. But yeah, Ben Johnson took it. It's a big sprinter's drug. Hamstring, rotator cuff . . . oh, it definitely works. Horses were taking it."

Clemens already was among the greatest pitchers of his generation, if not of all time. Clemens on a steroid regimen as alleged by McNamee was literally unbeatable. Clemens went 14-0 with a 2.29 ERA for the rest of the season. In his final 11 starts alone that season Clemens' game-by-game strikeout totals were 14, 8, 15, 6, 18, 7, 11, 7, 11, 15 and 11. Only one other time in Clemens' career did he strike out at least 14 batters four times in an **entire season,** and that had occurred when he was 10 years younger. And yet in 1998 he did it in just the last two months of a season in which he threw 234⅔ innings at the advanced age of 36. It was a freakishly phenomenal season, but like many achievements in 1998, gained little recognition because of the overwhelming fascination with McGwire, Sosa and the Great Home-Run Race.

The Yankees noticed. They traded an 18-game winner off their 125-win team, Wells, the same pitcher who had thrown a perfect game, too, to get Clemens from the Blue Jays at the start of their 1999 spring training camp. Clemens wanted his new buddy and trainer, McNamee, to join him with the Yankees. There was a problem, though. McNamee was under contract to the Blue Jays.

"He tried to get me out of my contract in '99," McNamee said. "I had a player's contract. And he wanted me out of there by the All-Star break. The only thing is [the Blue Jays] would have filed a grievance and I would have been unable to work with a team for six or seven years because I broke my contract. And that's why I didn't leave. I wanted to leave the door open to get back into Major League Baseball. So I let it go."

Without McNamee, Clemens did not pitch well in New York. Clemens' ERA jumped by nearly two runs in 1999 to 4.60, the worst mark of his career. He did win the clinching game of the World Series against Atlanta. Just weeks later, McNamee said, Clemens called him.

"You're not going back to Toronto," Clemens said.

"Okay," McNamee said. "I'll train you."

McNamee, the New York kid, was happy about coming home. There were a couple of issues that needed to be worked out, though. Clemens didn't want to have to fly McNamee around the country to train him while the Yankees were on the road, so he petitioned the Yankees to make McNamee a strength coach. But the Yankees already had a strength coach, Jeff Mangold. Did they need another one? They did if they wanted to keep Clemens happy and productive.

McNamee flew to Tampa to meet with Yankees general manager Brian Cashman and assistant Mark Newman. A deal was struck. McNamee would be named as the team's assistant strength coach, with a base salary, full medical benefits and complete access to the Yankees players and facilities. There was only one catch: Clemens would have to pay McNamee's salary. The Yankees would deduct the money from Clemens' salary and give it to McNamee. The arrangement suited Clemens, who now had his personal trainer with him at all times on the staff of the New York Yankees without the bother of having to make separate travel arrangements for him or the worry of trying to gain him access to club facilities. Even McNamee found it odd that one player, acquired in a trade, not even with the leverage of free agency, essentially appointed his personal trainer to the team, a team that had forged its reputation on turning unselfishness into championships.

"It was set up to fail," McNamee said. "Because I went in there to try to help and Roger put up a front and it was like me versus Mangold. Mangold was Joe's guy, but Roger would tell the players to go see me, not Mangold. And I hated going to work every day."

McNamee had trained Clemens, Andy Pettitte and pitcher C. J. Nitkowski in Houston that winter after the 1999 season. When McNamee arrived at the Yankees' 2000 spring training camp, it took only the first minute of the first stretching exercises of the first day of workouts for trouble to start. McNamee was leading the team in stretching when Cone, the respected elder statesman of the Yankees, yelled at him with only a modicum of humor that intentionally could not disguise his anger.

"What the fuck are you doing here leading stretching?" Cone yelled for all of his teammates to hear. "Did you get a quickie degree? What are you doing here? You're not supposed to be here doing this!"

Cone went on to trash McNamee so badly that the pitcher admits, "I was getting a little embarrassed because it was in front of the whole team." Cone, the old-school union man, was upset not only because he felt the Yankees catered to Clemens' wants by hiring him, but also because he regarded McNamee as a gate-crasher, somebody who had entered the elite club of Major League Baseball without earning his way there, which is how the players have to do it.

"McNamee's leading the team in stretching and he's Roger's guy," Cone said, "and then there's Jeff Mangold, who's another Gold's Gym guy from Jersey who wasn't qualified to have a big league job, I thought. I never understood why major league clubs would not use guys internally. Train them the way you want to train them and hire them in that position. I never understood that. None of those guys were ever properly vetted.

"I didn't like McNamee. Not that he was a bad guy. I never thought he was properly vetted. [Trainers] Gene Monahan and Steve Donahue were just like us. They had to go through the minor leagues. They were vetted. They rode the buses. They ate the ketchup sandwiches. They worked their way up to the big leagues. I always thought, There is another Gene Monahan in Double-A or Triple-A that has three kids and a family and needs a big league job. Why did McNamee get it? He went back and got a quickie degree? The guy was a bullpen catcher in '95 for me. Then all of a sudden he's gone, he comes back, he's doing some sports book? Basically, he's a hustler. And now he's a trainer.

"I didn't use either one of those guys. I used [trainers] Gene Monahan or Steve Donahue if I needed something. I never, ever understood that. That was more on principle than anything I saw. And yeah, there were whispers about what was going on, but we really didn't know."

What was going on was that the Yankees, like every team in baseball, were increasingly turning to steroids and human growth hormone, and those so inclined now had someone on the payroll and in uniform and on the team plane to provide information and access to those drugs at any time if they so wished. In 2000 and 2001 the Yankees would joke among themselves about guys who worked closely with McNamee, especially the ones who showed obvious strength and body-type changes. "He's on Mac's program" was the joke, which often was reduced to the simple shorthand of "He's on 'The Program.'" No one knew for certain the details of "The Program." No one wanted to know the details. These were the days of "don't ask, don't tell, don't care."

"They were on his program, guys like Roger and Andy and maybe [Mike] Stanton," Cone said. "I thought he had some GNC stuff he was putting in shakes, over-the-counter stuff, maybe creatine or andro or whatever you can get over the counter. I thought that's what he was doing. I had no idea he had kits [of human growth hormone]."

McNamee intentionally kept a low profile. He rarely spoke or smiled. That was his personality.

"If I could go through the day without talking to anybody, it was a good day," McNamee said.

Besides, he sensed the friction created by the assumption that he was "Roger's guy."

"Bernie, Posada, Mariano, Pettitte, they all knew me because I was there when they first came up," McNamee said. "But then the pitchers start talking and the players start talking and it's like a little bitch fest. 'Oh, go see Mac.' Then it was like I was doing my own thing."

"Go see Mac" and "The Program" became understood code for seeking out supplement options, legal or perhaps not. McNamee claims to be personally opposed to illegal performance-enhancing drugs.

"I had guys ask me general questions," McNamee said. "I would give the good and the bad and my recommendation would be not to do it. I can get 200 players now I talked out of doing it. Or said no to. But I never said I could get stuff to anybody. I think because of [Jason] Grimsley, Roger knew that I knew a guy, and because David [Justice] knew that I knew a guy and I knew that his stuff was legit, clean and whatever. And that's where the problem started. And I enabled that. And I shouldn't have."

McNamee also had a practical reason for not emphasizing steroids: they would devalue his work as a trainer. How could he claim credit for the benefits of a conditioning program, for instance, if a steroid shortcut available to anybody made the biggest difference of all? But by 2000 and 2001 the drug culture in baseball was so firmly established that ballplayers were going to cheat whether McNamee or any other strength coach was on board with it or not. The signs were too obvious. Wells, for instance, would later write in his 2003 book, **Perfect I'm Not: Boomer on Beer, Brawls, Backaches and Baseball,** that you could stand anywhere in the clubhouse and be no more than 10 feet away from illegal drugs.

"Yeah, that's a good guesstimate," McNamee said. "Guys were looking in each other's lockers, guys were searching . . . that was pretty much it. Some guys were open about it, some guys weren't.

"And you wouldn't believe the shit they were taking. I mean, it was like horseshit and crap. Like, they didn't know the toxicity levels. They didn't know orals. They were taking whatever the fuck . . . they were taking Ritalin, oral steroids . . . they were taking stuff that was bad for them. And then they're going out all night because they've got amphetamines in them, and they're drinking, and then they're sleeping all day, and then they've got to take amphetamines . . . It's a vicious cycle."

Amphetamines had long been established in

baseball to combat the mental and physical grind of the baseball season. But they became a routine part of the game.

"'If you're not cheatin', you're not tryin,'" Mc-Namee said. "That was the motto."

McNamee said players from the Blue Jays and Yankees during his year there would store their amphetamines in their lockers, but disguised in the plastic canisters of over-the-counter supplements.

"When you see that 'Ripped Fuel' thing? It was usually full of greenies," McNamee said.

He said obtaining amphetamines was easy. Players never even had to leave their own clubhouse.

"There was a guy in California, a Mexican guy," McNamee said. "He'd sit there all day in the clubhouse. Guys would sign bats for him, and he'd give them boxes of greenies. In Anaheim. He'd be sitting there with a satchel full of greenies. There was green and green-and-light-green. That's what they used to make the coffee with.

"We used to open 'em up and put 'em in the coffee in the clubhouse, which I took one time [in 1998] and didn't know. I almost had a heart attack. I was out stretching guys. One of the Blue Jays was like, 'Did you drink the coffee?' I said, 'Yeah. It's right near my locker.' He goes, 'Never drink the clubhouse coffee. Go to the back.' I'm like, 'All right. Thanks for telling me.'

"I didn't know one pitcher on Toronto's team that wasn't taking them, when he pitched. It's speed. Guys were beaning up to play golf after workouts."

The prevalence of amphetamines contributed to the general acceptance of illegal drugs in clubhouses. Steroid use had spread virally around baseball. Segui, for instance, was traded in the second half of the 1999 season from Seattle to Toronto, where he met McNamee. McNamee went to the Yankees the next year, where he met pitcher Jason Grimsley. McNamee gave Grimsley Segui's telephone number, knowing both were interested in performance- enhancing drugs. And then one day during that 2000 season, McNamee was sitting with Grimsley in the Yankees bullpen during a game when he happened to mention that he really liked the Lexus RX300 SUV.

"Really?" Grimsley said. "I know a guy who works with Lexus."

Grimsley gave McNamee the name and telephone number of his friend. His friend's name was Kirk Radomski. McNamee called him and arranged to meet him at a car-detailing shop.

"And that's how I met him," McNamee said.

Radomski and McNamee became friends and business associates. Much later, after the feds closed in on them, they also became star witnesses in the Mitchell Report. The connection became a convenient one for Grimsley, who was purchasing his drugs from Radomski. Why not, Grimsley figured, have McNamee do his legwork? He asked

McNamee to pick up his kits of human growth hormone from Radomski. McNamee obliged, even though he was putting himself into the dangerous area of drug distribution.

"He asked me to pick up some stuff for him and Knoblauch," McNamee said. "That's how that started. That was three times, and I stopped it, because I didn't feel good about it."

Members of the 2000 Yankees became good business for Radomski. At some points over the 2000 and 2001 seasons, according to the Mitchell Report, Radomski provided drugs for Grimsley, Knoblauch, pitcher Denny Neagle, outfielders Glenallen Hill and David Justice, and later for pitcher Mike Stanton. In addition, the 2000 Yankees included three other players who later admitted their drug use (though not necessarily specific to that particular year): Jose Canseco, Jim Leyritz and Andy Pettitte. Most infamously, the 2000 Yankees had a tenth player who would be tied to reports of performance-enhancing drug use: Clemens.

———

According to McNamee, Clemens came to him in the second half of the 2000 season looking for a boost. McNamee turned to his friend Radomski for steroids and human growth hormone. McNamee said he injected Clemens four to six times with the steroids and four to six times with the HGH. Clemens, who turned 38 years old in August that season, pitched far better in the second half than he had in the first, lowering his ERA from 4.33 at the All-Star break to 3.15 after it, while improving his record of 6-6 before the break to 7-2 after it. The Yankees finally saw the pitcher they traded for from Toronto. Did the players assume Clemens was on "the program"?

"I think the fact that I picked up some stuff for Knoblauch and Grimsley, there was an assumption they talked about it, too," McNamee said. "I would think you would have to assume that Roger was taking something. I never talked about it. And I didn't want steroids and growth hormone to be the be-all, and that's why Roger was performing well. I made that clear to Andy once I knew he knew. He understood that. I think you would have to be an idiot not to think Roger was taking something."

Of course, such thinking did not stop McNamee from writing a guest column in the **New York Times** later that same year that was titled "Don't Be So Quick to Prejudge All That Power." In it McNamee wrote, "The suggestion that steroids are the answer to the increased strength, recovery from injury and the improved performances of today's players is just wrong." He concluded his opus thusly: "Yes, the players today are stronger, faster and smarter than their predecessors. But their superiority is not because of steroid use, but because of the advancement in sports-specific science and commitment of the organizations to strength, conditioning and nutrition. To suggest otherwise is irresponsible and disrespectful."

It was, naturally, a complete lie. Baseball had become one fraud piled upon another.

"I did lie to the media," McNamee said. "Because I got tired of going to clinics and kids asking me about steroids. I went out of my way to say no, never, never, never . . . I lied. But to me, what was I going to do? 'Oh yeah, this is the way you should work out, but by the way, my guys take steroids.' So I had to answer the question. Me, as a trainer, can't say, 'I don't want to talk about it.' Because that's an admission of guilt.

"The fact that I enabled it was wrong. I shouldn't have done it. But it was a gray area for me. Because the way I got involved with Radomski had nothing to do with steroids. And it's a personality flaw, where you look at my job. My job is to protect these guys at all times. Before, during and after. So when these guys are already doing something that's wrong, I tried to help that. Because they're going to do it anyway. Was it wrong for me? I don't know if I would do the same thing again. I should have said no, but I can't. I have an inability to do that."

The 2000 Yankees won the American League East Division with 87 victories, stumbling badly to the finish by losing 15 of their final 18 games. They held off Oakland in the Division Series in five games, dispatched Seattle in the American League Championship Series—in which Clemens won

Game 4, 5-0, with the most dominating game of his postseason career, a one-hitter in which he struck out 15 batters and threw 138 pitches—and then took out the Mets in five games to win the world championship. (Radomski said he provided drugs to at least two Mets players on that team, Matt Franco and Todd Pratt.) The Yankees were the best team in baseball. And when it came to steroids, they were no different from anybody else.

———

"You had two guys from New York doing all the talking in the Mitchell Report," Torre said. "That's why you have more information on New York players. If people want to devalue the 2000 team, is that how we lost 15 out of 18 down the stretch? We dried ourselves out and then got a heavy dose for the postseason? One thing I've learned is that people are going to feel the way they're going to feel, regardless of what happened. You can talk until you're blue in the face and there's no answer that's going to satisfy everybody."

Said one former All-Star and steroid user who competed against those Yankees teams, "Everybody around baseball did what they could possibly do. It was the survival of the fittest."

Nobody said, "This has to stop"?

"Who would have?" the player said, laughing. "It's why the government regulates monopolies. If people could do it, they would fucking do it. Just like cheating on your taxes. If there's a gray area, you're going to find it, until the government said it's not a gray area anymore."

The player said that everybody in the game just understood that attitude was acceptable. "Now whether it was right or wrong, now you're talking about a moral issue, but there were no rules. You did what you did. It was the wild, wild west."

Torre came from a generation in which weight training and adding bulk were taboo. Steroids? He knew nothing about them. He never saw them. The players certainly weren't going to tell him what was going on, and he wasn't going to probe without invitation into their private lives.

"I've always tried to respect guys' privacy," Torre said. "I remember in Atlanta in 1982 we were going to the postseason and rumor had it they were going to check bats to see if any were corked. It was the time when loading bats was one of the things that was starting up. I remember having a meeting and saying, 'Guys, I never ask you what you do, but I know we've accomplished something very special here, by winning the division, and if they decide they want to check bats it could nullify everything we've ever done here. So if you were doing it, you better be careful. And if you weren't, don't even worry about it.'

"That's basically been my attitude—unless I see erratic behavior sometimes. Unless somebody acts funny. I just don't go into people's lockers. Plus, I didn't see anything. I walk all over the clubhouse. I walk in the trainers' room. I walk in the lounge. I walk in the weight room, and all that stuff. I never saw it.

"I never heard players talk about it. Jeter used to kid about it. He'd joke around, 'Yeah, watch me on steroids hit it to the warning track!' The thing that comes to my mind with steroids is it can cut your life short. The other thing is I don't think it's fair. The analogy I use is that it's like some guys are using metal bats and some guys are using wood bats. It's not right. It's dangerous.

"The one thing you have to remember is that baseball is business that has never interfered with putting asses in the seats. You can't tell me that with everything going on—Babe Ruth hits 60 home runs in 1927, Roger Maris hits 61 in eight more games in 1961, and then in 1998 two guys hit more than that—that nobody thinks it's suspicious? In 1998 when one guy hit 66 and one guy hit 70, baseball said it's great. And now baseball is pointing the fingers at everybody? That's the fraud to me."

Not all 10 members of the 2000 Yankees in the Mitchell Report were described as using drugs during that particular season, but the cooperation of McNamee and Radomski gave that team a higher profile than others in the report. For instance, outfielder and admitted steroid user Shane Monahan has said steroid and amphetamine use was rampant on the 1998–99 Mariners teams he played on. (Monahan also described hangers-on with club-house access brokering greenies-for-memorabilia transactions.) Nine players from those Seattle teams, both of which lost more games than they won, have been linked in various reports to performance-enhancing drugs. McNamee said the 2000 Yankees were no different from the 29 other teams when it came to drug use.

"I think the talent level was better," McNamee said. "You put ergogenic aids on top of that, you're going to get a better team."

McNamee said he told federal agents and Mitchell's investigators that both Toronto general manager Gord Ash and Yankees general manager Brian Cashman did not want to know if players were doping and that player agents were directly involved in procuring illegal drugs for their clients, but that Mitchell did not include those comments in the report. Gord Ash and Brian Cashman denied McNamee's assertion.

"I told the [federal] agents and George Mitchell's people that the [general managers] came up to me and said, 'We don't care what they're taking. I just don't want to know about it.'" McNamee said. "That wasn't in their report." Cashman denied McNamee's allegations, saying, "we thought we had a clean clubhouse. I never had a dialogue with him about what players may or may not be taking. Never, ever once." Ash also denied McNamee's allegation: "I don't recall that," Ash said.

McNamee described his relationship with Cashman as a friendly one. Indeed, McNamee said in 2007, six years after the Yankees did not retain McNamee as the assistant strength coach, Cashman called him regularly to consult on strength training issues regarding the team.

"If he didn't understand what was going on [with steroids], then he's a jackass," McNamee said. "[But] what was he going to do? If he wanted [a clean clubhouse] he would have had to have said, 'Hey, we're getting our asses kicked. Everybody take 'em.' That's the reality. I know that would have happened. You've got to be on a level playing field."

———

McNamee's run with the Yankees ended after the 2001 season. The team chose not to invite him back, principally because of an incident on October 6, 2001, at the team's hotel in St. Petersburg, Florida, while in town there to play the Tampa Bay Devil Rays. Police questioned McNamee in connection with a possible sexual battery incident after he was found in the hotel pool at 4 a.m. with a 40-year-old woman. Both were naked. The woman had ingested GHB, an odorless substance commonly referred to as a "date-rape" drug. McNamee was never charged. Though the Yankees cut ties with McNamee following that season, Clemens and Pettitte continued to train with him and would do so for a year.

In May of the following year, 2002, Pettitte gave McNamee a call. The trainer was on the road with the Yankees and Clemens, this time not as an official member of the team, but only as Clemens' personal trainer with no special access. Pettitte was in Tampa, where, while on the disabled list after making only three starts that season, he was working out at the Yankees' training complex to rehabilitate a strained left elbow.

"I need some help, Mac," Pettitte said.

It wasn't just McNamee's training help that Pettitte wanted. It was human growth hormone.

"You don't need to do that," McNamee told the pitcher.

"Yes, I do," Pettitte told him. "I'm going to do it. Are you going to help me or not?"

McNamee decided he wasn't about to change Pettitte's mind. There was only one thing to do.

"I'll help you," McNamee said.

"Good," Pettitte said. "Can you get it for me?"

"Yeah, I can get it."

Said McNamee, "I don't even know how I got it down there. I didn't travel with it."

Pettitte would go to the Yankees' training complex in the morning for 30 minutes of treatment. McNamee then would train Pettitte through conditioning and rehabilitation exercises. They would run through another training session at night. It was hard work, designed to get Pettitte back into the rotation as soon as possible while the Yankees, stuck in second place, tried not to fall too far behind the red-hot Boston Red Sox in the AL East. But the training regimen wasn't enough for Pettitte. Twice each day, once in the morning and once at night, McNamee injected Pettitte with human growth hormone. Pettitte was a churchgoing, God-fearing Texan, known in the Yankees clubhouse for his integrity and earnestness. If Pettitte was going to cheat, who wouldn't? Of course, even Pettitte did not consider injections of an illegally obtained performance-enhancing drug as cheating.

"I think he rationalized it with the information I supplied and why guys took it," McNamee said. "I think he just really wanted to heal. It wasn't a performance-enhancing issue. As far as I know, he never took steroids. Everybody thought he did, because when I started training him he went from 88–89 [miles per hour] to 96. If you have a photo of him taking steroids, I don't know. I don't know what to believe."

Torre never knew about Pettitte's HGH use. He learned about it at the same time as the rest of the world: when the Mitchell Report was released in December of 2007. Pettitte was in the middle of preparing a statement in which he would admit to using HGH when Torre called him.

"Andy, I'm just calling to see how you're doing," Torre said. "I'm not calling to ask any questions."

"Skip," Pettitte said, "I'm just getting ready to make a statement."

"I don't want to know your statement," Torre said. "I just want to see how you're doing."

"I'm okay," Pettitte said.

Torre noticed that Pettitte sounded anxious, or "jumpy" as he put it. After Pettitte released his statement, the pitcher called his former manager back.

"I'm sorry," Pettitte said. "I apologize to you, especially if I did anything to put you in a tough situation. I don't know how I did this. As religious as I am, I even question how God can help me make those kind of decisions."

"Well, Andy," Torre said, "we don't always make the right decisions. It's what life is all about. Just knowing you the way I know you, and not a lot of people know you like I do, you were torn because you thought, being on the disabled list, the most important thing was to get yourself back to earning your money and helping the team. You were willing to try something, and then you realized you didn't want to do this anymore. So what did you do? You stopped.

"It's what you did. Is it the right thing? The wrong thing? It's what you did. You certainly didn't have anything really devious in your mind at the time. You were just trying to get back to earn your money. You weren't trying to get back there to win a game for yourself."

"I feel badly about it," Pettitte said.

"And what about the other donkey?" Torre said.

Pettitte knew Torre was referring to Clemens.

"Roger is Roger," Pettitte said. "When I talked to him, he was Roger."

Torre immediately understood what Pettitte meant about his good friend: that a full-blown steroids scandal wasn't about to change Clemens from being the most cocksure cowboy on the planet. Clemens lived in his own world, surrounded by people who unequivocally verified it for him, and George Mitchell wasn't about to cause him any self-examination or doubt. Torre also understood how Pettitte fell victim to the culture of the times.

"It's like Bob Gibson said: 'To win a game you'd take anything,'" Torre said. "We'd all sell our souls. Winning is something that was first and foremost and that's what we wanted to do. Unfortunately, now what stimulates the need to do this is individual performance and not winning. It used to be all about winning. It was, 'Let's win this game.' 'Let's go to the World Series.' That was the motivation at the time. Now it's more a case of the motivation being, 'My numbers.' But yeah, as a competitor, you'd sell your soul."

Pettitte might not consider his HGH use to have been cheating or performance-enhancing. The Red Sox, of course, might view it a little differently. Pettitte was off the disabled list and back in the rotation on June 14. The Yankees trailed Boston by 1½ games. Pettitte made 19 starts thereafter and was one of the best pitchers in the league at that time, going 12-4 with a 3.29 ERA. With Pettitte's help, the Yankees overtook the Red Sox and won the division with 103 victories. The Red Sox won 93 games. They did not qualify for the playoffs.

———

At about the very same time Pettitte, with McNamee's help, was in a hotel suite in Tampa sticking needles loaded with HGH into the folds of the skin in his abdomen, and four years after Helling's first of several pleas to the players association fell on deaf ears, Ken Caminiti sat across from a writer in a lawn chair in his garage in Houston, surrounded by his show-quality muscle cars, and made an announcement that was a long time coming: the emperor had no clothes. Baseball, Caminiti said, was rife with steroid users. It was a moment that would change how baseball would be played and administered. It was the beginning of the end of The Steroid Era, at least its Wild West days with no laws in place in the game.

Not only did Caminiti, a former Most Valuable Player Award winner then in his first year of retirement, admit to using steroids himself, making him the first among the hundreds and hundreds of players who had used steroids to actually admit it, but he also expressed absolutely no remorse about having done so. Steroids were so prevalent, they had become the default choice if you wanted to make it as a big leaguer. How could you feel guilty about it if about half the players, as Caminiti estimated, were doing the same thing?

What he said was not shocking at all. Baseball had given itself over to steroid users for more than a decade, though, as Cone observed, the rate of those crossing over to the dark side had greatly accelerated over the previous four years. By 2001 it had reached its tipping point: clean players such as Helling began to see themselves as the minority, put at a competitive disadvantage by the growing acceptance that steroids simply were, like occasional brushback pitches, now part of the cost of playing baseball. Steroids were no longer part of a rogue element. They were de rigeur.

This important shift among the rank and file of players became clear in the second half of that 2001 season. Perhaps the breaking of the home run record yet again, this time by a garishly pumped-up version of Bonds, who hit 73 at the age of 36 after never having hit more than 49, helped fuel the intramural carping. Several clean players steered conversations toward this growing acceptance of steroids. They were concerned and angry, of course, though the thin blue line mentality among these union brothers and foxhole comrades prevented them from speaking on the record. One of them joked, though with black humor, about the "steroid starter kits" that made the users so obvious and ubiquitous: in addition to the needles, the steroid user needed acne creams for the pimples that otherwise would fester on his back, and a good razor or wax job to keep the body hairless, the better to show off the new, well-muscled, if bloated, physique. These players became increasingly body-image conscious, even if they fairly glistened from the watery, hairless musculature. Some players had slight trouble speaking clearly because the HGH swelled the size of their tongues and jaws. Some players could not push their batting helmet completely down on their heads because their heads had swelled.

Of course, steroids hardly were a secret in baseball then. Many media outlets had covered the topic, often with anonymous sources, and the Mitchell Report referenced many of those reports. But the topic never gained much traction, primarily because top Major League Baseball officials, union leaders and active players typically would not admit the scope of the problem or attach their name to a call for action.

By April of 2002, the increasing resentment among some players to steroid use was a sign that perhaps the "don't ask, don't tell, don't care" culture was about to crack. The worst-kept secret in baseball was the growing use and acceptance of steroids. Caminiti, who was a fierce competitor and bluntly honest character over his 15 seasons with Houston, San Diego, Texas and Atlanta, was the man who broke the coded silence in the pages of **Sports Illustrated.**

"I've got nothing to hide," he said.

Still, there was an obvious sadness about him. His virility was gone. Caminiti moved and spoke slowly. His famously intense eyes had gone cold and dull. He complained several times that his body could no longer produce enough testosterone on its own, having grown dependent on the synthetic forms he injected into his body.

"You know what that's like?" he said. "You get lethargic. You get depressed. It's terrible."

The story was enormous. What Helling had been trying to tell the players association for four years was now broadcast across every network and media outlet in the country. The secret was out, as much as some still didn't want to acknowledge the obvious truth. They wanted to perpetuate the myth.

"Everybody hates a snitch," said Cubs manager Dusty Baker, remaining faithful to the ballplayers' **omerta.**

Said Angels slugger Mo Vaughn, "Let me tell you why Barry Bonds hit 73 homers. Because he's a great hitter. Because the Giants moved out of Candlestick Park into a place where the wind doesn't blow as much."

Of course, this was the same Mo Vaughn who was one of Kirk Radomski's best customers. Mitchell's investigators found that Vaughn, who was referred to Radomski by Glenallen Hill, wrote at least three checks to Radomski in 2001 totaling $8,600 for kits of human growth hormone.

Radomski told Mitchell he personally delivered the drugs to Vaughn.

Then there was the post-Caminiti reaction of Jason Giambi of the Yankees. "I know this stuff is newsworthy," Giambi said, "but hopefully people don't buy into it. There's no miracle thing for this game. Either you have talent or you don't. One common thread of all the greats of the game, they've had longevity."

Of course, this was the same Jason Giambi, apparently short on requisite talent, who was pumping his body full of steroids and human growth hormone.

Try as they might, the ballplayers could not wish away the steroid issue. Three months after Caminiti spoke out, the players association suddenly dropped its long-standing and fierce opposition to random drug testing, and agreed to a new collective bargaining agreement that would require all players in 2003 to submit to anonymous "survey" testing. Before the union would even agree to do something about the steroid problem in baseball, however, the players bargained for an escape clause: a program just to find out if a problem even existed. Real steroid testing would take place starting in 2004 only if more than 5 percent of the anonymous 2003 tests came back positive—tests the players knew they would be taking in spring training. The players couldn't even keep from using the drugs long enough to beat the tests they knew were coming.

Enough ballplayers still flunked to trigger the real testing program.

"It does surprise me a little bit," said relief pitcher Mike Stanton, then with the Mets after his years with the Yankees. "But the tests don't like lie."

Stanton was surprised? Of course, this was the same Mike Stanton who, according to the Mitchell Report, met Radomski when he was a Yankee in 2001, and received from Radomski three kits of human growth hormone in 2003—the same year Stanton expressed surprise at the survey test results.

Rick Helling was at least one person who was not surprised at what happened to baseball. Baseball in the Steroid Era was one lie piled upon another over and over, starting with the lie that baseball didn't have a steroid problem at the time, continuing with the wanton disregard of federal law that there were no rules against steroids, advancing to the lie that steroids did not help anyone play baseball, moving to the lies that go on even to this day that no one ever seemed to know anyone who used steroids or, God forbid, actually used the stuff themselves, and including the lies that pass as the career playing statistics for the hundreds of players who knowingly chose to break the law and the seemingly archaic code of sportsmanship. The Steroid Era was baseball's Watergate, a colossal breach of trust for which the institution is forever tainted. It floats untethered to the rest of baseball history, like some great piece of space junk, disconnected from the moorings of the game's statistics.

Like Watergate, the Steroid Era eventually and assuredly led to an age of discovery, a sort of archaeology of the times in which some of the ugly truths bobbed to the surface or were unearthed by the brushing away of the lies. Reputations were ruined or damaged. Helling was right. It blew up in the players' faces. Two giants of the game, however, were hit the hardest of all, paying a steep price because their reputations were so outsized in the first place, and then because their personal trainers were ensnared in the legal unravelings of what had happened. One was Bonds. The other was the cocksure cowboy from Texas who helped deliver Torre's Yankees to two world championships.

4.

The Boss

George Steinbrenner would shovel debris out of six inches of gunky, green water while dressed in his loafers and slacks if it meant winning a World Series, which is exactly what he was doing in the eighth inning of Game 4 of the 2000 World Series at Shea Stadium. A fire had started in a third-deck trash container at Shea. When firefighters opened one standpipe to extinguish the fire, pressure built in another standpipe located over the Yankees' clubhouse. The pipe burst, spewing torrents of dirty water and eventually causing the clubhouse ceiling to collapse. Great waves of fetid water cascaded over the clubhouse, and headed in the direction of the Yankees' principal owner.

Steinbrenner's custom was to watch postseason games on television in the Yankees' clubhouse. "You would show up for a game early and he would be the first one there, sitting on the couch waiting for the game to start. He watched the whole game right there," said David Cone. Steinbrenner liked that the television cameras could not focus on him there, and he liked being able to communicate with his team during games. For instance, when hitting coach Chris Chambliss walked into the clubhouse during the game to look at videotapes, Steinbrenner barked at him, "We've got to get these guys going!" It was the old football coach in him.

As firefighters arrived to shut off the standpipe and to clean up the mess, Steinbrenner jumped in to help them. After they did the best they could to move the water out and shovel away the pieces of the demolished ceiling, Steinbrenner, soaked himself, took a wad of bills from his pocket and peeled off fifties and hundreds to give to the firefighters in appreciation of their effort.

Steinbrenner was the epitome of the hands-on owner. His presence was everywhere. Earlier on the same day the pipe burst, Steinbrenner ordered his clubhouse attendants to refurnish the visiting clubhouse at Shea Stadium with the team's own chairs, sofas and training tables trucked over from Yankee Stadium. The Boss was upset that the Mets provided only stools in front of each player's locker and he wanted high-backed leather chairs for his players.

"I can't have my guys sitting on these stools!" Steinbrenner said.

Nothing was too small or insignificant to be out of the purview of the owner of the Yankees. Indeed, Steinbrenner thought of himself as one of the guys, a former football player and coach who liked milling about the clubhouse and jabbering with the athletes, speaking their language and smelling the liniment. He would even sit in on scouting report meetings. Cone, more than any other player, recognized Steinbrenner's need to be a part of the jock culture and toyed with him about it.

"I would do stuff just to get him going," Cone said, "to make him feel a part of it. I liked having him around for that reason, because most people were too intimidated to say anything. I would always say, 'What was it like to coach Lenny Dawson? Tell O'Neill. C'mon. Tell him! Give him that pep talk like you gave Lenny!' I'd get him going. And O'Neill would hate it.

"George just wanted to be a part of it. He loved that. I remember one time we had a hitters' meeting before one of the playoff games at Yankee Stadium. George would hang out in the clubhouse for the entire postseason after hardly seeing it during the regular season. He would be involved with the hitters' meetings, the pitchers' meetings, the scouting reports—after not coming by all year.

"I remember we had our pitchers' meeting, and then George was back in the food room with all the hitters, and Chris Chambliss was going over all their pitchers. 'This guy's got this, and that . . .'

Gene Michael had the advance report. And the Coke machine was over in the corner buzzing. **Bzzzzz.** It drove George nuts. So he got on his hands and knees and reached around and he's trying to unplug it. **Bzzzzz.** He's moving that thing, he's trying to go around it . . . **Bzzzzz.** He's yelling at the clubbies, 'Help me move this thing!' Finally, he unplugs it. It stops making the noise. He gets back up off the ground.

"So we had just finished our meeting and I walk in there and I saw him in there and I looked at Tino's face. And Tino looks as tight as a drum after going over everything. Now George is going over everything, looking over Chambliss' shoulder. So I just screamed, 'George, don't you fuck up those guys in there!' He looked back at me like this, like, 'What the . . . ?' and everybody just looked up at me.

"I said, 'Get out of there, George! Don't you fuck them up!' Then I kind of waved, and he broke down and started laughing. Right then, Tino got up and they broke up the meeting.

"And George came up to me after that and said, 'You just better be ready!' I told him, 'I'll be ready, George. I'll be ready.'"

Cone was at it again with Steinbrenner just before the start of that fourth game of the 2000 World Series. O'Neill, famously intense and serious about his preparation, was walking by Cone in the redecorated clubhouse when the pitcher called out to Steinbrenner, "Time for a pep talk, George! O'Neill needs something. He doesn't look like he's ready to play to me."

O'Neill shot a cold stare at Cone. Said Cone, "He's looking at me and he's as tight as a drum. He's **bitter.** He's pissed at me for trying to stir things up." Cone, of course, kept up the banter.

"C'mon, George," he said. "Tell him! C'mon. We need O'Neill today, George. He doesn't look ready to go to me. Does he look ready to you?"

Said Cone, "George just loved it." O'Neill, however, took a very different view of Cone's gamesmanship.

"You," he barked at Cone, "get the fuck out of the clubhouse! Right now!"

Said Cone, "I thought he was going to kill me. That's the first time I saw Paulie look at me like that. And he wasn't kidding."

Cone had some more fun with Steinbrenner the next day, with the Yankees up three games to one and an opportunity to clinch the World Series. Once again, Steinbrenner arrived early to the clubhouse. Cone pointed out to him some strange cables that had not been in the clubhouse before. He found a microphone taped to the underside of one of the clubhouse tables.

"Look, Boss!" Cone said. "They're wiretapping us! The Mets are wiretapping us!"

Cone, however, knew the equipment belonged to Fox television in preparation for a possible clubhouse celebration.

"Cone knew how to push his buttons," said Lou Cucuzza, the Yankees visiting clubhouse manager. "He knew Steinbrenner had a distrust of everything, and was always concerned about wiretapping."

Steinbrenner took Cone's bait.

"Somebody," Steinbrenner called out, "go get a pair of scissors and cut it!"

For better or worse, Steinbrenner contributed immensely to the harsh desire to win around the Yankees. Unlike most of the other owners, who busied themselves with their business-world interests and found pockets of time to check on their baseball team, Steinbrenner went to bed at night and woke up in the morning with the same thought: **we have to win.** He was ruthless in his goal. "I saw George make a player cry once," said Brian McNamee, the former strength coach. "Might have been '93. John Habyan, a pitcher. He made him cry one day. It was sad."

Another time, Allen Watson, a relief pitcher, threw a bagel at a clubhouse attendant while goofing off in the clubhouse during spring training. Just as the bagel sailed across the room, Steinbrenner walked through the doorway. It was a case of perfect timing: the flying bagel hit Steinbrenner in the chest. The clubhouse fell ominously silent.

"Who threw that?" Steinbrenner demanded.

Watson raised his hand.

"I did."

"I figured it was you, Watson," Steinbrenner said. "That's why it didn't hurt."

And he kept on walking.

———

Intimidation, and the mere threat that he could go off at any time, was part of Steinbrenner's persona and leadership package. A person could sense when Steinbrenner was lurking because Yankees employees would grow tense and anxious. He kept everyone on edge, which is exactly how he liked it.

"One thing about this organization," said Cucuzza, "when The Boss was on top of everything, especially in Florida for spring training, everything had to be perfect. There was no being lax on anything. You knew he would come around the corner at precisely the weakest moment and be all over you. He knew just when to show up. You might be taking a break after working 20 straight hours. As soon as you put your feet up, boom, he walks in. 'Hey, I don't pay you to relax!' He constantly did that.

"The thing about George was you knew where you stood with him. I knew how tough he could be on the players and Joe, but there was no gray area. You knew where you stood. That by far has been the biggest change. When he was at his height some people couldn't stand him because he was so tough. Now you hear they wish The Boss was back."

One time during spring training, Cucuzza and his interns were assembled in his office to review the ground rules for their PlayStation football tournament. Suddenly he glimpsed Steinbrenner walking into the clubhouse. "I immediately went into a Vince Lombardi speech," Cucuzza said. **"'And another thing, make sure you keep this place spotless. . . .'"**

Steinbrenner walked past Cucuzza and said to him, "That's the way to go."

Cone was one of Steinbrenner's rare employees who was not intimidated by him and delighted in disarming him. There was another key person who was not so bossed by The Boss: Torre. Of course, it helped that Torre made a huge deposit into his goodwill account with Steinbrenner immediately upon being hired; he won the World Series in his first season. Their relationship, however, hit a key turning point the following year, 1997, when Torre proved he was not the "muppet" for Steinbrenner that the New York press had expected.

——

On August 10, 1997, Torre brought in Ramiro Mendoza to start the fourth inning against Minnesota in relief of Kenny Rogers with an 8-2 lead. Mendoza gave up three runs on seven hits over three innings. The Yankees still won the game, 9-6, but not comfortably enough for Steinbrenner. He called up Bob Watson, the general manager, and

When Torre was named Yankee manager on November 2, 1995, he was not a popular choice.

Jim Leyritz's 8th-inning home run against Atlanta in Game 4 of the 1996 World Series was a pivotal moment in the Yankees' comeback from a 0-2 deficit in the series.

The big hit in the clinching Game 6 was a triple by Yankees catcher Joe
Girardi. It was the Yankees' first title in 18 years.

John Wetteland, the Yankees closer and World Series MVP in 1996. As good as Wetteland was, he was let go to make room for Mariano Rivera the following season.

Bernie Williams was a force at the plate and a Gold Glove–caliber center fielder. Classy and graceful, Williams won a batting title and was one of the best clutch hitters in play-off history.

WALTER IOOSS JR./SPORTS ILLUSTRATED/GETTY IMAGES

Paul O'Neill and Tino Martinez epitomized the intensity and selflessness that characterized the great Yankee teams and were adored by the fans.

RON FREHM/AP IMAGES

Scott Brosius was a terrific defensive third baseman, who played hard and handled the bat well.

Andy Pettitte never was considered the ace of the staff, yet won 170 games in a Yankee uniform and pitched brilliantly in many big games.

Jorge Posada emerged as an offensive force at catcher and was the most vocal and fiery force in the clubhouse.

The greatest closer in baseball history and the essential element in the Yankees' dominance: Mariano Rivera.

said he wanted Mendoza shipped to the minor leagues. Mendoza had a 4.34 ERA and had earned Torre's trust as an emergency starter, a long reliever and a groundball-throwing machine who could get out of jams with double plays. Watson called Torre after the Minnesota game to tell him Steinbrenner wanted Mendoza demoted.

"Just make sure," Torre told Watson, "that George knows that when we do it and the writers ask me why, I will tell them that George wanted to do it—that he wanted to send him out. I didn't."

Said Torre, "I couldn't in good conscience say, 'We're sending him out. He didn't do the job.' Everybody knew how I felt about him. The kid had been pitching his ass off and then one afternoon he gives up a base hit."

Watson relayed Torre's message to Steinbrenner. The Boss suddenly changed his mind. Mendoza wasn't going anywhere.

"That was a good lesson I learned early on," Torre said. "It was really my first confrontation with George. He backed off. Because he didn't want that responsibility of people knowing it was his call."

The divide-and-conquer dynamic Steinbrenner created with the Yankees encouraged some employees to stake out their own turf, to curry favor with The Boss or damage the standing of others to elevate their own. What Steinbrenner saw as a system to keep his employees perpetually on edge, Torre saw as divisive and unproductive.

"You'd like to believe that we all want everybody to get better and the whole team to get better and never give a shit who gets credit for it," Torre said. "People would get in George's ear. All these people would make suggestions and never be accountable for what went wrong. When it did go wrong, it was, 'Well, he's the manager' or 'He's the pitching coach.'

"Sometimes I may get a message from Cash: 'George wants to talk to you.' I'd call him and there would be something he wanted to get on me about. Usually I'd beat him to the punch. I'd call him. I'd say, 'We're struggling.' He'd give you the huff and puff, but nothing that other managers didn't put up with. George always wanted to make me feel uncomfortable because he wanted that control over you.

"The one phone call I got from George that I'll never forget was when he criticized me for not using Mariano in a tie game in extra innings. I told him, 'I'm not going to have him go out there and pitch two, maybe three innings. I can't do that. This is only one game.' He said, 'Oh, yeah?' That's what he'd say to me. I said, 'Yeah. Right, wrong or indifferent, I'm not going to do it.' But then we got waxed two straight games against the Mets and then on a Sunday morning he called me up to tell me to keep my chin up. That's the way George was. When you were suffering, he'd come and help you. Otherwise, he'd be this tyrant who would second-guess a lot of stuff that you did or didn't do."

Torre did his best not to allow Steinbrenner to make him feel uncomfortable, a tactic that frustrated Steinbrenner because it undermined the control he sought. Unlike most of Steinbrenner's managers, who played by The Boss's rules and felt beholden to him for the job, Torre came to the Yankees as a complete outsider to the franchise who had been fired three times and wasn't sure if he ever was going to get a fourth chance. He was playing with house money. He did not manage under a fear of his losing his job, thus depriving Steinbrenner of one of his main weapons. Another manager might have demoted Mendoza, for instance, and simply covered for Steinbrenner with a handy organizational lie. Not Torre. On top of that kind of disarmament, Torre received high critical praise from the media and opponents for his management of the team, another annoyance to Steinbrenner and another threat to the control The Boss wanted over his manager.

"He was resentful of the credit I got," Torre said, "and I addressed it with him. The thing that bothered me is I was getting this credit so he would try to find little things to tweak me with, just to get my attention. I'd tell him, 'Not a day goes by where somebody credits me that I don't mention your name. They don't always write that, but I can't help that. Just understand that.' He always denied that. He'd say, 'No, I don't care about that.' I knew better."

Steinbrenner especially was on edge in that 2000
World Series, ankle-deep in water and chest-deep in
the pressure of maintaining the Yankees' status as
New York's premier team. The Yankees simply
could not afford to lose to the Mets, of all teams, especially at a time when Steinbrenner was planning
the launch of his regional sports network. The Mets
were a confident team hardened by the pressures of
New York and, unlike the 1998 Padres and 1999
Braves, were not about to roll over to the mighty
Yankees and their home-field advantage. "Yankee
Stadium? I don't give a hoot about it," Mets reliever
Turk Wendell said on the eve of the series. "We've
played there before. It won't be a surprise." Wendell, who grew up a fan of the Red Sox, added,
"The Yankees have tortured us for years and years,
and beating them would be sweet for me."

The 2000 Yankees, however, were no longer so
mighty. They represented another incremental decline in the dynasty from that 1998 pinnacle.
Knoblauch, 31; Martinez, 32; Brosius, 33; O'Neill,
37; and Cone, 37—all had down years as they
began to show some age-related attrition. Denny
Neagle, a midseason acquisition to the rotation, was
a bust, a precursor to the many times the Yankees
would get burned by bringing a National League
pitcher over to the American League. The Yankees
finished sixth in the league in runs and sixth in

ERA. They were good, but nothing special. The Yankees won only 87 games, fewer than eight teams in baseball, including the Cleveland Indians, who didn't even make the playoffs.

The Yankees held a nine-game lead with 18 games to play and still had to sweat out a first-place finish over Boston, losing all but 2½ games of that lead. They finished the season in a 3-15 tailspin in which they lost games by scores of 11-1, 15-4, 16-3, 15-4, 11-1, 11-3 and 9-1.

"I have no clue what happened in September," Torre said. "The second inning we're down six-nothing every day. I had a meeting before a game in Baltimore when I said, 'Guys, you want the champagne **before** the game? Because we keep holding on to this champagne, waiting to clinch. Might as well drink it early.' I was just trying to do something to relax them.

"But then all of a sudden you get to the postseason and the pressure is off. All of a sudden that 15 out of 18 doesn't count anymore, so the pressure's off. You don't have to worry about losing the lead."

Though the 2000 Yankees seemed vulnerable based on their regular season production, their postseason know-how served them well. They survived a five-game series against Oakland in the Division Series, winning Game 5 on the road with Andy Pettitte starting, Orlando Hernandez, Mike Stanton and Jeff Nelson in the middle and Mariano Rivera at the end—all of them postseason stalwarts.

The Athletics started journeyman Gil Heredia and found themselves down 6-0 before they took their first at-bat.

"It was our first time in the playoffs in eight years," said Billy Beane, the Oakland general manager. "We had a young, highly emotional bunch. We won the first game, we had a good team, we carried the adrenaline for a game or two, but when we played Game 5, it was almost as if the Yankees said, 'Enough is enough. We've played with the mouse long enough. It's time to get it over with.'"

The Yankees then dismissed Seattle in six games in the American League Championship Series, losing only in the two games started by Neagle. Clemens helped turn the series with the greatest game of his postseason career, a one-hit shutout with 15 strikeouts and 138 pitches to win Game 5, 5-0, a game in which he announced his nasty intentions by buzzing Alex Rodriguez with a pitch early in the game. "That game was incredible," Torre said. "I remember him knocking Alex back, and Alex looking like, 'What are you doing?' And that was it."

———

The Yankees advanced to a Subway Series against the Mets, though by evidence of the advance billing, the World Series itself seemed relegated to only a backdrop to the hyperpublicized personal war between Roger Clemens and Mike Piazza.

Clemens had started against the Mets that year on July 8 at Yankee Stadium. Piazza had worn out Clemens in his career. In 12 at-bats, Piazza had raked Clemens for seven hits, including three home runs, and nine runs batted in. McNamee, Clemens' since-estranged trainer who used to help Clemens warm up in the bullpen before games, said he told Clemens just before the game, "Listen, you've got to cut that shit out. I mean, the guy . . . you've got to end that shit." McNamee said Clemens responded, "Don't worry."

Piazza was the leadoff batter of the second inning of a scoreless game. Clemens obtained a called strike on the first pitch. His next pitch, a fastball, sailed toward Piazza's head. Piazza threw his hand up and ducked his head slightly at the last moment, but the baseball drilled him right on the front of his helmet. Piazza immediately fell limp to the ground in the manner of someone who had been shot. The Mets believed Clemens had thrown at Piazza intentionally. Piazza had to be removed from the game. While Piazza was being examined in the Mets' clubhouse, Clemens called there to talk to him, to see how he was feeling. There was some confusion about what happened next: whether Piazza was unable to take the call at that moment or whether he flat out refused to take the call. All Clemens knew was that his attempt to talk to Piazza was rebuffed.

"The worst I've seen him upset was when he hit Piazza," McNamee said. "He said, 'Mac, he won't pick up the phone. What should I do?' I said, 'Fuck 'im.' He goes, 'No, man. He won't pick up the phone. I've got to do something.' I said, 'Listen, I know Franco. You want me to go, I'll go get Franco.'"

Mets reliever John Franco and McNamee both had attended St. John's.

"So I went over to the clubhouse and I grabbed Franco," McNamee said. "I'm talking to John right outside the clubhouse and I'm going, 'Yeah, John. Roger just feels bad. He's in the locker room and he wants to speak with Mike.' And he goes, 'He's in there. He's a pussy. Fuck 'im. He's in the trainer's room.'

"And I went back and I told Roger that. And that's when Roger went on the offensive, saying, 'Who gets hit and has a press conference?'"

Said Torre, "Piazza wouldn't take the call in the clubhouse, but that's understandable. I mean, we all thought Roger was that same person when he pitched against us and didn't know him. I mean, I hated him as an opponent for the shit that he did.

"I remember it was right before the All-Star break, and the All-Star Game was in Atlanta and Bob Gibson was there. He told me, 'The guy never moved. He just sort of stayed there.' I said, 'Yeah, because the last thing he thought was that he was going to get hit in the head. Just wait 'til I step in, dig in, and throw the ball over here where I like it so I can knock the shit out of it.'

"Roger didn't throw at him. I mean, I'm not saying he didn't try to push him back off the plate. I'm not saying he didn't do that, but he certainly didn't have any intention of hitting him."

It was made-for-tabloids stuff. It was a bitter feud between two superstar players, Yankees versus Mets, New York versus New York. Clemens, finally earning his keep with the Yankees after a transitional year in 1999, played the role of the bad guy.

"The whole Piazza thing in 2000 kind of dominated that year for him and everything surrounding it," Cone said. "Steve Phillips, the Mets general manager, really escalated things. He was very angry and very aggressive in his postgame comments. He shut down the weight room the next day when we went to Shea Stadium. Yankee players weren't allowed in the Mets' weight room the next day. He just kept it going. He said, 'Keep the players away from each other.' There was too much animosity. He escalated things. I thought that was a little out of line for a GM. That could have been handled by the players and managers. He unnecessarily escalated the situation, but he was upset."

For the World Series, speculation was rampant about what would happen when Clemens and Piazza met again. Sports channels and news channels played endless loops of the July beaning. Would Clemens hit Piazza again? Would the Yankees pitch Clemens at Shea Stadium, where, under National League rules, he would take his turn at bat and be subject to getting hit himself as a retaliatory act by the Mets?

"We didn't need for that to happen," said Torre, who slotted Clemens in Game 2 for the safety of pitching at Yankee Stadium. "Roger told me, 'Whatever you'd like me to do.' I think Mel got to me and said that he'd rather not pitch at Shea, but he'd never admit that to me. Mel was remarkable. He'd get a sense for everything, or pitchers would talk to him before they'd talk to me, which is understandable."

Mel Stottlemyre, Torre's trusted pitching coach, was undergoing aggressive treatment for a bone marrow cancer known as multiple myeloma. At great risk of infections, he could not perform the duties of the pitching coach that year, but he continued to serve Torre as an adviser. Steinbrenner invited him to Yankee Stadium for the first two games of the World Series. They would watch the games together from Torre's office, the two of them eating cheeseburgers.

The Yankees, as they always seemed to do in October, somehow won Game 1, even though they left 15 runners on base and were losing, 3-2, with one out in the ninth inning with nobody on base against Mets closer Armando Benitez. The Mets' lead should have had a cushion to it, but the Yankees prospered from a baserunning gaffe by Timo Perez in the sixth inning. With two outs, Perez might have scored from first base on a double off the wall by Todd Zeile, except for Perez falling into a jog when he assumed the ball was going to clear the wall for a home run. Derek Jeter, with yet another of his exquisitely timed comic-book heroics, made Perez pay for the mistake with a perfect relay throw to the plate for the final out of the inning.

Still, the Mets had the Yankees down to their final two outs with the bases clear when Benitez pitched to O'Neill. What happened next was the quintessential championship Yankees at-bat: a 10-pitch walk. "It set the tone for the series," Torre said. "It was just a dare: 'You can't get me out.' It was the loudest walk you've ever experienced."

O'Neill fell behind Benitez, one ball and two strikes. One hundred four times during the regular season Benitez had put hitters in a 1-and-2 snare, and only 19 times did they ever escape from that snare to reach base, leaving a lowly 18 percent chance of reaching base. O'Neill fought his way out of the predicament with the Yankees' trademark persistence forged from that **desperation to win** from 1998. He fouled off two pitches, let two more go for balls, fouled off two more, and finally watched the tenth pitch sail out of the strike zone for ball four.

The rest of the rally carried the same familiar earmarks of Yankees ingenuity: two opposite-field singles, one by pinch-hitter Luis Polonia and another by Luis Vizcaino, and a sacrifice fly by Chuck Knoblauch and the game was tied. Watching the

Yankees rally like that over and over was like watching an old woman knit: knit one, pearl one, knit one, pearl one . . . the repetition of executing simple tasks created something big. The Yankees would win in the 12th inning by stitching together a walk and three hits, the last of them an opposite-field single by Vizcaino off Wendell.

———

Game 2 brought the main event, the wrestlemania matchup of Clemens versus Piazza. Torre was sick of the hype, even angry about it. The feeling in Yankee Stadium that night was a rabid one, three months of hostility brought to a boil, fired by the incessant media fascination with the two stars. Torre spoke briefly to his team before the game.

"Let's not get caught up in the emotion of what they're trying to make this about," Torre said. "We still have baseball to play, a team to beat."

By then Torre had come to like and trust Clemens, who in his second year with the Yankees had become more a part of the team. There was less hiding around the back rooms of the basement of Yankee Stadium.

"He was easy for me," Torre said. "I have my rules about the national anthem and stretching. I'd get them sometimes and sometimes I wouldn't notice. All of a sudden Roger would come out to the field and say, 'Skip, I just put three hundred on your desk.' Because I don't look for everybody when they come out for the national anthem. I don't think there was anything phony about Roger. He was who he was. And he was a good teammate."

Clemens treated every one of his starts as if preparing for Armageddon, none with more emotion than Game 2 of the 2000 World Series. He had not pitched for seven days since dominating the Mariners with that one-hitter, the bulk of those days consumed by media reports of another showdown with Piazza. He also was worried about his mother, who would be sitting in the wheelchair section of Yankee Stadium, with an oxygen tank to counter the effects of emphysema. She was there when Clemens pitched the 1999 World Series clincher, but had to leave after five innings because she grew so nervous and anxious that her breathing became more difficult. Clemens was also emotional about seeing the ill Stottlemyre in the clubhouse before the game.

There was so much to think about even before throwing a pitch. Clemens lost himself in his usual pregame preparation, which typically began with cranking the whirlpool to its hottest possible temperature. "He'd come out looking like a lobster," trainer Steve Donahue said. Donahue than would rub hot liniment all over Clemens' body, "from his ankles to his wrists," Donahue said. Then Donahue would rub the hottest possible liniment on his testicles. "He'd start snorting like a bull," the trainer said. "That's when he was ready to pitch."

Said Donahue, "Roger was a warrior and a fighter. His intensity was not the same as David Cone's. You didn't even talk to Coney when the game started. Roger could talk about fishing, hunting, umpires.

"Between innings, almost every inning, was like a prizefight with Roger. It was like he was coming back to his corner in between rounds. He'd come in and you'd have to have your surgical gloves on, ready to go. He might say, 'Give me the red hot on the back.' Or, 'Give me some grease on my elbow.' You really had to pay attention when he had two outs, because the first thing that would come off were the shirts. He had all dry shirts lined up. Then we'd have two or three grades of hot stuff lined up. He'd get the medium on the back and the next-to-hottest on the elbow and he'd get all greased up and then you'd have to put talcum on him so he could put his shirt on over the grease and then he'd go back out there for the fight."

Clemens went out for his usual bullpen warmup. Mike Borzello would catch him at the start. McNamee would observe, always checking some cranky body part—back, hamstring, groin—that needed extra observation. Posada would arrive in time to catch the last 20 pitches, with McNamee assuming stances as a lefthanded and righthanded batter. "Whew! How many times did he almost smoke my ass!" McNamee said. Clemens would finish by working through pitch sequences on two virtual batters. Then he would wipe the sweat from his brow, rub it on the Babe Ruth monument in Monument Park for good luck, and get down to the business of intimidating grown men with the flight path and velocity of a thrown baseball.

It was 8:05 p.m. when Clemens threw his first pitch. He would say later that night, "I don't remember ever being more ready for a start, but I also knew I had to control it somehow."

He was positively ferocious from the start, blowing pitches past the Mets with the heat and force of an acetylene torch. Timo Perez, the first batter, struck out on a 97-mph fastball. Edgardo Alfonzo whiffed on a ridiculously fast 94-mph splitter. Piazza was next. The crowd was nearly barbaric in its frenzy. Clemens clearly was more amped than his usual warrior-like self.

"I was anxious all day," he said after the game, at 2 a.m. in the Yankees' parking lot, still edgy. "I really had a hard time with it. I felt like I couldn't go up and in, which I normally would do on him, because what if I did? What if one got away? With all the talk it really wore me down. I kept telling myself, 'You've got to get a hold of your emotions.' Everything was building up to it. It was so hard to get a hold of my emotions."

The first two pitches were 97-mph missiles that Piazza took each time for strikes.

"You couldn't even see the plate with all the flashbulbs," McNamee said. "I was in the bullpen, and you couldn't even see the batter after all the lights."

Clemens tried a splitter next, but missed, running the count to 1-and-2. The next pitch was an inside fastball, full of anger and machismo, a buzz saw of a pitch that bore through the handle of Piazza's bat as he tried to hit it. Objects flew every which way in the manner of an explosion. One piece of the bat flew toward the left side of the infield. The handle stayed in Piazza's hands. The ball flew into foul territory off first base. The biggest remaining part of the bat, the barrel, sheared off with a shard at one end, bounced toward Clemens. There was so much going on, so much in his head, so much emotion coursing through his body, that Clemens could not process the inventory of what was happening at that moment quickly enough. He picked up the barrel as if fielding a grounder—in fact, he would say that his first thought was that he was fielding the baseball. And when he realized it was a useless piece of wood in his hands, he threw it—threw it, he said, toward what he thought was a safe area out of play, simply to get this damn piece of wood, by extension, this piece of Piazza, off the field.

Piazza, however, happened to be right near the flight path of the barrel. Piazza was confused himself. He had no idea where the ball was, so he began jogging toward first base, just in case it might be in play somewhere. The bat careened and cartwheeled not too far in front of him. Piazza was stunned.

"What is your problem?" he yelled at Clemens. "What is your problem?"

Clemens did not respond. He spoke to home plate umpire Charlie Reliford about how he thought it was the ball.

"That was just Roger's pent-up frustration," Mc-Namee said of the bat-throwing incident, "because that was the first time he saw him since July. He was hyped. That was just emotion. It was nothing. He didn't throw the bat **at** Piazza.

"And Roger reads every fucking one of the stories. His sisters read everything and talk to him. He finds out about it. He's got people all over the Internet. That cockamamie story about the ball, that's bullshit. I think he was just so hyped up and focused."

Said Torre, "Roger was on another planet, obviously. He gets the bat and he throws it away, just throws it off the field. Piazza, not knowing where the ball was, he started running. Clemens knew it was a foul ball, and he just threw the bat toward the dugout. Turns out Piazza ran into it almost."

Reliford moved between Clemens and Piazza. Both dugouts emptied. The situation was quelled quickly. On the next pitch, Clemens retired Piazza on a groundball to second base. Clemens, still highly emotional and amped, ran off the field and kept going, past Torre, up the runway and into the clubhouse. This time it had nothing to do with changing his shirt. Stottlemyre jumped up from eating his cheeseburger with Steinbrenner in Torre's office and made his way toward Clemens.

"I didn't mean to do that!" Clemens said.

When Stottlemyre reached Clemens he found a most surprising sight. Clemens, the intimidating warrior who put hot liniment on his balls, who snorted like a bull, who threw 97 miles an hour with more than a hint of danger affixed to his pitches, sat there crying uncontrollably.

While Clemens, with Stottlemyre's help, pulled himself together, his teammates scored two runs for him. By the eighth inning the Yankees led 6-0 and Clemens was nearly unhittable. He faced 28 batters. Two managed hits, none walked, nine struck out and only five managed to get the ball out of the infield, safely or not. The Mets put up five runs in the ninth off Jeff Nelson and Mariano Rivera—Piazza hit a home run off Nelson—but the night belonged to Clemens and the Yankees, 6-5.

"Competition," Mets catcher Todd Pratt said that night, "brings out the best and worst in people."

———

The next day, a workout day before Game 3, Cone asked Torre if he could speak to him for a minute. Torre had not yet announced his starting pitcher for

Game 4. He had Orlando Hernandez lined up for Game 3—a game the Yankees would lose, 4-2, when El Duque was touched for two runs in the eighth—but had yet to decide between Neagle and Cone for Game 4.

"Joe didn't have a lot of faith in Neagle," Cone said. "Neagle rubbed him the wrong way for some reason. He thought he was a little flighty. There was something about him he didn't like."

Cone, though, was far from a sure thing. He had pitched only one inning in the ALCS against Seattle, a mop-up inning at that in a 6-2 game. The body of the inspirational leader of the championship Yankees teams was breaking down. Cone suffered through a dreadful season, going 4-14 with a 6.91 ERA.

"I got to a point in my career where I learned how to manage the pain," Cone said. "I learned how many Advil I had to take or when I really got in trouble I could take something heavier, Indocin or other anti-inflammatories. I had been through it enough that I knew how to manage the pain. What I didn't know was how short my stuff was getting. I almost got too good at managing the pain, because I didn't recognize my stuff got short. Lots of hanging sliders that year. My slider just stopped breaking."

Toward the end of the season Cone dislocated his left shoulder diving for a ball.

"I shouldn't have been on the playoff roster," he

said. "I was throwing with one arm. You really need that drive from the front side. For the rest of the year I had nothing."

Cone threw no harder than 85 miles an hour in that one inning against Seattle. He knew Torre was considering a start for him, which is why he asked to speak with the manager on that workout day.

"Hey, look, Joe," Cone told him. "I'm pretty comfortable I can give you a couple of innings of relief. But I'm not sure what I can give you as a starter."

Said Cone, "That was the first time I ever admitted that. To anybody. To admit that I can't do it."

Torre thanked him for his honesty and announced Neagle as the Yankees' Game 4 pitcher.

Jeter hit that important first-pitch home run off Bobby Jones to begin Game 4. The Yankees pushed the lead to 3-0 by the third inning, but Neagle gave back two of the runs by serving up a home run to Piazza in the bottom of the third.

It was still 3-2 in the fifth when Piazza came up with two outs and nobody on base. Torre walked out to the mound. Neagle was one out away from qualifying for a World Series win. But Torre wanted no part of watching Neagle pitch to Piazza a second time. He signaled to the bullpen.

Torre managed postseason games with cutthroat urgency, a policy that began in his first postseason series as Yankees manager with advice from Zimmer. Torre starter Kenny Rogers was getting hit hard by the Rangers in the second inning of Game 4 when Zimmer turned to Torre and said, "You might want to get someone up in the bullpen."

"What?" Torre said. "It's only the second inning."

"You can never let these games get away from you," Zimmer said.

Torre pulled Rogers after only two innings, down 2-0. The Yankees won the game, 6-4. He never forgot Zimmer's lesson.

In Game 4 of the 2000 World Series, Neagle was the latest version of Rogers. He handed Torre the ball and walked off dejectedly. Neagle would later explain, "I'm a victim of not having done it long enough for Joe."

The bullpen door swung open, and out jogged the clubhouse rascal whom O'Neill wanted to maul before the game, the same guy with the 4-14 record, the 85-mph fastball, the dislocated shoulder and the heart of a lion. It was time for one last Yankee moment for David Cone.

"He couldn't get me or you out," Torre said, "but I knew you plant some thoughts in Mike Piazza's head. 'Oh, shit. Now I've got to look for more than one pitch.' When a certain hitter like Piazza knows he's going to get that one pitch eventually? He'll kill you. But with Coney, he goes out there and throws buckshot at you. He's all over the joint."

Cone figured at some point in the game he might be called on to face Piazza. He just didn't figure that point would come with Neagle one out away from qualifying for a World Series victory.

"It just goes to show you: Joe didn't care," Cone said. "One thing Joe set the tone on early on was that he was not going to play favorites. Yeah, he was a little bit of a riverboat gambler in terms of strategy. But he was going to put the team on the field that gave him the best chance to win at that point. If that meant sitting Tino in the postseason, sitting Boggs, taking Neagle out with two outs in the fifth and not letting him face Piazza one more time, he was going to do it. He didn't care who you were or what was going on. He was going to do whatever he was going to do to help the team win. Guys didn't like it, but too bad. Tino didn't like it. But he accepted it. He dealt with it."

Cone's savvy served him well. He knew, for instance, that Piazza was the type of hitter who liked to take a strike. "To me that's half the battle," Cone said, "knowing which guys will spot you a strike or not."

So even after Cone missed with his first pitch, he came back with a fastball that caught a lot of the plate. Piazza took it for strike one.

"That," Cone said, "was a pitch he could have mashed. But I was really confident he wasn't going to swing at the 1-and-0 fastball. And once I got the strike I threw him two sliders, one he swung at and missed and one he barely fouled off. Decent sliders—kind of sweeping, Frisbee sliders.

"Then Posada called a fastball in, so I thought maybe I'll miss in with it. It got a little more of the plate than I wanted. It was up just enough. The last thing he was looking for was a fastball anywhere in there. It was just luck of the draw. He reacted late and just missed it—popped it up."

Said Torre, "He was looking off speed, and he threw him an 85 mile an hour fastball down the middle and he hit a pop-up."

It was a triumph of trust. Torre wanted Cone on Piazza even with an 85-mph fastball. And Cone came through for him. It was the last pitch Cone would throw in his great career with the Yankees. Cone was going to pitch another inning, but Torre used Jose Canseco to pinch hit for him with two outs and two on. Canseco whiffed. Nelson, Stanton and Rivera took care of the final 12 outs to keep the final score at 3-2.

———

The Yankees the next night won the World Series for the last time under Torre. It was the perfect coda, straight out of the 1996–2000 Greatest Hits songbook. There was, of course, a comeback; they trailed 2-1 in the sixth inning. There was Jeter playing the superhero again; he tied the game with a home run. There was terrific starting pitching; Andy Pettitte allowed two unearned runs in seven innings. There was the prototypical game-winning rally of Yankee ingenuity; the Yankees had two outs and nobody on base in the ninth when Posada drew a nine-pitch walk from Al Leiter. Brosius added an infield single and Luis Sojo added a groundball single that, coupled with an error, sent two runs home for a 4-2 lead. And, of course, at the end there was Rivera, getting the final out on a fly ball by Piazza, the potential tying run.

After Sojo's game-breaking hit, technicians and carpenters from Fox hustled to the Yankees' clubhouse to begin erecting the platform for the presentation of the Commissioner's Trophy. But there was a problem. The door was locked. They knocked on it, announcing themselves.

Steinbrenner shouted, "Don't let those bastards in!"

He was superstitious about having anyone assuming the Yankees had the world championship in hand. No one, he decided, was coming into his clubhouse until after the last out. Commissioner Bud Selig, with word reaching him in the stands, was apoplectic. His television partners needed to get in! Kevin Hallinan, Major League Baseball's director of security, called a Yankees official in the clubhouse and told him that the Yankees were risking an enormous fine from Selig if Steinbrenner didn't open the door immediately. Steinbrenner sent word that the only person he would talk to was Paul Beeston, one of Selig's assistants and a friend of Steinbrenner's from Beeston's years running the Toronto Blue Jays. Beeston, in fact, was friendly enough with Steinbrenner to have pulled a prank on him a few years earlier when he helped arrange an owners meeting in which all of the owners came dressed as Steinbrenner: gray slacks, navy blue blazer, white turtleneck.

Beeston banged on the door. "George. It's Beeston! Open the door," he called out.

Steinbrenner opened the door a bit, just wide enough for Beeston and no one else to slip through before he slammed it shut. Beeston calmly negotiated with Steinbrenner to open the door and let the TV people do their job. Steinbrenner eventually relented, but not without warning Beeston, "But if anything goes wrong, this is on you!"

Only a few minutes later, Rivera leapt in the air after getting Piazza to fly out to Bernie Williams. Steinbrenner was crying on the shoulder of a very relieved Beeston. Soon the champagne was flying yet again. It never grew old. Every champagne celebration was full of exuberance and joy, though with each year more and more relief crept in there as well.

"We had a blast afterward," McNamee said. "I was sitting on top of the refrigerator in that little room. And George came up to me and shook my hand. Said, 'Congratulations!' I don't think he knew who I was. I just know for like a good 30 minutes after the champagne was gone almost everybody on the team was in that room. Guys were laughing. And every five minutes somebody would say, 'And this is for Turk Wendell!' So we toasted him like 10 times. Like we'd be talking, 'Hey, isn't this great?' and then some guy would raise his hand and go, 'To Turk Wendell!' And everybody would be cheering. It was pretty funny. They might have had a chance if he didn't open his mouth. Oh, he pissed everybody off. That Yankees team was not that good."

––––––

Didn't all the October nights in those years seem to end the same way? Watching the Yankees in the postseason those years was like watching a **Gilligan's Island** episode. No matter what outrageous plot twists and red herrings were thrown into the opening minutes of the show, you knew how it was going to end: Gilligan was still going to be on the island when they ran the credits. Likewise, no matter if the Yankees fell behind or were tied or were confronted with a rally, you knew they were going to come out ahead.

From 1998 through 2000, the Yankees won three consecutive world championships by playing .805 baseball in the postseason, going 33-8. Even as their talent waned, they seemed to know their way around the postseason better than anyone else, as if they had the only map to the buried treasure. Pitching, of course, was their compass. They allowed zero, one or two runs in 23 of those 41 games. But there was something else, something else that existed inside and between these players. It was something so strong that they took all the common logic of "small sample sizes," the randomness of when two good teams meet in the playoffs, and the difficulty of having to get through three rounds of playoffs, and they blew up all of what is now that conventional wisdom. Those three Yankees teams, for instance, were 15-3 in playoff games decided by one or two runs. Were they that lucky? Or were they that good?

"The randomness existed then," said Beane, the father of the modern philosophy that the playoffs are "a crapshoot." "But at some point you are like UCLA basketball under John Wooden. They won, what? Twelve titles in a postseason where you can get knocked out in one game? At some point a team becomes so good that they overcome the randomness. The '98 Yankees were one of the greatest teams I ever saw. That team was almost as good in '99 and 2000. They were without a doubt the UCLA of baseball in that time. They had everything you'd want a baseball team to have, and they were young, and let's face it, when you're that good it's a pretty overwhelming environment for another team to go in and try to beat them. They were that much better than anybody else."

Four times in all, Torre's Yankees rode down the Canyon of Heroes in Lower Manhattan while honored with a parade. Four times they added to the Yankees' legacy as the most prestigious franchise in sports, with 26 world championships in all. Yet there was a downside to the glory. Steinbrenner, who was desperate for a winner when Torre arrived, having endured 17 years without a title, now had come to expect these championships. Each title brought him a little less joy. The Yankees could do no better than to fulfill an obligation.

A short time after the 2000 World Series, with the Yankees having dispatched their crosstown rivals in a bitterly fought series, and the YES network cleared for launch with what remained the pre-eminent team in sports, Torre and his wife were getting ready to board a plan for Europe when his phone rang. It was Steinbrenner.

"I'm not giving the coaches a bonus this year," The Boss said.

Steinbrenner had handed out $25,000 bonuses to Torre's coaches when the Yankees won in 1996, 1998 and 1999.

"George," Torre said. "How can you give the coaches a bonus when we beat San Diego and then when we beat the Mets you can't give them a bonus? That's crazy."

"Well," Steinbrenner said. "They're **expected** to win."

A few weeks later, Steinbrenner called Torre again. It was New Year's Eve.

"I'm going to give the coaches a bonus," Steinbrenner said.

Who knew what changed his mind? All Torre

knew was that he was happy for his coaches, but still angry that Steinbrenner didn't believe they deserved a bonus in the first place.

"Still, you go through the same act with George," Torre said. "You thank him, you tell him what a great owner he is, and how much you appreciate it. You mean it, but you're also thinking, **Why is this necessary?** But see, that's the only control he had. That's what he used to get my attention. Because he wanted to see me squirm. So it was basically a game.

"At least you had access to him. I worked for Ted Turner and I worked for August Busch, and it was easier to work for George because you had access to him. You could talk to him. You could get to him. You could get your point across. You could never get to those guys to talk to them."

Steinbrenner's declining appreciation for what his team accomplished, however, was taking a toll on the morale of the organization. His scouts and player development people, for instance, did not receive their 1999 World Series rings until more than a year later—until **after the 2000 World Series,** and when they did receive them they turned out to be fake ones. The ring company eventually sent them word to return the rings so they could correct the "mistake."

Still, no 2000 World Series rings were forthcoming for the scouts, numbering about two dozen. Morale worsened when they were instructed not to bring up the subject of World Series rings at organizational meetings. It worsened still when they heard or saw Steinbrenner cronies such as actor Billy Crystal and singer Ronan Tynan wearing World Series rings. The daughter of one scout wrote a scathing letter to Steinbrenner about the withholding of rings from the people who worked so hard behind the scenes to help build a championship team. Steinbrenner relented and eventually ordered a ring for that one scout. Another player development official put his request in writing; he insisted that he would not sign his next contract until it included the promise of a 2000 World Series ring.

Nearly all of the scouts, however, never did receive a 2000 World Series ring. The bit of black humor among them, considering how long it took them to receive the 1999 World Series rings, was that the Yankees would have to win another World Series for them to receive the 2000 World Series rings. But no rings were ever forthcoming for the scouts and, in fact, Cashman told **Newsday** in 2006 after he assumed full authority in baseball operations that those people would not be receiving them. As the years went by, the jilted scouts began to refer to each lost Yankees season after 2000 as the result of what they called The Curse of the Rings. The Yankees have not won a World Series since.

5.

Mystique and Aura

In the middle of the sixth inning of the seventh game of the 2001 World Series, Joe Torre retreated to the clubhouse to use the bathroom. George Steinbrenner was waiting for him as Torre walked up a short flight of stairs. The Yankees owner had taken his customary position in the clubhouse to watch his team play in the postseason.

"What do you think?" Steinbrenner asked him.

Torre knew exactly what Steinbrenner wanted: another shot of reassurance. "He was a wreck," Torre said. Many times over the years Torre had calmed Steinbrenner's jangled nerves and fears. It was Torre's nature to be reassuring, even going back to 1962, during the Cuban Missile Crisis, when he was in the Air National Guard and was in charge of 50 troops at Lackland Air Force Base in Texas. One night while on a march the troops were moaning about the possibility of being sent off to a war. "Don't worry," Torre told them. "We're not going off to war." The troops believed him and immediately felt better. Torre had no inside information himself. He simply figured if they did not go to war, he would look smart, and if they did go to war, well, they would have bigger things to worry about than what their dorm chief had told them.

It was the same way with Steinbrenner. Torre told The Boss the Yankees would win with rookie pitchers in a doubleheader against the mighty Indians in 1996, and they did. He told Steinbrenner the Yankees would win four games in a row against the powerful Braves in the 1996 World Series, and they did. He told him Orlando Hernandez was ready to pitch the pivotal Game 4 of the 1998 ALCS, and Hernandez threw a gem. He told him Andy Pettitte was too good to trade, and Pettitte went 75-35 for Steinbrenner.

This time, however, was different. As Torre stood there in the visiting clubhouse of Bank One Ballpark, he looked Steinbrenner in the eye and realized he could not tell Steinbrenner what he wanted to hear. Torre had no words of reassurance this time. Fact was, with Arizona Diamondbacks pitcher Curt Schilling on top of his game, and the Yankees' offense looking mostly anemic throughout the series, not even Torre could muster an optimistic picture to give Steinbrenner. The reassurance well was dry.

"Boss," Torre said, "I wish I could give you something positive. But I don't know if we're ever going to score a run here. I wish the hell I knew, George."

That the Yankees were still playing at all, down 1-0 to Schilling and the Diamondbacks in Game 7, was in itself a colossal achievement. The dynasty was running low on fuel. Age continued to bring the Yankees down another notch from their 1998 pinnacle. For the third straight season since that 1998 juggernaut, the Yankees' run production diminished—they scored more than a full run a game less than they did in 1998 and dipped below an average of five runs per game for the first time since a dismal 1992 outfit that lost 86 games. The 2001 Yankees' on-base percentage, once the prideful signature of a team that grinded out every at-bat, sunk to .334, which would be the worst in Torre's 12 years with the Yankees and the franchise's worst since that 1992 team.

The Yankees resorted to stealing bases—they stole 161 bases, the franchise's second-most since 1916—and trusting that their pitching would carry them through close games. Clemens won the Cy Young Award with a 20-3 record, while Mike Mussina, the free agent prize signed to replace Cone, led the staff in innings, ERA and strikeouts. Mariano Rivera saved 50 games while the Yankees went 30-18 in one-run games, the first time the Yankees won so many games by the slimmest possible margin since 1980. The youthful Athletics, with 102 victories and a dynamite rotation that recalled the 1995 Braves and the deep, resourceful Mariners, with a league-record 116 victories, were the ascendant teams, the Yankees' likely successors.

The Yankees, on their way to 95 wins, went largely unchallenged in the second half in the American League East, thanks to a long fade by the Red Sox.

On the morning of September 11, Torre woke up to a comfortable 13-game lead over Boston. He was getting out of bed when his phone rang. It was his car service, calling about a scheduled appointment to take Torre to an appearance in Manhattan later that morning.

"I guess it's canceled," the man from the car service said.

"What's canceled?" Torre said.

"You haven't heard?"

The man told him about the plane that had crashed into one of the twin towers of the World Trade Center. Torre turned on the television, only to see a second plane strike the other tower.

"My first thought was my daughter," Torre said. "She was not quite six yet. I was trying to flip the TV stations around to make sure she had some cartoons or something. My wife was working out, and she came up and I told her. She had the TV on in the kitchen and me and my daughter were in the living room. It was absolutely frightening.

"I thought about my son. He used to be at the World Trade Center. I tried to get a hold of him on the phone. My sister-in-law Katie, one of Ali's sisters, was a flight attendant with American Airlines. She was in another country. That was our priority at that point, to find out where everybody we knew was. My son was living in New Jersey at the time. He was just on the other side of the Holland Tunnel, the Jersey side."

Life in America was put on anxious hold. Many of the mundane pursuits of everyday living, such as air travel and Major League Baseball, were meaningless in the great vortex of grief and anxiety that consumed the country. Some of the players fled to their families. Roger Clemens, for instance, drove from New York to Texas. On September 15, the Yankees who were still in town gathered after a workout to visit the Jacob Javits Center, which had been transformed into an emergency staging area, St. Vincent's Hospital, where survivors were expected to be treated, and the New York Armory, another staging area that had become a gathering place for families looking for lost loved ones. Derek Jeter, Bernie Williams, Chuck Knoblauch and several of the coaches joined Torre on the goodwill mission.

"It was obviously emotional," Torre said. "You go to St. Vincent's Hospital and there was nobody there. I think we went up and saw a firefighter who had smoke inhalation. But no people from the building that were in it when the plane hit.

"The most emotional part was the Armory. You go to the staging area and you see the workers and you shake their hands. And there were people waiting on results, DNA results, to see where their loved ones were. That was the toughest one, because we walked in—I didn't even want to go in. But then I remember that Randy Levine sent somebody in, or he might have gone in, just to see what the mood was. And the people who were in there wanted us to go in there.

"I think I realized at that point in time there was a purpose for us being there. We didn't know all these people, who were certainly devastated and huddled around in different groups. You'd look around and see that they had counselors or priests or rabbis in different family settings. We sort of just walked in there and looked around. And then somebody looked up and sort of waved us in, a family member. They brought out pictures of the family members they were waiting on, pictures of them wearing Yankee hats. Big Yankees fans, which was pretty moving."

The Yankees were a part of their community at a time of great need. Williams, for instance, walked up to one grieving woman.

"I don't know what to say," Williams said, "but

you look like you need a hug." And the center fielder of the Yankees reached out and embraced her.

"I realized at that point," Torre said, "we had to take a certain perspective for the rest of the season."

Word reached Torre that the Yankees would fly to Tampa the next day, a Sunday, to play the Devil Rays for one game only on Monday, and then fly to Chicago after the game for a series against the White Sox.

"I thought, That doesn't make sense. I don't have players here," Torre said. "I argued with George and he relented."

The plan changed. The Yankees would not fly to Tampa. They would fly to Chicago to work out Monday and resume the season Tuesday. Torre held a brief meeting with his team before the game.

"The 'NY' on our caps," he told them, "is all about New York, and not about the Yankees."

Orlando Hernandez, the Cuban émigré who had come to America for its freedoms, stymied the White Sox that night with seven shutout innings as the Yankees won, 11-3. The Yankees had become not just New York's team, but also America's hometown team. "There were lots of big banners in Chicago supporting New York," Torre said. "It was like an out-of-body experience watching all that stuff. You didn't know how important it was, what we were doing. It was just sort of feeling your way through it."

Clemens was the Yankees' starting pitcher the next night.

"I remember him getting focused," McNamee said. "When it's a big game we can have a 20-minute conversation and he won't remember it. He knew what it represented. I said, 'Listen, man. You understand the importance of this game.' We always talked like this. Sometimes it would get in, sometimes it wouldn't. That's how I worked. That's how I would treat a guy in preparation. We talked, and it was huge. I just tried to make sure that he didn't try to do too much, which he's capable of trying to do. That's how the conversation went, but he had that look on his face, just a glare. The next day we'd talk about it and he wouldn't even know what the fuck I said."

Clemens, following the lead of Hernandez, pitched well, taking the ball into the seventh inning as the Yankees won again, 6-3. The White Sox stopped them the next night, 7-5, in a game in which Chicago pitcher Kip Wells hit Williams in the head with a pitch. Williams' mother, who was at the game, rushed to the trainer's room to check on her son. Williams checked out fine. He returned to the Yankees' bench in the fifth inning in good spirits.

"You know when you get hit in the head and they check your eyes and ask you different questions?" Williams said to Torre in the dugout.

"Yeah, sure," Torre said.

"Well, the doctors asked me questions," Williams said. "They asked me what day it was and I said I didn't know. When they looked concerned I said, 'But I never know what day it is!'"

Baseball, with its leisurely pace and everyday rhythm, slowly returned to normal, and maybe even provided a small diversion to help bring the country closer to its normal bearings. The Yankees treaded water the rest of the season, winning nine times, losing eight times and tying once. Fact was, the wreckage of the twin towers still smoldered at Ground Zero and rescue workers and emergency personnel still combed through the debris. Every time the crowd sang "God Bless America" at Yankee Stadium, Torre would tear up, just knowing the world was a changed and darker place.

"I got choked up because the camera would always find children," Torre said, "and having a young child myself, you realize these children are not going to have the freedoms that I had. They're not going to be as trusting as I was. And that was sad. Still is."

In the Division Series, the Yankees again drew Oakland, a dangerous team one year wiser and one year more experienced. The Athletics won the first two games at Yankee Stadium, needing only one win in the next three games, with the next two at home, to knock out the three-time defending world champions. Torre held a team meeting on the workout day when they arrived in Oakland. He wore a cap given to him by Yogi Berra that said "It Ain't Over til It's Over," which he carried for the rest of the post-season.

"Let's not think about how we have to win the rest of the games in this series," Torre said. "Let's just win one game. Trust me, if you win one game your momentum switches and there's an element of doubt on the other team's side."

The Yankees turned around the series by winning Game 3, the Flip Game, 1-0, behind the pitching of Mussina and the timely improvisational skills of Jeter. By the third inning of the next game they were comfortably ahead, 4-0, on their way to a 9-2 victory to bring the series back to Yankee Stadium and a decisive Game 5. Once again, Clemens would get the ball in a big spot.

"Clemens' locker was next to mine," Donahue said. "I remember him coming in that day. He was trying to take off his T-shirt, and he was struggling just to do that. I said, 'Holy shit. He's hurting.' I said something to him about how he was feeling. He just said, 'I'm okay.'"

A short time later, Torre confronted Clemens in the trainer's room. He needed to be convinced by Clemens that he could help the Yankees win the game, give them five decent innings, and not just go out there gamely with a bum shoulder and cranky elbow for the sake of being able to say he gave it a shot.

"Roger, I need you to pitch today," he said. "But I don't need you coming off the mound, limping or whatever, and taking your hat off and being a hero. I need a fucking win. I don't need somebody who tried."

"Joe," Clemens said, "I can do it."

Clemens lasted until there was one out into the fifth inning, leaving with a 4-2 lead and two runners on, one of whom would score. The Yankees went on to win, 5-3. Rivera, Torre's ultimate postseason weapon, secured the final six outs on 23 pitches, all but five of them strikes.

"I thought in 2001 we had narrowed the gap," Oakland's Beane said. "They were the better team. We almost got lucky. Everyone likes to say the key game was the Flip Game, that if Jeremy Giambi slides he's safe. Let's assume he does slide and is safe. That only makes it a tie game. And Rivera could probably go two or three innings."

The Yankees then stopped cold the 116-win Mariners, dispos-ing of them in five games, including a 12-3 blowout in the clincher. Seattle had scored the most runs and allowed the fewest in the American League, but the Yankees in October seemed to operate on postseason muscle memory. Martinez, Williams and O'Neill—all Old Guard stalwarts—each hit home runs. Cone, viewing the Yankees from afar that season as a member of the Boston Red Sox, gained a greater appreciation for his former fellow soldiers, with whom he had shared many foxholes, as they again somehow found a way back to the World Series.

"It was definitely bizarre seeing it from the other side," Cone said. "I learned that with the Yankees involved, it was a typical Red Sox year. We were in first place half the year looking in the rear-view mirror the whole time. Plus we had injuries. You could see it coming.

"The thing I appreciated more and more from the other side was how good Bernie and O'Neill and Jeter were after facing them. How good Bernie was really caught me. Watching Bernie all those years we always thought, tremendous talent, batting champion, but when we always asked him, 'What are you thinking about when you're hitting, Bernie?' you'd get, 'Nothing. I'm blank.' And that was Bernie.

"So facing those guys you see how talented they really were—how tough an out Jeter was, Tino, O'Neill, Bernie . . . It was about how good they are, how tough they are and how much they can grind it out, especially for a pitcher like me who throws a lot of pitches and is trying to trick them later in my career. I got a really good appreciation for how many good at-bats they get, which leads them to grind it out, and they just keep coming over the course of the year.

"That was Joe's big saying over the years: 'Keep grinding it out.' I really felt it on the other side. I appreciated it much more. I saw it sitting there. It's a little more stark reality when you're facing them trying to get them out. And if it wasn't this guy, it was the next guy. It was somebody different every day. I really got the sense of that, too."

———

The 2001 World Series, the first major sporting event after 9/11, began in Phoenix under such heavy security that all manhole covers in the vicinity of Bank One Ballpark were welded shut. Then Curt Schilling and Randy Johnson applied the same procedure to the Yankees' offensive. The Diamondbacks won Games 1 and 2, 9-1 and 4-0, while allowing the Yankees a total of six hits—the fewest ever over the first two games of a World Series except for the clampdown job by the deadball-era 1906 Cubs on the White Sox. So chipper were the Diamondbacks feeling about themselves that as the series shifted to Yankee Stadium, Schilling famously dismissed the nearly supernatural powers associated with the Yankees' home-field advantage. "When you use the words **mystique** and **aura**," Schilling said, "those are dancers in a nightclub. Those are not things we concern ourselves with on the ballfield."

The Yankees didn't hit all that much better back at Yankee Stadium for an emotional Game 3, a night that began with President George W. Bush throwing out the first ball, a declarative strike down the heart of the plate, from the pitcher's rubber.

(Torre knew something was different when he saw a seventh, unfamiliar umpire at home plate when the teams exchanged lineup cards; it was an undercover Secret Service agent.) The Yankees scratched out two runs on seven hits, but that still was good enough for a 2-1 victory because Clemens threw three-hit ball for seven innings, allowing only one run. When Torre removed him—Rivera, with his twoinning high-tech weaponry, would close it out with six uninterrupted outs—he grabbed Clemens and told him, "You never have to prove yourself again."

What happened over the next two nights is the stuff of legend, an Americanized King Arthur tale of such improbability that the passage of centuries might leave open to debate its historical accuracy. But it really did happen: not once but twice, the Yankees hit a home run when they were down to their last out and trailing by two runs—and then won the game. Only once before in the 98-year history of the World Series had a team hit a game-saving home run from such a bleak position (and that once-a-century shot happened 72 years ago), and here the Yankees did it **two times in a row?** It was crazy stuff. It was exactly the kind of stuff a grieving city needed, if only to start believing again in **something** in a suddenly senseless world.

The Yankees were one out away from losing Game 4 on Halloween night, 3-1, when Tino Martinez—0-for-the-World-Series, and batting with

O'Neill at second base—whacked the first pitch he ever saw from Byung-Hyun Kim off the facing of the bleachers in right-center field. Only Mule Haas of the 1929 Athletics ever before had staved off a World Series defeat from two runs down with two outs by slamming a home run. Jeter won the game with a home run in the 10th that, even for him, represented impeccable timing. Jeter had stepped into the batter's box at the stroke of midnight, then consumed nine pitches and four minutes to get to the game-winner that made a Mr. November out of him.

At the stadium the next night, somebody held up a sign during Game 5 that said, "Mystique and Aura Appearing Nightly." Sure enough, the show began at exactly the same time: with the Yankees down to their last out, trailing by two runs, with Kim on the mound. This time Brosius, who had not hit a home run since September 21, and batting with Posada at second base, walloped a home run into the delirious crowd in the left-field seats.

"He hit that ball," Torre said, "and it was like, 'I don't even know what I'm seeing here.'"

Said Jeter, "Unbelievable. You'll never see anything like that again. Never. We did it two days in a row. That was as exciting as anything that has happened here. That and the 2003 Boston game, Game 7—those are the three loudest times I've ever heard it at Yankee Stadium."

It wasn't a walkoff homer; it was a knockoff

homer. This time the Yankees won on a 12th-inning single by Alfonso Soriano.

It was hard to make sense of what was going on. The Yankees were batting .177 in the World Series and had scored only 10 runs in five games—and yet they were one win away from winning their fourth consecutive world championship and fifth in six years. The Diamondbacks, meanwhile, left Yankee Stadium down three games to two knowing they had been two outs away from being world champions.

"This," Arizona pitcher Brian Anderson said that night, "is beyond nightmare. All I know is that we need to get out of this place. Fast."

———

Mystique and Aura, however, did not travel. Back in Phoenix for Game 6, the Yankees absorbed their worst beating in the 213-game World Series history of the franchise, 15-2. Reliever Jay Witasick, while getting only four outs, gave up nine runs, as many as the Yankees did in the entire 1999 World Series. His pounding took place after Arizona hammered Pettitte for six runs on seven hits, whaling away at his pitches with such assuredness that the Diamondbacks seemed to know what was coming. As it turned out, they did. After the game, injured Arizona pitcher Todd Stottlemyre told his father, Mel, the Yankees' pitching coach, that the Diamondbacks figured out that Pettitte was tipping his pitches from the set position. They knew every time Pettitte brought his hands to his belt in a high, looping path, he was throwing a breaking ball. If he brought his hands to his belt in a more direct path, it was a fastball. Mel Stottlemyre broke the news to Pettitte the next day, before Game 7.

"Mel wasn't going to tell me," Pettitte said. "He didn't want to tell me. Todd wanted me to know because we had only one more game and I wasn't pitching. To this day Mel knows what it was. I didn't even want to know. I just changed my whole delivery. I went to a high set. I didn't even want to look. I didn't even want to see it. It just made me sick.

"Because I never felt so good. I felt real good as far as my elbow. I felt strong that year. I won the MVP the series before against Seattle. I was just on a good roll. My stuff was so good and I felt so strong.

"Then by the time you get to the last start of your season, and you'd lost the other one in Game 2—and they made me work so hard over the first three innings—that by Game 6 I was just worn down. They wore me down. I didn't think anything had happened as far as tipping pitches. I just chalked it up to I had a bad outing. It's tough to swallow.

"That was brutal. But again, everything happens for a reason. It makes you want it more the next time. But you hate it because you know how precious those opportunities are."

Game 7 came down to a clash of titans, Clemens and Schilling, marking only the fourth Game 7 matchup of 20-game winners. Clemens, 39, was the oldest Game 7 starter ever. Schilling was pitching on three days and exceeding 300 innings for the year. The duel unfolded as good as advertised, much to Steinbrenner's nervousness. It was scoreless until the bottom of the sixth, when Danny Bautista smacked a double off Clemens to drive in Steve Finley.

The Yankees answered back, nicking Schilling for the tying run in the seventh on singles by Jeter, O'Neill (on what would be his final plate appearance as a Yankee) and Martinez. Clemens struck out Schilling to start the bottom of the inning, but when he yielded a single to leadoff hitter Tony Womack on his 114th pitch, Torre removed him. Mike Stanton pitched out of the inning to preserve the tie, but now Torre had a decision to make with Stanton's spot in the batting order due up third in the eighth inning.

"Who's going to come in and pitch the eighth inning?" Zimmer asked him.

"Mendoza," Torre said.

"You can't bring in Mendoza," Zimmer said. "You've got to bring Mo in."

"We're on the road," Torre said. "Who the fuck am I going to save this game with?"

"I know. But you'll kick yourself in the ass if you never get Mariano in the game."

"But what the hell am I going to do? Who am I going to trust with a lead?"

"So, what about Mariano now?"

"Yeah, sure—if Sori hits a home run here. It'll solve the whole problem."

Torre barely had finished getting the words out of his mouth when Soriano golfed a pitch from Schilling over the wall in left-center field to give the Yankees a 2-1 lead. Now, with a lead, the decision was obvious: it would be Rivera, the ultimate weapon, for the last six outs.

Rivera was devastating in the eighth inning against the heart of the Arizona order. Steve Finley did manage a groundball single, but Rivera fanned the other three hitters, Luis Gonzalez, Matt Williams and Bautista. He threw only 14 pitches in the inning.

The Yankees went quietly in the ninth against none other than Randy Johnson, who came out of the bullpen in the eighth inning the night after throwing 104 pitches in his Game 6 victory.

———

So it came down to this: Mariano Rivera on the mound with a one-run lead against the bottom of the Arizona lineup. Steinbrenner was standing in front of the bathroom mirror, combing his hair, preparing to soon accept the Commissioner's Trophy for a fourth straight year. Meanwhile, unbeknownst to Steinbrenner, Fox technicians slipped through a side door of the clubhouse and began hanging lights and cable to prepare for the postgame celebration. A Yankees security official, carefully, so as not to tip off Steinbrenner, whispered to them to try to shoo them away.

"You know, you can't be in here," the official said.

"We've got to set up," one of them said. "It's the ninth inning."

"But you can't be in here! The Boss will go nuts."

Well, this one did look like a lock for the Yankees, even with the television crew defying Steinbrenner's superstition. These were the forces in the Yankees' favor:

- Rivera was undefeated in 51 career postseason games.
- Rivera successfully had converted 23 consecutive postseason save opportunities.
- The Yankees were 155-1 (.994) in franchise history when leading a postseason game after eight innings.
- The Yankees were 45-0 under Torre when leading a postseason game after eight innings.
- The Yankees' bullpen was undefeated in 52 consecutive postseason games (10-0).
- The Yankees were undefeated under Torre in postseason games decided by one run (10-0).

- The Yankees were 11-0 in postseason
  series since 1998.

What happened next was as stunning as the paranormal events of Halloween night and its follow-up at Yankee Stadium. There were no home runs this time. The Diamondbacks, borrowing from the Yankees' Championship Baseball 101 textbook, formed the equivalent of an emergency bucket brigade—employing eight players in a span of 14 pitches to hit, bunt and run their way to one of the greatest endings to one of the greatest games of all time.

The endgame began when Mark Grace, choking up on his bat as a defense against Rivera's great cutter, fought off Rivera's signature pitch for a single to center field. David Dellucci pinch ran for Grace. The next batter, Damian Miller, dropped a bunt near the left side of the mound. Rivera, a slick, athletic fielder, pounced on it, wheeled and threw hard to Derek Jeter covering second base in an attempt to get the force-out.

Rivera made his great career with the cutter, a pitch that bores toward the hands of a lefthanded batter, away from a righthanded batter. But a fielder trying to quickly make a play on a bunt has no time to worry about grip. Amid the randomness of reaching into his glove and pulling out the baseball as it came to rest in the leather, Rivera incidentally came up with a grip that approximated a two-seam

fastball, a pitch that has the exact opposite movement of his cutter, a left-to-right action. Rivera's
throw began tailing, tailing, tailing away from
Jeter's glove hand. Jeter began to position himself
and stretch for it.

But something wasn't quite right.

As the Yankees took the field for the bottom of
the ninth inning, Jeter had moved noticeably slower
and stiffer. Maybe this was a perfectly awful time to
be paying the price for his nonstop hustle. Jeter had
ended the regular season on a hitting tear, and carried it into the Division Series against Oakland.
Over 15 games he batted .375, including .444
against the Athletics in the playoffs. He was playing
some of the best baseball of his life at the peak age
of 27. And then, in the eighth inning of Game 5 of
that series, Terrence Long of the Athletics lifted a
foul pop fly toward the seats near the left-field line
at Yankee Stadium. The Yankees were leading, 5-3,
and were five outs away from advancing to the
ALCS, but Oakland had one runner on base against
Rivera. Jeter hauled after the pop-fly, knowing he
was nearing the stands. Just as he caught the ball,
Jeter smashed into the padded concrete wall with
his hip and flipped into the stands, landing hard.

The Yankees won the game, but Jeter, just like
that, suddenly stopped hitting. He was 2-for-17
against the Mariners and then 4-for-27 against
the Diamondbacks, making him a .136 hitter after
falling hard into the stands. If he was hurt, Jeter, of

course, told no one, not even Torre. But as Rivera's two-seam throw to second base tailed away from him, Jeter was unable to stretch enough to catch it while keeping one foot on the base. The throw flew wide of his glove. It was an error on Rivera, and now the Diamondbacks had runners on first and second with no outs rather than having a runner on first base with one out—one play that essentially tripled Arizona's run expectancy from 0.54 runs to 1.51, according to 2007 run-expectancy models.

"He couldn't extend to get that throw," Torre said.

Even in an interview seven years later, Jeter was not about to make even the slightest concession to any injury limitation.

He was asked if he was hurt in Game 7.

"I was all right."

Told it looked like he was dragging his legs going out to the field, he replied, "I was all right."

Pushed, he said, "You know what? You get to a point, especially that late in the season, everybody's got something wrong with him."

He was reminded he had banged into the stands to get a pop-up versus Oakland.

"I was all right."

It's not an excuse if it was an injury, but Jeter still insisted.

"I was all right."

He paused.

"No, I was all right. I don't remember. It was a long time ago."

If he was healthy, would he have caught the throw from Mo? Got a glove on it?

"No. Mo threw a two-seamer . . . Maybe . . . No, I don't think. Nuh-uh. Even if I caught it we wouldn't have got him. I think it was Dellucci. We probably wouldn't have got him."

When Jeter was 24 years old and after the Yankees won the 1998 World Series, George Steinbrenner gave a book to him as a present: **Patton on Leadership: Strategic Lessons for Corporate Warfare.** Steinbrenner inscribed it, "To Derek. Read and study. He was a great leader just as you are and will be a great leader. Hopefully of the men in pinstripes." When it came to physical ailments, Jeter lived a philosophy that was Pattonesque. For it was Patton who said, "If you are going to win any battle, you have to do one thing. You have to make the mind run the body. Never let the body tell the mind what to do. The body is never tired if the mind is not tired."

Jeter was all right.

———

Just after Dellucci slid into second, putting the tying run in scoring position, Steinbrenner walked around a corner of the Yankees' clubhouse and was stunned by what he saw: television crews setting up for the trophy presentation!

"Get out of here!" he shouted. "You're jinxing

me! Get out of here!" And he quickly shooed them out a door and into a hallway.

The Yankees were in trouble now: no outs, two on and another bunt play in order. Torre walked out to the mound, where he and the infielders converged around Rivera.

"Get an out," Torre told them. "I'm not worried about second and third with Mariano. Just get an out."

A pinch hitter, Jay Bell, bunted the next pitch. Rivera fielded quickly and fired a strike to Brosius at third base for the force-out. Brosius let himself relax as soon as he caught the ball for the out, never bothering to consider a throw across the infield to try to also get Bell at first base.

"I don't know if I planted the seed with Brosius when I said, 'Get an out,'" Torre said. "The guy at first base, he's out easily. What a surprise that was, because he caught the ball and he sort of just walked in, and the guy was like two-thirds of the way to first base. All he had to do was throw it. And we had a double play. But he was so good instinctively, and it was right there in front of him. It wasn't like he had to turn. He just never threw the ball. The game may have wound up with the same result. Who knows? But it would have been a little tougher for them because they would have had two outs."

Another pinch runner, Midre Cummings, replaced Miller as the lead runner at second base. The next batter, Tony Womack, turned hard on a 2-and-2 pitch, sending it into right field for a double. Cummings sped home with the tying run. Bell, carrying the winning run, stopped at third base on the double. Rivera hit the next batter, Craig Counsell. Now the bases were loaded, there was one out, and Luis Gonzalez was the hitter. Torre had a choice to make: play the infield back to try for a double play, or play the infield in to try to cut down at the plate the potential winning run of the seventh game of the World Series.

"I had no choice," Torre said. "At that point you play the infield up. If someone hits a groundball off Mo it's going to be an 87-hopper somewhere. You're not going to get a double play. And I hate to think of watching the winning run cross the plate while we're trying to get a double play, I don't care how slow the runner is."

Since Rivera became the Yankees' closer in 1997, hitters had taken 33 plate appearances against him with the bases loaded. In those situations they batted just .071, with just two hits, four sacrifice flies, one walk and just one double play.

Gonzalez had struck out and grounded out meekly against Rivera in the World Series, employing his usual wide-open stance in which his right pinkie and ring finger rest on the knob of the bat. This time, employing the Diamondbacks' default defense mechanism against Rivera's cutter, Gonzalez choked up two inches on the bat.

"It was the first time I choked up all year," he would say later. "I told myself, Whatever you do, just try to put the ball in play somewhere."

Gonzalez fouled off one pitch. The next pitch was a classic Rivera cutter, boring toward Gonzalez's hands. He swung. The bat cracked deeply just below the trademark upon contact. The baseball floated toward the left of Jeter and over his head. He was powerless to do anything about it, though he lunged in vain as the ball seemed not so much to fall but to parachute to a soft landing where the infield dirt meets the outfield grass. Bell bounded home happily with the winning run.

———

It was over. The World Series was over, sure. But the championship Yankees as everyone had known them, as they knew themselves, ceased to exist, too. From 1998 through 2001, seven players took almost 15,000 at-bats for the Yankees, representing 67 percent of the team's total at-bats on four straight pennant-winning teams: Posada, Martinez, Knoblauch, Jeter, Brosius, Williams and O'Neill, or as they were known familiarly inside the walls of their clubhouse, Sado, Tino, Knobby, Jeet, Bro, Bernie and Paulie. The Old Guard. Each year the Yankees could dicker with left field and the designated hitter spots, but the Yankees essentially were a set team for four years—and Martinez, Jeter, Williams and O'Neill even traced their Yankee roots to at least the 1996 championship, too. The Yankees were a remarkably tight group and a remarkably durable group. But as they took off their uniforms after the Game 7 defeat, they knew it would never be the same again. The contracts of Martinez, Knoblauch, Brosius and O'Neill were all expiring. O'Neill had made known his intention to retire.

"I came into the clubhouse," Torre said, "and George was there. He was, like we all were, stunned. I don't think we had any conversation. It was tough after the game because you knew you were saying goodbye to a lot of players. I had a meeting, and then I went over and hugged them all. You weren't going to have Knoblauch back, you weren't going to have O'Neill back, Tino, Brosius—he was another one. Like O'Neill, he went right home, too."

Steinbrenner didn't want to linger. He left quickly to congratulate Diamondbacks owner Jerry Colangelo. On his way there he ran into Johnson and Schilling in a hallway. The two pitchers had accounted for all four of Arizona's wins and 59 percent of its outs in the series. They were dripping with champagne. Steinbrenner congratulated them. After shaking hands with Colangelo, Steinbrenner didn't know what to do with himself, except he did not want to go back to the Yankees clubhouse. So he walked to one of the Yankees' family buses and sat by himself. It was much too soon after the game for anyone else to be there, and when family members finally did begin to make their way out of the ballpark, some would peek into the first bus, see a brooding Steinbrenner, and decide to keep walking to the second bus. It was a difficult loss for Steinbrenner to accept.

"What do you say?" Torre said. "We had Mariano on the mound with a lead in the ninth inning. Of course, you get the question, 'Do you play the infield back?' Sure—and watch the winning run cross the plate on a soft-hit ball to shortstop. I didn't lose any sleep over it other than the result. There was really nothing. Now, did I do everything right? I don't know. But I know one thing: I wouldn't have done anything different."

Rivera stood in front of his locker and answered wave after wave of questions. He was neither angry nor sad. He was matter-of-fact about it all. In other words, even upon blowing the seventh game of the World Series, he was the same old Mariano.

"I made the pitches I wanted to make and they hit them," Rivera said. "That's baseball. I did everything I wanted to do. They beat me. They can say they beat me."

No one better represented what was being lost than O'Neill. He took off his uniform for the last time and changed into a black shirt and gray pants. He was 38 years old and maybe as willing as ever, but his body was betraying him, as happened in the first inning when he tried to stretch a double into a triple. His legs could not carry him quickly enough. O'Neill's on-base percentage had declined for five consecutive seasons since 1996. The 2001 season was his worst in pinstripes. It was time to go, he decided.

"Paul O'Neill was a great example of what we were about," Torre said. "He knew, 'I've got to find a way to do this.' And that's the kind of attitude you have to have. Watch Jeter do it. Bernie Williams would do it, even without being an instinctive player. I wish I could explain it better than that. It's just something when you're around guys every day, it's that secure feeling you have to go out there and you're going to let them play.

"There's a certain amount of keeping track and keeping a little grip on certain things, so somebody doesn't go off half-cocked or somebody doesn't lose their direction, but aside from that you trust these guys to play the game. I can honestly say that when the game's over that you just go home. If it wasn't good enough, it wasn't good enough. You knew they were out there giving it everything they had."

For O'Neill, there were no more watercoolers to topple, no more batting helmets to slam, no more bats to heave across the clubhouse toward his locker and no more pitchers who weren't good enough to get him out but somehow did. He was at peace that night, maybe not with the result of Game 7, but that he had given baseball the best effort that he could. After packing his bag he smiled softly as he caught the eye of Nick Johnson, a 23-year-old first baseman who had made his major league debut that August.

"Did you learn anything?" he asked Johnson. "It's yours now. You've got to keep it going."

6.

Baseball Catches Up

Less than 48 hours after one of the most exciting and emotional World Series ever staged, including that historic Game 7 in 2001, and before the Diamondbacks even had time to stage a victory parade, Major League Baseball owners celebrated the occasion by voting at a meeting in Rosemont, Illinois, to put two teams out of business, beginning with the 2002 season. After watching the Yankees play in four straight World Series with three and even four times as much revenue as ten other franchises, they decided the economics of the game were so out of whack that the bottom of the baseball food chain simply needed to be eliminated. Such teams, they decided, were beyond hope. "There are certain markets where baseball cannot succeed," commissioner Bud Selig said that day.

"Remarkably, there was strong sentiment to contract **four** teams."

The Montreal Expos were one obvious choice for obliteration. They were being owned and operated by the other 29 franchises, a ward of the baseball state. They averaged only 7,643 fans a game and generated a major-league-low $34 million in revenue. The Minnesota Twins, fresh off an 85-win season in which their attendance jumped 70 percent to 1.7 million, were considered the other team most likely to be excised, if only because their owner, Carl Pohlad, seemed to be a willing accomplice. Florida and Tampa Bay, while seemingly weaker franchises, also were mentioned, though stadium leases and threats of lawsuits made their elimination more problematic.

Not coincidentally, the contraction vote occurred at a time when the owners were trying to reach an agreement with the players association on a new collective bargaining agreement. "No, this is not a negotiating ploy," Selig said. "It's absolutely not that."

If nothing else, the contraction vote put two options in front of the players: either the weaker teams get more money from the richer teams, or they, and the jobs that go with them, get whacked. The Yankees were becoming too good for baseball's own good. Their success at generating gobs of money was blowing up the ideal that baseball afforded all teams a somewhat equal chance of winning. The

Yankees generated $242 million in revenue in 2001, more than the Expos, Twins, Marlins and Royals combined. Their payroll had more than doubled since 1996, to $112 million. While other teams saw their narrow windows of building a championship team close because of the cost of free agency, the Yankees kept the core of their team together because they never lost a player they wanted to keep.

The best such example of the power of their largesse occurred when Bernie Williams nearly signed with the Boston Red Sox after the 1998 season. During that season the Yankees had offered Williams $37.5 million over five years. After the season, their offer was up to $60 million for five years. As a free agent, though, Williams fell into the arms of the Red Sox, who lavished him with a $91.5 million offer over seven years.

The Yankees, meanwhile, turned their attention to White Sox slugger Albert Belle, whose temper and volatile behavior might sorely have tested the winning camaraderie of a team coming off 125 wins. Torre played golf with Belle in Arizona on a recruiting visit, and came away thinking the Yankees had such a strongly established clubhouse culture that not even Belle could screw it up.

"I asked him, 'What do you require?'" Torre said. "He said, 'I just require that you hit me fourth in the lineup.' I in essence said okay because it wasn't a big deal and I knew over time practicality would bear out that you may have to hit fifth or something on occasion. But that's all he said to me: just playing every day and hitting fourth. He was very easy to talk to. The thing I judged about Albert Belle was he played 160 games a year. How bad can it be? I didn't worry about the clubhouse. You know you usually can hook on to something where you say, 'Well, let's figure it out.'"

The Yankees offered Belle the money they offered Williams: $60 million for five years. Belle came back and asked that the deal be restructured for $52 million over four years. Steinbrenner signed off on it. Belle was about to become a Yankee with one simple "yes." But with the deal in place, Belle changed his mind because of second thoughts about playing under the scrutiny of New York. He ran to the comfort of the Baltimore Orioles and their last-ditch $65 million offer. Suddenly the Yankees were about to lose Belle to the Orioles and Williams to the Red Sox. What to do? They quickly came up with another $27.5 million for Williams, or $50 million more than what they had offered Williams during the season. Steinbrenner closed the deal himself at $87.5 million over seven years.

The Yankees had the money to get their way, and it was just as true in 2001 when they needed to replace Tino Martinez, Scott Brosius, Chuck Knoblauch and Paul O'Neill—a first baseman, a third baseman and two corner outfielders. Among the free agents that winter was Barry Bonds, fresh off his record 73 home runs with the San Francisco Giants, but with a reputation for an ego even more outsized than his increasingly enormous body. "I had no interest," Torre said. "His name may have been thrown around, but there was never any serious talk about him. The one I was interested in was Johnny Damon."

———

The prize attraction for the Yankees, however, was Damon's Oakland teammate, Jason Giambi. Giambi was a devastating all-fields hitter who won the 2000 Most Valuable Player Award, was the MVP runner-up in 2001, and improved his batting average in every one of his major league seasons: .256, .291, .293, .295, .315, .333, .342. Giambi, who was drafted as a skinny infielder who was projected to hit about 15 home runs a year, grew into a monster of a hitter who slammed 47 doubles and 38 home runs in 2001. If there was a downside to Giambi it was that he was about to turn 31 years old and seemed to be growing larger and increasingly less mobile, with an impending future as a designated hitter written all over him.

Cashman and Steinbrenner asked Torre what he thought about the Yankees' signing Giambi. Torre told them he was against the idea. Torre told them he preferred to bring Martinez back for one year while grooming Nick Johnson to take over as his replacement at first base and to spend the big money on an outfielder such as Damon.

"I liked Giambi," Torre said. "In Oakland he hit the ball the other way, got as many walks as he got . . . he was great. I just thought at the time you had Tino and you had Nick Johnson. I just felt Giambi would sort of hamstring us. Even though he was a first baseman, he wasn't part of what we prided ourselves on: playing well defensively. He ties your hands. The biggest problem we had was a lack of flexibility. Once you have a guy who is basically a DH, you eliminate a lot of flexibility and the ability to utilize more players.

"They wanted Jason. George really liked the big boppers. I was outvoted, which was fine."

Steinbrenner asked for everyone's opinion in writing. Torre knew that when players did not perform well for the Yankees, Steinbrenner liked to blame him and Cashman, telling one of them, "He's **your** guy! You wanted him!" In 2003, for instance, Torre would suggest that the Yankees sign 37-year-old Todd Zeile for their bench. Zeile could play third base, first base, pinch hit and even provide some insurance as an emergency catcher. "I knew he could handle pressure and I just thought he'd be a good addition for us," Torre said. The Yankees did sign Zeile and he was awful. He batted .210 before the Yankees released him in August.

"Whenever you lose a couple of games George

would look to punish you by getting rid of a person," Torre said. "He did it with Billy Martin and Art Fowler, Billy's pitching coach. That year it was 'Zeile, Zeile, Zeile.' That's all I heard. It was like he was the reason we were losing. He wasn't even playing. I remember telling George one day at one of those luncheons at Malio's in Tampa, 'I recommended Todd Zeile. I thought he'd be good. I still think, batting average aside, that he's a good extra guy on this club. It's not like he runs errands for me. I didn't want him to get coffee for me. I got him here to try to make us better.' "

When it came to Giambi, Torre wanted to avoid Steinbrenner laying his buyer's remorse on him. He was happy to have his objections on the record, Torre wrote down and handed to Steinbrenner that his idea was to stick with Tino for one more year while grooming Johnson, rather than signing Giambi. Sure enough, two years into the deal, as Giambi's batting average plummeted almost one hundred points from where it had been in Oakland, and especially in the third year, as Giambi's steroid-jacked body began falling apart, Steinbrenner wanted to blame Torre for the signing of Giambi.

"Cashman stood up for me," Torre said. "He told him, 'No, no. He didn't want him.' Because he was blaming me for Giambi. He kept blaming people for shit that didn't work."

The Yankees signed Giambi to a seven-year contract worth $120 million. One day, while Torre was in Hawaii, Cashman called and said the signing came with one condition on which Giambi had insisted.

"In order to get him we've got to take his trainer, Bobby Alejo," Cashman said.

"Why do you do this to me, Cash?" Torre said half-jokingly. "That makes my job tougher. How can I tell the other guys on the team they can't bring in their guy if he gets to bring in his guy?"

Said Torre, "Obviously he needed somebody to push him, his father or somebody."

It made for a whole different dynamic in the Yankees' clubhouse. The team famously packed with grinders, all-around players and self-starters had just paid $120 million for a slugging DH in training who needed his personal trainer with him at all times. The Yankees put Alejo on the payroll essentially to be Giambi's personal assistant. The days of Paul O'Neill and the low-maintenance grit he represented were officially over.

"We were in the dugout during a rain delay once," Torre said. "Jason was at one end, toward the first base side. Alejo comes out of the runway and said to him, 'Go ahead. Run.' From one end of the dugout to the other he yells. There's no shame here? You need to be self-motivated here. You don't need somebody to push you. He had to tell him everything. Jason relied on that. You knew it was going to be the start of something different.

"Jason was a good guy, a good, huggable bear.

He can get along with anybody as far as I'm concerned, a team concept guy who knew individual numbers didn't amount to a whole lot. He was a gamer. The pressure of the game didn't bother him, even if he didn't always work hard enough. In spring training I would remind him, 'To be a regular player you've got to take your regular complement of groundballs.' And then I'd have to remind him two or three times during the year."

As the Yankees were wrapping up the Giambi negotiations, Giambi lobbied the Yankees to sign his buddy Damon to play left field. The Yankees decided they had a better idea; they signed Rondell White for $10 million over two years, leaving Damon to sign four days later with the Red Sox for $31 million over four years.

"Giambi tried to talk them into signing me," Damon said. "Rondell beat me to the punch. I heard there was one person who didn't want me there." Damon declined to identify the person with the Yankees who did not want him.

White was 29 years old and coming off a .309 season with the Cubs, but he was a major injury risk. White averaged only 109 games per year over the previous four seasons in what should have been the prime of his career. When the New York press asked him about his expectations for the 2002 season, White replied, "To stay on the field." It was an answer that hardly rang with inspiration.

Cashman admitted at the time, "Is there a risk associated with Rondell? Certainly. Maybe a little higher than some players. But given the choices on the market, he's a better risk than some others."

Both Giambi and White, as the Mitchell Report would uncover, also happened to be symbolic of how performance-enhancing drugs were changing the game and the difficulty in how durability could be evaluated by baseball front offices. According to the Mitchell Report, White bought human growth hormone and the steroid Deca-Durabolin starting in 2000 from former Mets clubhouse attendant Kirk Radomski. The report said, "Radomski recalled teaching White 'a lot about steroids and HGH' and 'walking him through the HGH injections for two hours on the phone one night.'"

What kind of player were the Yankees getting in Rondell White? As a young player with the Expos he once stole 25 bases in 30 tries. But as he broke down more he ran less and, according to what Radomski told Mitchell, turned to drugs to "stay on the field." Or were the drugs contributing to the muscle problems that kept him off the field? Were the Yankees getting a player in his peak years or a steroid-addled injury risk?

As it turned out, White was finished as a top-flight everyday player. The White-over-Damon decision turned out to be spectacularly awful for the Yankees. White played in 126 games for the Yankees in 2002 and batted .240 with a .288 on-base percentage. He was so bad that only two Yankees outfielders were ever worse at getting on base while playing that many games in one season: Andy Kosco in 1968 and Wid Conroy way back in 1907. The Yankees dumped White on the Padres after just one year of watching him make out after out.

———

The Yankees had been such a set team in their championship years that all they required was tinkering around the edges. But when they faced the challenge of making major alterations after their core broke up after the 2001 season, the results were mixed, with the mistakes leading to more mistakes. This is what they came up with: Giambi replaced Martinez; Robin Ventura, who was turning 35 years old and who was acquired in a trade with the Dodgers, replaced Brosius; White replaced Knoblauch and a platoon of Shane Spencer and John Vander Wal replaced O'Neill. They also added setup reliever Steve Karsay, another known injury risk, who, after giving them one good year, was paid $17 million to pitch 12⅔ innings over the next three years.

The missteps continued during the season. When the right-field platoon revealed itself to be a bust, the Yankees traded for the famously overpaid and undermotivated Raul Mondesi. They also traded Ted Lilly, a 26-year-old lefthander with a 3.40 ERA, to get Jeff Weaver, a soon-to-be-26-year-old righthander with a fragile personality who had been durable on the mound but only a little better than average with Detroit.

"I thought trading Ted Lilly in essence for Weaver was terrific, and I was wrong," Torre said. "I remember telling Jeter about the chance to get Weaver and he was excited, because he didn't like facing Weaver. Again, I think that's another situation where New York played a part in not being able to realize your ability."

Just how bad was Weaver? There have been 188 pitchers who threw at least 200 innings in their careers with the Yankees. Weaver pitched the worst of all of them, posting a 5.35 ERA. Weaver was another reminder of the challenge of doing business in New York. Because of the expectations and scrutiny in New York, the Yankees face a longer checklist of evaluative items on a player than do other teams before pulling the trigger on a signing or trade. They must ask not just "Can he play?" but also "Can he play in New York?" The years following the 2001 World Series would be littered with expensive mistakes of exactly that kind like Weaver.

"I was more like a deer in the headlights when I got there because I really wasn't sure," Giambi said. "In Oakland, I was that leader, that guy. But all of a sudden you walk into a room with guys with just as many years in the big leagues as you do. In the beginning I was just more getting acclimated to trying to fit everything in. You realize after a while there are just so many people who need so many things, especially when you're the new kid on the block, the fresh story. Because before you know it you can find yourself saying, 'Oh, I've got a game to play now?' It happened.

"There are so many newspapers and they're all trying to vie for the same reader and they all have to have something different. They have to ask you different questions. That's where you learn how to fit in. Give people what they need or change your story a little bit or give them a little bit different quote and try to take care of them.

"I don't think it was bad, it was more like, 'I've got to get this under control.' The Yankees are the ultimate place to play if you're a player because it's all you can ask for. You have fans that are fanatical. You have your media. You're a traveling rock show. The Yankees are a traveling rock band."

Not everyone was made for the stage. The 2002 Yankees, and those teams that followed, found themselves playing under tremendous pressure. No longer was it just the pressure of New York, but now it also was the pressure of trying to re-create the success of the Old Guard Yankees—and without that indomitable will that those men uniquely shared.

"With Paulie's retirement that kind of changed the core," Mike Mussina said. "You're asking about a leader, and I don't think it was **a** guy. It was a group. It was like six or seven guys who kind of worked together as a committee, not necessarily one guy.

"It was just about winning the game that day, whatever they had to do. They could be 0-for-4 in the eleventh inning but fight their way for a walk. Whatever that small thing it took, that's how that group of guys played the game. You start losing guys who have been involved in most of the championships, that's big. It's hard to keep the same feeling when it's not the same people."

Without the Old Guard core, or at least their playing values, the Yankees could never again live up to that mandate. And forced to find suitable replacements for those players, many of whom were homegrown, the Yankees did not run a productive enough farm system to sustain that culture. And when they needed to look outside the organization for those replacements, they found a changed landscape in baseball from when Watson, Michael, Torre and Steinbrenner reengineered the 1995 Yankees into champions.

———

Informational and economic revolutions were percolating around baseball. When the Yankees were winning championships, the teams they were competing against in the American League East were being run by men with mostly traditional scouting backgrounds who would never again run another team: Gord Ash in Toronto, Dan Duquette in Boston, Syd Thrift in Baltimore and Chuck LaMar in Tampa Bay. Most people in baseball, in fact, were just like them, running teams in dowdy, old-school ways that were made largely ineffective by the Yankees' growing edge in resources. In the new century in places such as Oakland, Cleveland and Boston, young minds were studying and understanding baseball in new, cost-effective ways. They knew they could not outspend the Yankees. The answer was to outsmart them. It wasn't until the 2003 publication of the bestseller **Moneyball,** by Michael Lewis, which laid bare how Oakland general manager Billy Beane built winning teams on the cheap by exploiting "market inefficiencies," that the Yankees and other teams in baseball understood the gains in research and development that were happening in the labs of these cutting-edge teams.

"There has to be a certain point that the game gets elevated," Mussina said. "I think Michael Jordan, Larry Bird and Magic Johnson in the NBA made everybody else have to be better. The league had to get better. Wayne Gretzky made everybody else have to be better in the NHL or he was going to embarrass them forever. So the league started to get better. I think the Yankees of the '90s forced everybody else to find a way to be better because what they were doing wasn't good enough. So they found a way to be better, so it elevated the game another notch.

"Like Jordan going away or Gretzky going away, the Yankee dynasty, it went away. We tried to hang in there. We've been in the playoffs every year, but it's not the same."

The new-age general managers, freed from the shackles of conventional thinking, enjoyed an edge on the teams still doing business with old-school ways. They rooted for the old men to keep their jobs, and mourned when another team made the switch and joined the information revolution. They knew where to go to pick somebody's pocket to find undervalued, cost-efficent players. One general manager said he went to the same pigeon time and time again to pluck future big leaguers out of his farm system. The first reaction of the traditionalists to **Moneyball** was to deride its paint-by-numbers approach to evaluation. It was an easy shot to take. Beane's A's, after all, never made it to the World Series and they were built on as timeless a philosophy as ever existed: a perfect storm of talented and cheap starting pitching. Between 2000 and 2003, the Athletics made the playoffs every year largely because Tim Hudson, Mark Mulder and Barry Zito started 57 percent of the team's games in that four-year period while costing Oakland the total sum of $7.2 million, or about $10 million less than the Yankees paid for 12⅔ innings of Steve Karsay in the last three years of his deal. But even the most crusty traditionalists eventually had to concede that **Moneyball** at the very least changed the dialogue in the game. If you were a dinosaur, it was something best kept to yourself.

"It's a sensationalized book that doesn't completely accurately depict what happened," said

Mark Shapiro, general manager of the Indians. "But it does pose the questions that should be asked. What are our decision-making processes? How are we making decisions? How do they fit into a strategy and a plan? I don't think **Moneyball**—leaning objectively all the way in making decisions—is the right way to go. The beauty of this game is that the reality is we're dealing with human beings. But if I were an owner, I would certainly have the right to ask, 'What are our processes? How are we making decisions? How do our decisions mesh with each other as we implement a plan, a strategy? What are we doing at the levels beneath the major league team that support that plan? To facilitate us making the best decisions possible? In an inefficient environment, how can we be as efficient as possible? How can we find value?'

"Those kinds of questions have got to be asked by owners. What I think is—and this is theory—is that owners started getting asked by their friends. It's a small fraternity. David Glass of Kansas City starts getting asked by his friends, 'Hey, did you read that? That's pretty incredible. Do you guys do that?' Now all of a sudden they go down and they look at a conventional old-school general manager, and they're probably not satisfied with the answers they're getting in response."

The intellectual revolution took off. Teams now wanted not just a Billy Beane of their own, but a Paul DePodesta, the Harvard economics graduate who at the age of 26 became Beane's righthand man and the brains behind the numbers and at 31 became the general manager of the Los Angeles Dodgers. The game that depended largely on washed-up former players and reassigned company men to build a 25-man roster became a multi-billion-dollar business that attracted well-educated minds to build **organizations,** even **systems.** When Beane, for instance, promoted David Forst, another Harvard grad with a sociology degree, to replace DePodesta, he posted an opening for Forst's former position as an assistant general manager. He received 1,500 résumés, including one from a chap who wrote, "I apologize, but I won't be available until June because I am completing my astrophysics degree from Oxford." Beane wound up hiring Farhan Zaidi, a PhD in economics from Cal Berkeley who earned an undergraduate degree in behavioral economics.

"Guys that maybe 15 years ago spent four years at Goldman Sachs and then moved on to private equity are applying for jobs with baseball teams," Beane said. "I remember when I sheepishly had to inform Farhan the amount of money we were paying him to start. The point being is that the résumés you see now are amazing. Partners in law firms are ready to give it up to work in baseball.

"I'm talking about entry-level positions, below Farhan, paying $30,000 starting salary. The people that got to Wall Street and want to work in sports are by nature very competitive. And because they are smart and competitive, the ultimate reward is they make a lot of money. Not that everyone makes a lot of money, but it's there to be claimed. That's the way it should be. I wouldn't even be able to apply for this job in another ten years. And it doesn't bother me."

———

The rise in intellect meant that all organizations began to better understand the value of the players. For instance, after the 2002 season, the Red Sox encountered little competition for free agent third baseman Bill Mueller. He did not hit for power and he did not hit for an especially high batting average, the two traditional yardsticks for offensive "value," and thus the two components tied most directly to pay. Splitting the 2002 season with the Cubs and Giants, Mueller batted .262 with seven home runs. The Red Sox signed him for three years (with the third year left to their option) at a total cost of $7 million. What the Red Sox knew then that most others did not, however, was that Mueller was far better than the average player at getting on base. And the more runners you put on base the more runs you could score. His career on-base percentage was .370. Mueller won the American League batting title in his first year with the team and helped the Red Sox to the world championship in his second year.

Four years later, Dave Roberts, a career .270 hitter with little power, went on the free agent market. By 2006, teams understood the value of on-base percentage and were paying for it. Roberts, like Mueller, did not have traditional value in terms of a high batting average or home runs. His value was getting on base. Roberts did not reach base as readily as did Mueller—his career on-base percentage was .344—but still he was better than the average player at getting on base. The Giants gave Roberts $18 million over three years, a whopping 129 percent increase over Mueller's value just four years earlier. Finding the next Bill Mueller became increasingly difficult with the rise in intellect. And if more teams were better at identifying the value of talent, then more teams had a better chance of putting together a winning ballclub.

"There are fewer inefficiencies to exploit," Shapiro said. "It becomes harder and harder, particularly as the teams with the great resources become well run and more efficient in the way they operate. The opportunities are fewer and farther between. And that has created some of the parity you're seeing. Obviously, I still feel like there are opportunities in certain areas, but they're harder to find."

Said Beane, "It used to be ten to twelve years ago I could call up Brian Cashman and there was always a yin and yang with teams. He could take my expensive players and I could value his younger players. It was a case of what was most valuable to each franchise. You could always find a dance partner.

The biggest thing happening now is the ability to properly value what is the most valuable commodity in the game: the cost-controlled young player at a minimum salary who is productive at the major league level. Everything revolves around that.

"The Boston Red Sox are incredibly bright. They still have the resources to get the high-priced player, but they also value the young player with great player development. They can have the best of both worlds. The dangerous thing is when you have really smart guys that have a lot of money and are running those teams, quite frankly, when you look at Boston there's no reason to think they won't continue to win. The fact of the matter is you arguably have the brightest front office with lots of resources and an ownership group that supports it. They've turned the Red Sox into an international brand name with their on-field performance and marketing that brand. They created a Manchester United, an international brand."

Intellect and player development is where Boston lapped the Yankees. The Red Sox, for instance, became so insatiable about the power of information that they deployed expert number crunchers to the NCAA headquarters in Kansas to input every available statistic on all college players in history into a database. They then cross-referenced those numbers against the performance of those college players who made it to the big leagues, and from there they devised their own tables of how college performance might help predict major league performance—information that would become critical in their draft-day decisions. They also hired a renowned trainer specifically dedicated to keeping pitchers healthy, understanding that arms and shoulders required a very different expertise and maintenance than the bodies of position players. (The Yankees, meanwhile, stumbled so badly looking for answers to conditioning issues that in 2007 they hired a "director of performance enhancement" out of a country club in Florida. Marty Miller had not worked in baseball in 10 years. After five hamstring injuries on the Yankees in four weeks, he was fired one month into the season.)

When the Yankees won, they did so with a very similar model to what is in vogue today: a core of cheap, homegrown players. On the 125-win 1998 world championship team, for instance, Jorge Posada, then 26, Derek Jeter, 26, Mariano Rivera, 28, and Andy Pettitte, 26, were paid a combined $5.55 million. Bernie Williams, 29, another product of their farm system, was the team's highest-paid player at $8.3 million.

"The template wasn't much different than it is today," Beane said. "As that core gets older it sort of needs to be rejuvenated to some extent. After around 30, 31 years old, you start to get depreciating performance due to age. You still need to have those 25-year-olds entering their prime. Free agents complement the core."

The Yankees never replicated that sort of young core, in large part because they did not give their farm system the same priority they gave their 25-man roster, especially as their frustration grew with not winning it all.

"The Yankees have never been able to do both," said one veteran general manager. "They've tried to change and do some deconstruction, but it's so complicated over there, so institutional, so multi-headed, that Cashman has a hard enough time just tearing things down to build them back up. They are smart and they have talent. They got pretty lucky internationally with Wang, Cano and Cabrera—Arizona could have had all three in the Randy Johnson deal. That really helped them be-cause they had terrible drafts up until 2006.

"But it's so hard to deconstruct there that they went so far in the other direction. They rushed starters and made mediocre prospects untouchable. It was too dramatic a pendulum swing."

_____

Another executive cited the declining health of George Steinbrenner as a factor in the Yankees falling behind the curve. Cashman's hold on base-ball operations, which he seized in 2005, became more complicated with a committee to answer to, involving Hank and Hal Steinbrenner, Randy Levine, Felix Lopez and Lonn Trost.

"They started to catch up," observed the executive, "and they started, according to my conversations with Cashman, to understand what was happening to them with the Red Sox. They started to react to that and started to do things much more effectively and the dysfunction kind of went away for about two years. And now the dysfunction is right back. Cashman is wasting his time on things I don't have time to waste my energy on. Factions are starting up again."

Said the Indians' Shapiro, "Don't make the mistake, whatever is happening now, to think those teams with resources don't have a distinct advantage, particularly with how the Yankees were for a brief period of time and how the Red Sox are now."

Teams moved beyond the popular conception of **Moneyball** long ago essentially because on-base percentage was no longer an inefficient market. So if all teams now recognize on-base percentage as well as the value of young players, what is the next inefficient market to exploit in order to make up the ground on the Yankees' growing edge in resources? Beane laughed and said, "Just saying that gives me a headache. Every part of the game is measured now versus the dollar investment. It's about turning over every rock. It's more and more difficult. I think that's a good thing. I have no chip on my shoulder about being antiquated."

The race is always on. The A's have tried to develop proprietary defensive metrics to identify undervalued players by way of their glove work. The

Red Sox then set about working up their own defensive metrics based on Class-A and Double-A players—trying to snatch them **before** they got to the big leagues. Such a think-tank culture helps drive the game forward and fosters the spirit of parity: if the real currency of the game is intellect rather than money, then why can't anybody truly win?

One area several teams are exploring as the next possible strategic advantage is biomechanics. Every team will agree that acquiring and developing pitching is the foundation to championship teams. But what good is great pitching if your pitchers aren't healthy enough to pitch? For all the planning and scheming it takes to build a roster, a team's season generally comes down to whether its rotation stays healthy or not. Even Torre's Yankees were proof of that. Here is the breakdown of Torre's rotations according to how many starters made at least 25 starts:

25+ GS	YEAR
2	2005
2	1997, 2001, 2002, 2004, 2007
3	1996*, 1998*, 2000*, 2003, 2006
5	1999*

* won World Series

Torre won his four world championships only in the years when at least four starters took their regular turns. On the other hand, in the six years when he had to patch staffs together—when no more than three starters gave him regular work—his teams were knocked out in the first round four times and never won the World Series.

Championships, then, might seem to turn on the vagaries of fortune, on the sheer luck of staying healthy. But what if health is not left to chance and can be controlled to a certain extent? What if data, and the analysis of that data, could improve a team's chances of keeping its pitchers healthy? Then you might have the next market inefficiency.

Glenn Fleisig, PhD, and Dr. James Andrews did their best to explain this concept to major league trainers and executives at a special presentation in 2002. Fleisig and Andrews helped establish the American Sports Medicine Institute in Birmingham, Alabama, a nonprofit clinic devoted primarily to injury prevention.

"We said, 'Hey, we've got this biomechanics thing going,'" Fleisig said, "'and we want to get into the prevention of injuries.' We went for the home run: a contract arrangement with Major League Baseball in which we would screen all pitchers. We can figure out who is at high risk of getting hurt. They all said, 'Great idea, but that's not how baseball works. Thirty different teams don't work as one company.'"

So ASMI opened its doors to individual teams. The A's were the only team to come through in

2002. The Indians, and then Red Sox, soon followed. The clinic now attracts 10 teams. ASMI puts reflective markings on a pitcher's body and uses eight special motion-capture cameras, using technology developed by Hollywood movie production companies, to film the pitcher's delivery and feeds the information into a computer. What comes out of the computer is a 35-point diagnostic checkup, measuring everything from the length of the pitcher's stride to "shoulder horizontal adduction," a biomechanical term for how far back the pitching shoulder flexes. ASMI captured so many pitching deliveries this way over the years that it established normative range guidelines for proper mechanics. They found that the greatest pitchers, such as Roger Clemens, don't do any phase of the delivery that is off the charts, but rather are exceptional because they fall in the normative range across the board.

"What we're studying," Fleisig said, "is how the principles of physics help people move and what are the patterns. What makes you the most efficient pitcher, where you obtain the most velocity with the least stress on the elbow and shoulder."

The biggest payoff to the data has yet to be unlocked: Once you have it, what do you do with it?

"It's a huge challenge," Fleisig said. "My number-one priority is to find out what's wrong with pitchers. What to do with it is a huge question. Some things might need to be improved on by the pitching coach and some by the strength coach."

The Indians, for instance, sent pitcher Jeremy Guthrie to ASMI in 2004. His diagnostic report indicated that his "maximum upper trunk angular velocity"—in layman's terms, it's the answer to whether his upper trunk rotates faster than his pelvis in his delivery—fell just short of the normative range. Guthrie clocked in at 1,059 degrees per second, just outside the normative range of 1,078 to 1,370 degrees per second. What did the Indians do about it? Nothing. Guthrie otherwise checked out fine with no major red flags.

"It's so rare when you actually make a meaningful change with a guy," Shapiro said. "Occasionally you can work stride direction, when the ball comes out of the glove, little things like that might actually help."

Pitching is an act of violence. Once the pitcher loads the baseball in the cocked position, the arm rotates forward at 7,000 degrees per second. "That is the fastest measured human motion of any activity," Fleisig said.

While in that loaded position, the shoulder and arm bear the equivalent of about 40 pounds of force pushing down. The biomechanical experts at ASMI were curious about how much more force an arm could take, so they brought cadavers into the lab and pulled and pushed upon the shoulder joint to find its breaking point. The cadavers' ligaments blew apart just after 40 pounds of force. "So a pitcher is just about at maximum," Fleisig said.

No wonder pitchers break down: they have pushed their shoulders and arms to the edge of the breaking point. Pitching, unlike most sports activities, has reached the limit of what is humanly possible. So while sprinters continue to run faster, swimmers swim faster, golfers drive the ball farther and football players get bigger and faster, the pitcher has reached his peak. You will not see a pitcher throwing a baseball 110 miles per hour. The arm and shoulder are maxed out. Pushed any further, the shoulder would blow up, like a blown engine.

"That's why the role of research in baseball is not to get the pitcher to throw faster," Fleisig said, "but to lower the risk of injury."

Said Beane, "At some point what's really going to happen is we are all going to employ actuaries, like insurance companies. In some ways we have now become pseudo-actuaries. You may hire actuaries in your office to figure out the probability of injuries occurring, given the amount of money you're putting in. Biomechanics is certainly a fascinating area to explore. One pitcher can be both the riskiest and the best investment we make. It makes sense to explore why."

———

Dovetailed with this information revolution was the seed money to encourage innovation. Selig and the owners did not follow through on their threat to contract two teams, but the gambit did succeed as leverage toward establishing an increased revenue-sharing system that funneled more money from the rich teams—most especially, from the Yankees—to the poor teams. The revenue-sharing system in 2001, for instance, transferred $169 million. By 2008 the amount transferred had more than doubled to $408 million.

Simultaneously, baseball developed lucrative sources of national income that didn't exist when the Yankees were winning the World Series. On January 19, 2000, for instance, Selig convinced the owners to share equally in all profits generated from the Internet. Baseball had no idea what kind of money was at stake—especially Selig, a technophobe who was computer illiterate. But Selig understood that if each team were left to make its own way on the Web, the rich teams such as the Yankees, Mets, Red Sox and Cubs would only grow richer, extending the resource gap between them and the other clubs.

"I said at the time, and I didn't understand the full magnitude of it," Selig said, "that this will go down as being similarly important to when Pete Rozelle talked the National Football League owners into sharing television money. I believe history will show that to be correct."

Major League Baseball Advanced Media was created in 2000 to handle the sport's digital assets, with MLB.com launching in 2001. By 2007 it was generating almost $400 million in revenue, much of it from selling tickets, subscriptions to game packages and as one of the Net's most adept providers of streaming video. Suddenly baseball owners were getting equal cuts of national revenues that never before existed. In addition to MLBAM, they also enjoyed payouts from such revenue streams as satellite radio and satellite television and Major League Baseball International. Moreover, many clubs seized control of the resale-ticket market, using the Web to claim the secondary-ticket market revenues that previously went to scalpers on the black market.

The effect of these changes was that by 2008 every team in baseball knew before it sold a single ticket or negotiated its own local media packages that it started with a nut of $29 million, up from $16 million in 2001. It was the equivalent of the bank handing you money in a game of Monopoly before a die is cast.

The extra money did not close the gap on the Yankees' financial might. Indeed, the Yankees were getting the same one-thirtieth cut of the revenue streams as, say, the Kansas City Royals. But what the growing national revenues allowed poorer teams to do was to make financial commitments to their young players that might not have happened previously. And if these teams could lock up their young stars, it would mean postponing their free agency, and postponing free agency would mean fewer choices for the Yankees when it came to making up for the deficiencies in their farm system.

"More teams have signed guys who are prearbitration eligible, arbitration eligible and even to cover free agency," said Chris Antonetti, the Cleveland assistant general manager. "That happened with Roy Halladay, Chris Carpenter and, with us, C.C. Sabathia. There have been a lot of guys where that happened. What that does, especially because of the timing of it, is limit the available players in their prime years. So if you sign a starting pitcher through his two through eight years? Those are going to be the years of his highest leverage."

Here is an example. In March of 2006, the Indians signed center fielder Grady Sizemore to a six-year deal worth $23.45 million, with a club option tacked to the end of it. That meant the Indians control Sizemore's services through 2012. Without the contract extension, Sizemore could have left the Indians as a free agent after the 2010 season at age 28—smack in his prime—with the Yankees no doubt prepared to outbid everybody in baseball for his services. In all likelihood, the Indians would have faced the necessity of having to trade Sizemore before or during his walk year to gain a greater return on his loss than simply two compensatory draft picks. The contract extension, though, keeps Sizemore off the market, and away from the Yankees, for at least another two years and until after his 30th birthday.

274 JOE TORRE AND TOM VERDUCCI

"If we didn't have Grady signed we'd probably be looking at trading him at some point," Antonetti said. "What the central fund money has done is allowed us to retain our core guys. That's mostly what it's allowed us to do.

"For the teams in the middle and smaller markets, the central revenues are becoming a larger percentage of their revenues. Whereas for the larger market teams, that's not happening. Their revenues continue to grow with new ballparks and TV deals, radio deals, raising ticket prices, attendance . . . they're still increasing their local revenues. Our local revenue is far smaller, but the growth in central revenue becomes more and more important for us."

With clubs able to afford to delay free agency for their best young players, free agency became less of a guaranteed lifeline for the Yankees. When Toronto locked up Roy Halladay, for example, the Yankees were left to troll for Carl Pavano and Jaret Wright.

"Start with the fact that free agency is inefficient by nature," Shapiro said. "Because almost all of the players are past their prime as they hit free agency. You're paying top dollar for declining talent. Start with that. Then reduce the overall talent base in terms of quality, to the point that you've got competitive frenzy for the limited talent that is out there? You're exponentially increasing the inefficiency. And then, to add a more cyclical trend now, with more and more players tied up to deals, there is going to be less and less talent out there."

Though the Yankees kept generating more local revenues, the rise in intellect, the sharing of revenue and the tapping of more national revenue streams created a competitive balance in baseball that had not been seen since the 1980s. The Yankees now had to worry about not just old foils such as the Red Sox and Braves, but also the Angels, Marlins, Tigers and Indians—all of whom knocked them out of the playoffs—while teams such as the Astros, Rockies, Cardinals and White Sox were going to the World Series for the first time in a generation, if ever.

After the 2001 World Series, 12 franchises played in the next seven World Series, including nine that had not been there since 1987 and five who made it the year after posting a losing record. The trend toward parity has only accelerated. Since 2005, the eight World Series slots have been filled by eight different franchises. In 2007, no team repeated as division champion for the first time since 1988.

"The big market clubs will always be big," Selig said. "Even they understood this system was in their best interest. You're never going to get a completely even playing field. But if you're a fan in New York or Boston or Chicago or Los Angeles, and if you know three-quarters of the clubs coming in don't have a chance to win, what's going to happen? You know, people aren't dumb. I think it's worked out extraordinarily well."

After 2001, the Yankees could no longer count on other general managers to be pigeons or for cash-strapped teams to dump their best young players on the market or for teams that were down to stay down. They could no longer count on a core of New York–proven winners on their own roster or another wave of players from their minor league system to fortify it. Into the headwinds of all of those forces, though, the Yankees stubbornly counted on the same old outcome: to win the World Series. Anything else was a failure.

"It reached a point with us where it was six months of preparation for one month of important baseball," Mussina said. "And that wasn't written on the chalkboard anywhere, but it had become that way. I mean, the machine that had been created, the monster that was being created, that's what it was all about. It wasn't about getting to the playoffs anymore. It was about getting there and winning. It didn't matter how you got there, just get there and win."

Leaving themselves only two options in this new realm of baseball, win the World Series or fail, the Yankees came to know only failure.

———

By 2001 the so-called Greatest Rivalry in Sports, the shorthand account of the competition between the Yankees and the Boston Red Sox, was no more a rivalry than what existed in the cartoons between the roadrunner and the coyote. The 2001 Red Sox gave what even for them was a virtuoso performance of the doomed foil. They finished in second place behind the Yankees for the fourth time in what would be eight consecutive such finishes. They won just 82 games, winding up 13½ games behind the Yankees. The Red Sox had the best pitcher in baseball in Pedro Martinez, but their attempt under general manager Dan Duquette to support Pedro with a collection of castoffs and aging veterans—Frank Castillo, Hideo Nomo, Rolando Arrojo, David Cone and Bret Saberhagen all had seen better days—failed miserably. Even the great Pedro broke down, giving them only 18 starts in 2001. The Red Sox fired Jimy Williams as manager and replaced him with pitching coach Joe Kerrigan, who presided over the team mailing in a 17-26 finish.

Quite simply, there was no rivalry. In the six seasons since Torre took over as manager of the Yankees, New York was 67 games better than Boston and won the head-to-head competition 45-35. The Yankees had won fourteeen postseason series, including four World Series, and the Red Sox had won one postseason series, while a World Series championship remained almost unfathomable for the accursed franchise.

It was not a fair fight upon any ground, includ-

ing the business side. In 2001 the Yankees generated 52 percent more in revenues than the Red Sox.
Boston drew fewer fans than fifteen franchises—
fully half the teams in baseball—including such
middle-market franchises as the Rangers, Brewers,
Rockies and Orioles. The Yankees essentially built
their dynasty with little resistance from the Red
Sox, with the exception of the 1999 season when
Pedro Martinez, at the height of his mastery, willed
them into the American League Championship Series. Even then, however, the Yankees dismissed
them in five games. The Red Sox won the only
game Martinez started in that series, but lost the
others behind fading starters Kent Mercker, Ramon
Martinez and Bret Saberhagen.

The rivalry as we know it did not begin until December 20, 2001. On that day the Red Sox partners, operating the team under a trust arrangement
from the estate of former owner Jean R. Yawkey,
voted to sell the team to an investment group
headed by John Henry and Tom Werner. Larry
Lucchino, who would be named club president,
joined them. The group paid $660 million for the
Red Sox, Fenway Park and 80 percent of the New
England Sports Network, the regional sports network that carries Red Sox games. No baseball team
ever sold for even half that amount.

The sale was bad news for the Yankees. Henry,
Werner and Lucchino were true baseball insiders,
friends of commissioner Bud Selig, who knew from

their previous stakes in big league teams how to play by Selig's unwritten rules. (Henry had owned a small piece of the Yankees, then the Marlins, while Werner had owned the Padres and Lucchino had served as president of the Orioles and Padres.) These men knew how to make deals and make money in the provincial world of baseball, having long ago covered the learning curve that even the sharpest of businessmen must traverse when they join the game. They represented the biggest threat to the Yankee dynasty. Within hours of their purchase, they fired Duquette. They promoted assistant general manager Mike Port to serve as general manager but only on an interim basis, vowing to take as much time as necessary to find a dynamic young architect that fit their vision for the team.

Kerrigan lasted only two weeks into spring training, the owners waiting until their purchase was closed in February. Lucchino called a team meeting one day in the team's clubhouse at its spring training site in Fort Myers, Florida, to introduce Grady Little to the players as their manager. Little, who had served as Williams' bench coach for three seasons, was a safe, popular pick. Immediately after Lucchino introduced Little, Martinez was so happy he danced naked around the clubhouse, cracking up his teammates by shaking his member.

The owners made a more important hiring that same spring training to far less fanfare, crude or otherwise. They named a 28-year-old Yale graduate to serve as an assistant general manager to Port. Theo Epstein, who grew up one mile away from Fenway in Brookline, had started out in baseball as a summer intern for Lucchino's Baltimore Orioles in 1992, 1993 and 1994. Epstein followed Lucchino to San Diego, where he worked two seasons in the Padres communications department before moving to baseball operations in 1997, all the while earning a degree from the University of San Diego Law School. He was whip smart, full of questions and at the front of a generation of young, computer-savvy executives and analysts who believed some of the answers for evaluating players and constructing teams could be found in a careful parsing of the game's copious statistics.

Change, however, did not come immediately to the Henry-Werner-Lucchino Red Sox. During the first half of the 2002 season, Port and his baseball operations people and scouts would hold frequent conference calls that sounded not very different from the way virtually all clubs had conducted business for generations. One of those conferences included a discussion about acquiring an outfielder.

"Hey," one scout piped up, "how about that Doug Glanville? He's pretty good."

"How about Marquis Grissom?" interjected another scout. "I've always liked him."

The conference call went on in the same manner: baseball men talking baseball, trusting their gut and little else. (The Red Sox eventually traded for

Montreal outfielder Cliff Floyd, giving the Expos pitching prospects Sun-Woo Kim and Seung Song.)

"That was pretty much the methodology," Epstein said. "People would sit around talking about the players they heard of and who might be a good fit. There were no numbers studied, just subjective analysis. Old school? It was really old school. And not good old school. So we basically started to integrate some new techniques behind the scenes."

In the back offices at Fenway, Epstein, Jed Hoyer and other young assistants in player development were running their own kind of lab, crunching numbers and asking questions in their new-school way. For instance, it was the statistical analysis done by Epstein and the back-office upstarts that helped lead to the Red Sox trading for lefthanded relief pitcher Alan Embree in June of 2002. The Red Sox gave up two pitching prospects of little import to San Diego to get Embree, a journeyman making $500,000 who had bounced from the Giants to the White Sox to the Padres to the Red Sox within 12 months. But Epstein liked Embree's strikeout rate—more than one per inning. Embree would be an important part of Boston's bullpen over four seasons.

"We weren't empowered to make the final call," Epstein said of the back-office analysts. "But gradually over the course of the year we started to integrate some of these techniques. It became rather obvious what John Henry was looking for in a new

GM, and because of John's thinking, I felt empowered to create a new system."

Henry believed in numbers. They made him a rich man. In 1981, at the age of 31, Henry established an alternative asset money management firm that proudly took human emotion and subjective analysis out of play. It made trading decisions based on a proprietary, objective system that analyzed trends in each market. By 2005 John W. Henry & Company, Inc. held assets of $3.8 billion. By 2006 Henry was estimated to have a net worth of $860 million. Henry saw no reason why data-based analysis should not work in baseball, too. After all, he had long been a baseball fan himself, and about 20 years earlier had discovered the work of statistical analyst Bill James and other so-called sabermetricians.

"We took our cues from the way his mind works," Epstein said. "He's really an empirical-based thinker. Very logical, very analytical, very objective. That led him down his career path, where he figured out trends in the market and discovered a formula. His belief is that you can look at the market objectively and the trends lie in the numbers, and even if you get battered in the short term, ultimately it's going to work out. It's empirical.

"Sabermetrics really appealed to him. He saw a great analogy between the financial markets and baseball. He understood the worst decisions to be the subjective ones, the older-school decisions, and he wanted someone to approach baseball operations in the same systematic way he knew from the markets. He's even more devoted to a systematic approach than I am. I take a more balanced approach.

"Right around then the landscape was definitely changing around baseball when it came to decision making. The default modus operandi in the game, the old school approach, was about to undergo a sea change. It was a time of great change, and you saw a change in the type of people making the decisions."

The 2002 Red Sox won 93 games, but still missed the playoffs in what was a transitional year in the organizational culture. Henry still needed a point man to run the baseball operations in a manner that dovetailed with his objective analytical approach to the markets, and by November he knew exactly who that person was: Oakland general manager Billy Beane, but Beane turned him down for family reasons.

He considered J. P. Ricciardi, who had been Beane's righthand man in Oakland, but Ricciardi had been hired only a year earlier by the Toronto Blue Jays to be their general manager, and he wasn't about to walk away from that contract, not even to be the general manager for a team in his home state of Massachusetts. Henry then turned to his third choice, who also happened to be the one Billy Beane recommended: Epstein. On November 25, 2002, one month before his 29th birthday, Epstein was named general manager of the Boston Red Sox. That same month, Henry hired James, the high priest of the sabermetric movement, and the next month he hired Josh Byrnes, a 32-year-old Haverford College graduate who had served under Mark Shapiro in the Cleveland Indians front office. The cultural shift in Boston was now complete. The Red Sox would run their organization with a heavy emphasis on statistical analysis to help find and exploit undervalued markets. They were the Athletics, only with a lot more money. With the new ownership and with Epstein's youthfulness, they also now had the bravado to be a true rival to the Yankees. They were now equipped to compete with the Yankees on their turf, even if that turf was in Nicaragua.

On Thanksgiving, only days after being named the Red Sox general manager, Epstein telephoned his girlfriend from Logan Airport in Boston. He was supposed to be enjoying Thanksgiving dinner at her parents' home.

"Sorry, but I can't make it," Epstein said. "I'm on my way to Nicaragua."

One of the legendary pitchers in Cuba, Jose Contreras, had defected the previous month while in Mexico pitching for the Cuban national team. He was in Nicaragua essentially to skirt major league draft requirements and become a free agent. The Yankees badly wanted the man Fidel Castro himself had dubbed El Titan de Bronze (The Bronze Titan) as an homage to the courage of 19th-century Cuban general Antonio Maceo. The Red Sox, however, conceded nothing to the Yankees. Indeed, Epstein's trip to Nicaragua was a symbolic beginning to Boston's mission to go eye-to-eye with the Yankees.

"Our scouts loved him," Epstein said. "They thought he could be a number-one starter in the big leagues, with some risk involved. You could not do the same statistical analysis as you could with a major league pitcher, and the issue of leaving his country and family was part of the risk. But right then two things became clear about us: we wanted to have no fear, and we wanted to be the type of organization that could take a risk and not back away because it might make us look bad. We didn't want perception to be part of the decision-making process. For too many years this organization was obsessed with tomorrow's newspapers and the Yankees. There was such a focus on what the Yankees were doing and looking silly in the newspapers that it almost paralyzed the club."

Before Epstein left for Nicaragua, he received a call from Louie Eljaua, his director of international scouting. Eljaua had arrived there first, taking one of the 12 rooms at the hotel in the remote Nicaraguan town where Contreras and his agent, Jaime Torres, were staying.

"Hey, man, it might be good if you booked a room not just for yourself, but book all the rooms in the hotel," Eljaua told Epstein. "That way other teams won't be able to stay here. The nearest place is miles and miles away."

Epstein loved the idea. The Red Sox bought up all the rooms. When he arrived there Epstein could not believe how well the plan worked. They had the place to themselves, he and Eljaua stayed up late with Contreras and Torres, drinking whiskey, smoking Cuban cigars and talking about a new life in Boston with the Red Sox. Epstein told Contreras that the Red Sox employed a bullpen catcher who was born in Cuba and would provide him with daily support and friendship.

"We probably won't be the ones with the highest offer," Epstein said, "but other teams won't give you the support and welcome that we will."

Contreras loved everything that he heard about the Red Sox. They enjoyed more conversation, whiskey and cigars before finally turning in.

"I went to bed sure he would sign with the Red Sox," Epstein said. "The next day I see two shadowy figures going in and out of his room. They're from the Yankees. I see him on his cell phone."

The Yankees had dispatched two operatives with a simple order: don't come back unless you have Contreras signed. If you don't sign him, your jobs won't be here when you get back. It wasn't long before Contreras asked to see Epstein. El Titan de Bronze had tears in his eyes.

"It's nothing personal," he told Epstein. "I had a better offer. They wouldn't take no."

The Yankees gave Contreras $32 million over four years, blowing away Boston's offer of $23 million over three years. Legend has it that Epstein reacted by heaving a chair in his room and breaking furniture, a story he denies.

"I did not break anything," he said. "I may have thrown a few of my possessions across the room."

Lucchino, speaking to the **New York Times** then, reacted by throwing insults.

"The Evil Empire extends its tentacles even into Latin America," Lucchino said.

The Red Sox had lost to the Yankees. Again. Dog bites man. But Epstein saw victory in this defeat.

"We **were** bold," Epstein said. "But we still had to be disciplined and focus on value. We did that with our offer. Our goal in player acquisition was to set a value and never get into a free agent bidding war. Don't get in without a strong sense of what our walking away point was. It's almost like a small-market approach to get the most bang for every buck. At the same time, we had showed we had changed. We were really following through on our goal to be really bold and not worry about looking stupid if things didn't work out."

What followed in the immediate wake of the Contreras imbroglio was one of the most fertile and efficient off-seasons in the history of the Red Sox, a haul that would soon make possible the attainment of their Holy Grail, the world championship more than eight decades in the waiting.

The 2002 Red Sox had finished second in the American League in runs and third in on-base percentage, but nonetheless gave far too many at-bats to inefficient hitters such as Tony Clark, Rey Sanchez, Jose Offerman, Carlos Baerga and Shea Hillenbrand. Epstein knew his team needed hitters who were better at getting on base. In the next three months Epstein added designated hitter David Ortiz, first baseman Kevin Millar, second baseman Todd Walker, third baseman Bill Mueller and out-fielder Jeremy Giambi while also adding pitchers Mike Timlin and Bronson Arroyo. The seven play-ers cost him a total of three nonprospects from his minor league system and $13 million in salary for the 2003 season. Epstein operated in the manner of an expert serial pickpocket. He was so good the rest of baseball didn't even know what hit them, espe-cially months before **Moneyball** would tip off the old-school guys on what the new-school guys were up to.

"The quick application of some basic principles yielded immediate results in 2003," Epstein said. "We took a look at the roster and we saw we had su-perstar talent on the top of the roster. But after our 10 best players there were a lot of areas that needed improvement. We thought if we could get above-league-average players at getting on base we'd be much better off. We needed guys to get on base. We had too many dead spots in our lineup. We also knew at that time you could get guys who got on base inexpensively. You could still find those guys and they were still good values. You can't now. But back then batting average correlated to salary, not on-base percentage. Now it's the opposite. All those guys had great years and had a really dramatic effect on our offense."

Every hitter Epstein obtained in those heists was better than league average at getting on base. Walker (.353 OBP in 2002) and Giambi (.414) were obtained in minor trades. Mueller (.350) was signed as a free agent. Ortiz (.339) was signed for $1.25 million after the Minnesota Twins cut him rather than pay him about that much in arbitration. Millar (.366) was signed after the Florida Marlins had placed him on waivers to allow him to play in Japan; the rest of baseball interpreted those waivers as the necessary formality of a player leaving the States, while the Red Sox saw the move as an opening to grab yet another player who could get on base. Other teams were angered at having been caught napping, or, in their minds, simply respecting the unwritten rules in the game.

"It gets back to our first priority: be bold," Epstein said.

Giambi would break down with injuries, but Walker, Mueller, Ortiz and Millar were major contributors. Epstein's stealth offseason brought an immediate and huge impact. The 2003 Red Sox won the wild card playoff spot with 95 victories (six fewer than New York) and were the greatest slugging team in baseball history, knocking the 1927 Yankees out of the record book with a .491 slugging percentage. They hit a franchise-record 238 home runs and led the league with 961 runs, the second most in franchise history. A club-record six teammates hit at least twenty homers: Millar, Ortiz, Manny Ramirez, Jason Varitek, Nomar Garciaparra and Trot Nixon. Of Boston's 95 wins, 40 of them were comeback victories, including 13 in which they had trailed by three runs or more.

"The '03 team had a bunch of guys that just didn't know any better," Epstein said. "It didn't matter how badly we pitched, we knew we could kick your ass and beat the ball around the park."

Within two years, the savvy ownership of the Red Sox had assembled a true rival to the Yankees with team-building tools and know-how that were ahead of the curve. In 2003, the Red Sox, little more than a cooperative sparring partner for the Yankees during New York's championship years, were good enough and cocky enough to push the Yankees to the brink of a tipping point: one game to decide the American League championship, if not the arrival of a new paradigm coming to baseball. One game. It was, quite simply, one of the greatest baseball games ever played.

7.

The Ghosts Make a Final Appearance

David Wells had been a colorful nuisance during his first stint with the Yankees, and the same was true when he rejoined the team in 2002. He might sometimes throw his arms up in burlesque disgust if a teammate made an error behind him, he might quarrel with Torre and pitching coach Mel Stottlemyre, he might let himself get too heavy and he might stay out at night a little too late, but the incidents, even one involving a police report in 2002, mostly could be written off as the incidental cost of his immaturity, like bothersome toll booths on the highway to his usual 17 wins or so. The 2002 incident, for instance, occurred at an East Side diner where a heckling fan punched Wells, knocking out his two front teeth and bloodying

him. Wells had pitched one of his classically efficient games that Friday night, September 6, beating
Detroit, 8-1, in a complete game with no walks that
took just 2 hours, 28 minutes—all the quicker so
Wells could get to the business of trolling the Manhattan bar scene. Wells threw back shots of tequila
at a Soho club before heading to the diner for something to eat, not expecting it to be the flying fist of a
five-foot-seven diner patron.

Torre called Wells into his office the next day.

"What time did this happen?" he asked Wells.

"It was about a quarter to one or something,"
Wells said.

It was a boldface lie. Wells apparently forgot that
911 emergency calls, of which he had placed one
that night, are dated and placed in public record. "I
just got my teeth knocked in, all right?" he barked
at the 911 operator during a two-minute screed in
which he slurred his words and repeatedly cursed at
the operator. "Nine motherfucking one one," he
spat out through his bloodied mouth.

It was soon apparent beyond any doubt that
Wells had lied to Torre about when the incident occurred. He was off only by about five hours. Wells
had placed his 911 call at 5:49 a.m.

"I had no report at the time to the contrary,"
Torre said. "I always want to believe my players, but
he just out and out lied."

Lying tore at the trust between Torre and his players, which was the very foundation of his entire managerial philosophy. Wells' lie immensely bothered Torre because of that willful destruction. It encroached upon the absolute worst kind of betrayal in Torre's book between a manager and his players: insubordination. In 1981, for instance, Torre was managing the Mets when he and Bob Gibson, his pitching coach, saw two players, Ron Hodges and Dyar Miller, in the bar of the team's hotel, which was off limits to the players.

"Go over and tell them to finish their beer and leave," Torre told Gibson. "I'm not looking to catch people, but just tell them to finish up and go out."

The players told Gibson they would take their time with their beer, thank you. They did not leave.

The next day, Torre called Hodges and Miller into his office. They were joined by Rusty Staub, the respected clubhouse leader, whom Torre invited to have on hand as a witness, as a form of documentation. "Guys," Torre told Hodges and Miller, "I'm sending you home. I told the clubhouse guy to get your luggage off the truck. You're not going with us to Philadelphia. You're going home."

As Torre explained, "I hated doing it. But I had to. It was insubordination."

Miller looked in astonishment at Torre and, referring to Mets general manager Frank Cashen, said, "Does Frank know about this?"

"Not until I tell him," Torre said.

Torre told Cashen about it while the two players were on their way back to New York.

Cashen asked Torre the next day, "Do you realize this thing was over one beer?"

"Yep," Torre said.

"If you lift the suspension," Cashen said, "I can have them in Philly in time for the game tonight."

"If I lift the suspension," Torre said, "you might as well take the rules and stick them up your ass."

What Wells did—lying to him face-to-face—was a betrayal of Torre and the Yankees that as the manager saw it walked right up to the line of insubordination.

"That was probably the one incident that came closest to insubordination," Torre said. "But that became an issue for the front office, not under my discipline, because it was a legal matter."

Wells survived the incident, as he always did with the Yankees, with almost no collateral damage. Not only did he make his next start as scheduled, he also won all his starts the rest of the season, going 3-0 with a 1.64 ERA to finish with a team-leading 19 wins.

Wells continually pushed the boundaries of what it meant to be a Yankee. He was a counterculture iconoclastic party boy in the buttoned-down pin-striped world, the rebel without a pause, but some-how always managed to survive on the strength of his golden left arm. No matter how much Wells drank or cursed or ranted or lied, he was blessed with a rubber arm, and a kind of stealth athleticism that could allow him to repeat his finely balanced delivery, the key to throwing a baseball precisely where he wanted over and over again, as routinely and as exactly as dotting **i**'s and crossing **t**'s in the most elegant handwriting imaginable. Wells could wake up Christmas morning in a snowstorm after an all-night bender and paint the outside corner with his fastball. Maybe even blindfolded. His mechanics and his arm were that good.

"When you're on a team that's mature," Torre said, "a guy like David Wells can be a real benefit because he can pitch and everybody understands that, understands that this guy can help us so let's do everything we can to help him. And if it's kissing his ass or whatever it is, let's do it. It depends on the group. It's something you don't know until you get them together and what their makeup is."

According to Mussina, "Boomer was high-maintenance. Boomer was even loud **and** high maintenance. And I like Boomer. He's funny. I never took him too seriously. I had no problem playing with him, whatever else happened. I didn't have any problem playing with Boomer."

At spring training in 2003, however, Wells finally pushed the envelope of his rebellion too far, at least with the front office. He pushed it far enough that not even his golden arm could save him from the wrath of George Steinbrenner. His crime? Wells wrote a book, **Perfect I'm Not; Boomer on Beer,**

Brawls, Backaches and Baseball. It was an immediate problem for the Yankees when the galley
proofs circulated that February. Wells claimed he
was "half drunk" when he threw his perfect game in
1998, estimated that up to 40 percent in the big
leagues used steroids (a number he reduced to 25
upon the book's release), took some veiled shots at
teammates Roger Clemens and Mussina, and said
you could stand anywhere in the Yankees clubhouse
and be within 10 feet of a supply of amphetamines.
Wells could show up teammates on the field, stay
out all night long and lie to the manager, but writing a book that impugned the integrity of the Yankee franchise finally put him on ground where
Steinbrenner said, "Enough." It became an important episode for Torre, far more significant than the
2002 lying incident, because the shrapnel that flew
from the book fallout would forever damage Torre's
standing with the front office.

Steinbrenner was outraged about the book, and
deliberated for a few days about what he should do
with Wells. "He's given Darryl Strawberry and
Dwight Gooden second chances," Wells told reporters, referring to two former drug users whom
Steinbrenner personally signed with the Yankees. "I
deserve a second chance."

Steinbrenner summoned Torre to a meeting at
Legends Field in Tampa. Torre rode the elevator
from the lobby, on the ground floor where the clubhouse was located, to the fourth floor and the exec-

utive offices. Torre walked into the conference room and found Steinbrenner with general manager Brian Cashman, assistant general manager Jean Afterman, chief operating officer Lonn Trost and public relations director Rick Cerrone. Also in the meeting, by way of speakerphone from New York, was president Randy Levine.

Steinbrenner looked at Torre and said, "What do you think we should do about David Wells?"

"What I would do if I were you," Torre told Steinbrenner, "is call him up here and tell him to shut the fuck up."

"No," Steinbrenner said. "I want you to tell him . . ."

Torre cut him off.

"I'm not telling him anything," Torre said. "This has nothing to do with me. If you have something to say to him, **you** say it to him. Simple. It will be over with. Call him up here. Tell him."

Torre knew Steinbrenner had a weakness. As often and as easily as Steinbrenner could berate people, he never liked to do so on a one-on-one basis. Said Torre, "He always wanted to do it with two other people there. He wanted to scare you in front of other people." Steinbrenner wanted no part of dealing with Wells himself.

"Here's what I want you to do," Steinbrenner told Torre. "I want you to make him the eleventh pitcher on the staff."

Steinbrenner wanted to punish Wells by taking

him out of the starting rotation and banishing him to mop-up duty in the bullpen. The Yankees had been 23-8 when Wells started for them the previous season.

"I can't do that," Torre told Steinbrenner. "I don't like the son of a bitch all that much, but I can't do that. He can still win, and he's still going to help you win ball games."

Steinbrenner and Torre began arguing back and forth, Steinbrenner insisting Torre bury Wells, Torre explaining he would be punishing Wells' teammates if he did that, Steinbrenner telling Torre it was his job to discipline his players, Torre telling Steinbrenner that this was an off-the-field issue that was his responsibility . . . and on and on it went. Until Torre had enough. And Torre had enough not just of this argument about David Wells. He also had enough of Steinbrenner.

"You know what?" Torre told Steinbrenner. "I'm sick and tired of this shit. You keep pounding at me, pounding at me, pounding at me . . . It bothers me. I probably shouldn't tell you that. But it bothers me."

Suddenly, the voice of Levine was broadcast over the room via the speakerphone on Steinbrenner's conference room table. Levine started to say something, but Torre immediately cut him off.

"Randy," Torre said, "shut the fuck up."

The room went silent for just a moment, a small moment, but one packed with awkwardness.

Said Torre, "I found out Randy had been trying to find a way to get rid of me from that moment on. Understood."

Levine wasn't there for the bulk of the championship Yankees seasons. He hopped aboard the championship train only in time for its last stop, joining the club in January of 2000. He had no connection to the rise of the dynasty and the groundwork of trust Torre formed with his players and he had no connection to baseball operations. Levine was there because he was a smart, savvy political operative who knew how to steer the Yankees through the labyrinth of rules, regulations and red tape as they planned the equivalent of the two most mammoth offshore drilling projects to find revenues to keep them at the economic forefront of the next century: the launch of their own regional sports network and the construction of a new Yankee Stadium.

Levine knew how to get things done in New York City. Before joining the Yankees he served as the city's Deputy Mayor for Economic Development, Planning and Administration. He was a graduate of George Washington University and Hofstra School of Law. Levine quickly became an important force with the Yankees, providing a daily presence in New York while Steinbrenner spent more and more time in Tampa. Reporters learned to tap him for leaks, someone who anonymously would push the Yankee agenda as Steinbrenner slowly retreated from feeding the tabloids, the art of the leak a skill Levine sharpened in politics as one of Mayor Rudy Giuliani's most trusted advisers.

Levine's political bearings clashed with Torre's emphasis on organizational and personal trust. Torre believed an organization operated at peak efficiency only when all relationships were built on trust and that the shared vision of winning overrode, even muted, individual agendas. He believed in people. But too often Torre cringed at the quickness and coldness with which the Yankees on Levine's watch could turn against one of their own. The Yankees' reaction to a player in crisis often included exploring the possibility of getting out from under the responsibility of having to pay the player. They sometimes sought to excise wounds, not heal them. Among those about whom they were quick to investigate contractual relief starting in 2000 were Bubba Trammell, an outfielder suffering from depression who, unannounced, simply did not show up for work one day; Chuck Knoblauch, who wanted to quit because of a mental block about throwing the ball from second base; Jason Giambi, because of his reported BALCO grand jury testimony in which he admitted steroid use; Carl Pavano, who seemed to look for reasons not to pitch and didn't tell the Yankees about two cracked ribs suffered in an auto accident; Kevin Brown, who broke his hand in a fit of anger; and Johnny Damon, because of his retirement thoughts caused by a kind of battle fatigue.

The most infamous and longest-lasting case of the Yankees turning against one of their own involved Giambi. On the day after Giambi's grand jury testimony was reported by the **San Francisco Chronicle** in 2004, the newspapers were awash in leaks from the Yankees that they already were investigating the possibility of voiding his contract. The same scenario occurred in 2007 when Giambi implicated himself in steroid use by telling a reporter he was part of a playing culture that "was wrong for doing that stuff." (Of course, the legal ground upon which the Yankees were standing seemed as unstable as a sinkhole, considering they specifically removed the word **steroid** from his contract when they signed him, changing the language to more generic references such as **controlled substance,** in the belief, they said, that broader language offered them better liability protection.)

Indeed, the desire to get out from under Giambi and his contract would bubble between 2004 and 2007 just about every time Giambi wasn't hitting or was hurt. During one such time, Torre said, Levine tried to see if the Yankees could cut Giambi without pay on the grounds of insubordination for refusing an assignment to the minor leagues. "Cash told him, 'We can't do that,'" Torre said.

During another front office campaign against Giambi, the team physician, Dr. Stuart Hershon, would walk into Torre's office on a daily basis to say why Giambi was available to play.

"He would come down, with word from George and Randy, to find out why Jason wasn't playing," Torre said. "He looked very uneasy."

"He's able to play," the doctor told Torre one day. "He can play."

"I know," Torre said. "I'm choosing not to play him."

Said Torre, "It appeared that they wanted the fact that he was refusing to play to come out of that. They never asked me to say Jason in fact refused to play. They never included me in any discussions. I just didn't think he was one of our best options at the time."

For a third straight day Hershon poked his head into Torre's office to again find out what was going on with Giambi. It would be the last such day.

"You know, Doc?" Torre said. "Get the fuck out of my office. I don't want to hear it anymore. If George has a problem with it, fine. But don't tell me who to play. Stay out of my office."

———

Torre always did hate confrontations, probably because he grew up in an abusive household under the iron fist of his father, Joe Sr. But he loathed nearly as much as confrontations the damage people could do by scheming covertly.

"The thing I can't stand, and I guess it goes on in

a lot of businesses, is when stuff goes on behind people's backs," Torre said. "If something needs to be addressed, I address it. As much as I hate confrontation, I have to do it. Avoiding it is torture. I remember when I was managing St. Louis, and I had a meeting with Kenny Hill, a pitcher, and said, 'You seem to get to a point in a game where you seem to lose your focus.' And then he said, 'Well, Tom Pagnozzi, he does this and he does that . . .' Pagnozzi was the catcher. I said, 'Whoa. Timeout. Tommy, come over here.'

"Kenny Hill was mortified, because here I am calling over the catcher he was talking about. I said, 'Let's get this thing solved. We're not going to hurt each other's feelings. Let's find a way to make this better by working together.' But that's what I do. I bring players in."

The 2003 spring training meeting over Wells at Legends Field with Levine, Steinbrenner, Cashman, Torre and others ended without a resolution. Indeed, it took Steinbrenner and the Yankees two weeks to come to a resolution about what to do. Wells clearly was bothered by the criticism fired at him from inside and outside the organization over the book. On February 28, before a spring training game in Clearwater against the Phillies, Wells told Torre and Cashman that he wanted to quit.

"David," Torre told Wells, "your name is on the book."

"I didn't know that stuff was in there," he said.

"David, did you go over the pages in the book? Did you do any of that?"

"No."

"Well, I don't know what to tell you."

"I'm going to quit."

Torre knew Wells was speaking out of frustration. Torre had been here before—listening to a hardened, admired big league player with world class skills and millions of dollars tell him he wanted to quit. Wells followed Knoblauch and would precede others among those Yankees who reached a breaking point and wanted to walk away from baseball. All of them were reminders of the frailty of the human spirit, even among the physically strong and the sports celebrities considered to "have it all" and to be living the charmed life. Wells was highly emotional when he met with Torre and Cashman.

"Don't quit," Torre told Wells. "Just don't quit. Go home now and come back tomorrow. Just think about it. Nobody wants you to quit. You just have to talk to these players and do what you have to do to apologize to them to make this whole. But don't just quit. You've got too much to offer."

Wells stuck around. The Yankees, after negotiations with Wells' agent, settled on fining Wells $100,000. A short time later, **Sports Illustrated** arranged a photo shoot at Legends Field for what would be the cover of the magazine's baseball preview issue. The idea would be to pose Steinbrenner surrounded by the Yankees' six starting pitchers to whom he was paying a combined $46.5 million: Roger Clemens, Andy Pettitte, Mike Mussina, David Wells, Jeff Weaver and Jose Contreras. Wells refused to be included, still smarting from the book contretemps but also because he had accused **SI** in the past of doctoring an action shot of him to make him appear fatter (a wildly inaccurate accusation, of course). "You Can't Have Too Much Pitching (Just Ask George)" read the cover.

"So there it was: me, Andy, Roger, Weaver, Contreras and George, and not even Boomer in the picture," Mussina said. "Now, I don't know what else you want for a staff, but that's about as good as it goes. That's as good a group of people as I probably ever had a chance to play with."

So stacked were the Yankees with starting pitchers that their number **six** starter (Weaver and Contreras shuttled between the fifth spot and long relief) could have been the number one starter on many other teams. They were as good as advertised. Clemens, Pettitte, Wells and Mussina all pitched more than 200 innings, marking only the 12th time in franchise history the Yankees had four such workhorses, but the first time ever in the era of the five-man rotation. All four won at least 15 games with only single-digit losses, making the 2003 Yankees rotation one of only 12 in baseball history to be so successful; the only other Yankees rotations in that group occurred way back in 1927 and 1932.

The staff issued the fewest walks per game of any
Yankees team since 1906.

Torre always believed the blueprint for a championship team began with the rotation, and the
2003 Yankees represented one of Torre's strongest
staffs. His starters threw 1,066 innings that year, the
most in his 12 years with the Yankees, and won 83
games, exceeded only by the historic 1998 team.
The 2003 Yankees rolled to 101 victories and had
the pitching to extend the dynasty to what would
have been a fifth world championship in eight
years. Alas, they fell two wins short of the title, losing to the 91-win Florida Marlins team that ran
into a hot spell at the right time.

———

That the Yankees even made it to the 2003 World
Series was in itself a memorable achievement. It
took every game and every inning of the American
League Championship Series, and then some, at
that. It took a kind of noise and a kind of intense
emotion the likes of which never quite before or
after ever shook the grand old stadium. It took one
of the greatest baseball games ever played. It took
what would be the last miracle in the Bronx.

———

On October 16, 2003, a Thursday, United States
defense secretary Donald Rumsfeld composed an
internal memo to his top advisers, under the subject

heading "Global War on Terrorism," in which he wrote, "It is pretty clear that the coalition can win in Afghanistan and Iraq in one way or another, but it will be a long, hard slog." That same Thursday, President Bush met privately in a hotel suite with California governor-elect Arnold Schwarzenegger. Had the same men convened only thirteen years earlier you would have been talking about a meeting with slightly less gravitas, considering it would have been the man running the Texas Rangers baseball team chatting up the star of **Kindergarten Cop.** The world on October 16, 2003, could seem as confusing and changeable as ever, and perhaps nowhere else more so than at an empty Fenway Park in Boston. For on that morning grounds crew workers carefully painted the 2003 World Series logo on the grass behind home plate. The World Series was scheduled to begin two nights hence in the home park of the American League champion. As the workers at Fenway rolled and brushed the paint on Fenway's lush turf, there was one small detail yet to be worked out before the festivities: the Red Sox still had to play Game 7 of the American League Championship Series at Yankee Stadium that night against the Yankees.

The Red Sox no longer looked the role of the cartoon coyote against the Yankees. They had grown into a rival of the most authentic, worthy and anxiety-inducing sort. And Torre knew it. Hours before Game 7, Torre sat in his office at Yankee Stadium and wondered if the Yankees could beat Boston one more time, as agonizing and draining as he knew even the victories had been against the Red Sox.

"Oh, they were better than us in '03," Torre said. "Let's put it this way: they scared me more than they ever did before. Of course, they always scared me. You can't help it when it's the Red Sox. But eventually you say to yourself, 'When is this shit going to end? How long do we keep beating them before the law of averages catches up to us?'

"Growing up in New York, I knew about the wars between the Dodgers and Giants 22 times a year. But not being personally involved in it, other than as a fan, I had never experienced anything like the whole Red Sox–Yankees thing. It was personal. I mean, Don Mattingly said he didn't want his son to be drafted by the Red Sox. That's how deep-seated it is. It becomes personal among the players."

Mel Stottlemyre, Torre's trusted pitching coach, stepped into Torre's office before Game 7.

"You've got Moose in the bullpen tonight," Stottlemyre said.

Said Torre, "I've got everybody in the bullpen tonight."

Mike Mussina, "Moose," had started and lost Game 4 three days earlier. Mussina had pitched well, taking the ball two outs into the seventh inning, but Boston starter Tim Wakefield had pitched better. Mussina left with a 3-1 deficit in a game the

Red Sox would win 3-2, a game in which Boston manager Grady Little pulled Tim Wakefield after seven innings and 100 pitches so relievers Mike Timlin and Scott Williamson could get the final six outs. Mussina had appeared in 431 games in his professional career entering Game 7, postseasons included. None one of those 431 appearances came out of the bullpen.

"We might use you out of the pen," Stottlemyre had told Mussina. "But if we do, we won't bring you into the middle of an inning. We'll only have you start an inning. That way you'll have plenty of time to warm up."

One of the beauties of baseball is its forgiveness. There is always another at-bat, another game, another chance to right a wrong, and those redemptive opportunities, unlike in other sports, are made possible on a daily basis. A team plays 162 games in 181 days. A batter will get 600 chances. A pitcher will face 900 batters. A season will offer 750,000 pitches. The sheer volume of opportunity is what gives the game its rhythm and soul.

Until you get a Game 7.

Game 7 flips baseball inside out, replacing near-endless opportunity with urgency. Injected with a heavy dose of finality, baseball in a Game 7 scenario is thrillingly different. There have been only 47 decisive Game 7s played in the history of baseball.

None were ever more anticipated, none were more fraught with tension and ill will, than Game 7 of the 2003 American League Championship Series. The starting pitchers alone guaranteed something historic, if not downright dangerous. The Yankees started Roger Clemens. The Red Sox gave the ball to Pedro Martinez. Between them Clemens and Martinez had won 476 games in the major leagues, a record total for any Game 7 pitching matchup. They had combined to win nine Cy Young Awards. They were not only among the best pitchers of their generation, they also were among the most feared. Both Clemens and Martinez used the baseball not just to beat you but to intimidate you. They threw at and near batters regularly with a frontier justice mentality, the kind of machismo that mostly had disappeared from the game. Clemens liked to use a euphemism for such intimidation tactics; he called it "moving a batter's feet," and he would say so with the matter-of-fact casualness associated with moving someone's furniture. Martinez, meanwhile, quickly had developed such a reputation for throwing at batters that one of them once charged the mound certain that Pedro had hit him on purpose—a pitch thrown with a perfect game intact. Morever, Martinez and Clemens never cared much for each other.

Already Game 3 at Fenway Park in Boston had proved the explosive properties at play when you mixed the Yankees and Red Sox and Clemens and

Martinez. The two aces started that game and considered mayhem. The Yankees did not like Martinez, so much so that when Martinez later became
a free agent following the 2004 season, several of
them would go out of their way to tell Torre the
Yankees should stay clear of him.

"When he was a free agent there was some idle
chatter about him coming to the Yankees, but there
was genuine dislike from our players," Torre said.
"They didn't want him around and they told me so.
We didn't like him. We didn't like him for a reason.
I mean, he would get away with throwing at people.
There was one game in New York where he hit Soriano and Jeter back to back and put them both in
the hospital.

"This is a guy who can put the ball where he
wants. And he certainly has the right mentality:
that if you're going to pitch somebody in, you miss
in and hit them. I don't see anything wrong with it.
It's better than missing over the plate and the guy
hits a home run. That's what you try to teach and
not a lot of guys can do that. We used to hate
Clemens for the same reason when he was on another team."

Beside his penchant for pitching inside, Martinez irritated the Yankees with his bench jockeying,
another old-school tactic that seemed out of place
in the modern game. He would insult the Yankees
from the Boston dugout. Catcher Jorge Posada was
a favorite target. Martinez would question Posada's

intelligence and call him "Dumbo," a reference to the catcher's prominent ears. It was a shrewd tactic, for Martinez knew that Posada was an emotional player, and the more Martinez riled Posada the more Posada became distracted. Posada was a career .191 hitter against his tormentor entering the 2003 ALCS.

In Game 3, however, the Yankees would not let Martinez have his way with them. Boston staked Pedro to a 2-0 first-inning lead off Clemens, but the Yankees, led by the fiery Posada, fought back with aggressive hitting against Martinez. Posada opened the second inning with a double and later scored on a single by journeyman outfielder Karim Garcia. Derek Jeter hit a home run in the third inning to tie the score. And by the fourth inning, the Yankees were so emboldened by their hacks against Pedro that they turned the tables and were razzing him from their dugout.

"You've got nothing!" they yelled at Martinez.

It was Posada who started another rally in the fourth, this time with a walk. Nick Johnson followed with a single off the Green Monster in left field, a shot that sent Posada to third. Hideki Matsui drove the next pitch into right field for a ringing double that bounced into the stands, scoring Posada. Now the Yankees, led by Posada, were all over Martinez with catcalls from the dugout. Martinez was facing Garcia, a lefthanded batter, with first base open and a righthanded hitter on deck.

His first pitch to Garcia was a fastball that whistled straight for Garcia's head. Garcia ducked, and the ball glanced off his left shoulder.

The Yankees were outraged. The way they saw it, Martinez threw at Garcia intentionally, having grown frustrated with their aggressive swings and mouthing off from the dugout.

"Was Pedro trying to make a point? I'm sure he was," later said one of Martinez's teammates, pitcher John Burkett. "Roger does it, Randy Johnson does it at times and Pedro does it. I don't think he was trying to hurt him. He was trying to send a message. It was, 'Fuck this, I've got to put a scare into somebody.' And he did."

Martinez claimed the pitch carried no intentions. It simply got away from him.

"Why am I going to hit Karim Garcia?" he said. "Who is Karim Garcia? Karim Garcia is an out. He's not the out I want to let go."

The catcalls continued from the Yankee dugout. The next batter, Alfonso Soriano, hit a groundball to shortstop that the Red Sox turned into a double play, but not before the enraged Garcia slid hard into second baseman Todd Walker in an attempt to disrupt the pivot and to vent his anger at being hit. Garcia picked himself up off the dirt and glared angrily at Martinez as he jogged across the infield toward the third base dugout. Martinez rightfully interpreted Garcia's stare as a message that Garcia believed Martinez had purposefully tried to hit him.

"Why am I going to try to hit you?" Martinez yelled at Garcia. "You're my out!"

"Motherfucker!" Garcia yelled back.

"You're the motherfucker, you dirty bastard!" Martinez shouted.

"When I said that," Martinez said, "Posada jumped up on the dugout steps and started screaming at me in Spanish. I could hear him yell at me and then he made a comment about my mother. Posada is Latin. He should know if you don't want to fuck with someone you don't say anything about their mother.

"One thing in the Dominican culture you have to be very careful about is saying anything about someone's mother. You say something about someone's mother, you're picking a fight right away. If I even see someone raising his voice to his mother, you're going to get slapped in the mouth. Posada is from Puerto Rico. Being Latin, he should know that."

Martinez no longer cared about Garcia. He turned his attention to Posada in the dugout. Martinez raised his right index finger and pointed it to the right side of his head and yelled something in Spanish at him. Martinez said he yelled, "I'll remember what you said." Posada and the Yankees heard and interpreted something very different. They saw Martinez's actions as a clear threat that he was going to hit Posada in the head with a pitch the next time he batted.

Clemens, of course, would not let such actions go unanswered. The question was not if he would respond with a militant pitch—just a little something "to move somebody's feet"—but when. A jam in the sixth inning of a close game, with one out, a 4-2 lead and the tying runs on base, did not appear to be the proper opening for retribution, but Manny Ramirez figured differently. The Yankees always discussed in their pregame scouting report meetings that Ramirez was uncomfortable with inside pitches. The reports said you could get Manny off his game by occasionally throwing balls on his hands, off the plate. Such warning shots could make Ramirez less bold about diving into outside pitches. (The reports also included notations that such pitches typically had no effect whatsoever on David Ortiz, Boston's other big slugger and confirmed Yankee-killer. Ortiz would respond to any such pitches simply by spitting into his palms and resuming his customary, aggressive place practically on top of home plate. Unlike Ramirez, the Yankees regarded Ortiz as unable to be intimidated.)

Clemens uncorked a high fastball that, while somewhat inside, did not come all that close to hitting Ramirez. Still, Ramirez, sensing as all of the Red Sox did that Clemens would not let the fourth-inning incident with Martinez go unchallenged, thought Clemens threw at him. Ramirez ducked and then, bat in hand, stormed toward the mound. The players and coaches from both dugouts immediately dashed toward the middle of the field—except for one 72-year-old Yankees coach who made a straight line toward the Boston dugout. Don Zimmer had seen and heard enough of Martinez. This incident, Zimmer figured, was caused by Martinez and his years of throwing at hitters and mouthing off at the Yankees. He saw Pedro in his red warmup jacket across the field and that's where he headed. Zimmer didn't know what he was going to do when he got there; he just knew he was fed up with Martinez.

"The only thing I remember," Torre said, "is when I was going out of the dugout Zimmer was on my left and maybe a step or two below me. I was going to say, 'Zim, you stay here,' but I knew it was fruitless. I mean, me stopping him, or anybody stopping him, it wasn't going to happen. It's the last I remember Zim. And then I was in the middle of the scrum with everybody else in the middle of the field, and I heard Zim or somebody yell something near their dugout, and I look over. He's already on the ground."

Zimmer had charged Martinez in the manner of a bull in a ring, and a stunned Martinez had responded in the manner of a matador. He sidestepped Zimmer and pushed Zimmer to the ground.

"He reached for my right arm," Martinez said. "I thought, Is he going to pull it? Is he trying to hurt me? I tossed him down."

The sight of this 72-year-old man tumbling to

the ground, his bald pink head, capless, against the dark green grass in front of the Boston dugout, was so jarring as to effectively end what otherwise might have been a full-scale brawl. (Clemens said at first he thought the prone, round body might have been that of teammate David Wells.) Zimmer was unhurt, though the Yankees would insist he be strapped to a gurney and hauled away in an ambulance to a hospital. Zimmer was, however, deeply embarrassed. He called a news conference the next day and, through tears, apologized for his actions. His contrition did not stop New York City mayor Michael Bloomberg from suggesting that Martinez would be arrested if he had acted that way in New York.

"Whatever kind of baseball they want to play, we're going to play, but we didn't start that," Clemens said after the game, barely containing his anger toward Martinez. "Sometimes when you get knocked around the ballpark, you get your ticket punched. I've had it many times. These guys have done it to me. If you don't have electric stuff and you're not on and guys are hitting balls they shouldn't be hitting, you might stand somebody up. But just because you are getting whipped, you don't hit [somebody] behind somebody's neck . . .

"I wasn't a part of all that. I went in there and I was trying to strike Manny out, and bottom line is he started mouthing me and the ball wasn't near him. If I wanted it near him, he'd know it."

Torre pulled Clemens after he pitched out of that sixth inning by getting Ramirez to ground into a double play. Clemens might have lasted longer, but Torre figured Clemens had spent himself physically and emotionally in such fitful battle. He had noticed the veins bulging on Clemens' neck. The Yankees couldn't get through the game without one more fight, this one a bloody one in the New York bullpen between a Fenway Park security guard, pitcher Jeff Nelson and right fielder Garcia, who hopped the fence. The rivalry had become sheer madness, so when Torre needed order restored, he turned to the reliable coolness of Mariano Rivera. The closer took care of the final six outs of a 4-3 victory with no runs, no hits and no incidents, requiring just 19 pitches to do so.

The outrageousness of Game 3 established the animosity and competitiveness of the series that would build toward the seventh game. Starting with Game 3, the teams alternated wins over four games in which each one hung in the balance into the ninth inning. So it would come down to this: the Yankees and Red Sox playing each other for the 26th time that year—the most two teams had seen of one another in baseball history—and a Yankee Stadium reprise of the Martinez-Clemens pitching matchup. To add to the drama, the game stood a chance to be the last time Clemens pitched in the big leagues. He had announced his intention to retire after the season, an intention that actually took four years to consummate. But the expectation at the time was that this might be his last game.

Martinez did not sleep well before Game 7. For one reason, his body clock was askew from a weary travel schedule. In the previous 19 days he had flown from Boston to Tampa to Oakland to Boston to Oakland to New York to Boston to New York. For another reason, Martinez was anxious, even fearful, of the hostility he might find in New York after the incidents from Game 3. He read and heard comments that he should be thrown in jail for what he did to Zimmer, and that fans were going to come to Game 7 armed with rocks and batteries to throw at him in the bullpen. His brother, the former pitcher Ramon Martinez, wanted to watch his kid brother pitch with the pennant on the line at Yankee Stadium, but Pedro would not allow it.

"Stay in Boston," he told Ramon. "Anything can happen."

Martinez made certain not to leave his hotel room while in New York. On the day of Game 7 he ordered some Dominican food delivered to his room rather than venturing out for lunch. He took the team bus to the ballpark, rather than trust a New York cabbie to bring him safely to the ballpark. The Yankees never liked Martinez much, but now he felt the wrath of the citizens of the city for having flung an old, huggable man to the ground.

Burkett, knowing this was likely to be his final season, had toted a video camera throughout the playoffs. It was rolling in the clubhouse before Game 7. One of his favorite images, taken unobtrusively, is of Martinez, sitting alone, facing into his locker, his face taut with concentration and anxiousness.

Martinez embraced the challenge, clearly outpitching an ineffective Clemens in the early innings. Boston whacked Clemens for three runs in the third inning, while Martinez was giving the Yankees nothing. Kevin Millar ripped Clemens' first pitch of the fourth inning for a home run, and it was 4-0. The Red Sox didn't stop there. Trot Nixon walked and then Bill Mueller lashed a single to center field. The Yankees were on the cusp of getting blown out, already down four runs to a sharp Martinez with Boston runners at first and third and no outs. Torre had little choice but to pull Clemens from the wreckage before it grew even worse. Clemens walked off the field in that slow, ambling cowboy walk of his, but the Yankee Stadium crowd was in too foul of a mood to send him off to his retirement with polite applause.

―――

When the bullpen door swung open, an accidental reliever walked out. It was Mussina. There he was making the first relief appearance of his professional life and having to do so by parachuting into the middle of an inning—exactly the scenario Stottlemyre had told him would not happen. Trouble was, Stottlemyre did not tell Torre he promised Mussina he would relieve only at the start of the inning. All Torre knew was that the game was on the line right now and it was time to break glass in case of emergency. Mussina was his best option.

Mussina first had to face Boston catcher Jason Varitek. He struck him out on three pitches. Next up was center fielder Johnny Damon. Mussina induced a groundball to Jeter, who turned it into an inning-ending double play. Just like that, with six pitches to two batters, Mussina had authored his signature moment as a Yankee. Until then he had acquired the reputation of a nearly great pitcher. Reliable, yes, but always somehow short of real greatness. He had never won 20 games in a season, had come within one strike of throwing a perfect game against Boston in 2001, and had lost four straight postseason decisions for the Yankees, including two in the 2003 ALCS alone.

Mussina's relief work grew in stature as the game unfolded. The Yankees finally broke through against Martinez when Jason Giambi whacked his first pitch of the fifth inning for a home run. Meanwhile, Mussina tacked on two more shutout innings. He had thrown 33 pitches and kept the Yankees within range of Pedro when Torre decided to take him out after the sixth inning, turning to lefthanded reliever Felix Heredia to face Damon and Todd Walker, two lefthanded hitters due up for Boston.

Told he was done for the night, Mussina turned to Torre in the dugout and said, "I thought you weren't going to bring me in in the middle of an inning."

Said Torre kiddingly, because he was unaware of what Stottlemyre had told him, "Well, I guess we lied to you."

Then Torre turned serious. He drew closer to his pitcher and told him, "All I can tell you is you pitched the game of your life here. If anybody ever questions how you handle pressure, you answered that right here. Don't you ever forget that."

"Thanks," Mussina said.

"Oh, and one more thing," Torre said. "Maybe when we come back next spring we'll take a look at you out of the bullpen."

"No, no. No, thanks," Mussina said.

Torre, of course, was kidding, but Mussina's clutch relief work had allowed some levity and hope in a game the Yankees still trailed by three against a determined, if somewhat weary, Martinez. The lack of sleep, the anxiety about the cauldron of New York, the three weeks of crossing times zones . . . all of it sapped a bit of energy from Martinez. Even though he cruised through the sixth inning, Martinez came off the field, sat next to assistant trainer Chris Correnti and offered something revealing: "Chris," he said, "I'm a little fatigued."

In the seventh, Martinez locked down the first two outs without apparent difficulty. But then Giambi hammered his second home run of the game to cut the lead to 4-2. Now Martinez only needed to dispatch Enrique Wilson to end the inning. Wilson normally would be the last guy you would want taking an at-bat when you were down to the last seven outs of your playoff life. Quite simply, Enrique Wilson was one of the worst hitters ever to play for the New York Yankees. He appeared in 264 games for the Yankees and batted .216. Only four men in the history of the franchise ever hit worse with that much time in pinstripes: Bill Robinson (.206, 1967–69), Jim Mason (.208, 1974–76), Lute Boone (.210, 1913–16) and Steve Balboni (.214, 1981–90). Moreover, Wilson was neither especially fleet nor adept in the field. His value essentially came down to one specific and unexplainable skill: he could hit Pedro Martinez. Wilson was a career .500 hitter against Martinez, with 10 hits in 20 at-bats, including a freakish 7-for-8 performance that year alone. Torre started Wilson at third base on those numbers alone, though his regular starting third baseman had given him no reason why he should stay in the lineup. Aaron Boone, looking overmatched, was hitting .125 in the ALCS, with two hits in 16 at-bats. Naturally, Martinez could not get Wilson out. Wilson reached base with an infield single. Garcia, whom Martinez had treated as his plastic duck decoy for Game 3 target practice, smacked the next pitch for a single.

Martinez had so cruised through most of the

game that he had thrown only 11 pitches out of the
stretch position before Garcia's hit. But now that
the Yankees had the tying runs on base and Soriano
at bat, Martinez had to tap whatever reserve tank
of energy he possessed. Soriano fought Martinez
through a grueling six-pitch at-bat. On the last
pitch, Soriano swung and missed for strike three. It
was Pedro's 100th pitch of the game. As Martinez
walked off the mound he gave thanks to God by
pointing to the sky. Red Sox Nation recognized the
body language. It was Pedro's usual coda to a full
night's work, his signature signoff. It was the look of
a man who was done, who had delivered his team
with 100 pitches to a 4-2 lead and within six outs of
the World Series. Martinez's teammates recognized
the look. As Martinez walked into the third-base
end of the Boston dugout, shortstop Nomar Garciaparra threw his arms around Martinez in a hug, a
gesture of appreciation for the game he pitched. At
the other end of the dugout, nearest to home plate,
Boston pitching coach Dave Wallace pulled his
pitching log notebook and a pencil from his pocket
and ran a line through Martinez's name. Pedro, to
the coach's best assumpton, was done. Underneath
Martinez's scratched-out name Wallace wrote "Embree." Alan Embree, a lefthanded pitcher, would
start the eighth inning to match up against Nick
Johnson, a lefthanded hitter and the first Yankee
due up in the inning. Wallace and Correnti congratulated Martinez on his effort, a job well done.

"After the seventh," Martinez said, "Chris and Wallace told me that was pretty much it. They were going to talk to Grady."

At that moment, Martinez figured he was done for the night. Such a moment is all it takes to trigger the shutdown of a pitcher's competitive systems. Rebooting is never quick and easy.

"Your energy level drops," Martinez said of that mental shutdown. "As soon as you think you're out, even for 30 seconds, you get tired and out of focus."

Martinez, slipping on his warmup jacket, was getting ready to leave the dugout for the clubhouse. Suddenly Little approached him.

"I need you for one more [inning]," the manager said. "Can you give me one more?"

Martinez was stunned. First of all, he had already assumed that he was done. And second of all, how was he supposed to answer the question? Was he even permitted, in the unwritten macho code of the game, to refuse the manager's request and say he wanted to come out of a Game 7?

"I didn't know what to say," Martinez said later. "Do I come out after the sixth or seventh? If anything happens, everyone will say, 'Pedro wanted to come out.'

"I wasn't hurt. I was tired, yes. I never expressed anything about coming out. The only way I would say that is if I was physically hurt. The only way."

So Martinez told Little he would try to give him another inning. Little must have sensed the fatigue and the hesitation in Martinez, because he decided on a backup plan.

"I'll tell you what, Petey," Little told him. "Why don't you try to start the eighth. I might even send you out there just to warm up."

Embree would be throwing in the bullpen. He would be summoned at any sign of distress, even if it occurred as Martinez threw his warmup pitches.

"Help is on the way," Little told Martinez.

David Ortiz provided another kind of assistance when he popped a home run off David Wells in the top of the eighth inning, extending Martinez's lead to 5-2. Torre had used Heredia to face two left-handed hitters and Jeff Nelson to face two righthanded hitters when he had called on Wells to neutralize Ortiz. It didn't work. Now Torre had used five pitchers, including Clemens, Mussina and Wells, who among them had won 709 games in the major leagues, and still found himself down three runs to Martinez with six outs left. Martinez marched out to the mound for the last of the eighth inning believing he would be removed as soon as the Yankees put anybody on base.

"At that point, I thought I was batter-by-batter," he said.

As Martinez threw his warmup pitches, Embree threw in the bullpen, ready to go. Righthanded re-lievers Mike Timlin and Scott Williamson were available, too. The three relievers had dominated New York throughout the series, allowing only one run in 11⅓ innings and just five hits in 36 at-bats. Little would later tell club officials that as well as they had pitched, he did not trust them to keep their nerves under control in such a pressurized spot. He trusted no one more than Martinez, even a fatigued Martinez. Indeed, Little trusted Martinez so much that even though Martinez himself thought his place in the game was a batter-by-batter proposition, Little intended for him to pitch the entire inning, even if runners reached base.

"It's the way we've always done it," Little said. "Ninety percent of the time when we send Pedro back out there he completes the inning. He gets out of his own jams. I can hardly remember the times I had to go get him. I'd rather have a tired Pedro Martinez out there than anybody else. He's my best."

Until Game 5 of the AL Division Series against Oakland, Little had removed Martinez only seven times mid-inning in his 60 starts for the manager—four of those seven hooks came against the Yankees—and only once after the seventh inning. But in a subtle bit of foreshadowing, Martinez had been unable to get through the eighth inning of that clinching game in Oakland. Little pulled a weary Martinez after two hits in that inning, and then used four relievers to secure the final six outs to make possible the New York–Boston steel-cage match.

Ten days later, Little faced the same predicament, only this time with a World Series berth on the line: a fatigued Martinez starting the eighth inning with a rested, reliable bullpen behind him. He would play this one differently than he had the game in Oakland, and it would cost him his job.

Martinez started that eighth inning well enough, getting Nick Johnson on a pop fly to shortstop. But Johnson had extended Martinez through another seven pitches in that at-bat. The last of those pitches was clocked at 93 miles per hour. The speed sounded impressive enough, but Martinez knew it was an inadequate gauge of how he was feeling.

"Even when I'm fatigued, I can still throw hard," Martinez said. "My arm speed may be there, but location is where I suffer and that's because my arm angle drops. I throw three-quarters, yes, but it's three-quarters steady. If I start to get tired, my arm drops a little more and that causes the ball to stay flat over the plate. My velocity doesn't change, but I can't spot the ball as well when I'm tired. That's what happened."

Five outs away. The Red Sox were just five outs away from going to the World Series and from smashing their inferior status to the hated Yankees. Of course, the Boston paradox at the time, typically referred to as the Curse of the Bambino, is that each out brings the club as close to infamy as it does fulfillment. Each step offers the horror of a trapdoor.

"As Game 7 was going on the drama kept building," Burkett said. "You have people on our team thinking, 'I don't want to be the one to make the mistake.' You know, the Bill Buckner thing. I'm sure it entered people's minds."

After getting Johnson, Martinez jumped ahead of Derek Jeter with two fastballs for strikes. If Babe Ruth, and his 1918 trade from Boston to the Yankees, is the root of all things evil for the Red Sox franchise, Jeter is the talisman of the Yankees' modern dynasty. So many of the team's signature moments and improbable rallies featured Jeter:

- He started the 12th inning rally, and scored the winning run, in Game 2 of the 1996 AL Division Series against Texas, the pivotal win that saved the Yankees from going down two games to none in the best-of-five series and was the springboard victory to their dynasty.
- He hit the disputed home run (the Jeffrey Maier home run, courtesy of fan interference) to rescue the Yankees in Game 1 of the 1996 AL Championship Series, just when they were five outs away from losing to Baltimore.
- With the Yankees down 6-0 in the sixth inning of 1996 World Series Game 4— the Braves seemed a lock to extend their series lead to three games to one—Jeter started the epic comeback with a single.
- After the Yankees lost Game 3 of the 2000 World Series to the Mets, Jeter

restored equilibrium to the series by ripping the first pitch of Game 4 for a home run off Bobby Jones.

- With the Yankees facing elimination in Oakland, he saved Game 3 of the 2001 AL Division Series by appearing from seemingly nowhere to fetch an errant relay throw and improvising a flip throw to the plate to cut down the would-be tying run.
- He hit a walkoff home run in the tenth inning to win Game 4 of the 2001 World Series against Arizona.

Jeter was still only 29 years old, but already owned several lifetimes worth of huge postseason moments. He had grown so comfortable in big spots, especially at Yankee Stadium, where the Yankees sometimes seemed to be paranormally good, and every break seemed to go their way, that he would tell first-year Yankee third baseman Aaron Boone, "Don't worry. The ghosts will come out eventually."

Against Martinez in Game 7, Jeter would provide yet another signature moment. Boston catcher Jason Varitek called for another fastball at 0-and-2, wanting this one so far out of the strike zone that he practically was standing when he gave a target for Martinez. Pedro did throw to the spot, very much up and very much away, but Jeter swatted at it anyway, lining it hard into right field. Trot Nixon, the Boston right fielder, took a poor path to the ball, running more shallow to his right than the hard-hit ball required. By the time Nixon corrected his mistake it was too late. The ball sailed over his head and bounced off the padded blue wall as Jeter dashed into second with a double.

The hit was largely forgotten amid the madness that was still to come, but it was one of those subtleties of execution that can drive baseball men mad. Yankees fans saw the clutch hitting of Jeter, while inside the Red Sox dugout they saw the possible second out of the eighth inning squandered by an outfielder's path to the baseball. In the immediate aftermath of the game, one of the Red Sox would grab a reporter and ask, "Tell me, was Jeter's ball catchable?" Told that it was, crestfallen, he sighed, "I thought so."

Martinez, who figured he would be done as soon as a runner reached based, glanced toward his dugout, but no one came. Bernie Williams, a switch-hitter who hit 24 points worse against left-handed pitchers that year, was due to bat next with Hideki Matsui, a lefthanded hitter, behind him. Fox analyst Tim McCarver said on air at that time, "You get the feeling [Embree] will be the pitcher for Matsui one way or the other."

Once again Martinez brought the hitter to the brink of expiration with another two-strike count, this time 2-and-2 to Williams. And once again,

Martinez could not finish the job. He threw a 95-mph fastball that caught too much of the plate. Williams pounded it for a hard single that sent Jeter dashing home to cut the deficit to 5-3.

As expected, with the lefthanded Embree ready to face the lefthanded Matsui, Little left the dugout and walked to the mound. But then something very much unexpected happened: Little walked back to the dugout without Martinez. Writers in the press box howled, "What is he doing?" Said McCarver on the air, "This is the most blatant situation for a second guess in this series, whether to bring Embree in to pitch to Matsui or not. If you're not going to bring him in against Matsui, when are you going to make that move?"

Martinez had thrown 115 pitches. He was fatigued. He had taken the mound in the eighth inning thinking one runner might bring about his removal, and here two of them had reached base by hitting the ball hard and he was **still** in the game. Once again Little had put much of the decision-making process in the hands of a proud pitcher who did not want to say no.

"Can you pitch to Matsui?" Little had asked Martinez on the mound.

"Yeah, of course," Martinez had replied. "Let me try to get him."

Little's question regarding Matsui left Martinez thinking this would be the last batter he would face.

"He didn't ask me about anybody else," Martinez said. "Just Matsui."

For a third consecutive batter, Martinez obtained two strikes, this time with another 0-and-2 count after Matsui looked at a fastball and curveball. And for a third consecutive batter, Martinez could not execute a pitch to finish off the at-bat. Varitek called for a fastball up and in.

"We've probably thrown Matsui 80 pitches up and in," Martinez said, "and he's never hit that pitch."

Again Martinez missed slightly with his location. The pitch wasn't far enough inside. Matsui blasted a line drive down the line that bounced into the stands for a ground rule double. Martinez had given up only two extra-base hits all year on 0-and-2 counts. Now he had done so twice in a span of three batters with the American League pennant only five outs away.

The Yankees had runners at second and third. Now Martinez thought for certain he was out of the game. Little had asked him only about Matsui, and Martinez had failed to retire him. He had thrown 118 pitches and no longer had the strength to finish off hitters. But Little didn't move from the dugout. The howls from the press box grew louder. The next batter was Posada. One more duel among the archenemies.

"I was actually shocked I stayed out there that

long," Martinez said of the eighth inning. "But I'm paid to do that. I belong to Boston. If they want to blow my arm out, it's their responsibility. I'm not going to go to the manager and say, 'Take me out of the game.' I'm not going to blame Grady for leaving me out there."

By now, Yankees closer Mariano Rivera was throwing in the bullpen. The crowd, with a shark's intuition for the vulnerability of its prey, was gleefully frenetic. Once again, Martinez forged a two-strike count. He missed with a cut fastball before throwing three straight curveballs, getting a called strike on the first, missing with the second and getting a swinging strike with the third. Varitek called for a fastball at 2-and-2. And for the fourth consecutive time, the Yankees jumped on a two-strike fastball for a hit. Posada did not hit it well—the 95-mph pitch jammed him—but he did hit it fortuitously. His little pop fly plopped onto the grass in shallow center field.

Williams scored, with Matsui following him home with the tying run. None of the Red Sox, as if stunned by what was happening, bothered to cover second base, so Posada easily chugged into the bag for a double. A tremendous wall of sound rose up, the kind of roar that comes not just from the throat but also from the soul. Down three runs to Pedro Martinez and down to their final five outs, the Yankees had tied the game with four straight two-strike hits.

"That," Posada said, "was the loudest I have ever heard Yankee Stadium."

Suddenly, Rivera ran off the bullpen mound. The Yankees' bullpen was a two-tiered arrangement. The throwing area is at field level, behind the left-center-field wall, and above that, up a short flight of stairs, is a sort of staging area, with a small dugout and bathroom. Without a word of explanation, Rivera climbed the steps, ran into the bathroom, closed the door behind him and, with the joyous music and noise shaking the concrete walls of the stadium, starting crying.

"I started crying because it was just too much," Rivera said. "I needed to be pitching, yes, but that's how awesome the moment was. I didn't want anyone to see me. I didn't want people to see me standing there with tears coming out of my eyes."

At that moment, Little was walking to the mound. At last, he signaled for Embree to replace Martinez. In Boston, where more people were watching than saw the Patriots win the Super Bowl eight months earlier, those that did not weep cursed. There had been 1,053 postseason games played in the history of baseball. In only 13 of them did a team lose after leading by three or more runs with no more than five outs to go. And only twice did a team blow a lead that big and that late without using the bullpen. Those two historic postseason meltdowns occurred just three nights apart: first when Cubs manager Dusty Baker lost Game 6 of the NLCS with Mark Prior on the mound against Florida, and then when Little lost ALCS Game 7 with Martinez unable to stop the Yankees. Two losses, three days apart, with matching DNA. Two out of 1,053. A one-tenth of one percent match.

"That eighth inning rally was what we were all about," Torre said. "Never giving up and just finding a way. What we were able to do against Pedro was what we always tried to do: just making Pedro pitch and work until you can get to a point in the game where he is vulnerable. Whether he is in the game or not, and you can question the decision either way, what makes that inning possible is all the at-bats before then that made him vulnerable."

Embree, of course, and then Timlin proceeded to navigate the rest of the inning without another run scoring. With Martinez out of the game, Torre lifted the now-useless Wilson to have Ruben Sierra pinch-hit against Timlin. The Red Sox intentionally walked Sierra, upon which Torre put his erstwhile starting third baseman into the game to pinch run: Aaron Boone.

Torre then turned to Rivera to preserve the tie. Rivera did so in the ninth, the tenth and the eleventh innings. It was his longest outing in seven years. Torre had only Gabe White and Jose Contreras, the Game 6 losing pitcher, as his next options behind Rivera.

"Every inning we thought that was it for him,"

Burkett said, "and every inning we were like, 'Oh, shit, he's still pitching.'"

The Boston bullpen didn't blink, either. The Yankees were 0-for-8 against Embree, Timlin and knuckleball pitcher Tim Wakefield, who had entered the game in the tenth inning. Boone, with his two hits in sixteen at-bats in the series, was the first batter of the eleventh for the Yankees.

"Boone," Torre said, "was just a mess. He was a good kid. He just couldn't keep his feet on the ground. He was just too excited. He just kept swinging at fastballs all the time. It didn't matter who was throwing it or where it was."

Boone did not have to worry about chasing fastballs against Wakefield. He was going to see knuckleballs. Torre called over Boone as Boone grabbed his bat from the dugout rack.

"Listen," Torre said. "Just when you go up there, try to hit a single up the middle or right field. It doesn't mean you won't hit a home run to left."

Boone nodded and walked to the plate. It was sixteen minutes past midnight on what was now Friday morning. The series and the rivalry hardly could have been more tied. The game was tied at five runs each. The series was tied at three wins each. Each team had scored exactly 29 runs. If you took it back further, back to when the Red Sox were sold and Henry, Werner, Lucchino and Epstein began to run a smarter, more efficient ballclub that wasn't afraid to poke a stick in the Yankees' eye,

New York and Boston had played each other 44 times. The difference between the two of them over 44 skirmishes was only two wins and five runs, each slight edge held by the Yankees.

Wakefield threw his first pitch to Boone, a knuckleball, slightly inside and up. Boone swung and connected with it, so solidly that he knew in an instant it would be a home run. The baseball flew, as Torre had imagined, toward the left-field seats.

Inside the Yankees clubhouse, Clemens, who for seven innings had contemplated the possible end to his career, heard the sound of history, like a freight train rumbling through a concrete tunnel. Clemens was sitting in a small side room off the main clubhouse, across a narrow hallway from Torre's office, when he recognized that sound. The sound came above him—the Yankees' clubhouse was tucked under the first-base stands—and he knew it was the sound of thousands of those blue plastic seat bottoms snapping upright almost simultaneously as the fans jump to their feet. The baseball was still in the air as Clemens dashed out of the room toward the clubhouse door and the narrow ramp leading to the dugout.

There was bedlam, and there was relief—relief at having somehow held back this strengthening force that the Red Sox had become.

"The one thing I saw," Torre said, "was Manny Ramirez turning around in left field and trotting off the field. Everything after that was blank except for one thing: seeing Mariano out there on the mound, kissing the rubber or whatever he did."

Rivera is a deeply religious man. He had prayed in the clubhouse before the game for strength and courage. "A good conversation with the Lord," is what he called it. He had been humbled into tears in the eighth inning, crying in the privacy of the bullpen bathroom. But this . . . this victory . . . it was too much to keep emotions private. He ran straight for the mound and flung himself onto the dirt on his hands and knees. Through tears again, this time for all to see, he thanked the Lord for pulling him through. It was an odd sight: the Yankees jumping upon one another around Boone at home plate while Rivera wept in supplication.

"That," Torre said, "was an emotional night. I'm not sure what was most emotional: that game or the three games at Yankee Stadium in the 2001 World Series. In all my years in New York, that Game 7 and the games in 2001 were the best of all."

The Red Sox slunk without a word back to their clubhouse. Several players were crying. Once inside, the door still closed to reporters, Little spoke briefly, telling the players they should hold their heads high with pride. Relievers Todd Jones and Mike Timlin also spoke, making a similar point.

Sometime later, amid the profound sadness in the Boston clubhouse, Little and Martinez shared a hug in a brief, private moment. Then the manager looked at the pitcher whom he trusted more

340 JOE TORRE AND TOM VERDUCCI

than anyone else and talked about what would come next.

"Petey," Little said, "I might not be here anymore."

Martinez tried to cheer him up.

"Why?" Martinez said. "It's not your fault. It's up to the players. Any other situation I get the outs and you're a hero."

Little, however, knew too well how baseball in Boston worked. The blood was on his hands, and Boston held little room for forgiveness for those who could be blamed. He couldn't come back. Truthfully, Little had been something of a placeholder anyway, a guy whom the Red Sox players knew and liked, who was available in spring training and who would fill the seat inoffensively until the new owners could establish a new, process-oriented culture around the team and find the right manager to dovetail with it. Little, who didn't totally buy into the growing emphasis on statistical analysis, wasn't that guy. The horror of Game 7 ensured the end of his days, and Little knew it. Martinez tried to comfort Little with the same words generations of Red Sox players and fans practically had made their motto:

"It wasn't meant to be."

So ended the eighty-fifth consecutive season for the Boston Red Sox and their congregation without a world championship. Boston was bound by history and New York empowered by it. The angst of the Sox did not go back to the first century B.C., but the Roman poet Catullus back then captured in an epigram the essence of such frustration when he wrote, "I hate and I love. Perhaps you're asking why I do this? / I don't know, but I feel it happening, and it's torture."

The torture of the Red Sox would be no more. Aaron Boone was the last twist of the knife. The rest of baseball had caught up to the Yankees, and the Red Sox were at the forefront of this revolution. There was no way to know it at the time, of course, but the home run by Boone was the ending to more than just one of the greatest ballgames ever played. It was the very last magical moment of the Torre Era. It was the last time the Yankee Stadium ghosts would come out to play. It was the last time the Yankees would douse one another with champagne at the stadium to celebrate yet another postseason conquest. It was the last time the Yankees could claim a truly superior position over the Boston Red Sox.

"I felt tremendous disappointment that night," Epstein said. "I grew up in Boston. I understood and felt the Yankee rivalry and the domination by the Yankees. I felt like I understood it, but sitting there watching Aaron Boone's home run leave the park I felt baptized, immersed in it.

"I thought our new approach to things was working, even though we ended up losing Game 7 in that fashion. I thought about how far we had come, but in the end we were back where we always were: playing second fiddle to the Yankees. It was pretty obvious where the flaws were. They were in the pitching staff. We had tried to cobble a league-average pitching staff and just hit the living piss out of the baseball. But now we knew that if we could add an elite starter and a dominant closer, that would make a huge difference. That was the quickest way to improve the club. By adding two elite guys, we thought that would close what was left of the gap between us and the Yankees."

———

The Marlins were not a particularly special team throughout the regular season. They ranked eighth in runs in the National League and seventh in runs allowed, making them the only one of the 28 teams to reach the World Series in the wild card era to rank seventh or worse in both categories. But they became the first success story of commissioner Bud Selig's plan to spread the wealth and success around baseball.

Of the $49 million the Marlins spent on payroll (ranked 26th among 30 teams; the Yankees were first at $153 million), $21 million came from revenue-sharing checks written by other teams. Of course, no team contributed more to the revenue-sharing pot than the Yankees, who kicked in $52.6 million, and no team except the Montreal Expos, a team owned and operated by Major League Baseball, received a bigger handout than the Marlins. Three years after baseball included the Marlins on its hit list when floating the idea of contraction, the Marlins were beating the Yankees in the World Series with help from the Yankees' own money. The Yankees were helping to arm the enemy, who signed $10 million catcher Pudge Rodriguez as a free agent and traded for $4.5 million closer Ugueth Urbina, a rental player at that, given his impending free agency.

If the dynastic Yankees, in their last days then of such exalted repute, were emblematic of the traditional baseball powerhouse, the Marlins were the epitome of Selig's new vision of the postmodern champion. A team that finished 10 games out of first place, was a middle-of-the-pack team in run production and prevention and had 43 percent of their payroll covered by other teams became world champions—that in the season after the Anaheim Angels, another wild card team on the receiving end of the new revenue-sharing system, also ran roughshod through the Yankees in the Division Series on their way to the world championship.

"This is the first year of a lot of changes," Selig said to reporters after the Marlins won the World Series. "I told all of you last year the Anaheim Angels were the first real beneficiary of revenue sharing. Now you're seeing this, and I'm delighted."

The Yankees actually led the World Series two games to one before a series of critical breakdowns in Games 3 and 4. The first occurred in the 11th inning of Game 3, when Aaron Boone batted with the bases loaded and one out against Braden Looper. Boone failed to put the ball in play, striking out. John Flaherty ended the threat by popping out.

Torre, having used a pinch hitter in the inning for Jose Contreras, who threw two shutout innings out of the bullpen, needed a pitcher for the bottom of the 11th. With the first four hitters due up being righthanded, Torre had only two righthanded options: Weaver and Mariano Rivera. Using Rivera in a tie game on the road, Torre figured, did not make much sense. Weaver could cover more innings. He had started 24 times during the season, though his 7-9 record, hangdog demeanor on the mound and trouble adjusting to the New York cauldron of criticism made for a rough year. With Rivera available for a maximum of only two innings, that gave the Yankees only one at-bat, one chance, to hand Rivera a lead to protect. Otherwise, who would close the game after that? Weaver?

"I had no options," Torre said. "People say bring in Mariano. I had no options. It was an extra-inning game on the road. There was never any consideration of other options. I never was between anybody, I know that."

Weaver was lights-out in the 11th inning. He zipped through three straight Florida hitters with only eight pitches.

"I was so happy for him," Torre said. "People

were basing their criticism of him in Game 4 on what happened before, when he was bad. But we finally got him to a point where he was controlling his emotions better. But the result reverted to what he was before, so people say, 'It's the same old guy.'"

Weaver's Yankees career ended with one pitch—actually three, if you count the two pitches out of the strike zone to Marlins shortstop Alex Gonzalez to start the 12th. Gonzalez, batting eighth, was a .256 hitter during the season. But with a 2-and-0 count, Gonzalez, a good fastball hitter, turned into Hank Aaron. He was a .636 hitter on 2-and-0 counts, with seven hits in 11 such at-bats. Weaver obliged him with a fastball and the game was over just like that, the ball clearing the left-field wall.

After the failures by Boone and Weaver, more breakdowns occurred in Game 5, and those were physical. The first happened during batting practice. Torre was standing behind the batting cage on the field when first baseman Jason Giambi, who was in the lineup batting sixth, and who had been taking groundballs at first base, approached him.

"Skip, my knee," Giambi said. "I can't move. I can't really move. I know you wanted me to tell you if it was a problem."

Giambi feared that he could not defend against the bunting ability of Juan Pierre and Luis Castillo, the speedsters at the top of the Florida lineup. He feared his mobility was not good enough to get to groundballs. "The infield there in Florida is really fast," Giambi said. The way Giambi saw it, this was no time to play the role of the tough guy and see if the knee would hold up, even if it was the World Series.

"What happened was I had blown out my knee that year," Giambi said. "That was the year Derek went down, Bernie had gone down, Nick Johnson had gone down earlier that year. That's where Joe was: 'I need you to play. I need somebody to anchor this lineup.' I hit fourth all year and my knee was torn to shreds. Joe and I had talked before. 'When we get to the playoffs, you're the DH, and if we get to the World Series, we'll just talk about it.' Because Nick was back and he's a great defensive player."

So Torre told Giambi he would take him out of the lineup, which already had been announced to the media, and replace him with Johnson.

"Okay," Torre told him, "I'll just tell the press it was my decision."

Torre told reporters, "I saw him limping around. I asked him about his knee. He hemmed and he hawed, and I said, 'Why not just play Nick Johnson?'"

Giambi told the media, "I didn't want to cost us on defense."

It was a decision that was both difficult and curious, depending on the angle from which it was viewed. On the one hand, Giambi believed he might hurt the team if he tried to play. On the other hand, he took himself out of the lineup of the fifth game of the World Series—his first World Series, and a World Series that was tied at two games each.

"Of course, Jeter would come up to me and say, 'What happened to Giambi?'" Torre said. "He could never understand how people could do that. He had no patience for that stuff. 'What happened to this guy?' if he didn't play. 'What's the matter with him?' for somebody, anybody. He had absolutely no patience for that stuff."

Said Giambi, "You wait your whole life for that, but that's kind of how I was brought up in Oakland. 'Hey listen, we need to win as a team.' It breaks your heart, trust me. But sometimes you have to think not about yourself, but about the team."

Giambi did come off the bench as a pinch hitter that night. He hit a home run.

There was yet another major problem before the game even started. Torre was standing next to Mel Stottlemyre during the national anthem when the pitching coach told him, "You may need to get another pitcher ready."

Minutes earlier, Wells had told Stottlemyre that his back was stiff and that he might not be able to pitch. Wells threw a one-two-three first inning with a 1-0 lead, walked off the mound, threw his glove on the bench, announced "I can't go," and kept walking right into the clubhouse. Only 24 hours earlier at a news conference, Wells had bragged to the media about his lack of conditioning when someone asked him to reveal the secret to his success. "Goes to show you don't need to bust your ass every day to be successful," he crowed. The audience broke into laughter.

Boomer's act wasn't so funny in Game 5, not when he stuck the Yankees bullpen with eight innings to pick on the night after a 12-inning game. Contreras coughed up four runs in three innings, Brad Penny pitched well for the Marlins, and the Yankees lost again, 6-4. Watching Giambi and Wells go down was like getting hit on the same commute by not one, but two flat tires. The timing was awful and the results were worse. The Yankees were done, though there still was the formality of a Game 6 to wrap up the series. Florida righthander Josh Beckett took care of the clincher with a five-hit clampdown on the Yankees, 2-0.

Oddly, the Yankees outhit, outhomered, outscored and outpitched the Marlins in the series. Their vaunted rotation lived up to its preseason cover billing, posting a 1.91 ERA in the series (though the Wells exit was harmful because of its brevity). Still, the Yankees lost. Why? The series could have gone either way. A sacrifice fly here, a hit there, a little back and core maintenance training regimen there, and who knows? Maybe it simply was the karmic tariff for all those October nights and weeks that had fallen their way, the stuff that made bright, reasonable people believe in the forces of mystique and aura. Maybe the Marlins were a collection agency sent by the baseball gods, or possibly Bud Selig, whose new world order of baseball democracy was just dawning. Eight different franchises would play in the next five World Series— none of them having been there since 1987 and none of them being the 26-time world champion New York Yankees. Maybe by somehow losing the 2003 World Series, the Yankees actually provided a reminder of just how great and prolific were those championship Yankees teams.

"You know, we made it look easy," Jeter said. "We knew it wasn't easy, but we made it look easy. And people automatically assume, 'Well, your payroll is this, and you've got this player, that player, this all-star, that all-star . . . you should win.' No, it just doesn't happen like that. You have to have a lot of things go right. We were in six World Series? It's not easy, you know what I mean? Nowadays? Six World Series in 12 years? That's tough to do, man."

8.

The Issues of Alex

Because Aaron Boone's car was in the repair shop on January 16, 2004, he was unable to get in his daily workout.

And because he was unable to get in his daily workout, he was apt to say yes when a buddy of his called and asked if he'd like a ride to come with him to play in a pickup basketball game.

And because he played pickup basketball that day, Boone was running to save a ball from going out of bounds when he suddenly stopped at the sideline and reached to flick the ball back toward him.

And because Boone stopped short, a friend of his in the game, who also had been chasing the ball but who could not stop in time, plowed into him, tearing the ligaments of Boone's left knee.

And because Boone blew out his knee, Alex Rodriguez became a Yankee.

And because Alex Rodriguez became a Yankee, the Yankees' clubhouse and the personality of the team, already sliding further from the O'Neill-Martinez-Brosius band of brothers comportment, would never be the same.

Talk about car trouble.

"When Alex came over it became strained in the clubhouse," Torre said. "I can't tell you for sure who you can put a finger on there, or if it was just one of those things that was pretty much unavoidable with the strong personalities."

Boone's decision to play a little game of pickup basketball was the baseball equivalent of Mrs. O'Leary leaving a lantern a little too close to her cow, or of five small-time burglars breaking into the Watergate complex in Washington. History, Voltaire observed, is little else than a picture of human crimes and misfortunes. The misfortune of Boone changed baseball history, most especially the neo-Peloponnesian War between the Boston Red Sox and the New York Yankees.

"I don't think we're ever going to live long enough to see us outspend the Yankees in the off-season," Red Sox general manager Theo Epstein said after the Yankees replaced Boone at third base by trading for Rodriguez from the Texas Rangers on February 16, 2004, exactly one month after Boone's idea of a cardio workout ended with his knee shredded. "We'll devote our energies hopefully to a day real soon where we beat them on the field in October."

That day would be as soon as possible, which is to say the very next October. The arrival of Rodriguez in New York just happened to coincide with the flipping of roles between the Yankees and Red Sox. Athens would prevail over Sparta at last. The championship banners flew in Boston now, not in New York. Rodriguez hit 208 home runs and won two Most Valuable Player Awards in his first five years as a Yankee. But in those five seasons, the Yankees won zero pennants and went 10-14 in postseason games. The Red Sox, meanwhile, won two pennants in those five years, both of which were capped with World Series triumphs, and went 28-14 in postseason games.

In the five years before Rodriguez was a Yankee, the Yankees won four pennants and were 42-24 in postseason games; the Red Sox won zero pennants and were 10-12 in postseason games. The roles completely reversed.

Rodriguez, who played nearly every game and produced at an elite level, at least before October rolled around, surely wasn't the main cause of the role reversal. No team exploited the changing baseball marketplace in those years better than the Red Sox. The ballclub's business acumen produced tremendous gains in local revenues atop the growing national revenues dispersed from the Central Fund pool, and its baseball acumen not only made for a fertile player development program, but also promoted wise spending because of state-of-the-art valuations on players based on complex statistical analysis and old-school scouting methods. At the same time, the Yankees' fallow player development system and scattershot approach to player acquisition—overpay in the increasingly inefficient free agent market—made for a recipe of their own quicksand. The more they flailed, the more they sunk.

Nonetheless, Rodriguez was conspicuous by the awesome disparity between his skills and his inability to use them in the clutch. Rodriguez hit .245 in the postseason as a Yankee, or 61 points worse than his career average. From the fifth inning of Game 4 of the 2004 ALCS—the onset of the dynasty's demise—through 2008, Rodriguez hit .136 in 59 postseason at-bats, including 0-for-27 with 11 strikeouts with a total of 38 runners on, every one of whom he left on base. The Yankees went 4-13 in that stretch when A-Rod went AWOL, losing consecutive series to the Red Sox, Angels, Tigers and Indians. Such colossal performance anxiety from such a talented player seemed almost unfathomable, even before one's very eyes.

"When it comes to a key situation," Torre said, "he can't get himself to concern himself with getting the job done, instead of how it looks.

"There's a certain free fall you have to go through when you commit yourself without a guarantee that it's always going to be good. There's a sort of trust, a trust and commitment thing that has to allow yourself to fail. Allow yourself to be embarrassed. Allow yourself to be vulnerable. And sometimes players aren't willing to do that. They have a reputation to uphold. They have to have an answer for it. It's an ego thing."

Fairly or not, Rodriguez, by the sheer timing of his arrival, but also by dint of his outsized talent and knack for calling attention to himself, was the unmistakable shorthand symbol for why the Yankees no longer were champions and suffered at the rise of the Red Sox. Whether hitting 450-foot home runs or sunbathing shirtless in Central Park or squiring strippers, Rodriguez was like nothing ever seen before on the championship teams of the Torre Era: an ambitious superstar impressed and motivated by stature and status, particularly when those qualities pertained to himself.

"Alex monopolized all the attention," Torre said. "I don't think that's important. We never really had anybody who craved the attention. I think when Alex came over he certainly changed just the feel of the club, whether or not that was because of certain assumptions people had just made by Alex being there, that he was this kind of player.

"For me success was still going to be about pitching. But seeing his personality concerned me because you could see his focus was on individual stuff."

About midway through that 2004 season, for instance, Rodriguez was walking past Torre in the dugout toward the bat rack. Torre offered him some encouragement to help him relax.

"You know, you'll be fine," Torre told Rodriguez. "It just takes a little time to adjust to playing here."

Said Rodriguez, "Well, my numbers are about the same as this time last year."

Torre was disappointed in his response.

"I wasn't talking about numbers," Torre said. "I was talking about getting used to playing in this environment and what you were expected to do. The expectations with the Yankees are about winning, and people aren't really concerned about what your stats are."

Maybe there was some risk introducing Rodriguez to the Yankees culture, but how risky could it really have been to add the most talented player in the game, who was only 28 years old, who had hit no fewer than 41 home runs for six years running, and who had won two straight Gold Gloves at shortstop? Truth be told, the Rangers had come to realize that Rodriguez, or at least his $252 million contract, was a mistake they needed to unload. They were a last place team with him, and they wanted out from the financial commitment so badly that they first tried to trade him to Boston in December—the deal to renegotiate Rodriguez's contract downward fell apart over a difference of $15 million over seven years—and then they kicked in $67 million to ship Rodriguez to the Yankees for the dynamic second baseman Alfonso Soriano. How badly did Texas want Rodriguez gone? By 2025, when the last of his deferred payments to Rodriguez is due, Rangers owner Tom Hicks will have paid Rodriguez $140 million for only three years of service, all of them on lastplace teams. Hicks found that alternative more bearable than keeping him.

The Yankees had tried to replace Boone with Los Angeles third baseman Adrian Beltre, but they could not work out a trade with the Dodgers. The Yankees signed journeyman Mike Lamb to play the position. On February 8, about three weeks after Boone tore up his knee and one week before spring training was to begin, agent Scott Boras called Brian Cashman to talk about one of his clients, first baseman Travis Lee. The conversation included some idle chatter about the state of the Yankees.

"I'm having trouble finding a third baseman," Cashman told Boras.

The agent made a little joke, kidding on the square, about how maybe Cashman should be interested in another client of his: Alex Rodriguez, who only two weeks earlier had been named captain of the Rangers, if for no other reason than to cover up the fact that the team had just tried to ship him off to Boston.

Cashman was immediately interested, if slightly surprised. Rodriguez was a shortstop. With Jeter firmly entrenched there with the Yankees, and with

Boone out for the season, Cashman wondered if Rodriguez would be willing to move to third base. Boras said he would get back to Cashman. He called Rodriguez.

"You'd have to decide what the position means to you," Boras told him, referring to shortstop, "and understand what you'd be giving up for a chance to win. Think about it."

Rodriguez called Boras back the next day.

"Let's do it," he said.

The next day the Rangers, still trying to put on a happy face after their forced reconciliation with Rodriguez, held a conference call with Rodriguez, Boras, Hicks, general manager John Hart and manager Buck Showalter. The idea was to say wonderful things about the future of the Texas Rangers, with their newly named captain at the forefront in shaping the direction of the team.

Boras just happened to throw a bomb into the room. He made sure to mention on the conference call that Rodriguez might consider a trade to New York. Hicks scoffed at the idea.

"Alex isn't going to play third base," Hicks said. "He's always said that."

"Alex," Boras said, as if asking the question for the first time, "what do you think about third base?"

"I wouldn't rule it out," Rodriguez said. "It's something I'd consider."

Silence fell over the line.

358 JOE TORRE AND TOM VERDUCCI

"Frankly," Boras said at the time, "Tom Hicks was stunned."

The next day Hart and Cashman were negotiating the framework of a deal to send the newly minted Rangers captain to New York. Within 72 hours it was done. Rodriguez was a Yankee, even if an accidental Yankee at that. Of course, he said all the right things then about yielding his alpha status with the Rangers to a more deferential one with Jeter's Yankees.

"Once Scott brought it to my attention, it made perfect sense," Rodriguez said about moving to third base in order to be a Yankee. "I began to think about the pinstripes. I felt the allure of the tradition and opportunity to win and asked myself, 'Why not do it?'

"You know the best part? Getting there while I'm still young and knowing I have seven years to play with Derek and set my legacy as far as being a part of Yankees history. Getting there at 37 and playing two years wouldn't be the same."

"I began to think about the pinstripes?" "The allure of the tradition?" "Set my legacy?" Who spoke like that?

You could have shined the entire fleet of New York City cabs for a year with all that polish. The only problem with such a rosecolored view was that putting Rodriguez and Jeter in the same clubhouse was in itself a risk. The two of them were once close friends as young stars in the 1990s, often staying at one another's apartment whenever Jeter's Yankees played Rodriguez's Mariners. But a rift developed in spring training 2001 with the publication of a story in **Esquire** magazine by Scott Raab about Boras and Rodriguez. In the piece, Rodriguez went out of his way to take shots at Jeter. Indeed, it was Rodriguez who brought Jeter into his conversation with the writer, doing so decidedly without any polish whatsoever.

"The thing about [New York **Daily News** columnist] Mike Lupica that pisses me off," Rodriguez said in the story, "is that he makes me look like the biggest dickhead in the world, and then he takes a guy like Jeter and just puts him way up there."

Rodriguez then added this infamous dagger: "Jeter's been blessed with talent around him. He never had to lead. He can just go play and have fun. And he hits second—that's totally different than third or fourth in a lineup. You go into New York, you wanna stop Bernie and O'Neill. You never say, Don't let Derek beat you. He's never your concern."

Jeter was hurt. The demeaning attack was unprovoked from someone he had considered a friend. Rodriguez drove two hours from the Rangers' spring training camp to apologize to Jeter, but it was too late. Jeter requires fierce, unqualified loyalty from friends and teammates. You are either with him or not, and there is no allowance for switching sides or absolution. In that sense he is demanding, even coldly so, with the requirements of his inner circle. Rodriguez was forever compromised in Jeter's eyes. Putting them on the same team, on the same side of the infield, with Jeter manning Rodriguez's natural position, holding the captaincy and the unquestioned alpha status in the clubhouse, was a chemistry experiment of such flammable possibilities it was best approached with a haz-mat suit and titanium safety goggles. It did not go well for the better part of three years, with a kind of begrudging neutrality becoming the best possible outcome by year four. By 2007, battleworn and still suffering by comparison at Jeter's most-favored-nation status in New York and in the clubhouse, Rodriguez took to keeping the earbuds from his music player in his ears whenever walking around the clubhouse, mostly to prevent the media from engaging him. Of course, inauthenticity even dripped from that simple act; Rodriguez later admitted he often did not have music playing while doing so.

Back in 2004, at first Rodriguez did his best to try to fit into the Yankee culture—his cloying, B-grade actor best. He slathered on the polish. People in the clubhouse, including teammates and support personnel, were calling him "A-Fraud" behind his back.

"He **was** phony," said Mike Borzello, the former Yankees bullpen coach and one of Rodriguez's close friends, "and he knew he was phony. But he didn't know how to be anything else at that time. Then he started to realize what it's all about and what people feed off of, and thought, 'Hey, I can really be myself.' "

Put another way, New York could sniff out a phony in a heartbeat.

"Right," Borzello said, "and eventually he realized, 'I don't have to rehearse. I can just do it in one take if I just say what I really feel and show the emotions that I really have as opposed to acting like I don't care or knowing your questions before you ask them so I can give the answer I think you want to hear.' He stopped doing that. But sometimes he'll revert back, and that's when guys make fun of him. We made fun of him about everything.

"I used to tell Alex all the time, I said, 'You come to the stadium and you try to get everyone to look at you. Meanwhile, they already are looking at you. You're Alex Rodriguez. I don't understand that.'

"And he would say, 'Well, I like to play with a certain style.' Bullshit. I said, 'You do things on the field that draw attention to yourself that are unnecessary, and you want people to know how good you are, how smart a baseball player you are. And we already know that. Just play. Stop saying, 'Look at me.' We're already looking."

Players notice. For instance, one Rodriguez self-styled flourish that irritates other players is how he recognizes the depth of outfielders when on second base. Players are taught in that situation to gauge where the outfielders are positioned before the ball is hit. If the right fielder, for example, is playing especially deep, the runner may be more apt to break for home on a bloop in that direction or, under the direction of the third-base coach, to anticipate continuing home on a base hit toward that side. It is part of basic baseball fundamentals that requires only a quick look at each outfielder before the ball is pitched. Rodriguez, however, would turn that subtlety into a grand gesture for everyone to notice. He would turn and make an obvious pointing motion toward each outfielder, in a manner not unlike a football referee signaling a first down three times. You couldn't miss it, which is exactly why it drove other players nuts. One spring training, for instance, while one American League team was reviewing good base-running habits, the instructor and several players gave over-the-top parodies of Rodriguez's triple-point technique in the middle of the drill, mocking the obviousness of it. Everyone cracked up.

"He points to make sure you know how smart he is, that he checks the outfielders," Borzello said. "So now, if you remember in center field at Yankee Stadium, there was a window in the bullpen. I'd be sitting there and when he would get to second I would do it. So it got to the point where he'd get to second and immediately look out, and I would point. And he would go ahead and point. I said, 'What are you doing? Stop it. Stop it. It looks so stupid. We know you're smart. We know you know the game'—because he does."

Rodriguez did impress his teammates with a relentless work ethic. They found him to be the baseball equivalent of a gym rat. He knew everything going on around baseball and he never stopped working. One night in 2007 he showed up in the dugout 10 minutes before the first pitch with blood dripping from his hands and knees. "What the hell happened to you?" somebody asked.

Rodriguez explained that he just had been running full tilt on the treadmill in the weight room when the belt broke and he went flying off the back end of the machine, skinning his hands and knees as he was thrown into a wall. Who the hell ran at sprinting speed on a treadmill right before a game was about to start? The most talented player in baseball did. That was A-Rod, too.

"Nobody has ever worked harder in my memory than this guy," Torre said. "Jeter, I'm sure he does his weight work in the wintertime. In the summertime he gets dressed and gets the hell out of there. He doesn't hang out. Nobody's in better shape than Alex. Nobody works harder than Alex. For a star player, who gets there as early as he gets there, and still he might hear Coach Larry Bowa say, 'You need to take groundballs.' And he'll do whatever it takes. He'll do it all the time. He's just a workaholic."

Said Bowa, "If he missed a slow roller, the next day he's out there early and we're working on slow rollers. If he missed a backhand, the next day we're working on backhands. This guy would be the first one to admit, 'I need to work on that,' or, 'I didn't approach that ball the right way, so let's go work on it.' And that's why he's such a great player."

The hardest worker on the team, however, also established himself as the one requiring the most maintenance. One of the first things Rodriguez did as a Yankee was to ask for his personal clubhouse assistant. The Yankees typically employ four or five young adults in their clubhouse and another three or four in the visiting clubhouse to run all sorts of errands, such as picking up and washing dirty laundry, cleaning and shining spikes, ordering and stocking clubhouse food, etc. They are drones known as "clubbies" to the players. Rodriguez wanted his own clubbie. The Yankees had never heard of such a request. Rodriguez was familiar with one particular visiting clubhouse clubbie from his visits to Yankee Stadium when with Seattle and Texas and asked that the clubbie be reassigned to attend only to his needs.

"But Alex," said Lou Cucuzza, the visiting clubhouse manager, "he works for me. I need him."

Rodriguez and Cucuzza struck a deal. The clubbie would still work primarily in the visiting clubhouse but also would be considered "on call" for Rodriguez to use him on an as-needed basis. The as-needed part virtually became a full-time job. Rodriguez would have his personal clubbie lay out his practice and game clothes each night, in the manner of a dresser for a king. When Rodriguez needed something—such as a bottle of water during batting practice or stretching—he would call his clubbie and the clubbie would come running.

One time, in Detroit, where his personal attendant was not available, Rodriguez was jogging off the field after batting practice, saw a Comerica Park visiting clubhouse attendant, a young kid in his first months on the job, and simply barked, "Peanut butter and jelly."

"He always wanted his guy assigned to him," Cucuzza said. "I knew a little bit about what he had in Texas, where there was a strained relationship between his guy and the equipment guy. It can be tough trying to run a clubhouse. But we know Alex wants that. It's a comfort thing for him. When Alex does need something, we try to get it done. The bottom line is to keep the players happy."

The championship Yankees, though, never had such a needy player. The maintenance that Rodriguez required was not a huge distraction, but it did raise some eyebrows in the clubhouse.

"He definitely needs more attention than anybody else," Cucuzza said. "Does it cause a problem? Early on we had heard the rumors about when he was in Texas, when he was the one-man show. But you come into the Yankees and it's a whole lot different than the Texas Rangers. You still need to fit in. You didn't see that [neediness] with the Yankees.

Jeter was a product of the old regime. He's definitely low maintenance. Rocket was low maintenance. He could tell you in May who he was leaving tickets for in August. It was all written down."

Rodriguez's neediness included being liked by his new teammates, but the maintenance of Alex Rodriguez required so much work—the look-at-me mannerisms on the field, the personal clubhouse valet, the phoniness of trying too hard to say things to the media that sounded bright or insightful— that it turned off teammates. He was hyperaware of how he looked to others and how he was perceived. It was a self-awareness that crept into his at-bats in clutch situations, causing performance anxiety, and his teammates knew it.

Two seasons into Rodriguez's term with the Yankees, word reached Torre that Rodriguez had complained to a team official that he didn't feel accepted on the team. So one day in spring training Torre found Rodriguez alone in the clubhouse food lounge and sat next to him to talk about it.

"I'm somewhat naïve," Torre said, "because I'm not in that clubhouse all the time. I'm mostly in my office and when I am out there everybody seems to be on their best behavior when I walk through. But I said to him, 'Alex, do me a favor: at least go get a cup of coffee by yourself, instead of sending somebody to get you a cup of coffee.'

"A little while later he goes out of his way to find

me. He's carrying a cup of coffee. 'Look, skip' he said, 'I got my own cup of coffee!' That wasn't even the point. It was just an example. The point was, just be one of the guys. He didn't get it.

"But see, Alex needs that. He needs to be that level above. That's been the intimidating part of being with the Yankees because he's up there in the rarified air, but so are a lot of those other guys. How much money he makes? That doesn't mean anything to them."

By the end of May in the 2006 season, a small group of players were complaining to Torre about how Rodriguez did not fit the team concept of the Yankees. Torre already had engaged in several discussions with Rodriguez to try to help him become "one of the guys." Nothing seemed to work.

"His goal was to be the best player in baseball," Torre said. "He was very much aware of what was going on elsewhere in baseball. He seemed cluttered up with these things."

No one doubted that Rodriguez was a hard worker and a great player who wanted to win. He won two Most Valuable Player Awards in his four years playing under Torre and rarely missed a game. But coupled with his will to win was a neediness to be noticed, to acquire as much status as possible, and to be liked—and the best way to measure his quest for such attention was through his individual statistics. In a Yankee clubhouse still vainly trying to hang on to what was left of the core values of the championship teams, the A-Rod way seemed awkwardly out of place.

"I can relate to some of the things Alex feels," Torre said. "Obviously, I was never as talented as Alex, but my self-esteem was based on what I did on the field. It feels like that's what's going on with him.

"He could never walk away from this game and all of a sudden have people talk about somebody else. Jeter could just disappear and go sit on a quiet beach somewhere and not be bothered.

"And it's sad because I know when I played, even in my good years, if I went 0-for-4 and didn't get a hit in a key situation, I wouldn't even want to go out to dinner. I felt damaged, I guess. I let people down. It took me a long time to get over that. With Alex, it's a lot different because he will conjure up in his mind that it wasn't that way. He'll disappear into his dream world and reason with himself.

"But Alex is all about the game. He needs the game. He needs all of those statistics. He needs every record imaginable. And he needs people to make a fuss over him. And he's always going to put up numbers because he's too good. It means a lot to him, and good for him."

When Rodriguez won his first MVP as a Yankee, in November of 2005, Torre called him to congratulate him. This was right after the Yankees lost the Division Series to the Angels, during which Rodriguez batted .133 with no runs batted in and flogged himself by saying he had "played like a dog."

"Alex, this thing is always going to haunt you because people are always going to find reasons not to give you credit, even winning the MVP," Torre told him. "I'm proud of what you did and you should be proud of what you did. You're never going to satisfy people. Just understand that. It sort of makes the criticism easier to deal with."

Rodriguez then held a conference call with reporters upon the announcement of the award, and this is what he said: "We can win three World Series (and) with me it's never going to be over. My benchmark is so high that no matter what I do, it's never going to be enough."

Torre saw the comments and shook his head.

"I told him he could never satisfy people to give him perspective. No good could come from him making that idea public. I just wanted him to understand that I and his teammates appreciated what he did."

———

Rodriguez may have had his quirks and foibles, but those were trivial matters compared to the biggest issue his presence brought to the Yankees clubhouse: the uneasy dynamic between him and Jeter. It was a problem for both of them. For Rodriguez, the problem was that he knew he was a better player than Jeter but he could not enjoy anything close to

Jeter's preferred status in and out of the organization. Jeter had the Yankee pedigree, the four championship rings, the captaincy, the national endorsements and that off-the-charts likability factor that flummoxed Rodriguez. Jeter didn't hit or field like Rodriguez, so for a guy who measured himself by his statistics, Rodriguez wondered how Jeter could be held with so much more reverence than himself. In his own way, Rodriguez was fascinated with Jeter, as if trying to figure out what it was about Jeter that could have bought him so much goodwill. The inside joke in the clubhouse was that Rodriguez's preoccupation with Jeter recalled the 1992 film **Single White Female,** in which a woman becomes obsessed with her roommate to the point of dressing like her.

During the World Baseball Classic in 2006, a clothes designer who was friends with Gary Sheffield gave some USA players designer jeans in a hip-hop style. Jeter and Rodriguez received their jeans in Tampa. One day, while Team USA was working out in Arizona, Rodriguez noticed the designer jeans hanging in Jeter's locker. "Oh, you're wearing those?" he asked Jeter. Rodriguez promptly had his jeans overnighted from Tampa to the team's training base in Arizona.

"I think Alex fit into the clubhouse that first year," Borzello said. "I just don't think he fit in anywhere else. I don't think he fit in, especially with the media. It just didn't work. He didn't understand it.

I think he had to realize that what you had done up to that day didn't mean anything to the fans. I mean, you didn't do it here so no one cared. I think that was something he had to adjust to.

"Plus, he didn't do all that well by his standards. I just think it was a constant struggle for him to do like Roger tried to do, show everyone how good I am. 'You guys know, but watch.' And trying to do it, we weren't able to succeed that year for the most part."

The problem for Jeter with Rodriguez in his clubhouse was not so much the **Esquire** article. Those quotes were three years old by the time the two of them became teammates, though as Borzello said, "Derek is a very stubborn person, and he doesn't have a lot of people he allows close to him. And when he does, if you burn him, I think he's very resentful of that. He opens the door for so few people that when he does open the door for you and you screw him over, in his mind, he becomes much more guarded."

The bigger problem for Jeter was discovering what Rodriguez was like as a teammate. Jeter already was chagrined to see the camaraderie of the championship teams disintegrating around him ever since O'Neill, Brosius, Martinez and Knoblauch left after the 2001 World Series. He could look around the clubhouse in 2004 and 2005 and see random veterans who just seemed to be passing through, people such as Kevin Brown, Kenny Lofton, Randy Johnson and Tony Womack. Rodriguez, with his hyper self-awareness, was the most visible and controversial symbol of the Yankees moving further away from what Jeter knew as the definition of championship teams. Jeter and Rodriguez were wired way too differently—saw very different versions of what it took to win—for the Yankees to recapture that togetherness of the championship years.

"Their motivations are completely different," Mussina said. "It will always be that way. I mean, there's nothing wrong with either one of their motivations. It's just that it's not the same motivation. And I think that group that Derek learned to play with—O'Neill and Tino and those guys—the motivation was all the same. They knew they weren't the greatest players in the league, but they knew if they did their job as a group, they could win.

"Derek's not the greatest player in the league. Even in his best years. But he knows how to win. He knows how to get the hit in the big spot. He knows what it takes. He knows how to run the bases. And he's got pedigree now. And it doesn't matter to him what the consequences of failure might be. There's no fear of that.

"Alex may end up calling attention to himself, but he's not loud about it. Alex has this motivation to be the best player in the game. When all is said and done, he wants to be the best player ever. That's his motivation in this. That's fine. That's good. Everybody needs a motivation, whatever it is."

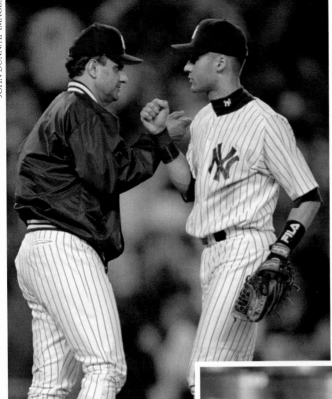

The unquestioned star of the Yankees was shortstop Derek Jeter, who combined Hall of Fame–level skills with a team-first mind-set, a ferocious competitive drive, a willingness to play hurt, matinee-idol looks, and an aptitude for great plays in key situations. The bond between Torre and Jeter was unshakable.

Torre handled the notoriously brutal New York media with aplomb and honesty.

Early on, Torre stood up to owner George Steinbrenner, earning his respect. Steinbrenner was unpredictable and volatile, but the emotional owner gave Torre space as long as the Yankees kept winning championships.

Torre often was criticized for his management of the pitching staff, mostly involving players who had not earned his trust. But for years, the Yankees were successful because the team rarely lost when leading after six innings.

Steinbrenner and the front office people in Tampa often tried to get to Torre by attacking his coaches, especially pitching coach Mel Stottlemyre and bench coach Don Zimmer. Zimmer would leave with some bitterness after 2003.

The Yankees' storied past was both an inspiration and a burden to the team and to Torre. Yogi Berra had stayed away from the Stadium for many years after a feud with Steinbrenner, but returned often after a reconciliation, to the delight of the fans.

Reggie Jackson was a special advisor to the team. He tried to help Alex Rodriguez with the pressures of being a superstar in New York.

Torre considered General Manager Brian Cashman a good friend, but by the end of his time in the Bronx they had grown apart.

The incredible 1998 season, in which the Yankees won 114 games in the regular season, was highlighted by David Wells's perfect game on May 17, 1998.

Scott Brosius was the MVP of the 1998 World Series, in which the Yankees swept the Padres.

Another title season in 1999, another perfect game, this time by veteran righthander David Cone.

1999 was the first season Roger Clemens pitched for the Yankees. He won two World Series titles and a Cy Young Award in 2001 but later allegations about steroid use would cloud his legacy with the team.

The dynamic between Jeter and Rodriguez never was an open war that sent collateral damage flying about the rest of the clubhouse. Indeed, they operated more along the lines of a cold truce. But everybody in the clubhouse could feel the frost emanating from the Jeter-Rodriguez dynamic.

"I don't think it's helped the team," Borzello said. "That team is a machine, though. It's resilient. You deal with so much there that most things don't faze you. You come in, do your thing. There are enough guys who do get along well that I don't think anyone is fazed by it. I don't think other players care that those two got along. It was never arguing or shouting. It was just sort of a cold shoulder.

"It doesn't help. You would rather that the stars are in the same place, pulling together, but I don't think it affected the other players. It just affected the feel in the clubhouse, and it separates the team off the field because Alex is going to go one way with a group of guys, Derek is going to go another way with a group of guys, and it's never going to be a group of 10 or 12 or 15 guys together."

Said Bowa about the relationship between Jeter and Rodriguez, "I think it's workable, but it is what it is. I saw the article they're all talking about, and obviously Derek took it real personal, and if Alex could do it over again, he'd probably redo it. He wouldn't say that. I think Jeet has gradually forgiven him a little bit, but I don't think they're ever going to be, as they say, buddies."

The bottom line was that Jeter and Rodriguez were vastly different people. Jeter did not care too much about his statistics and place in history; Rodriguez was consumed not only about his status in that regard but all things baseball.

"He's a fan of baseball first, and he happens to be a great player," Borzello said. "But he's a baseball fan. Whether he ever made it in baseball, he would be watching baseball all day long if he could.

"I'm telling you, we'd go from Yankee Stadium after the last out, get in the car, talk about the game, go to his house and watch the West Coast games on the baseball package.

"I remember him going to Derek Jeter's house once, me and him. He was going to get a haircut. Jeter had someone who cut hair at his house. So we went over there and we sit down and Alex turns on the TV, waiting for the guy. And Jeter's walking around. And Alex goes, 'Where's the baseball package? Jeet, what channel is the baseball package on?' And Jeter goes, 'I don't have that stuff.' And Alex goes, 'How come you don't have the baseball package?' He couldn't believe it, like, 'What else do you do?'

"So it was just so funny because Derek will never watch a baseball game other than the one he's playing in. They're just complete opposites. I remember Alex's reaction to it was like, 'How is that possible?'"

The third year of Jeter and Rodriguez living under the same clubhouse roof was the worst—"I could feel the tension," Bowa said—and never more so than on the afternoon of August 17, 2006, for a game at Yankee Stadium against Baltimore. The Orioles hammered the Yankees that day, 12-2, dropping the Yankees' first-place lead over the Red Sox to 1½ games on the eve of an enormously important five-game series in Boston. In a signature moment, easily the worst moment of the blowout defeat to Baltimore, neither Rodriguez nor Jeter attempted to catch a pop-up between the two of them on the left side of the infield. When the ball plopped to the infield dirt, neither bothered to immediately retrieve it. Instead, in silence, they sort of turned their backs to one another, each one of them as if in protest for not just letting the ball drop without an attempt to catch it, but for adhering to a completely different doctrine on what it took to win. They seemed at that moment, with a baseball landing between them, to have absolutely nothing in common.

Torre kept the clubhouse door closed after that game to air out his team, while specifically calling out Jeter and Rodriguez.

"I don't know who wants to catch that thing," Torre said, "but **somebody** has to catch the son of a bitch. It looks horseshit. It looks like you don't care. I don't know whose fault it was and I don't care. The only thing I know is that it can't drop. So you guys better figure it out.

"Now we all have two ways to go from here,

going up to Boston. If you take this up there, the way you just played, you're in trouble. Basically, you better leave this shit here. This was shitty. There's no excuse for it. We stunk. Now let's see what we're made of."

The Yankees would sweep all five games from Boston in Fenway Park, essentially salting away another division title.

———

After the game with the pop-up debacle, Cashman consulted with Torre on not only that play but also the Jeter-Rodriguez dynamic.

"Cash totally blamed Jeter on the basis of the shortstop having priority on a pop-up," Torre said. "There were times I had to defend Jeter. Cash went over backwards sometimes thinking the captain should be more proactive than what Jeter wanted to be in the relationship with Alex. I know I'm a little partial to Derek, so you have to take it into consideration, plus he's hurt and he still plays. He never looks for anything more than going out and playing. I'm not saying he does things one hundred percent of the time that he should do. But as far as competing, he's always there for you."

Cashman was already miffed with Torre and Jeter for not throwing enough public support toward Rodriguez during a three-month slump that summer in which fans at Yankee Stadium booed the third baseman with gusto. Rodriguez hit .257 over

the slump and played awful defense, kicking groundballs and bouncing throws. The New York newspapers reflected his poor play with headlines such as:

"Do You Hate This Man?"

"Personal Hell for Alex Is Getting Worse by
the Day"

"E-Rod"

"K-Rod"

"Alex gets a hit . . ."

Cashman looked to Torre and Jeter to help get
Yankees fans off Rodriguez's back. He told Torre,
"You've got to tell Derek he has to come out and
support Alex and tell the fans to leave him alone."

"I can't do that," Torre said. "Because if you ask
Jeter to do that and he starts doing it, then people
will say, 'Why didn't he do that last year?' I can't do
that. He's a teammate. He and Alex know each
other. It's not like he needs to get to know this guy
or he's misreading him. They've been together long
before we met them."

Torre wasn't going to ask Jeter to tell the fans to
ease up on Rodriguez. He wasn't going to ask Jeter
to do something he didn't want to do anyway.

"My job as a player is not to tell the fans what to
do," Jeter said then. "My job is not to tell the media
what to write about. They're going to do what they
want. They should just let it go. How many times
can you ask the same questions?"

Jeter was asked if he had seen anyone criticized
as much as Rodriguez.

"Knobby," he said, referring to error-prone former second baseman Chuck Knoblauch. "Clemens for a whole year. Tino."

Has A-Rod's treatment been worse?

"I don't know," he said. "I don't think about that. I'm just concerned with doing what we can to win. That's it. I don't worry about that other stuff."

Shortly before the pop-up episode, Rodriguez agreed to meet with Reggie Jackson over dinner. Jackson was concerned that Rodriguez was tone deaf to what was happening in his own clubhouse. Jackson knew that players were trying to help Rodriguez to get on track, whether it was at the plate or fitting into the team structure, but that Rodriguez wasn't getting the message because he was convinced that everything was perfectly fine.

Jackson began by telling Rodriguez he knew what it was like to struggle as a Yankee, and knew it to be much worse than what Rodriguez had known. Jackson said teammates would leave notes in the clothes in his locker telling him they didn't want him on the team. He told Rodriguez that manager Billy Martin so beat it into his head that he was a bad defensive player that on the night he famously hit three home runs in the 1977 World Series Jackson played a routine double to right field into a triple out of sheer passivity caused by fear he'd screw it up. Jackson also relayed a story that he once was mired in such an embarrassing, horrific streak of strikeouts that when he stepped into the batter's box he said to Tigers catcher Lance Parrish, "Tell me what's coming and I promise I'll take a turn right back into the dugout no matter where I hit it. I just want to look like a pro a little bit." (Parrish replied, "Fuck you"; Jackson, to his immense satisfaction, managed to ground out.) Reggie wanted A-Rod to know he really didn't have it that bad.

Jackson later told this parable to make a point about how Rodriguez refused to admit he was struggling or to accept the advice of teammates: A man is trapped in his house as floodwaters rise. Twice he refuses help, once from rescuers in a boat and then, when the man seeks refuge on his roof, from rescuers in a helicopter.

"No, thanks. I've got faith," the man said each time.

The next thing he knows the man is face-to-face with God in heaven.

"But I put my faith in you!" the man cried.

"Yes," God replied, "and I answered your faith and tried to help you twice!"

The Yankees soon reached the point of frustration in their effort to help Rodriguez. Jason Giambi came to Torre and said, "Skip, it's time to stop coddling him."

Recalling that conversation, Torre said, "What Jason said made me realize that I had to go at it a different way. When the rest of the team starts noticing things, you have to get this fixed. That's my job. I like to give individuals what I believe is the room they need, but when I sense that other people are affected, team-wise, I have to find a solution to it and take an approach that is a little more serious."

Torre asked Rodriguez to sit down with him in his office in the visiting clubhouse in Seattle. He wanted to snap back Rodriguez from this false world he lived in, to have Rodriguez recognize what everybody else in the room did: that he was struggling and needed help.

"This is all about honesty," Torre told Rodriguez. "And it's not about anybody else but you. You can't pretend everything is okay when it's not. You have to face the reality that you're going through a tough time, and then work from there."

That night, batting as a pinch hitter, Rodriguez struck out to end the game. He pounded the dugout railing with his bat on his way back to the dugout, walked up the runway and into the clubhouse and picked up a folding chair and threw it.

The trouble for Rodriguez as a Yankee was that everything he did, and especially everything that he didn't do, such as hitting in the clutch, winning a championship or staying out of tawdry gossip items, was compared and contrasted to Jeter, the Yankee template. Rodriguez, though recognized as the more talented player and certainly the far better slugger, could not win the comparison. With the Yankees under Torre, for instance, Jeter outhit Rodriguez with runners in scoring position, .311-.306, outhit him with runners in scoring position with two outs, .316-.274, outhit him in the post-season, .309-.245, and outhit him overall, .317-.306. Cashman, who had traded for Rodriguez and understood the value of his enormous production at bat, wanted to believe in Rodriguez, which meant the blame would go to Jeter if a pop-up fell between them or if the fans would not stop booing A-Rod. Torre, on the other hand, trusted Jeter like a son, and never did get the same sense of reliability from Rodriguez.

"My relationship with Derek has been great," Torre said. "Whatever I've asked him, he's been about as reliable as you can get. With Alex . . . When I'm having my annual charitable dinner, for the Safe at Home foundation, I only invite a few players, guys who live around New York, because it's in the off-season and I don't want guys to feel like they have to fly in, except when we honored the 1996 or 1998 team. So Alex said to me, 'Skip, why don't you invite me to your dinner?'

"I said, 'Alex, your wife is pregnant. I don't want to invite you if it means taking you away from her and from home. You're certainly welcome to come. We'd love to have you.' He said, 'I'll be there.' He canceled the day before based on his wife being due so soon. It didn't surprise me."

9.

Marching to Different Drumbeats

Joe Torre called Bernie Williams and Kenny Lofton into his office one day in the Yankees' 2004 spring training camp and closed the door. The two veterans, both competing for the center-field job, sat in upholstered chairs across from Torre, with the manager's desk between them and Torre.

"Guys," Torre said, "we've got a dilemma here."

The Yankees had signed Lofton that winter to a two-year, $6.2 million deal, essentially because they didn't trust Williams any more to be their everyday center fielder. Williams had batted .263 in a season in which he had missed 42 games after knee surgery. The Yankees' front office suspected that an aging Williams should be transitioned to life as a designated hitter, an idea Torre wasn't ready to endorse completely.

The Yankees had just watched Juan Pierre and Luis Castillo help the Marlins beat them in the 2003 World Series by giving Florida speed at the top of the lineup, and Lofton was the Yankees' attempt at a copycat move. It was a poor attempt. The signing was fraught with misguided thinking. For one, Lofton, then 36, was older than Williams, 35, and there was no evidence that he was an upgrade on Williams. Even in an injury-shortened season, Williams hit more home runs, drove in more runs and posted a better on-base percentage in 2003 than Lofton. Moreover, Lofton had turned into a baseball transient, unable to stay rooted with any team in the decline of his career and unwilling to concede he was no longer an everyday player. In 27 months he was the property of six teams, moving from the Indians to the White Sox to the Giants to the Pirates to the Cubs to the Yankees.

Lofton tried to be somewhat diplomatic and obligatory on a conference call with reporters to announce his signing. "If they want me to park cars," he said, "I'll do that." But Lofton wasn't about to start doing any grunt work in his baseball career. He thought of himself as a proud, All-Star-caliber center fielder and nothing else short of that. When Lofton was asked on the conference call about the possibility of replacing Williams, a Yankee icon, in center field, he replied, "They said they want me to play center field. I am a center fielder and they know that."

That was true enough, but was Lofton a better center fielder than Williams? Maybe, but maybe not. What was true was that the Yankees had signed an older player with a checkered reputation who was not clearly better than Williams.

Before the signing was announced, Torre called up Williams and told him, "We're getting Kenny Lofton. That doesn't mean anything is set for center field. We're going to start the season with the best center fielder, whoever that is."

It was a rotten scenario sure to displease both of them. Lofton, who never had accepted being a role player in his career, thought he was being signed to play center field, when actually Torre considered him to be coming to camp to compete for the job. Williams, the proud link to six pennant-winning teams, was stripped of his hold of the center-field job he had held for 10 seasons and forced to compete not with an up-and-coming prospect with young legs, but with an **older** player. But there was another problem, a corrosive one, to the bifurcated center-field scenario, a problem that revealed itself in the spring training meeting in Torre's office.

Every team is asked in spring training to submit to Major League Baseball the names that will be placed on the All-Star Game ballot. Each team is permitted to list three outfielders. The Yankees had Gary Sheffield, whom they had signed that winter as a free agent, established in right field and Hideki Matsui established in left field. No problem there. Center field, though, was an open competition between Williams and Lofton, and baseball officials needed an answer before that competition was to be decided.

General manager Brian Cashman asked Torre, "Who should we use in center field on the ballot?"

Said Torre, "We'll call them both in and work it out."

So Torre brought Williams and Lofton into his office to settle what he thought was a minor, procedural issue. If either one played very well in the first half of the season they would be selected to the All-Star Game anyway, whether they were listed on the official fan ballot or not.

"We've got to put an All-Star ballot together," Torre told Williams and Lofton. "You've both been around long enough. You know if you have a good year you get voted or picked. But right now it's just about being on the ballot and we have to make a decision."

Lofton had yet to play a game for the Yankees. Williams was a franchise star and a Torre favorite. Yet the manager would not favor one over the other.

"Here's what I'm going to do," Torre told them. "You're both All-Stars. You've both done it before. I'm going to put your names into a hat. Whoever comes out of the hat is the guy we put on the ballot."

Williams shrugged nonchalantly, as if to say, "Whatever. Fine." Lofton rolled his eyes and pouted.

Torre put two folded pieces of paper into his hat and started shaking the hat to mix them up. Suddenly one of the folded pieces of paper jumped out of the hat and fell to the floor.

"Let's use that one!" Lofton said.

"All right," Torre said. "Fine."

Torre picked up the piece of paper and unfolded it. He showed it to the two center fielders: "Bernie Williams."

Lofton dropped his head and shook it in anger. Torre was taken aback by Lofton's reaction.

"I thought, What does **that** mean?" Torre said. "He's probably not going to play enough to make the All-Star team, so what the hell's the difference anyway?"

Watching Lofton's reaction made Torre think he could leave nothing open to interpretation about this little game of chance. He reached into his hat and pulled out the folded piece of paper that said "Kenny Lofton" and showed it to him.

"I had to open it up to show him that he was on the other one, to make sure he didn't think there was two Bernies," Torre said. "That was a big deal to him, being on the All-Star ballot. It's too bad. And I had a taste of that kind of thinking on All-Star teams. It was always interesting when you watched all those guys from Cleveland when they came to

All-Star Games. They were so undisciplined. Colon, Manny, Lofton, Belle . . . they were just marching to their own drummer."

That was the real problem. The Yankees no longer had one drumbeat. It was obvious before the Yankees played a game in the 2004 season that the workmanlike, egoless culture of the championship Yankee teams was irretrievably gone. Sure, the Yankees began to change when they said goodbye to Paul O'Neill, Scott Brosius, Tino Martinez and Chuck Knoblauch after the 2001 World Series. But in 2003 they had successfully transitioned into a pitchingdominant team, clearly the best team in baseball until the Marlins, a 91-win wild card team, happened to throw some hot pitchers at them in October. The front office panic after that 2003 World Series did more to send the Yankees into a downward spiral, especially when it came to building a roster with team-centric grinders, than anything that happened after the 2001 World Series.

Not long after the 2003 World Series, Torre gave Brian Cashman a word of advice on Weaver.

"I remember telling Cash, 'You've got to get rid of this guy because emotionally he can't handle it, trying to come back from that,'" Torre said. "It's not like Eckersley giving up the home run to Kirk Gibson or Mariano giving up the home run to Sandy Alomar. This guy wasn't emotionally equipped to deal with that, especially in New York. I had become more comfortable with his pitching, like what he did earlier in that game, than I was earlier. But I couldn't sell it. There was just too much stuff that had happened."

Weaver would never throw another pitch for the Yankees. With a trade that winter, the Yankees turned Weaver into Kevin Brown, one pitcher who struggled with New York for another—only older.

———

In that one off-season the Yankees brought in Lofton, the surly, antisocial Kevin Brown, the infamously moody Sheffield and the needy, status-seeking Alex Rodriguez. In addition, the team shipped off its two best young hitters, Nick Johnson and Juan Rivera, to obtain pitcher Javier Vazquez, who came from Montreal wholly unprepared for pitching under the weight of expectations in New York. Of course, they still had Jason Giambi, the guy with his own personal trainer at his beck and call and who had removed himself from the starting lineup in the previous World Series and then been summoned to appear in front of the grand jury investigating the BALCO scandal. The Yankees were less of a team than ever before in the Torre years and more a collection of individual stars.

"You're mixing together people from all different teams," pitcher Mike Mussina said. "You're not going to get that precise, perfect blend with every group of players you put in uniform. And when you do find that perfect mix, you've got to hang on to it. It hasn't been the same mix, and it's nobody's fault. I don't blame any one player or any group of players for anything. It's just different."

When asked how long the Yankees were able to maintain the right blend of players who kept to the same mindset, Mussina said, "Until '03, until probably even during '03. Then Andy left after '03 and Roger left and Boomer left . . . So when '04 rolled around it was really different. We had very different personalities as compared to the other group, to the group that was here when I first came in 2001."

To the Old Guard of the Yankees, especially Derek Jeter, who had known nothing in his career except 25 guys buying into one mindset, the star system was a jarring change for the worse.

"I don't know if it bothered him or not," said Mussina, who witnessed the breakdown of playoff-caliber Orioles teams before signing with the Yankees, "but I know as a player who has watched good players be on a team, a good group of players, because I had a good group of players in Baltimore for a couple of years in a row, then, to watch a good group of guys just depart and then another group comes in and you see the whole dynamic of the clubhouse be different—be younger, not used to winning or not be about winning, it's about performing—I know it's got to be hard.

"I'm sure for him it was a big change and

especially having Alex, because Alex was the best, highest-paid player in the league, arguably. He was the highest paid, but he was arguably the best player in the league. You've got a new second baseman, you've got a brand-new third baseman . . . that's a lot to deal with."

Said Jeter, "The thing is we were winning and for the most part we had the same group together year and after, you know what I mean? Because we won, we were able to stay together. So as a group, we had pretty much gone through everything together. Whereas in recent years, when we lost, people changed. Different guys were in and out."

It wasn't just that the personnel changed; the culture changed. The tipping point to the end of the championship Yankees' culture, both in the clubhouse and its on-field foundation—strong pitching—was the almost casual loss of Pettitte to free agency. Pettitte was a rare commodity in baseball: he was lefthanded, durable, only 31 years old, coming off a 21-win season and hardened by the postseason experience and daily expectations of having played nine years in New York. Had he made his career somewhere else all those years, the Yankees, given their lustful ways in free agency, would have deeply coveted Andy Pettitte. But George Steinbrenner never did have a warm spot for Pettitte, always withholding his highest praise of calling someone a "warrior" and famously wanting him gone in an ill-conceived trade attempt in 1999.

Steinbrenner's lieutenants, too, constantly worried about Pettitte's throwing elbow, in part because Pettitte seemed to chronically worry about it himself. It was just Pettitte's honest nature to share his feelings about usual aches and pains. Other than the 2002 season, Pettitte's elbow was good enough to allow him to be one of the most reliable pitchers in baseball for almost a decade. From 1995, when he broke into the big leagues, through 2003, Pettitte threw more innings than all but nine pitchers in baseball and tied Randy Johnson for the second-most wins, behind only Greg Maddux.

But Pettitte was baffled by how little interest the Yankees showed in him when his contract expired after the 2003 World Series. For 14 of the 15 days after the World Series in which the Yankees held exclusive negotiating rights with him, the Yankees made no outreach to him. Finally, with Pettitte about to hear from other teams, the Yankees offered him $30 million over three years. Meanwhile, true to the Yankees' penchant of coveting what was not theirs, Steinbrenner occupied himself with personally negotiating a contract with Sheffield as the Astros, Red Sox and other clubs told Pettitte how much they wanted him. It was as if the Yankees were resigned to Pettitte leaving for his hometown Astros. Pettitte, though, said the Yankees' lack of interest in him pushed him toward Houston, ultimately giving Astros owner Drayton McLane his word and handshake that he would accept the Astros' offer of $31.5

million over three years, pending a physical and minor contractual details. Only then did the Yankees swoop in with a $39 million offer over three years, but it was instantly moot because of Pettitte's personal commitment to McLane. (Clemens, emboldened by his friend Pettitte signing with Houston, also signed on with his hometown Astros.) Even now, after having returned to the Yankees in 2007, Pettitte is sure the Yankees did not make a strong effort to keep him after the 2003 season.

"That's definitely how I felt," he said. "I'm so happy to come back here. But, I mean, back then they made the worst offer from among seven or eight other teams. After I already had talked to the Astros and told the owner I would play for him, **then** I get a higher offer. I couldn't go back on my word."

On the day the Yankees lost Pettitte, as if to cover the hit from the loss of one of the most popular Yankees, they completed a trade for Brown, who would turn a broken-down 39 the next March and, according to the 2007 Mitchell Report, had built his reputation as an ace with the help of performance-enhancing drugs that were now outlawed in the game.

―――――

It was shaping up as a miserable off-season for the Yankees. Already they had been caught napping while the Red Sox stole one of the best pitchers available and a guy who would tilt the balance of power in the New York–Boston rivalry. The Arizona Diamondbacks let it be known that they were shopping ace Curt Schilling. The righthander had veto power over any trade, and he told the Diamondbacks he would accept a trade only to the Yankees or the Philadelphia Phillies.

"I remember reading that," said Red Sox general manager Theo Epstein.

Indeed, the Yankees had talked to Arizona earlier that November about a trade for Schilling. The Diamondbacks put Nick Johnson and Alfonso Soriano on their wish list. The talks died, but the Yankees figured it was all part of the give-and-take of negotiations.

But the Red Sox, as they displayed in their wildcat pursuit of Jose Contreras the previous winter, had a new purpose under Epstein and owner John Henry: Be bold. Take nothing for granted. Don't worry about looking stupid. Epstein decided to make a run at Schilling while the Yankees attended to other business. He approached Arizona general manager Joe Garagiola at the general managers' meeting in Phoenix in the second week of November.

"I inquired about Schilling," Epstein said. "I kind of caught them at the right time because Garagiola seemed to be fed up with Schill and was frustrated that he had his hands tied with all the public speculation about New York or Philadelphia.

"I told him, 'We don't control the process. He has a full no-trade clause. But the part we can control is making a trade. Technically, we could make a trade and then bring it to him.'"

Garagiola said he would think about it. Two days later, Epstein called back. He detected some interest now from Garagiola.

"If you're serious," Epstein said, "if you don't mind coming to the altar and getting stood up, we don't mind. Why don't you take a look at our system?"

Garagiola was interested.

"Okay, we'll make you an offer," Epstein said. "It'll be like ordering from a Chinese restaurant menu. You can take two from Group A and two from Group B."

Epstein and his assistants worked up a menu for Garagiola of second-tier prospects. Nineteen-year-old shortstop Hanley Ramirez, who had just hit .275 in A ball, was in Group A. (Ramirez would eventually fetch the Sox Josh Beckett and become one of the biggest stars in the game.) Garagiola said the Diamondbacks liked pitchers Casey Fossum and Jorge de la Rosa from Group A, neither of whom Boston executives feared losing. From Group B he mentioned several names, but settled on Brandon Lyon, an injury-prone reliever, and Michael Goss, a 22-year-old outfielder who hit .245 with one home run in A ball, a guy whom the Red

Sox did not consider to be much of a prospect. Epstein couldn't believe his luck.

He turned to his assistants and said, "Guys, I think we've got something here."

One of them, Josh Byrnes, who eventually would become the general manager of the Diamondbacks, heard Epstein tell them the Diamondbacks were willing to accept Fossum, de la Rosa, Lyon and Goss for Schilling and deadpanned, "What time is the press conference?" It was a no-brainer for Boston.

There was only one problem: the Red Sox had a 72-hour window to convince Schilling to agree to the trade, a window that ran smack through Thanksgiving. The first thing Epstein needed to do was get Schilling on a plane to Boston. He would spread the word through the media of Schilling's trip so that thousands of Red Sox fans would greet him as he stepped off the plane at Logan Airport, an appeal to Schilling's considerable ego.

"There's no way he can say no!" Epstein said, delighted at the plan. It sounded great—until Epstein called Schilling to invite him to Boston.

"Dude, there's no way I'm leaving Phoenix," Schilling told Epstein. "I'm intrigued, but the only ones I really want to consider are Philadelphia and New York. If you want to come out, fine. But I'm not leaving."

Epstein would have to get on a plane to Phoenix.

396 JOE TORRE AND TOM VERDUCCI

He already was running on fumes. He had just finished giving free agent closer Keith Foulke a recruiting tour of Boston the night before, a night in
which they took in a Celtics basketball game and
afterward repaired for multiple refreshments in a
fine Boston establishment. The Red Sox needed a
manager—Grady Little was fired after the 2003
ALCS Game 7 fiasco with Pedro Martinez—and he
had interviewed DeMarlo Hale that day. Former
Phillies manager Terry Francona, considered the
front-runner, was due in Boston any day to take a
physical. Now Epstein, along with assistant Jed
Hoyer and Red Sox president Larry Lucchino,
would be taking an early-morning flight to see
Schilling on the day before Thanksgiving, but not
before Epstein and the baseball operations staff put
together a recruiting game plan.

The first thing they did was draft a letter to Curt
and his wife, Shonda, to be delivered the morning
before the Red Sox contingent arrived that Wednesday afternoon. The letter, signed by Epstein and
Lucchino, ran 1,165 words. It made reference to
how the Red Sox traded Schilling to the Orioles in
1988, and three years later, convinced they had not
make a mistake, the Red Sox had a report from one
of their scouts on Schilling that said, "Still a
thrower. Has arm strength but hasn't learned a
thing."

The letter then praised Schilling for his turnaround from those rough beginnings. Mostly, the

letter served as a substitute for a cheering throng at Logan: an appeal to Schilling's ego.

"At 37 years old," the letter said, "with a great résumé and an even greater reputation, it's clear to us that the next step in your career is baseball immortality. Baseball immortality—an enshrinement speech in Cooperstown, a plaque on the wall, a place alongside legends—is one of the reasons why the Schillings and the Red Sox are such a perfect fit. There is no other place in baseball where you can have as great an impact on a franchise, as great an impact on a region, as great an impact on baseball history, as you can in Boston. It is hard to describe what the Red Sox mean to New England. The players who help deliver a title to Red Sox Nation will never be forgotten, their place in baseball history forever secure.

"We are so close to the goal that has eluded us for 86 years. We would not have traded four young players or intruded upon your holiday if we did not sincerely believe that our time is coming very soon. The 2003 Red Sox were a talented and exciting team that came within five outs of reaching the World Series. As an ownership group and management team, we are committed to putting an even better team on the field in 2004 and beyond."

The letter went on to define Schilling's importance to that improvement, explaining that after the team's goal in 2003 was "to create a lineup that would be relentless one through nine," it now was about creating "a relentless pitching staff to match our offense. You are the key to the plan; in fact, you are the plan."

It concluded, "Curt and Shonda, quite simply, we think this is a great match. The timing and the purpose are perfect for both of us. We hope you feel the same way and we look forward to discussing anything that can help make you and your family more comfortable with Boston. See you this afternoon . . ."

The letter, the appeal to his ego, the attack while the Yankees slept . . . it was all brilliant tactical strategy by a smart, hungry organization. But the Red Sox weren't done yet with the recruitment of Schilling. They were just getting started.

Epstein knew Schilling was "a preparation freak," a guy who appreciated statistical analysis, kept voluminous notes and watched more video than a film critic. Schilling fit the profile, Epstein decided, of the perfect recruit for the techno-savvy Red Sox. Epstein ordered his staff to put together a disk to highlight all of the Red Sox's high-tech video and scouting equipment, which were among the most advanced in the game. In one disk they broke down massive amounts of video of Roger Clemens— Schilling's pitching doppelgänger, what with their four-seam fastball and splitter combination—pitching against the best hitters in the AL East. They also brought detailed scouting reports from one of the largest scouting staffs in baseball.

"This is how we can help you prepare," Epstein told Schilling when he presented the information at Schilling's home.

Said Epstein, "He ate it up."

Epstein also put esteemed sabermetrician Bill James to work. Two weeks earlier, Schilling had told the **Philadelphia Inquirer** that he would not approve a trade to Boston because, "I'm a righthanded fly-ball pitcher. In Fenway Park, that's not a tremendous mix." Epstein knew about that comment. He enlisted James to write a personal letter to Schilling that statistically proved that Fenway actually has been beneficial to righthanded fly-ball pitchers, including Pedro Martinez.

Epstein even came armed with information for Schilling's wife, Shonda, whom he knew to be active in community work. He brought literature on places to live in Boston, on the school systems and on the opportunities for community work.

Epstein also mentioned to Schilling that one of the candidates getting serious consideration for the Boston manager job was Francona. Francona had been Schilling's manager in Philadelphia and the two of them had remained extremely close.

There was one more argument to reinforce: the opportunity to make baseball history in Boston. The Red Sox had not won the World Series since 1918. A world championship for the Red Sox would rank among the most meaningful championships in all of sports. The opportunity appealed to Schilling's sense of baseball history.

"Right away we clicked as far as engaging in a baseball discussion," Epstein said. "The more we talked about his fit with the Red Sox and what it would mean historically, we knew we kind of had him on the hook. Then we had to find a way to make it work."

It was a strange and often tense negotiation at the Schilling house. Reporters, camped on the lawn, could peer through the windows to see Schilling and Epstein negotiating in the living room, and at night they could hear coyotes howling in the foothills of the nature preserve behind the house. Epstein ate Thanksgiving dinner at the Schilling house, but still had yet to gain Schilling's okay to the deal. The Red Sox petitioned Major League Baseball for an addition to the 72-hour negotiating window because of the Thanksgiving holiday, and they were granted one. They had until Friday afternoon to close the deal.

"They were really nail-biting negotiations," Epstein said. "It looked like we were going nowhere. I left after Thanksgiving dinner and I felt there was no way to get it done. We got a little more creative. As tough as the negotiations were, it would have been tougher to walk out of the house without him, knowing he was exactly the right guy for the club, to walk out and do the perp walk in front of all the cameras, all the while knowing we had delivered everything we could on a silver platter."

The persistence paid off. On Friday, the day after Thanksgiving and just in front of the MLB deadline, Schilling agreed to the trade and a two-year contract that would pay him $25.5 million, with a third-year option worth $13 million. There was one special clause added to the contract that, though illegal under baseball rules, somehow slipped through MLB officials. The Red Sox would pay Schilling a $1 million bonus if they won the World Series with him. Players are not permitted to carry award bonuses based on team achievements, but this one managed to become official.

"He'll be a king and a hero if they can win a World Series in Boston," said Diamondbacks owner Jerry Colangelo.

Epstein was ecstatic. He already had a dynamic offense, one that the previous season broke the all-time slugging percentage record of the famed 1927 Yankees. Now he had a strong stable of starters, with Schilling, Derek Lowe, Pedro Martinez, Tim Wakefield, Byung-Hyun Kim and Bronson Arroyo. As a bonus, Schilling was a confident, Type-A personality who brought the same swagger to the mound that players such as David Ortiz, Johnny Damon, Manny Ramirez and Kevin Millar brought to the batter's box.

"The intangibles were a great fit," Epstein said.

"Here was a guy who had pitched and won in Yankee Stadium and in big games. He was obviously fearless. The one thing you knew he was able to do is execute flawlessly, no matter what the situation. And he had a desire to be noticed. He had an ego. He liked being covered by the media, but in a legitimate way. He brought a fearlessness. He basically said, 'I'm going to Boston to end an 86-year curse, and I'll do Dunkin' Donuts commercials to let people know.' I think that rubbed off. That same kick-your-ass mentality we had on offense, Schilling brought that same attitude to the pitching staff."

———

The Red Sox's off-season would only get better. Pettitte left the Yankees 22 days later. Boston was thrilled to see Pettitte leave for Houston. The Red Sox actually had offered Pettitte the most money, more than $40 million. That gambit, however, not only was an unlikely attempt to coax him away from both his career-long team and his hometown team, but also as a shrewd strategic attempt to influence Pettitte's negotiations with the Yankees. How come, Pettitte was left to wonder, the Red Sox value me so much more than the Yankees after all these years in New York? Getting Pettitte out of the league was a victory in itself for the Red Sox, who despite their historically potent offense knew they had some vulnerability to lefthanded pitchers. The 2003 Red Sox slugged 49 points worse against lefthanders than righthanders. Pettitte was 13-5 in his career against the Yankees' greatest rival.

To compound the loss of Pettitte, the Yankees elected not to pick up the $6 million option on the contract of David Wells, yet another proven left-handed pitcher who had thrown at least 200 innings in eight of the previous nine years. Wells was headed toward back surgery to repair a herniated disk, an issue that did not stop the Padres from signing him to an incentive-laden contract in which Wells could earn $7 million. Wells had been 6-5 with the Yankees against the Red Sox.

In two months after a 101-win season, the Yankees had lost Clemens, Pettitte and Wells, who in 2003 had combined to start 60 percent of their games while compiling a record of 53-24. The team lost three starters with a combined career postseason record of 31-17, a .646 winning percentage. One of the greatest rotations in Yankees history, the **SI** cover boys from only nine months earlier, was torn apart.

To replace them, and to the delight of the Red Sox, the Yankees turned only to righthanded pitchers: Brown, who was 39 years old; Orlando Hernandez, who was 38; Jon Lieber, who was 34 and coming off an entire season missed to elbow surgery; and Vazquez, who was 27 and testing himself in the American League and New York for the first time. In 2004 the Yankees did not have a left-handed starter to use against the Red Sox—a flaw that would become fatally and infamously obvious come October—and only one righthander even close to having prime stuff, and that was the disappointing Vazquez.

Moreover, Yankee Stadium was a ballpark designed for lefthanded hitting, which could exploit the short porch in right field, and conversely for lefthanded pitching, which could exploit the vastness of the left side of the outfield against right-hand-dominant lineups. Yet the Yankees were ill-suited for their own ballpark—and by historic measurements. In 2004 the Yankees would use lefthanders (all of them journeymen) to start only 11 of their 162 games, by far their lowest such incidence in the previous half century, eclipsing the 27 starts by lefthanders on the 1992 team, the last time the Yankees fielded a losing club.

"To go from Clemens and Pettitte and Wells and myself to, I don't know . . . ," Mussina said. "I know Kevin Brown was on that staff, but we just couldn't count on him. The mentality was changed."

Said Mike Borzello, the bullpen catcher, "Pitching was the problem. After Pettitte, Clemens and Wells left in 2003, we went to an all-righthanded rotation. That was the beginning of the problem. Vazquez, Brown and then Pavano, Wright, Igawa, Farnsworth, Randy Johnson . . . They just didn't seem to work out. It never felt like we had the upper hand in pitching anymore. Before 2004 we never cared what the matchup was against the other team. We liked our guy against their guy, no matter where it fell in the rotation. But then it never seemed to be in our favor, never a case of 'We've got so-and-so tomorrow. We'll win.' "

———

While the 2004 Yankees marked an abrupt end to the franchise's run of championship-quality starting pitching, the loss of that key strength was exacerbated by what was happening around baseball. Starting pitchers were throwing fewer and fewer innings because of the convergence of several influences on player development, so workhorses such as Pettitte, Clemens and Wells actually were becoming more valuable than ever.

What happened to the workhorse starter? The analytical-minded Red Sox, as they did with most issues, assigned their statistical analysts to try to come up with objective answers to that question. They found that the decline in pitchers' workloads could be traced to manager Billy Martin's 1980 Oakland Athletics. Martin rode five young starters in their 20s into the ground. Rick Langford, Mike Norris, Matt Keough, Steve McCatty and Brian Kingman completed 93 of their 159 starts, a crazy workload. All of them broke down and never were the same. Martin had called so much attention to that staff because of their workload that when those young pitchers broke down, the entire baseball

world noticed. No manager or club wanted the no-
toriety of being arm-killers, so a new conservatism
began to grow.

The trend gained momentum at the end of the
decade when another Oakland manager, Tony
LaRussa, popularized the specialized bullpen, in
which he preferred to entrust late-game outs that
used to belong to a tiring starting pitcher to a series
of lefthanded and righthanded relievers, backed by
a closer. Also, by 1990 "pitch counts" began to appear in box scores, the effect being the placement of
a sort of governor on managers, who now had to
answer to a kind of "pitch count police"—fans and
media who would draw a direct line between an ar-
bitrarily high pitch count and a defeat or poor outing. Moreover, advanced research and data in the
growing field of sports medicine convinced the
medical experts that the greatest risk to a pitcher's
arm health came from overuse. With seven-figure
bonus payouts to amateur draft picks, the default
philosophy became one of increasing conservatism
when it came to pitchers' development and maintenance.

"The young kids, that's what we've conditioned
them to do: pitch less," Torre said. "It's our fault.
You have no choice because it's a bone of contention with everybody. A GM will tell you how
much we have invested in these guys and we can't
hang them out to dry. And even back with how we
were using David Cone in 1999, evidently Billy

Connors would tell George something about his pitch counts and George would scream at me or the general manager.

"To me, the pitch count is another of those number things that don't tell the whole story by itself. You can watch a guy have no problems throwing 120, 130 pitches, but he can throw 90 pitches with men on base every inning and be worn out. So that's where the number of pitches you throw is not indicative of being tired."

The workhorse starter was a dying breed in baseball, one of the most significant changes in baseball from the years the Yankees won World Series championships to the years they didn't. During Torre's 12 years as Yankees manager, here are the number of starts in which a pitcher threw at least 120 pitches:

YEAR	TOTAL	YANKEES
1996	444	20
1997	367	20
1998	458	25
1999	453	29
2000	454	31
2001	231	14
2002	225	12
2003	215	14
2004	183	4
2005	132	9
2006	119	1
2007	80	0

Two significant points emerge from the trend: the decline in 120-pitch games greatly accelerated right after the Yankees won their last world championship, and the decline for the Yankees themselves grew especially steep with that flawed 2004 staff.

Of course, with fewer pitches, starters were providing fewer innings. The number of times in baseball a pitcher worked eight innings, for instance, was cut by more than half in the 10 seasons from 1998 (736) to 2007 (362). Again, the Yankees' decline accelerated beyond the industry average. Their 1998 staff worked eight innings 42 times. The 2004 staff did so only 17 times, and by 2007 they were down to just 10. Perhaps no one disliked the trend more than an old-school guy like Andy Pettitte, who went from a career high of eleven 120-pitch starts in 2000 to zero in 2007.

"He would get real angry at the pitch count thing," Torre said. "We laughed at him. It wasn't a matter of how he would do for the next 10 or 15 or 20 pitches in that game, but how he would come out of it for the next time.

"Even in 2007, on the last Monday of the season, we took him out after six innings and 96 pitches. He was losing, 4-1. I said, 'Andy, it doesn't make sense for you to pitch anymore because we may need you again Saturday if we still need to clinch. I don't want you throwing a hundred-some pitches. I don't need you throwing another 15 pitches.'

"He said, 'Well, let me throw 12 more next inning.'"

Torre didn't budge.

"Eight more?" Pettitte pleaded.

"Get the hell out of here, will you please?" Torre said, laughing.

Said Torre, "He starts screaming at himself going up the runway. It was hysterical."

The 2004 Yankees could have used an old-fashioned workhorse like Pettitte, who was able and willing to go deep into games. Instead, Yankee starters that year obtained 371 fewer outs than did the 2003 rotation, the equivalent of nearly 14 full games less coverage.

The aged, overly righthanded pitching staff turned out to be as fragile as it appeared it was going to be. For only the second time since the franchise began in Baltimore in 1901, not a single pitcher threw 200 innings, won 15 games **or** qualified for the ERA title with a mark below 4.00. (The only other such team devoid of such a modest milestone were the 1988 Yankees, whose staff ranked 12th in a 14-team league.)

In the spring training camp of 2004, however, George Steinbrenner did not see those problems coming with his pitching staff. He was too busy patrolling the clubhouse area with his chest out and shoulders back. Steinbrenner was head over heels happy that spring about getting Rodriguez—especially after the Yankees got him only after the Red Sox blew their chance, when the players association would not allow Boston to renegotiate downward the value of his contract. Steinbrenner was walking around as flush as the high school boy who asks the prettiest girl in class to the prom and she said yes. The warning signs of his disjointed roster went unseen. So giddy was Steinbrenner that one day that spring training he walked into Torre's office and said, "What do you want to do next year?"

Torre was pleasantly stunned. It was an open invitation to a contract extension. Torre was working on the last year of his contract, and even though his Yankees had won four world championships and had come within three wins of owning six titles in nine years, they had not won the World Series in the relative eon of three whole years, and Steinbrenner hadn't breathed a word to Torre about an extension that winter after the Yankees lost the 2003 World Series in six games to Florida. Torre was heading into a lame-duck season with no idea about his future with the Yankees until that day when a starry-eyed Steinbrenner virtually invited him to remain with the team.

Steinbrenner then put his son-in-law, Steve Swindal, in charge of the negotiations of Torre's extension. It was a major assignment for Swindal, his first high-profile task in the crosshairs of the New York media. The assignment in part was designed to prepare Swindal for eventually running the team as Steinbrenner's successor.

"I certainly saw it as a great responsibility," Swindal said. "I didn't connect it to years later, that I am the heir apparent. That didn't cross my mind. I felt enormous responsibility to the fans. It was also important that Mr. Steinbrenner knew Joe and I had a very good relationship, built on mutual respect and trust.

"We were working on a two-year deal. At the last minute Joe said, 'What about an extra year?' I personally supported a third year. I said, 'I'll see what The Boss said.' He was supportive of it.

"Then we talked about a personal services contract added to it. Joe felt he wasn't going to manage after the three years, that he would retire. His thinking in this was that it would be his last contract. So we thought we could be creative and structure it in a way that it had added value. I used the quote, 'retire as a Yankee.' I thought it would be something that would be historical and appealing to him."

The Yankees announced on April 10 that they had signed Torre to a three-year, $19.2 million contract extension that carried him through 2007, with six additional years in which he would be paid $600,000 per year as a consultant. But the two sides never could agree on that postmanagerial portion of the contract.

"So I streamlined it, and making it cleaner I just told Steve Swindal, 'I'll split it with you. One-point-eight you put into my contract and you keep 1.8.' And that's what happened."

"I reported to George and George was pleased," said Swindal. "When we did the deal it made him the highest-paid manager in the history of the game. But I personally felt that Joe was a part of the Yankee magic and aura and had shown his success on the field and how he handles himself with the media. He had a part in our attendance rise and our success. All of that. I think he has a calming effect, through injuries, losing streaks . . . that calming influence. We've had teams of superstars and he had the ability to make everybody feel like one team rather than a collection of individuals. He had the ability to make the team feel as a team. That's his best attribute. He was always calm in rough moments."

The collection of egos and ailments that were the 2004 Yankees would test Torre like no other Yankees team. Once the season began, the off-season moves looked no better on the field than they did on paper. Lofton, almost predictably, would have been better put to use making good on his offhand offer to park cars for the Yankees. He broke down with leg injuries, complained about his spot in the batting order (Torre sometimes batted him ninth) and complained about not being the everyday center fielder (surprise!). Williams earned the bulk of the playing time in center field, and even while fighting wear-and-tear injuries to his knees and shoulders he posted better on-base and slugging percentages than Lofton, the man who was brought in to replace him.

As Giambi's body continued to break down, journeyman Tony Clark, 32, was Torre's most-used first baseman. Another journeyman, Miguel Cairo, 30, played second base and yet another, Ruben Sierra, 38, saw most of the time at designated hitter.

Alex Rodriguez struggled through what would have been a fine season for most players, but one that for him was his worst since 1997, when he was 21 years old. He introduced himself to Yankees fans by hitting .248 with runners in scoring position, including .206 with two outs in those spots, the kind of trouble in clutch spots that would become their knee-jerk association with him. There was no honeymoon for Steinbrenner's prize acquisition.

———

Worst of all, the pitching staff, with its 4.69 ERA, was pedestrian, clocking in slightly worse than the league average of 4.63. The Yankees put up numbers that equated to an 89-win team, according to the Pythagorean formula developed by James, the statistics guru. Torre, however, like a pilot landing a jet on a bobbing aircraft carrier in stormy seas in the dark of night, somehow delivered the Yankees to a second straight 101-win season, keeping them three games ahead of the Red Sox, who repeated as the American League wild-card entrant.

The best player on the team turned out to be Sheffield, whom Steinbrenner wanted instead of Vladimir Guerrero, against the preference of Cashman. Sheffield, 35, was eight years older than Guerrero, whose free agency was complicated by a back injury during the 2003 season, though Guerrero had returned to terrorizing pitchers at his normal rate when he rejoined the Montreal Expos lineup after that injury. Steinbrenner dealt with Sheffield directly, giving rise to the notion that he wanted to do well for a fellow longtime resident of Tampa.

"I know Cash wanted Guerrero, which is fine," Torre said. "My feeling was that I knew for sure that Sheffield wasn't going to be bothered by New York. Guerrero was coming from Montreal. If it was short term I wanted Sheffield. If it was long term I wanted Guerrero."

The Yankees signed Sheffield to a three-year, $39 million contract, with an option for a fourth year. The Angels signed Guerrero to a five-year, $70 million deal, with an option for a sixth year. The word that reached Sheffield after his signing was that Torre preferred Guerrero instead of him. The thought gnawed at Sheffield, even two months into the season. By May 26 a sullen Sheffield was hitting only .265 with just three home runs. The Yankees were playing in Baltimore that night. Sheffield walked into Torre's office at Oriole Park at Camden Yards.

"I just have to know something," Sheffield

told Torre. "Who wanted Guerrero and who wanted me?"

"I'll tell you exactly what I said," Torre told him. "If it's short term, I want you. If it's long term, I want him, because he's younger. But I've always respected you. As the opposing manager you scare me when you get to the plate. So if I feel that way, then I want you on my side. I'm telling you exactly what the conversation was. Whether you choose to believe it or not is up to you."

"Okay," Sheffield said. "I'm committed."

Sheffield instantly became a different player. That same night he whacked four hits, including a home run, and drove in six runs. The outburst started a 17-game stretch in which Sheffield hit .406 with seven home runs and 24 RBIs. It was classic Sheffield. His mood and his production could turn in an instant.

"It happened that night," Torre said. "It was like he turned it on. And he told me, 'Don't worry. I'll deal with everything.' Because if you notice, he never charges the mound or anything like that. He takes it out on you on the field. But that night in Baltimore, all of a sudden he started becoming a player and a ferocious hitter and a gamer. He played hurt, did all that stuff."

Sheffield was the fulcrum of a punishing offense that led the league in home runs and walks and finished second—to the Red Sox—in runs. By the end of the season Torre had stacked the top of his lineup with a devastating run of All-Star hitters: in order, Jeter, Rodriguez, Sheffield, Matsui and Posada. Giambi sometimes cracked the lineup, though he was a shell of himself, having missed half the season largely due to a benign pituitary tumor.

The Red Sox, however, could match the Yankees' thunder, and then some. They outscored the Yankees by 53 runs over the course of the season. Their biggest advantage, though, came from pitching. Boston's staff was the third best in the American League. New York's staff ranked sixth.

For a second straight year, the Red Sox and Yankees were on a collision course to meet in the American League Championship Series. The Yankees dismissed the Twins in the Division Series in four games. The Red Sox flicked aside the Angels even more handily, taking three straight from them. The New York–Boston rivalry was the epicenter of October baseball yet again, just as it had in 2003, although this time it would be as much about the previous November and December as anything else. The Yankees would try to beat Boston without a single lefthander in their rotation, or anyone in their rotation with pure strikeout stuff against a power-packed lineup. The Red Sox were fortified by Schilling, one of the best big-game pitchers in baseball, who was the grand prize for having outflanked the Yankees in November. Schilling had been everything the Red Sox had hoped, winning 21 games for them and fronting a remarkably strong and durable rotation. Schilling, Martinez, Lowe, Wakefield and Arroyo did not miss a turn, taking all but five of Boston's 162 starts.

The Yankees once commanded postseason series because they were so deep in starting pitching. By the 2004 ALCS, those days were over. The Red Sox had flipped the table on the Yankees. They had the superior pitching. The rivalry was about to take a turn of legendary proportions.

10.

End of the Curse

The Yankees–Red Sox rivalry may have been the best thing to happen to baseball, but both managers came to loathe it. Each time the Yankees and Red Sox would play one another, even in April—hell, even in **spring training**—there was an Armageddon quality to the proceedings. Baseball never was designed to be like this, not until October, anyway. The sport took great pride in the sheer volume of the season; "a marathon," as the players proudly liked to call it. But every game between the Yankees and Red Sox brought an NFL-like urgency to every game, every inning, every pitch. It ran counter to everything Joe Torre and Terry Francona tried to impress upon their clubs, knowing the wisdom of keeping their team on an even emotional footing. After just about every time the Yankees and Red Sox were done with one of these series, either Torre would call Francona or Francona would call Torre.

"Are you sick of this yet?" Torre would say.

"I'm glad it's over," Francona would say.

"You and me both, pal," Torre would reply. "See you in about six weeks."

Torre and Francona shared not only a unique vantage point to the rivalry, but an honest friendship. Torre had played with Francona's father, former big leaguer Tito Francona, and had recommended Francona for his first managing job with the Phillies to Philadelphia general manager Lee Thomas.

"I played with Terry's dad so I felt a closeness to him for that reason," Torre said. "I can still think of him as a kid. And I remember recommending him to Lee Thomas. Terry knew baseball, he was cerebral, and he wasn't showy. He was just a basic, good baseball person."

Torre and Francona believed that the whole Yankees–Red Sox dynamic had grown so big and so emotional that the managers dreaded it.

"It would wear you out," Torre said. "We had a common bond, because we both would feel the same way. We're both going through the same pressures. There really is no favorite. There's no one team that's clearly better than the other. It's like Michigan–Ohio State. It's doesn't matter how good your teams are. You're supposed to win. Each side.

"It's the media coverage that can wear you out. It's one game on the schedule and I know it's Boston. I know it's a team in your division. But I think the rivalry got out of hand as far as magnifying every single thing that went on in the game. It's absolutely exhausting. And you know what's interesting? The game is tense, but the game is even tenser only because you know you're going to have to explain the outcome in every small detail. The game itself, though, is great. It's everything else that wears you out."

From the time John Henry bought the Red Sox in 2002, when Boston began to make the commitment to look the Yankees in the eye and be a worthy rival, to the start of the 2004 American League Championship Series, when the Red Sox could best measure that progress, the Yankees and Red Sox had played 64 times, including the titanic 2003 ALCS. Each team had won exactly 32 of those 64 games.

Both teams had made significant in-season alterations to their clubs to get to the ALCS. For the Yankees, it meant dumping the object of the intense and expensive international bidding war they had engaged in with the Red Sox less than two years earlier: righthanded pitcher Jose Contreras. The big man who was supposed to be an ace for the Yankees struggled with his command and the subtleties of pitching, such as pitching out of the stretch and holding runners. He also had a particularly harmful and unforgiveable flaw with the Yankees: he could not pitch against the Red Sox. Contreras was 0-4 with a 16.44 ERA against Boston.

"He showed sparks of great pitching here and there," Torre said, "but he had a phobia against Boston and Boston just whipped his ass. He was tipping his pitches against them. They were in his head. They waxed him. They just waxed him.

"His stuff was good, but he had a lot of issues that I felt had to do with pitching in New York. I had gotten to the point where I said, 'He just can't help it.' He just didn't seem comfortable in New York."

On July 31, 2004, the day of the trading deadline, the Yankees were on their way toward beating the Orioles, 6-4, at Yankee Stadium when Brian Cashman called Torre.

"We can get Esteban Loaiza for Contreras," Cashman said.

Torre quickly checked with pitching coach Mel Stottlemyre before getting back on the phone with his general manager.

"Do it," Torre replied.

Loaiza was something of an enigma himself, and as a player with free agent rights after the season, only a rental return on the investment in Contreras. Loaiza was 9-5 for the White Sox but with a pudgy 4.86 ERA. The Yankees were his fifth team in seven years. He was 32 years old. Loaiza had won 21 games the previous season, but it was the only year in his life he won more than 11 games. In short,

Loaiza was nothing more than a spot starter. The Red Sox once had bought up all the rooms in a hotel to try to keep Contreras away from the Yankees, but now here was the celebrated El Titan de Bronze ingloriously being dumped for a rotation filler. And the Yankees didn't think twice about it. Neither did Contreras. Though he held a no-trade clause, he waived it without asking anything in return.

"At that time we were just looking for someone who could go out there and pitch," Torre said. "We could score runs. Our plan with our pitching was, 'Let's just try to stay in the game,' but even that didn't work sometimes.

"I didn't realize it when I first got to New York, but after having been there a little bit I understood that playing in New York was unlike playing in any other place. People either really embraced it, or they just really had a problem with it. I think Kenny Rogers had a problem with it. David Justice did well with it. Roger Clemens, after a bit, did all right with it. Randy Johnson, no way. I have to put Contreras in the group that had trouble with it."

———

The Red Sox made an even bigger, more stunning move on that same trading deadline day. Epstein organized an elaborate trade web of four teams involving seven players in order to dump an erstwhile star of his own, shortstop Nomar Garciaparra. The

Red Sox obtained shortstop Orlando Cabrera from the Expos and first baseman Doug Mientkiewicz from the Twins as part of the exchanges. That trade brought more dividends for Boston than the Contreras deal did for New York.

"We had a fatal flaw," Epstein said. "Our defense was terrible."

Under Epstein and Henry, the Red Sox not only embraced statistical analysis but also developed propriety formulas to measure performance. When they ran the numbers on Garciaparra's defense that season, they were astonished at what came out. He was, by a long shot, the worst defensive shortstop in the history of their database. The Red Sox did not rely solely on the numbers. The numbers were backed up by the observations of Red Sox scouts who occasionally checked in on their own team.

"Whether because of age or injury, he just wasn't getting to balls he normally did," Epstein said. "The pitching was really taking a hit, especially a groundball guy like Derek Lowe, in ways that you can't always see. We knew that teams that win the World Series typically have pretty rangy shortstops. Really, it was our whole infield defense that needed to be addressed."

The other element pushing Boston toward dealing Garciaparra was that he no longer seemed to be a perfect fit in a clubhouse that had become a band of crazy extroverts, who would become famously self-described as "idiots." Garciaparra was more the quiet, brooding sort, especially ever since spring training of 2003, when the Red Sox offered him what he considered to be a below-market contract extension.

"He was understandably upset," Epstein said. "He became isolated."

When Epstein put Garciaparra on the trade market, only one team, the Cubs, showed any interest at first. They offered to send Boston 24-year-old outfielder David Kelton, but they also wanted to swap pitcher Matt Clement for Lowe. Epstein said no thanks, and furiously went back to work. He eventually pulled enough strings to wind up with Cabrera and Mientkiewicz, two players renowned for their defense.

"Two minutes before the deadline I thought it was dead," Epstein said. "I must have made four dozen calls in the last half hour. It ended up happening right at the deadline. We thought it was the right deal. We knew Cabrera was good offensively but was underperforming. What we knew about his personality convinced us he would have no problem being put on the big stage with everyone watching. It was just what we needed. And we thought our firstbase defense had been equally shaky.

"We got two guys hitting about .230 at the time, but we thought it was what we needed. We had power, we had a really good pitching staff, but defense was killing us. These guys were exceptional defenders. It helped. Our starting pitching got on a huge roll. Starting in mid-August, they went 30-13."

If the Red Sox had outmaneuvered the Yankees the previous November, they had done so again in August. After the deadline deals, the Red Sox were the best team in baseball over the remainder of the regular season (42-18), 5½ games better than the Yankees (36-23).

"Over that year, for sure, I thought they were a better ballclub than us," Torre said. "But the games in the postseason have nothing to do with the season. At that point in time, you throw everything out the window. We certainly were conditioned enough to know that there was nobody on the field that could beat us. I mean, they got our attention and I'm sure we got their attention."

Boston's sweep of the Angels in the Division Series allowed the Red Sox to align their rotation to have Schilling and Martinez open the first two games of the ALCS at Yankee Stadium. It sounded great for Boston. Schilling, however, was a diminished pitcher. He had hurt himself while pitching in the Division Series, tearing a tendon sheath in his right ankle. A wholly ineffective Schilling was gone after three innings in Game 1, having buried his team in a 6-0 hole.

One out into the seventh inning, the Yankees led 8-0 and Mike Mussina was throwing a perfect game. The Red Sox suddenly showed their might, and before the Yankees could get five more outs it was 8-7 and Boston had the tying run at third base and Kevin Millar batting. Torre brought in Mariano Rivera and that was the end of Boston scoring. He retired Millar on a pop-up and the Yankees wound up winning, 10-7.

The Yankees also won Game 2, though they did so in far different form, with Lieber besting Martinez in a classic pitcher's duel, 3-1. Once again, Torre gave the ball to Rivera with a runner on third and one out in the eighth inning, and the great closer locked down another victory.

There would be no need for Rivera in Game 3. The Yankees won, 19-8, with a prodigious show of hitting in a game that had been tied after three innings, 6-6. The Yankees were rolling, up three games to none, a lead no team in the history of baseball ever had lost.

———

All was not perfect, though. Yankees starter Kevin Brown, who was supposed to be the ace of the staff, and who had battled back problems most of the year, had pitched horribly and did not look right. In only two innings, Brown gave up four runs on five hits and two walks before Torre sent Vazquez to replace him to start the third inning. (Vazquez, too, was hammered, yielding four runs on seven hits and two walks in 4⅓ innings.) It was only the latest episode to explain why Brown engendered no confidence from his teammates. Brown had a famously rotten temper and a surly disposition, attributes that did not serve him well at a time in his career when he could no longer throw as hard as he once did and didn't have the wherewithal to concede to his age and battered body in order to make adjustments.

Brown had missed seven weeks over the summer because of a strained lower back and also because of an intestinal parasite. On September 3, pitching against Baltimore, Brown was staked to a 1-0 lead when he gave up a run in the second inning, yielded another in the third, tweaked his knee while covering first base in the fifth, and was struck on the right forearm by a run-scoring hit in the sixth that stretched the Orioles' lead to 3-1. It was all too much for him and his short fuse to bear. After getting out of the inning, Brown stormed off the field and straight up the runway leading to the clubhouse. Stottlemyre, knowing Brown's low boiling point, and concerned about the shot the pitcher took off his arm, decided he should walk back to the clubhouse to check on the righthander. He found Brown standing in the narrow hallway outside of Torre's office, seething.

"Are you okay, physically?" Stottlemyre asked him.

"What's it look like?" Brown snapped back.

Brown wheeled away from Stottlemyre, walking into the main portion of the clubhouse. He stopped at a concrete pillar and hauled off on it, throwing a hard punch. Brown quickly bent over in pain, holding his hand.

"Tell me that wasn't your right hand," Stottlemyre said.

Brown didn't answer. Stottlemyre thought he saw that Brown was holding his left hand.

"Are you all right?" the pitching coach asked.

Still no answer. Brown kept ignoring his coach.

"Kevin," Stottlemyre said. "I need to know if you can go back and pitch or not. You gotta tell me something."

Brown looked down at his hand. Finally, he spoke.

"No," he said. "I'm not all right."

Stottlemyre knew the first order of business was to alert Torre because the Yankees would need to get a pitcher ready to replace Brown. He walked down the runway, back to the dugout.

"Joe," he said, "you're not going to be too happy with your pitcher."

"What'd he do?" Torre asked.

"He punched a wall," Stottlemyre said. "Might have broken his left hand."

Now Torre left the dugout and headed up the runway and into the clubhouse. He found Brown and immediately began to scream at him.

"That's the most fucking selfish thing I've ever seen anybody do!" Torre said. "I have no patience for that shit!"

"I'm sorry," Brown said.

Torre's anger and tongue-lashing quickly sub-
sided. He saw that the man in front of him was a
beaten man.

Said Torre, "At that point he was so demoralized.
He was never a fighter. He never wanted to fight
you. Neither was Randy Johnson, for that matter. I
like Kevin Brown. The difference between Kevin
Brown and David Wells is that both make your life
miserable, but David Wells meant to. I don't think
Kevin Brown meant to. I don't think Randy meant
to. And that's what I go on."

Brown came back from the broken hand to
make two starts before the end of the regular season, the first of which was a nightmare against
Boston in which he couldn't get out of the first inning. The Red Sox pounded him for six hits and
four runs in that abbreviated time. Brown simply
generated no good feelings from his team, and
ALCS Game 3, while ending up in a blowout victory, continued with Brown as the carrier of bad
karma, hardly the role the Yankees had in mind
when they traded for him and his $15 million per
year salary to take the sting out of losing Pettitte
and to provide a return volley to the Red Sox for
getting Schilling.

Buried within the Game 3 win was another troubling sign. Torre brought in setup reliever Tom
Gordon to pitch the ninth inning with the score
19-8. It was the third straight game in which Gordon was used. Why would Torre use his key eighth-

inning reliever in a blowout? Gordon badly was in need of a confidence boost. He appeared jittery in both Game 1 and Game 2, giving up two runs and failing to pitch cleanly in both outings. Torre thought giving him the ninth inning, with nobody on base and an 11-run lead, would relax Gordon and give him confidence that would carry over into the next time Torre needed him in a tight spot. Nonetheless, Gordon still appeared on edge. With one out he gave up a double to Trot Nixon. Then he uncorked a wild pitch. He did strike out Millar and retired Bill Mueller on a fly ball to end the inning without a run scoring. It represented progress for Gordon, but only by a small step.

Vazquez, Brown and Gordon all had struggled, but how much could that really matter at this point? The Yankees led the series three games to none. The Red Sox were as good as dead. In the history of Major League Baseball, the NBA and the NHL, teams trailing 3-0 in a best-of-seven series were 2-231. The Red Sox had a 0.85 percent chance of winning the series. The only teams to recover from the bottom of that well were the 1942 Toronto Maple Leafs and the 1975 New York Islanders. The Yankees were starting Orlando Hernandez in Game 4, the veteran righthander with a 9-3 career postseason record. The Red Sox were starting Derek Lowe, who had pitched himself out of the postseason rotation and was only getting the ball because the scheduled Game 4 starter, Tim

Wakefield, pitched in relief in Game 3 to save Francona from blowing out his bullpen in the rout.

A few hours before Game 4, Epstein watched Schilling muster his way through a bullpen session at Fenway Park, using a special bootlike spike to try to give support to his wobbly right ankle. No one was sure if he could pitch again in the series. Actually, no one was sure there were going to be any more games in the series.

On his way from the bullpen to the dugout, Epstein was stopped by reporters on the warning track, down the right-field line. They had obituaries and epitaphs to write about this Red Sox team and they wanted the team's general manager to cooperate. Epstein wasn't playing along.

"Guys," he pleaded. "We have one game to win tonight. That's our focus."

The line of questioning didn't end. A columnist, with the sound of the Yankees' bats still ringing in his ears after the 19-8 shellacking, asked Epstein, "Is what happened yesterday an indictment of the lack of professionalism in your clubhouse, especially contrasted to the Yankees? Is that a sign that you can't win with the kind of lawlessness in your clubhouse?"

"Guys," Epstein said, barely concealing his anger, "we might not win, but it has absolutely nothing to do with our makeup."

Epstein marched off into the clubhouse. He was hot. It wasn't the reporters that bothered him most.

It was how everything invested in this season, going back to the motivation to redeem the Aaron Boone game, to the stealth securing of Schilling, to the hiring of Francona, to the bold trade of Garciaparra . . . all of it could be washed down the drain without winning so much as one game against the Yankees.

"It was just a thought in the back of my head that wouldn't go away," Epstein said. "I was so pissed off about the possibility of getting swept. I'm thinking, I cannot fucking believe a team this good that played so well down the stretch and could so easily win the World Series is going to be swept by the Yankees. We cannot let it happen."

When Epstein looked around the room he saw reason to be encouraged.

"They were still really loose," he said of his players. "They had incredible makeup."

Millar, the first baseman who was always quick with a quote, a laugh or a joke, was walking around the room saying the same thing over and over again: "Don't let us win one! Don't let us win one!" It became the idiots' rallying cry.

As Millar recounted, "I was thinking, You better beat us in Game 4, because if we win it . . . look out. I didn't like our matchup in Game 4. I didn't know how we were going to do it, but don't let us win. Because now we've got Pedro in Game 5 and now we've got Schilling in Game 6, and in Game 7 anything can happen. So I knew once we could win that game, the entire pressure went to them. We didn't have any pressure. We were supposed to lose. We're down. Now we're just having fun. Now we're going to watch them choke. That's basically what it boils down to. We're going to have fun and keep battling. And those were great games."

The Yankees scored first, on a two-run home run by Alex Rodriguez in the third inning. It would be the last time Rodriguez drove in a base runner in the postseason in this series **and the next three postseasons combined,** a span of 59 at-bats overall in which he batted .136, including 0-for-27 with 38 total runners on base. The Yankees lost the lead when Boston nicked Hernandez for three runs in the fifth, then seized it right back with two runs in the sixth. The tie-breaking run scored on an infield hit by Tony Clark. Torre put the 4-3 lead into the hands of Tanyon Sturtze, not Gordon, and Sturtze came through with two scoreless innings.

Now the Yankees were six outs away from sweeping the Red Sox, with the heart of the Boston order due up in the eighth inning. Torre was absolutely sure who was going to get those outs: Rivera. Gordon's shakiness didn't even come into play now. Torre's closer was fully rested after three days off. Torre always worried about giving a near-dead opponent any reason for optimism. Rivera, even for six outs, was the surest option in baseball, the king of postseason closers. It was time to step on the throat of the Red Sox.

Rivera yielded a single to his first batter, Manny Ramirez, but it was classic Rivera for the rest of the eighth inning: three consecutive outs on 13 pitches (15 total for the inning) without the ball leaving the infield (a strikeout of David Ortiz and groundballs from Jason Varitek and Trot Nixon).

The Yankees went quietly in the top of the ninth against Keith Foulke. Three outs to go. The Yankees held an extreme advantage over Boston. In all best-of-seven series games, the road team leading by one run with three outs to go was 77-11, an 87.5 percent success rate. Representatives from Major League Baseball Properties carried large boxes into a back room of the Yankees clubhouse. The boxes held dozens of hats and T-shirts that said, "New York Yankees. 2004 American League Champions." There was no champagne being prepared yet. The Yankees were so experienced at those kind of celebrations—and so cautious not to jinx them—that their clubhouse staff learned to wait for the last possible out; they could set up for the party in under 10 minutes.

As Rivera prepared himself to leave the dugout to pitch the ninth, Torre thought of passing on to him a word of warning about the leadoff hitter, Millar. He thought about having Stottlemyre, or even himself, tell Rivera to be aggressive with Millar. He let the moment pass without saying anything. It is a decision that gnaws at Torre to this day.

"If there's one thing I can second-guess myself about," Torre said, "it was in 2004 with Mo going out in the ninth inning. I didn't tell Mel, 'Tell him don't get too fancy.' Or I was going to go to him and tell him, 'Don't get too fancy. Go after him. Don't worry about trying to make too good of a pitch.'

"The only reason I didn't say anything is I remembered the last time he faced him, in Game 2."

Rivera had faced Millar, representing the tying run, with Ramirez at second base, with two outs in the ninth inning of Game 2. The at-bat was relatively brief and emphatic: called strike, ball, strike swinging, foul, strike swinging for a strikeout to end the game.

"That's the only reason I didn't plant the seed," Torre said. "Because of how easy that at-bat was. I said, 'Fuck it.' Because I didn't want to plant a seed that wasn't there. It was so easy, the last time."

That Game 2 at-bat, however, occurred at Yankee Stadium, where Millar's pull-everything hitting philosophy was penalized by the expansiveness of left field. The Game 4 at-bat occurred at Fenway Park, where a fly ball to left field could easily be off or over the towering wall that seemed to loom right over a pitcher's shoulder.

"In that ballpark, you're trying not to make a mistake to him," Torre said. "It's a little different than in our ballpark."

On the other side of the field, Francona did not bother to say anything to Millar.

"No," Millar said. "There's nothing to say. In that situation, we're down by one, we're down 0-3 in the series, you've got Mariano Rivera in the game . . . there's not a lot of sunlight on us. But you know what? That's why you've got to play the game."

Millar was a .364 career hitter against Rivera in the regular season, with four hits, including one home run, in 11 at-bats, while also once getting hit by a pitch. Most hitters would begin the ninth inning while down one run trying to find any means possible to get on base, to grind out an at-bat in survival mode. But these were the idiots and this was Millar, who was one of the premier practitioners of the kind of brazen idiocy that served the Red Sox so well. There was only one thing on Millar's mind: try to jack a Rivera pitch over the Green Monster in left field.

"I've always had good at-bats against Mo," Millar said. "Decent numbers. But you don't want to make a living facing him. He's a power guy and I like the fastball, so I was just thinking one thing: get a pitch up and middle-in and hit it out for a home run. That was my thought process. Just try to hit a home run. There was no looking away. So I was basically in watch mode. If I could just get something up and leaking in and I was trying to pull, I thought that was our only chance. That's what I felt."

The "watch mode" approach served Millar well. Because he was going to swing only if the ball entered the area in which he was watching, Millar actually made himself patient. The downside of his approach is that he essentially conceded the outer half of the plate to Rivera, at least until he got two strikes. Rivera never got to two strikes. He missed with his first pitch. Millar fouled off the next. Then Rivera missed with three consecutive pitches, putting the tying run on first base with a free pass.

What were the odds that Rivera would walk the leadoff batter? Through 2004 in his regular season career, Rivera had faced 110 leadoff batters in the ninth inning while protecting a one-run lead. He had walked only four of them, and only twice did those walks presage a defeat. One of them occurred only one month earlier against the Red Sox, a game that suddenly looked eerily predictive. On September 17, Rivera began the ninth inning by walking Nixon with a 2-1 lead. Dave Roberts pinch-ran and stole second base as Varitek struck out. Rivera hit Millar with a pitch. Cabrera knocked in Roberts with the tying run. One out later, Damon knocked in the winning run with a single. Millar's walk in Game 4 gave the Red Sox that shred of belief that Torre wanted to avoid.

"You're looking in," Millar said of his approach, "and the thing is sometimes when you're aggressive at the plate in an area like that, your hitter's instincts will be to lay off. Whereas sometimes when you think you have to cover too much of the plate you start chasing more. I was just actually looking for one pitch. I was looking dead red and in. When you're facing Mariano you just hope he's not hitting his spots and you might have a chance. He's definitely tougher against lefties. He's not blowing up bats against righties that he does to lefties."

Francona sent in Roberts to run for Millar. Roberts was on his own, meaning he was free to attempt to steal second base whenever he thought he could get the bag. Roberts, however, was chilled, stiff and a bit jittery from sitting out the game for nine innings. Fenway Park, built in 1912, has no adequate area for someone to fully prepare himself for pinch-running on a cool night. Roberts had done the best he could, running in the narrow, short, wet concrete hallway that leads from the Red Sox dugout to a stairwell that winds to the clubhouse. When Roberts reached first base he had no intention of stealing second base on the first pitch; on September 17 he had waited until the third pitch.

Rivera made a pickoff throw to first base. Roberts got back easily. Then Rivera threw over again, and this time the play was a little closer. And then Rivera threw over for a third time, and this time it was closer still. Something unintended and important had happened with that sequence of three consecutive throws to first base: Roberts was now warm and his legs were loose. Rivera had done him a favor. Roberts now was fully immersed in the flow of the game. His plan had changed. He made up his mind to steal on the first pitch.

There was no fourth pickoff attempt. Rivera threw home with a pitch to the batter, Mueller. Roberts ran. The pitch was a ball. Jorge Posada, with a quick release, loosed a strong, accurate throw to second base. Jeter caught it, very close to the bag, and put a tag on Roberts. But it was too late. Roberts reached the base barely before Jeter applied the tag. The Red Sox had the tying run in scoring position with no outs.

Mueller was a .375 career regular-season hitter off Rivera, with three hits, including a walkoff homer July 24, 2004, in eight at-bats. Mueller took the next pitch for a strike, evening the count at 1-and-1.

"I give Tito a lot of credit for not bunting," Epstein said. "Back then Mariano really didn't use his sinker away to lefties. So if Bill Mueller makes an out, it's likely to be a groundball to the right side that gets him over anyway."

On the next offering from Rivera, Mueller grounded a hard single over the mound, over the second-base area and into center field. Roberts came bounding home with the tying run. The Red Sox were alive.

What were the odds? Through 2004 in his regular season career, Rivera had faced 231 lefthanded hitters with a one-run lead in the ninth inning. In only 10 such cases did Rivera blow the lead. Mueller was the only batter responsible for two of those failures: a single on May 28, 2003, and his walkoff home run three months earlier.

It was all so improbable. There was only a 3.6 percent chance Rivera would walk the lead-off batter in the ninth with a one-run lead. There was only a 4.3 percent chance he would lose such a lead while facing a lefthanded batter. And yet both of those occurrences, like the two longest shots in a daily double, had come through and paid off for the Red Sox. There was still a long way to go to get there, but was it somehow possible that even that longest of long shots, the 0.85 percent chance that a pro sports team could come back from being down three games to none, was suddenly in play?

"You start feeling it's possible after the walk," Millar said, "but the biggest at-bat of the whole thing was by Billy Mueller. You hear about the walk. You hear about the stolen base, but who drove him in? Billy Mueller got a single to drive in the son of a bitch. Then you hear about Ortiz's walkoff off Quantrill and Ortiz's at-bat against Loaiza, but Billy Mueller had the greatest at-bat of the postseason."

The Yankees would still have chances to win the game, getting four at-bats with the go-ahead run in scoring position in the 11th and 12th innings.

Every one of those at-bats ended in failure, by Rodriguez (line-out), Williams (fly-out), Clark (fly-out) and Cairo (strikeout).

Gordon, pressed into duty, gave Torre two shutout innings. Paul Quantrill, the Yankees' fifth pitcher, started the 12th. Ramirez greeted him with a single. Ortiz ended the long night with a walkoff home run.

"Everything flipped with that game," Millar said. "One hundred percent. I said that before the game."

The Yankees had not heeded Millar's warning. They had let the idiots win Game 4.

"I am very uncomfortable at that point," Torre said. "I mean, everybody else feels better than I do. We still have a three games to one lead. But the fact is we had our closer on the mound and we let them breathe."

The Yankees were in position to win Game 5, too. Trailing 2-1 in the sixth against Martinez, Jeter swatted a three-run double, yet another game-changing play in his long history of clutch post-season moments. But somehow, with multiple chances, the Yankees never scored again over what would be eight more agonizing innings. A series of bad breaks and bad at-bats began that same sixth inning, when the Yankees reloaded the bases after Jeter's double. With two outs, Hideki Matsui drilled a line drive into right field. Nixon, fighting the encroaching twilight, somehow found the ball and caught it for the third out.

"If that ball isn't caught, it opens up the game," Torre said. "It's over. Of course, when anything happens like that, I think it's a bad sign, because you never have enough runs."

The Yankees looked as if they would add to that 4-2 lead in the eighth inning, too. Cairo led off with a double against reliever Mike Timlin. Torre ordered Jeter to bunt him to third base to give Rodriguez a shot at bringing home a big insurance run. Again, the Red Sox had no fear pitching to Rodriguez with a base open, and Timlin rewarded their confidence. Timlin fanned Rodriguez on five pitches.

"Timlin just blew him away, basically," Torre said. "That to me stood out more than anything. It was not being able to get that third run."

Sheffield walked after Rodriguez's whiff, then Matsui lined out again, this time to left field, to end the threat.

Still, the Yankees had a two-run lead with six outs to go to end the series. What were the odds they could blow that? Among the 766 postseason games in best-of-seven series to that point, road teams with a two-run lead with six outs to go were 67-10, representing an 87 percent success rate. The Yankees still held a firm grip on the series. The game was in the hands of Gordon, who had pitched to one batter in the seventh, getting a double play. Gordon had been excitable all series, so unable to calm his anxieties that he had been throwing up in the Yankees bullpen before coming into the game.

"Flash always got very excited in the bullpen," said Borzello, the bullpen catcher. "There was nothing different about that game versus any other. Flash is high-strung and cares a lot. I don't think it's fear. I think it's more just the anxiety of not being out there yet. This moment is coming, and he knows it's there, and he gets anxious. I think he just reacts to that. I don't think he's scared. He's not afraid of anything, and he wants the ball, and he wants to win. People want to paint that as he was scared. I don't see that at all."

Gordon coughed up more than his lunch. His second pitch of the eighth inning was hammered by Ortiz for a home run. Now it was 4-3. Gordon then managed to get two swinging strikes on Millar, but then threw four consecutive balls to put the tying run on first base with no outs. To complete the symmetry of another key walk by Millar, Roberts replaced him as a pinch runner. Gordon fell behind Nixon, 3-and-1, and then Nixon slashed a single up the middle. Roberts scooted to third base. Gordon had faced three batters in the eighth inning with a two-run lead and retired none of them, going home run, walk, single. Torre brought in Rivera in what technically would be recorded as a blown save, but Rivera did well to get out of the jam—first and third, no outs—with only one run scoring a sacri-fice fly by Varitek.

"It's a blown save, but it certainly wasn't his fault," Torre said. "Tom Gordon, for whatever rea-son, was a mess out there."

The Yankees would never lead again in the series. They did nearly win it in the ninth when Clark smashed a two-out hit into the right-field corner that appeared would score Ruben Sierra from first base. But the ball hopped into the stands for a ground rule double, and Sierra was ordered stopped at third base, whence he stayed when Cairo lofted a foul pop-up for the third out. It was another bad sign for the Yankees.

They kept wasting chances in extra innings, too. In the 11th inning, with a runner at second base, Jeter lined out and Rodriguez flied out. In the 13th, Sierra struck out with runners at second and third. The longer the game went on, the tighter the Yan-kees looked. In extra innings they went 2-for-18 against four Boston relievers while striking out in half of those at-bats.

In the 14th inning, Torre had Loaiza, his seventh pitcher, on the mound for his third inning of work. Loaiza walked Damon with one out. He walked Ramirez with two outs. Then, on the tenth pitch of the at-bat and the 471st pitch of the game—which came five hours and 49 minutes after the first one—Ortiz smacked a base hit up the middle to send home Damon with the winning run.

The Yankees were stunned. They led the series three games to two but to everyone involved now it felt as if they were chasing Boston. They had played two games at Fenway that lasted a total of 10 hours, 51 minutes, two games in which they held leads in the eighth and ninth innings that statistically gave them win probabilities of 87.5 and 87 percent—and somehow they had managed to lose both of them. "It was draining," Torre said. The Yankees were going home to Yankee Stadium for Game 6, and their mission had changed, becoming psychologically more heavy and complicated. They were no longer trying to win the series. They were trying not to blow it.

The Yankees had Lieber to face Schilling in Game 6. Unbeknownst to the Yankees, Schilling had undergone an unprecedented medical procedure to keep the torn tendon sheath in his ankle from flapping open, a temporary suturing of the sheath that had been tried as an experiment on a cadaver. No one was sure if the suturing would hold up. Indeed, even as Schilling started to warm in the bullpen, blood started oozing from the area of the incision and through his white sanitary sock. There was some speculation that the Yankees would test Schilling's mobility early in the game by bunting on him. But Torre, unaware of the true extent of the injury, spoke to his team before the game about taking the same approach they always did against Schilling.

"I basically said, 'I don't believe this whole injury aspect of it,' Torre said. " 'You go out there and play your game.' We had pretty good success against him. So I didn't want to do anything different. 'Let's make him make the adjustment.'

"We just had to go play the game. And I just tried to add perspective, that we're home and that we have a 3-2 lead. But it's very difficult when you lose a couple of games. You sort of lose your footing."

The Red Sox, meanwhile, only grew bolder and looser with each win. Millar decided before the game that the team would not take batting practice on the field before Game 6.

"It was raining," Millar said. "It was like 47 degrees. They always play **Yankeeography** in New York on the videoboard. As a visiting player, you see that they get music to hit to and when we come up we get Yogi Berra and Mickey Mantle all the time."

Millar walked into the office of Francona.

"We're not hitting on the field today, Skip," Millar said. "We're not falling for the **Yankeeography** crap."

Francona barely looked up from his desk.

"Whatever you guys want," the manager replied.

The idiots were running the asylum.

As Millar walked out of the office, something caught his eye. "A big bottle of Jack Daniel's," he said. Millar got an idea. The Red Sox would all drink a pregame toast for good luck. He started pouring shots for guys into paper cups. Two days earlier the Red Sox were stuck at the bottom of a dark well from which no baseball team ever had recovered: trailing a best-of-seven series three games to none. And now here they were in Yankee Stadium, essentially flipping the finger at Yankee history as presented in **Yankeeography** hagiology, and lifting paper-cup shots of whiskey to toast themselves and their audacity.

"It was more of a joke, more just messing around," Millar said. "It's not like we got drunk. That's what I got heat for, people thinking we got hammered. We did a toast. The next thing you know, we won."

Schilling, on one good ankle and one gruesome one, was spectacular. This game was the very reason why Epstein had recruited him over Thanksgiving dinner. Schilling fired seven strong innings in which he allowed only one run, and that was a home run by Williams in his last inning, and permitted just four hits and no walks. The Yankees never did bunt on the man with the bloody sock. Boston won, 4-2, scoring all of its runs in the fourth inning, three of them on a two-strike, two-out, opposite field home run by Mark Bellhorn against Lieber.

"We had a little role reversal with Boston," Giambi said. "Until they got Schilling to go with Pedro, we could beat them. Then once they had that extra guy, that's what turned the table for them. That's where they turned the tide on us."

The series was tied. The Yankees had the look of one of those cadavers that made possible the procedure on Schilling's ankle. Torre had a huge problem as soon as Game 6 ended: he still did not know who was going to pitch for the Yankees in Game 7. The Yankees' lack of reliable starting pitching had come to a head. Over the previous winter the Angels had signed Bartolo Colon, the Astros had signed Pettitte, the Red Sox had stolen Schilling out from under the Yankees, and the Yankees had lost Clemens, Pettitte and Wells and replaced them with . . . Brown, Vazquez, Lieber, Hernandez and Loaiza. Mussina and Lieber were not available because they had pitched Games 5 and 6. Torre had no good options.

Hernandez wasn't an option at all. El Duque had told Stottlemyre he was not available on two days of rest after throwing 95 pitches in Game 4. (Lowe, his opposing starter who threw 88 pitches in that same game, was Boston's pick to start Game 7.)

Loaiza wasn't an option, either. He had only one day of rest after throwing 59 pitches out of the bullpen in Game 5.

Vazquez had three days of rest after throwing 96 pitches in less than five innings in his shaky relief outing in Game 3. Torre could not trust him. The Yankees thought Vazquez, who turned 28 that summer, would be exactly the kind of young gun their staff needed. He did look the part for half of a season, going 10-5 with a 3.56 ERA and earning Torre's selection for the All-Star Game. But mysteriously, and with no apparent injury, Vazquez became completely unreliable. He went 4-5 with a 6.92 ERA in the second half of the season.

"The biggest shock for me was Vazquez," Torre said. "He pitches Opening Day, I picked him for the All-Star Game, and it was ridiculous where he went after that. He was a huge pitcher for us, because all of a sudden we were getting younger. I remember Cash said to me, 'I can get Randy Johnson from Arizona, but they want Vazquez.' I said, 'I wouldn't make that deal.' That's what I thought of him early on. Later on, after the season, you could go ahead and give him up."

So Vazquez really wasn't an option to inspire any confidence. That left Kevin Brown, the 39-year-old pitcher with the bad back, the carrier of bad karma, and the guy who looked hurt and ineffective in Game 3 in only his fourth game since breaking his left hand in a childish fit of anger. Were the Yankees really going to trust Game 7 to Brown? Not even Torre was sure of that. The Yankees were never sure of his brittle physical condition. As soon as Game 6 ended, Torre went looking for Brown in the clubhouse. He found him in the players' lounge off the main clubhouse. Brown was sitting at a table, just past the bar area, with his back to the door of the clubhouse. Torre sat down in a chair across from him, with his back to the wall. Stottlemyre pulled up a chair, too. Other players were milling about.

"I was just trying to make a decision," Torre said. "We're trying to keep from choking to death at that point. Because Lieber pitched pretty well but he gave up the three-run homer to Bellhorn and that was the difference in the game. Everybody was as tight as a drum, which was understandable, because we had lost three games in a row."

Torre looked Brown in the eye and said, "You tell me: Can you pitch tomorrow? I don't need a hero. I need somebody who can do the job."

It was virtually the same speech Torre gave to a worn-down Clemens in the training room before Game 5 of the 2001 Division Series. Clemens assured Torre he could do it that night, and gave him five good innings.

"That's basically what I was hoping for from Brown, something to sort of settle the game," Torre said. "But he was so unlike anything I thought he was supposed to be. I watched him pitch in Texas and his shit was so good . . . But he was never satisfied with his stuff. He had issues. It was sad."

Torre continued with Brown.

"I need a pitcher tomorrow," he said. "You're one of my choices. I'm not going to give you the ball unless you understand what we need to do here. You need to look at me and tell me."

"I'll take the ball," Brown said.

Said Torre, "He gave me a positive response. I would have given it to Vazquez if I sensed it was something like, 'Well, if you want me to . . .' I didn't get, 'If you want me to.' To me, he was willing to take on the responsibility."

The Yankees' season, and the possibility of warding off the greatest collapse of all time, had come down to this: they were giving the ball to Kevin Brown, a guy with a bad back, and a guy his teammates did not particularly trust, understand or like.

"I thought, It's over," Borzello said. "It's over because Kevin Brown had no chance at all and neither does Javier Vazquez or anybody else. It's over. I remember standing in the outfield with Mussina and a couple of other guys during batting practice and we were just talking about it. 'We have no chance. There's just no chance of winning this game. We lost the series.' I remember that. I remember just standing in the outfield in Game 7 like we had already lost.

"People didn't trust Brown. He was never part of the team, and now our hopes were on him. We let it get to that point. And there's no way we're going to be able to survive. We had our shots. We had three games to do it and now it's come to this. We deserve to lose. I mean, of all people . . . Kevin Brown. Some guys hated him. Guys just didn't understand him. He always had something wrong, his back, this or that."

Said Mussina, recalling the team's feeling before Game 7, "We're finished. That was the feeling after Game 6. As soon as Game 6 ended."

There were no more Andy Pettittes or David Wellses or David Cones to turn to at a time like this. The 2004 Yankees had an entirely different DNA from the championship Yankee teams. Starting with the trade for A-Rod and his need to be needed, continuing with Lofton in spring training fretting over the All-Star ballot, Contreras and Vazquez being unable to pitch in New York, Sheffield moping for two months because he wasn't sure his manager wanted him, Giambi becoming a nonfactor because of his tumor and BALCO connection, and Brown, the broken-down lone wolf on whose cranky back rested all of the Yankees' hopes . . . The core of trust that had served the Yankees so well was now diminished by an influx of outside stars who brought their individual needs and anxieties into the equation.

"It goes back to David Cone," Borzello said. "David Cone never, ever would tell you anything was wrong with him. I remember charting a game, and the first three pitches of the game were 78 miles an hour. I thought they were splitters. And after the game—he went five innings, and he won the game—I walked over to him. I said, 'Coney, you were throwing 78 to 82, tops, with your fastball. Do you want me to hand this chart in?'

"Now this was before they started putting up velocities on the stadium scoreboards, so I'm the only one who knew how hard he was throwing. It wasn't on TV. It wasn't in the stadium. And he goes, 'Really? Yeah, I really didn't have much, did I?' I go, **'You didn't have much?'** He goes, 'You might want to bump it up so you don't scare anybody.'

"He never thought he couldn't win the game. And Kevin Brown was not that. It was, 'If I wasn't throwing 98 I can't win.' And guys didn't like that. It's a lack of competitiveness."

Torre knew his team was tight before Game 7, so he called a quick meeting in the clubhouse. He tried to relax his players by staying upbeat and asking other people to speak, including Yogi Berra and Hideki Matsui, who was always good for a laugh when he would end meetings in his thick Japanese accent with one of the few English phrases he had mastered: "Let's kick their fuckin' ass!"

Said Torre, "There is a little uneasiness at that point, and you'd like to bring a little levity into it. I was just trying to lighten the mood at that point. I just had a sense that Kevin Brown really wasn't a good sale in the clubhouse."

Naturally, the idiots on the other side of the field were, if possible, even looser than the game before. Lowe, the starting pitcher, was so loose that only then did he realize he had left his spikes back in Boston. Lou Cucuzza, the visiting clubhouse manager at Yankee Stadium, had to call a local sporting goods store to find spikes for Boston's Game 7 starting pitcher.

"We left our hotel rooms and all I said before we left was, 'Today we have a chance to shock the world,'" Millar said. "It's never been done. We were down 0-3. We were down in Game 4. We were down in Game 5. 'Today we have a chance to shock the world!' When we left our hotel rooms and checked out we knew we were going back to Boston that night after a chance to shock the world and that was the truth. How many times can you say that in your lifetime? The world is watching this game. The world knows the ramifications. That group, that team, changed the Red Sox franchise.

"Teams win championships. Not players. Our team was just too tight—sticking together, grinding things out. And that's what I try to stress to this day: teams win championships. Not salaries. Not looks. Not players. Teams."

The Red Sox had become more like the championship Yankees than the Yankees—except, of course, for the long hair, beards, irreverence and shots of whiskey. For Game 7 they stuck to Millar's Game 6 pregame preparation: no batting practice on the field, no **Yankeeography,** but shots of Jack Daniel's all around.

Game 7 was a blowout. It was over by the second inning. Brown was as bad as the Yankees feared. He faced nine batters and retired only three of them.

Ortiz hit a two-run home run in the first inning. The Red Sox loaded the bases in the second inning with a single and two walks, prompting Torre to replace Brown with Vazquez. Damon slammed Vazquez's first pitch for a grand slam. It was 6-0 before the Yankees even had a base runner or a chance to get their fourth batter to the plate.

"Looking back, he wasn't very good," Torre said of Brown, who had a 21.60 ERA in the ALCS. "It's the old thing about pitching hurt or pitching stupid. Pitching hurt, or playing hurt, is when you can go out there and still get the job done. Playing stupid is when you can't get the job done. Now you're letting everybody down."

The final score was 10-3. The rise of the Red Sox was complete. They had wiped out all of the ground the Yankees established over Boston as the superior team from 1996 through 2003. The Red Sox, better than any other franchise, had exploited the explosion of information and revenues that had changed the baseball landscape since the Yankees were winning titles. Most of the key players in the key moments of the 2004 ALCS were obtained as the Red Sox rode the cutting edge of player evaluation: Ortiz, Millar, Mueller, Roberts . . . all of them were obtained cheaply and without much competition because Boston understood the importance of measuring a player by his ability to get on base rather than the traditional but flawed yardstick of batting average. That advantage would go away as statistical analytical methods became mainstream, a factor in helping to usher in a parity in the industry that also conspired against the Yankees.

The last bit of ground Boston conquered to gain control of baseball's Peloponnesian War was represented by Schilling, the ace they squired out from under the Yankees while the turkey and stuffing were cooking. Torre always maintained that the foundation to the Yankees' championship years was pitching, particularly starting pitcher. While the Yankees lost their way on making evaluations and acquisitions on starting pitchers, the Red Sox knew Schilling was the last piece to the kind of championship rotation that the Yankees once flaunted.

"In past seasons, the Red Sox always started out really well," Torre said, "because they had guys who, whether it was a retread or whatever it was, would pitch well early. And then eventually the cream rises to the top and the guys who aren't as good would be exposed. And it really wasn't until they addressed their pitching that they became this force. They always had Pedro, but there was always a way we could get around Pedro. We could just hold them at bay until we could run up his pitch count to get him out of the game. Then we'd win."

The Yankees' superiority stopped dead cold in that 2004 ALCS. The Yankees were saddled not only with the worst collapse in baseball history, but also the insult of having the hated Red Sox spill champagne in their stadium. Torre brought his team together for a brief meeting after the game. He thanked his players for their effort. And when he looked around the room he realized that the Yankees, who once came to know the World Series as an expected extension of their season, were full of players who never had been there before.

"The sad part about this for me," Torre told them, "is the guys in this room that have never been in the World Series. Guys like Tony Clark, one of the classiest guys I've ever been around."

Said Torre, "Of course, the guy I didn't mention who was in the back of my mind was Don Mattingly. All those years with the Yankees, and he had never been to the World Series."

Torre picked up the telephone in his office and called over to the visiting clubhouse. He congratulated his friend, Francona. He asked to speak to Wakefield, the pitcher who one year earlier was near tears in that same clubhouse after giving up the home run to Aaron Boone. Now Wakefield was going to the World Series. After he hung up the phone, Wakefield said out loud, to no one in particular, "I'll never forget that phone call. That shows so much class."

So it was done. The 2004 Yankees were history. They would be remembered for all the wrong reasons. How did it go so wrong? What would most stick with the players about the failure to close out the Red Sox? Mussina thinks about those questions and he thinks about the same man who closed out all those championships before Mussina joined the Yankees in 2001.

"We were up 3-0 and Mo came in again with the lead and lost it," Mussina said. "He lost it again. As great as he is, and it's amazing what he does, if you start the evaluation again since I got here, he has accomplished nothing in comparison to what he accomplished the four years before. He blew the World Series in '01. He lost the Boston series. He didn't lose it himself, but we had a chance to win in the ninth and sweep them, and he doesn't do it there.

"I know you look at everything he's done and it's been awesome. I'll admit that. But it hadn't been the same in those couple of years. That's what I remember about the '04 series."

It wasn't long after Game 7 that Torre received a call from George Steinbrenner.

"Boss, I feel bad," Torre told him. "I'm sorry it happened. But you can't lose any sleep over this. I wish I could sit here and tell you I wish I had done something different. I mean, Game 7, we didn't have any options. And I mean, Game 4 you put Mariano Rivera on the mound with a lead in the ninth inning and you lose the game. Game 5, you have a two-run lead with Gordon on the mound and you lose the game. What do you change? You don't change anything."

But deep down, Torre knew Steinbrenner wasn't going to let go so easily of such a painful defeat. Torre's Teflon status as Yankees manager was gone. The lion tamer who somehow could always stick his head into the mouth of the big cat named Steinbrenner and emerge unscathed no longer had the same magic touch. He was on dangerous ground now. From this moment on, each year for him would become more difficult than the last.

"Obviously the embarrassment got to him," Torre said. "There was more after that with him. That's when this whole underground campaign started with me."

11.

The Abyss

If the 2003 World Series defeat to the Marlins caused the Yankees to lose their way in the subsequent off-season, the crushing 2004 loss to the Red Sox sent them even deeper and more horribly off course, like a ship wandering at sea without any instrumentation. Their response to losing to Schilling and the pitching-fortified Red Sox, the newly crowned champions of baseball, was to seek starting pitching over the winter, even if it meant rejecting a 27-year-old switch-hitting free agent center fielder coming off a 38-homer season, Carlos Beltran, who was willing to take a 20 percent discount to bring his young legs to the Yankees.

The Yankees were fixated on pitching, and this is what they came up with in one 22-day shopping spree they would quickly regret: Carl Pavano, Jaret

Wright and Randy Johnson. With that trio joining the creaky and cranky Kevin Brown, his ALCS Game 7 bomb added to his oversized baggage, the Yankees had one of the most physically and emotionally fragile rotations you could possibly put together, even if you tried doing so. Predictably, the Yankees' rotation in 2005 was such a mess that Torre needed 14 starting pitchers to get through the year. Only once before had the Yankees needed to put more starters to work, and that was during wartime, in 1946, when they used 16.

The 2005 Yankees were such a wreck, such a slapdash collection of parts that didn't fit or work, so full of organizational backbiting and clubhouse dysfunction, and another 60 degrees of separation removed from the championship Yankee teams, that at the end of the year pitching coach Mel Stottlemyre quit and Torre seriously questioned whether he should follow his friend out the door.

"I didn't know if I wanted to come back," Torre said. "That was the first year of my three-year contract. I was prepared to see if they wanted me, and if they didn't, I would find a way to get out of this thing."

The crushing defeat to the Red Sox brought out the worst in the Yankees: a quick-fix approach to team building, with little regard to the role character played in fitting into New York and in the Yankees clubhouse, and a sort of top-down anger and frustration over not winning the World Series for all of four years. Torre and Steinbrenner virtually stopped speaking to one another that year. The mood around the Yankees had turned so sour that by just the third game of the season—and the first defeat—fans at Yankee Stadium were booing the great and graceful Mariano Rivera. The closer entered that game against the Red Sox with a 3-2 lead and left the mound trailing 6-3. Only one of the five runs scored off him was earned.

"It was one of the only times I took him out of a game in the middle of an inning and the fans booed," Torre said. "That's the one time I was totally upset and shocked by the fan reaction."

Five days later, in Boston's opener, the Yankees stood there watching the Red Sox reap the spoils of war: the presentation of the 2004 world championship rings. There was much speculation about what the Yankees would do during the ceremony. Would they stay ensconced in their clubhouse? Torre held a brief meeting with his players after batting practice.

"The only thing I'm going to tell you, guys, is I'm not going to make you go out there," Torre said. "But they've had to put up with a lot of shit when we won. And I think we can just show what we're made of by understanding that they earned it. They won. You can't ignore it. So I'm not telling you to go out there. But I'm going out there when they're getting their rings."

Said Torre, "And everybody came out. It was

tough. Another one of those trips to the dentist's office. But it's one of those things that the more you think about it, the more uncomfortable it is, but you also have a better understanding. And I always try to nail perspective as a part of things."

The Yankee team that stood in the visiting dugout at Fenway Park that afternoon represented another rung down from the championship teams. General manager Brian Cashman would later describe this period of decline in the organization as heading toward "an abyss." And if there was a symbol of that impending abyss, it was Pavano. Torre had some inkling, but not a strong one, that Pavano might be a problem when he happened to run into him at a restaurant in West Palm Beach, Florida, over the previous winter. Torre was attending the wedding rehearsal dinner of a nephew. Pavano seemed slightly timid, even socially ill at ease. Torre, having watched players such as Kenny Rogers, Jose Contreras and Javier Vazquez underperform as Yankees because they were uncomfortable in New York, came away with a concern about Pavano, but the hesitation wasn't nearly as strong as the memory of watching Pavano throw nine strong innings against the Yankees in the 2003 World Series.

"He was at the top of my list," Torre said about the free agent market that winter. "I was just a little uneasy with some of the questions he asked. I reported back to Cash, and still that other image, the World Series image, kept coming back at me. I wasn't as put off by Pavano as much as I was about Kenny Rogers, when I sat with him back in '95."

Pavano and his agent, Scott Shapiro, embarked on a tour of the country to solicit offers. The Mariners, Red Sox, Tigers and Reds were among the many teams with strong interest in the right-hander. Pavano was getting a bevy of four-year offers—the Mariners were close to $48 million with escalator clauses that would bring him even more money—when Shapiro told him the Yankees were looking for an answer soon. The Yankees already had agreed to terms on a three-year, $21 million deal with Jaret Wright, who was coming off a 15-win season for the Braves but whose long history of arm problems made him a significant medical risk. They also were deciding on whether to bring back Jon Lieber. Pavano had grown up in Connecticut rooting for the Yankees. Shapiro gave Pavano the standard disclaimer about pitching for the Yankees: the expectations and attention are greater in pinstripes than anywhere else.

"I want to be a New York Yankee," Pavano told Shapiro.

There was trouble from the start. The Yankees signed Pavano for $39.95 million over four years. Pavano had been under the impression that he was getting $40 million from the Yankees, and he would soon fire Shapiro over the misunderstanding. Shapiro even offered to give Pavano the $50,000 himself by taking it out of his agent's commission, but that did not placate Pavano, who moved on to his fourth agent.

There were other troubling signs regarding Pavano. The Boston baseball writers invited Pavano, a Connecticut native, to attend their annual off-season dinner. Pavano agreed to it. On the day of the dinner, Pavano's girlfriend called up Shapiro and said, "Carl's not going to be able to make it. He wants me to tell you that he's sick, but he's not. But that's what he told me to say."

Shapiro wanted to arrange a casual dinner for Pavano with the New York press corps to ease his transition to the Yankees. It would be an informal question-and-answer, get-acquainted session with the writers covering the team. When Shapiro presented the idea to Pavano, the pitcher responded, "I don't want to meet with those fucking assholes."

On the day of Pavano's first game at Yankee Stadium, he met his mother in the executive lobby of Yankee Stadium and was mortified to see her wearing a Yankees "NY" on her cheek in face paint. "Take that crap off your face. You're embarrassing me," he sternly told her. The words were meant to be sarcastic, but Yankee officials standing there were uncomfortable with the manner in which Pavano rebuked his own mother in front of them.

"Whoa, did he just say that to his mom?" said a person who was there.

Pavano made 17 starts for the Yankees in 2005—he was hit hard, going 4-6 with a 4.77 ERA, a significant jump from his 3.00 the previous year in the softer National League—before shutting it down for the season in June with a sore right shoulder. The Yankees learned very quickly that Pavano was not cut out to pitch in New York.

"Partway through that first year," Mussina said, when asked when he came to that conclusion. "He said some stuff to me in the dugout about playing someplace else. He was referring to some other teams he had talked to when he was a free agent. He just didn't like being under the microscope. He couldn't play being under the microscope every day."

So Pavano's choice was not to play at all?

"That's what it turned out to be," Mussina said.

In August, while the Yankees were playing the White Sox, bullpen catcher Mike Borzello brought up Pavano to Tim Raines, the former Yankees outfielder who was a coach with Chicago.

"Tim Raines told me, 'Pavano? He's never going to pitch for you. Forget it,'" Borzello said. "I said, **'What?'** He said, 'The guy didn't want to pitch in Montreal. There was always something wrong with him. In Florida, same thing. He didn't want to pitch except for the one year he was pitching for a contract. I'm telling you, he's not going to pitch for you.'"

Raines turned out to be right. Over the life of the four-year contract Pavano made only 26 starts and won just nine games, or a cost of $4.44 million per win for the Yankees' investment. He missed extended stretches of time because of the sore shoulder, a bruised buttocks, two broken ribs suffered in a car accident about which he failed to notify the team, a strained elbow and eventually major elbow surgery. His Yankees teammates wrote him off as a guy who milked any physical ailment as an excuse not to have to pitch.

"The players all hated him," Torre said. "It was no secret."

Said Borzello, "Guys on that team despised him. One day Jeet walked by him and said, 'Hey, Pav. You ever going to play? Ever?' Wow. That was a damaging comment, coming from Jeter. He didn't say a whole lot, but when he said something like that, it was pretty piercing."

There was one time Torre called bullpen coach Joe Kerrigan and Pavano into his office, because Kerrigan reported that a defiant Pavano had told him, "I'm not blowing out my arm for this organization."

"Pav," Torre said, "this organization gave you $40 million and has been patient with you. What I want to know is, for what organization would you be willing to risk blowing out your arm?" Pavano said he couldn't remember saying such a thing to Kerrigan.

What bothered Torre most about Pavano was that the pitcher had no sense of his responsibility to his teammates. Pavano made that clear in 2006 when he hurt himself in the car wreck, when he drove his 2006 Porsche into a tractor trailer. The accident occurred just when the Yankees were about ready to activate him from a rehabilitation assignment. Torre telephoned Pavano and told him, "It's nice to go out. I know you like to go out, but you've got a commitment here. You've got a bunch of players that need for you to be a pitcher."

Pavano never did get it. "He was always a little skittish when you talked to him," Torre said.

At the end of that season, Cashman was ready to send Pavano home. The pitcher was on perpetual rehab in Tampa, and he wasn't going to be able to help the Yankees down the stretch.

"No," Torre told Cashman. "Have him come to St. Pete on the last road trip."

Torre knew Pavano's teammates loathed him, and he wanted them to be able to vent their frustration to the pitcher rather than carrying it over into a new season. He wanted Pavano in the Yankees clubhouse when the team played the Devil Rays in St. Petersburg.

"Let them get this shit out of the way," Torre told Cashman. "They can see him, get on him, whatever they're going to do to him."

Cashman agreed and told Pavano to come to the games in St. Petersburg. When Pavano arrived Torre explained to him why he wanted him there.

"You're going to have to get this shit out of the way," he told Pavano.

When Pavano showed up in the Yankees clubhouse, something far worse than cruel jokes and frat-boy razzing took place: nothing. The Yankees said nothing to him. They wanted nothing to do with him. He had turned himself into a nonperson.

"Unfortunately, nobody got on him," Torre said. "That's a bad sign. They ignored him."

The next spring, Mussina made it clear that the Yankee players had no confidence in Pavano. He told reporters about Pavano's injuries and extended absences, "It didn't look good from a player's and teammate's standpoint. Was everything just coincidence? Over and over again? I don't know."

It was a stunning and rare public rebuke among teammates, a violation of the unwritten code among teammates. But Pavano was so far removed from the natural bonds of a team that Mussina felt free to fire away. Torre called both Mussina and Pavano into his office. He knew Mussina, in the strictest sense of the code, was out of line, but he also knew that Mussina's feelings about Pavano represented the feelings of the entire clubhouse, and it was good for Pavano to know he faced major repair work when it came to his relationship with his teammates.

"Moose didn't do the right thing, the way he went about it," Torre said. "But they did talk and they got past that, and all of a sudden he started to get some support back.

"Andy Pettitte had elbow issues in 1996, and you just have to realize, 'I'm either going to pitch or I can't play this game anymore.' Pav, unfortunately, never faced that reality. In saying that, am I saying he wasn't hurt? No. Not at all. But would it have made a difference if he had pitched, based on where he wound up, anyway? You're still capable of getting people out.

"He's a guy with all these issues in his life and he's not sure what's important and what isn't. Was he afraid of failing in New York? It must be that way, because I talked to Larry Bowa, and he saw the bulldog on the mound when he pitched against the Phillies, and I saw it in the World Series. We just didn't see that with the Yankees."

Pavano was not some idle mistake. It was part of a trend. The collection of expensive pitchers imported to the Yankees who were ill-suited for New York, either because they were too emotionally fragile or broken down, was growing at a staggering rate. Weaver, Contreras, Vazquez, Wright, Brown, Pavano . . .

"I'm certainly not a player evaluator," Mussina said, "but I generally believe that players are who they are over a period of a certain number of years. They may have a good year here or they may have a bad year here, but in general they play at a certain level, the players who are around long enough. The time a player is coming up to be a free agent, like in his sixth year, let's say all of a sudden he has a year that shoots up. Everybody looks at it like, 'Oh, now he's got an idea.' It's not his rookie year. There are four or five other years in there. Let's look at all of them.

"So you're giving guys—and just using Pavano as an example—you give a guy that's two or three games under .500 for his career a four-year contract for $40 million. Well, I don't understand that. I don't understand that."

———

Brown, of course, because of the 2004 ALCS Game 7 debacle, also was symbolic of poor pitching evaluations steering the Yankees into the abyss, as Cashman called it. His 2005 season began just as 2004 ended: with a bad back and awful results. He started 2005 on the disabled list, the fifth time in six years he had to be put on the shelf.

When Brown did try to pitch again, he was wretchedly bad. He was, for all intents and purposes, finished as an effective big league pitcher. Moreover, the fans at Yankee Stadium, who would always associate him with the Game 7 abomination, had no use for him, and his teammates barely more than that. On May 3, 2005, Brown took the mound in St. Petersburg against the Devil Rays with an 0-3 record and a 6.63 ERA. His tenure with the Yankees was about to get even uglier. The Devil Rays gave Brown a brutal beating in the first inning, scoring six runs on eight hits before Brown could so much as get a second out. The symphony of hits and base runners played out to a staccaco beat:

single, wild pitch, single, ground rule double, run-scoring groundout, single, double, single, single, single. The score was 6-0 after one-third of an inning. After Brown finally managed to get the two outs to end the percussive treatment, he stomped off the field, kept going past Torre and marched up the runway to the clubhouse, shouting as he passed the manager, "I'm done!"

Torre and pitching coach Mel Stottlemyre looked at one another as if to say, "What now?" Brown was infamous for his temper, but was quitting in the middle of a game really an option? Torre turned and left the dugout, taking the runway and then the stairs that led into the visiting clubhouse at Tropicana Field. Torre saw Brown's jersey, hat and glove strewn about the floor, but he didn't see Brown. He did see Mussina, sitting in one of the clubhouse chairs.

"Where is he?" Torre asked.

"I don't know," Mussina said, "somewhere back there." He motioned toward a back room off the clubhouse. Mussina had seen Brown storm into the clubhouse, fling away his jersey, glove and hat, grab his cell phone from his locker, and disappear, snapping, "I'm done! I'm going home!"

Torre followed in the direction where Mussina pointed. He turned a corner, and suddenly was stunned at what he saw: Kevin Brown, 40 years old, a six-time All-Star, a two-time ERA champion, a man who had won 207 major league games and earned more than $130 million playing baseball, was curled up on the floor in a tiny crevice in the corner of a storage area in the back of the clubhouse.

"What are you doing?" Torre said.

"I'm not going to go out there and pitch anymore," Brown said.

"What are you going to do?"

"I'm going to go home."

"You might as well go home."

There was no response from Brown. Torre continued.

"Because just remember: if you're going to quit on those guys, you can't ever come back. You can **never** come back. Just understand that. What you just told me? That's what it means. If you're not going to go back out there, you can't even stay here."

Brown wore that thoroughly beaten look, the same look he had nine months earlier after he broke his left hand punching a concrete pillar.

Meanwhile, the top of the second inning was in progress, and there was one out already. The Yankees would need **somebody** to pitch the bottom of the inning real quickly. Nobody was throwing in the bullpen. Nobody else knew what was going on with Brown.

"Listen," Torre said to Brown, "why don't you just get your glove, go back out there and pitch, and let's talk about it later."

Brown stood up, walked past Torre and into the main clubhouse. He fired his cell phone clear across the room in the direction of his locker. He picked up his shirt, his hat and his glove and he walked backed toward the dugout. Kevin Brown threw four more innings, surrendering two more runs.

"He never did bother coming in to talk," Torre said. "He was banged up. But I think he had some emotional issues. There were a lot of demons in this guy. It was sad."

The Yankees lost the game, 11-4, and they lost again, and again and again after that as part of a 1-9 stretch that dropped their record to 11-19, marking only the fifth time in franchise history they posted so many losses in the first 30 games. The other four teams to start so poorly turned out, in fact, to be horrendous teams. Those teams, from 1912, 1913, 1925 and 1966, all lost at least 85 games and finished out of first place by 55, 38, 28½ and 26½ games, respectively. Such was the inglorious company of the 2005 Yankees.

There exists a mythology that the championship Yankees teams under Torre operated on autopilot, blissfully riding their talent and their will to preordained titles. No team requires no care. Even the most beautiful garden in the world, as amazed and occupied as we might be by its natural beauty, is the work of hours of pruning and weeding and feeding and fastidious attention to detail. The championship teams required their own maintenance, from, among others, the insecurities of Chuck Knoblauch, to the immaturity of David Wells, to the self-critical nature of Tino Martinez, to the overflow intensity of Paul O'Neill, to the neediness of Roger Clemens, and to the overbearing intrusion and influence of George Steinbrenner. Greatness is the ability to mask the difficulty of a task—to make the difficult appear easy. Those Yankee teams epitomized greatness.

But the Yankees in the middle oughts made nothing look easy. They were rocked by organizational and clubhouse dysfunction that made the maintenance of the team a noisy, constant and exhausting job, like keeping a belching, balky furnace going in the basement of an apartment building. The problems became apparent in 2004 because of the mix of players introduced and worsened in that 2005 season. Not four weeks after the Brown meltdown, Mussina asked to speak to Torre about what he perceived to be a lack of focus and preparation by some of the players. They went to lunch while the team was in Milwaukee.

"I laid some things out," Mussina said. "It was about players I thought weren't going about it the right way. The '05 team had some issues the first half of the season."

What the Yankees lacked in talent, particularly when it came to starting pitching, was exacerbated by odd personalities and individual agendas in the clubhouse. The mix of players wasn't working, taking the Yankees further and further from the roots of their championships.

"It's all a continuation of the end of the other group, the group that left after '01," Mussina said. "After '01 we lost some guys and after '02 we lost some guys, and after '03 we lost the pitching staff. Whatever semblance of that other team there was, it certainly was gone after '03. It started phasing out after '01, but after '03 it was just Derek and Posada and Mariano and Bernie who were left. Everybody else was new. The mix wasn't the same."

––––––

Only days after Mussina voiced his concern to Torre, and on the same trip, and still only one month after the Brown meltdown, another blowup occurred. This time it involved Gary Sheffield and Torre. As the struggling Yankees lost another game, this one in St. Louis, Sheffield appeared to loaf after a ball in right field. Torre, unhappy with the general effort he was getting from his team, held a clubhouse meeting after the game in which he singled out Sheffield and rookie second baseman Robinson Cano for what he thought was a lack of hustle.

In the days after the meeting, Torre noticed that Sheffield was moping around him. He called him into his office.

"Do we have an issue?" Torre asked.

"Yeah," said Sheffield, who explained he took exception to Torre accusing him in front of the team of not hustling.

"I was trying to deke the runner," Sheffield said.

"Well, if you weren't loafing, I apologize," Torre said, "because that's what it looked like to me. What else we got?"

"Well, it was in the paper," Sheffield said of Torre calling him out.

"Do you think I told them?" Torre asked.

"I don't know," Sheffield said.

"I don't do that," Torre said. "I wouldn't do that. Obviously, it came from somewhere else. There were a lot of people in the room. I can't control that. There's no reason for me to go to the media with that."

Said Torre, "He seemed to believe me, but he was always a suspicious person."

Two years later, speaking to HBO, Sheffield used that clubhouse meeting as evidence to support his opinion that Torre treated black players differently than white players.

"The only thing I ever wanted to do as a manager was to make sure everybody felt they were being treated fairly," Torre said. "That's why when Sheffield said something it really blew me away. Because I really went ass over teakettle to try to accommodate him. If I had something he needed to hear, like if he brought his son into the clubhouse, which wasn't allowed, I'd ask Jeter to tell him because he had a relationship with him. If it came from a player it didn't seem somebody was trying to tell him what to do again.

"At the time I knew none of what he said was true. I just didn't want to fan the flames at that point in time. I had been around the game a very long time, so if there had been an issue I'm sure it would have come out that I slighted people or didn't treat them right. That came out of left field."

What the 2005 Yankees needed most of all to establish stability and a presence was an ace. They needed a Schilling, the guy Boston general manager Theo Epstein successfully hunted to bring a "kick your ass" attitude to the Red Sox pitching staff. The Yankees were so sure they had that guy in Randy Johnson that their entire front office elected unanimously to pursue Johnson, who was 41 years old, rather than Beltran, a fleet, athletic everyday player in his prime. They were dead wrong.

(Beltran had given the Yankees a last-minute, discounted offer before signing with the Mets. Said Torre, "Cash said no, you can't have everything. Beltran wanted to come to us, so he could hide among the other trees. Nobody wants to be that guy to lead. That's what makes Jeter so unique in what he does. Alex, to his credit, wants to be that guy, but as long as Jeter is there he's very aware of that.")

Johnson had thrown a perfect game, logged

245⅔ innings, won 16 games and struck out a National League–best 290 batters in 2003 with Arizona. He fit the profile of the stopper the Yankees so desperately needed—the statistical profile, anyway. He was, in fact, a sensitive, hyperaware person who, in the growing tradition of Weaver, Contreras, Vazquez and Pavano, was uncomfortable with the constant criticism and noise that came with playing in New York. Such awkwardness was apparent from his very first day, when he swatted away a news cameraman on the streets of New York while in town for his physical.

"I was in Hawaii when it happened," Torre said, "and I talked to him on the phone. I said, 'Do what you have to do. If you want to apologize, apologize. Just let it go.'

"But that really wasn't his fault. They never should have put him in that situation. They should've put him in a car or a van and taken him to the hospital. That was our security decision. That was a bad decision. He really had trouble recovering from that, because all of a sudden now all this pressure was on him, because people don't like him to start with. And he would read every single word that was written."

Johnson was struck by two baseball neuroses that were amplified in New York: he fretted about what was said and written about him and he worried constantly that other teams were decoding "tells" in his delivery to know what pitch was coming. They most certainly were not the typical qualities of a "kick your ass" staff leader.

Johnson did not pitch all that badly in New York. He took the ball with regularity. From 2004 through 2007, only four times did a pitcher give the Yankees 200 innings. Johnson did so twice, as many as all other Yankees pitchers combined in those four years. He also won some games, posting a 34-19 record. But he was also hit too hard and was lost too deeply in his own cloud of worry to give the Yankees anything close to the vibe of being a true ace. In those two seasons, for instance, he gave up 95 and 114 earned runs, the two worst such seasons of his long career. His combined ERA in those two seasons with the Yankees was 4.37, which ranked an unimpressive 55th among all ERA qualifiers in that span.

"The biggest surprise to me was how Randy Johnson could get rattled," Torre said. "I wish I knew this about him in the 2001 World Series when we played against him. You could rattle him. Every start with Randy it would be, 'This guy has my pitches, that guy has my pitches...' There wasn't one team that didn't have a person that told him they were getting his pitches that he would take to heart. I mentioned it to Randy and I said, 'It's not about the pitches. It's about location. Throw that pitch where you want it and you'll get them out.'

"He was always so concerned about that. 'Are

they getting my pitches? Do you think they're getting my pitches? The guy hit this pitch.' I'd go, 'You
just threw it down the middle. When they start laying off pitches they should be swinging at, then
yeah.' But he was the biggest surprise for me. He
was probably the most self-conscious superstar I've
ever been around. By far."

Torre spent hours with Johnson trying to make
life easier for him in New York. He would tell Johnson that he shouldn't worry about criticism because,
based on his prolific career, he could never satisfy
fans and the media, anyway. "You're not going to
satisfy people unless you strike out 10 or 12 every
game," Torre would tell him. "Even if you win ballgames, they're going to want to know why you didn't
strike out more. So don't even worry about it."

One day Johnson came to Torre with a newspaper in his hand. "Look at this!" Johnson said. "This
is my apartment! They have pictures of my apartment!"

"Randy," Torre said, "why do you even look at
the fucking newspaper?"

Other times Torre would see so much passivity
out of Johnson on the mound that he would tell
him, "I need to see your teeth out there. You have to
growl." Then Johnson would pitch a good game
and say to Torre, "Is that what you mean?"

"Yeah," Torre said. "Just do what you do like that
and find out how good it is, that's all."

And then it would be gone, the fire snuffed by

something the newspapers or radio put out there about him or that nagging worry that hitters knew what was coming.

"I brought him into the office, I'd talk to him in the trainer's room, we'd sit in the dugout . . . a number of places," Torre said. "It was sad more than frustrating because when we got him I thought we finally had someone you could hook your wagon to, and that wasn't the case."

———

The 2005 Yankees employed a pitching staff with an average age of 34.2 years old, making it the oldest staff in franchise history. They finished ninth in the American League with a 4.87 ERA. Their relative ERA, essentially a measurement of how they compared to the league average, was the Yankees' second-worst in the previous 70 years, exceeded only by the 1989 club that lost 87 games and finished fifth. Bill James' Pythagorean formula pegged the Yankees, with that kind of pitching, as worth 90 wins, which would have kept them home for the playoffs with the fifth-best record in the American League.

Instead, somehow they won the AL East again with 95 wins. (The Yankees actually finished in a tie with the Red Sox, but were awarded first place by virtue of winning the season series against Boston, 10-9. The teams had split their previous 90 games, 45-45.) A clear pattern had developed. The Yankees' pitching was getting worse and worse and the clubhouse becoming more populated with ill-suited players, but Torre still not only was getting these teams into the playoffs, he was also consistently getting these teams to overperform. The 2005 team was Torre's eighth straight team that won more games than it should have been expected to win. Those teams outperformed Pythagorean expectations by an average of 5.25 wins.

In a way, by somehow dragging themselves into the playoffs in the later part of those years, those teams were covering up what otherwise would have been even more obvious flaws. The Yankees had nothing close to championship pitching anymore. But they wore the same uniforms as the 1996, 1998, 1999 and 2000 Yankees, still had Jeter and Williams and Posada and Rivera and Torre, still had the highest payroll in baseball, so therefore they were expected to simply show up and win the World Series as if nothing in baseball had changed in the past five years. They were bound to fail in October.

The Yankees drew the Los Angeles Angels of Anaheim in the Division Series, a series in which the Angels, who also won 95 games, held home-field advantage by virtue of beating the Yankees head-to-head during the season, 6-4. After the Yankees managed to split the first two games in Anaheim, their season fittingly was funneled straight into the hands of Johnson, who would get the ball in Game 3, the swing game, at Yankee Stadium. The Yankees' answer to Schilling was abysmal.

Johnson could not get so much as one out in the fourth inning. He faced 17 batters and gave up nine hits. He left with two runners on base in the fourth inning with the Yankees behind, 5-0. All season he never gave off the real glow of an ace, and the reality was all too obvious in Game 3.

"That's the game where you've got a decided advantage," Torre said, "and you've just got to go ahead and grab it by the throat. He just never seemed to be comfortable doing it. He never took the ball and said, 'All right, guys. Follow me.' You never had the feeling that that was what you were going to get. There's no question that New York is a different place to play. Everything you do is magnified and criticized. He was uncomfortable pitching in New York.

"He's the one that's supposed to be intimidating. He pitched a horrible game and it's like it didn't surprise him. It surprised Roger Clemens every time he pitched a horrible game."

The Yankees, who could still bang the ball with anybody in baseball, hit their way out of the 5-0 hole and actually took a 6-5 lead into the sixth inning. But the Angels battered the Yankees bullpen for six unanswered runs and won, 11-7.

The Yankees did send the series back to Anaheim by rallying to win Game 4, 3-2, with two runs in the seventh inning. But their pitching, old and creaky, caught up with them again in the deciding game. Mussina, 36, bothered by a strained groin muscle, staggered off the mound in the third inning, having put the Yankees in a 5-2 hole. They lost, 5-3.

———

Shortly thereafter, Stottlemyre quit as pitching coach, worn down by the fractious relationship between Yankees officials in New York and Tampa, the latter often choosing to intervene in major league pitching matters. Stottlemyre also quit, however, because he knew Torre's relationship with Steinbrenner had worsened, and he knew one of Steinbrenner's favorite tactics to tweak his manager was to fire one of his favored coaches. Stottlemyre wanted out before Steinbrenner had the chance to use him as a pawn in his war with Torre.

Torre, too, wasn't sure he wanted to come back to what the job had become. He knew, coming off the bitter 2004 ALCS defeat, that he had little favor left with Steinbrenner. The two of them had engaged in almost no communication throughout the 2005 season. The incidence of criticisms, second-guessing and statements handed or leaked to the media had picked up. Torre was bothered, too, that Yankee officials were feeding questions to YES network reporter Kim Jones designed to corner Torre or to put him in an unfavorable light. The questions themselves didn't bother Torre so much. It was more that Torre, who built his entire relationships with people on trust, understood that the very people who were paying him to help the Yankees win were intentionally trying to undermine him on the team's own network.

"I was getting paid to do a pre- and postgame show for the YES network," Torre said. "And they took the fact that they paid me as an opening to tell somebody what to ask me and try to ask tough questions—which I don't know what a tough question is when someone is talking about the game. I mean, they ask you a question about the game, you answer the question. You knew she was uncomfortable asking certain questions, about why'd you bring him in or why'd you do this. It just didn't match up.

"And then they admitted it. 'Well, you're getting paid.' They felt they had the right to do that, which is crazy in my mind. So after the season was over I said, 'Forget it. We're not going to do it anymore. I don't want your money. I'll answer any question you want, but let's not put a dialogue together designed to put me in a bad light.'

"It was so obvious that it was all about trying to make me look bad. And I don't know what question was so tough, anyway. If I brought in a pitcher and he got his ass kicked, what's so secretive about that? Everybody saw what happened. I made a decision and it didn't work. It's not like I said, 'I have to make a decision. Let me flip a coin. Okay, I'll bring this guy in.'"

Torre went home and tried to decompress from a draining season. For a few days he spoke to no one in the organization and no one in the media. He didn't know whether he wanted to manage the Yankees anymore, in great part because he didn't know if they wanted him. After Torre had done enough brooding around the house, his wife, Ali, said to him, "Why don't you go down and talk to George?"

"You're right," Torre said.

———

He had not called Steinbrenner virtually all year, nor had he discussed his relationship with Steinbrenner with the media, and it was time to break the cold war and see if George really did want him back.

"I disconnected," Torre said. "I hadn't talked to him. It was all secondhand smoke I was getting, which was the worst."

To keep the trip as quiet as possible, Torre chartered a private plane to Tampa. Steve Swindal, the team's managing partner, asked Torre if he minded if Randy Levine flew down with him. "No, not at all," Torre said.

Levine met Torre at the airport. The flight was delayed.

"Maintenance problem," Torre told Levine. "The ejection seat for you needed to get fixed."

They chuckled at the gallows humor. Levine told Torre on the plane ride to Tampa, "We want you back," so Torre's mood was brightened a bit by the time he walked into the meeting. Torre and Levine joined Steinbrenner and Swindal. They met in Steinbrenner's office at Legends Field, with Steinbrenner seated at his desk like the captain at the helm. Torre took a seat to Steinbrenner's left.

"The only reason I'm down here," Torre said, "is I want to see if you want me to be the manager."

Torre wasn't sure what reaction he would get from Steinbrenner to that opening. He had decided well before the meeting that "if there was any hemming or hawing, or if they didn't want me, I would have said, 'Let's figure a way out of this.'"

Steinbrenner did not hesitate.

"Yes, I want you to manage," he said.

Torre was relieved.

"I can't work for someone if the only reason they're keeping me on is they're paying me," Torre said. "I want to be comfortable knowing when I do things, they're on my side, that they're pulling for me to do something right."

The rest of the meeting was quick and easy. Torre did say that the disconnect between Yankees officials in New York and Tampa needed to be resolved; Steinbrenner agreed. Torre also promised to call

Steinbrenner every ten days or so. "I'll make sure we stay connected," he told him.

———

There was one loose end that required immediate attention, and, though Torre did not know it at the time, it would contribute to a rift in his professional relationship with Brian Cashman and, by extension, to the beginning of his end as Yankees manager. The Yankees needed a replacement for Stottlemyre as the pitching coach. Torre mentioned that his choice would be Ron Guidry, the former Yankees pitcher who had served as a spring training instructor.

"I knew he hadn't done it before," Torre said. "But he handled stress well. He did a lot of work in spring training."

Guidry was nothing close to the kind of coach Cashman wanted, and Cashman's power in the organization was growing immensely. As the Yankees played poorly during the first half of the 2005 season—after the 11-19 start, they were still a .500 team as late as July 1—Steinbrenner rode Cashman mercilessly.

"This is on you and Joe!" Steinbrenner would warn Cashman.

It was an old, favorite tactic of Steinbrenner. He loved to make people individually responsible for the outcomes of others. It was designated scapegoating, and what Steinbrenner loved about it was that it kept those placed under his warning perpetually uncomfortable. He hated his employees to be comfortable. He wanted his people to be on edge constantly.

The criticism bothered Cashman only because Steinbrenner made him accountable for decisions for which he had little input, or even argued against. Steinbrenner also loved the divide-and-conquer strategem to keep his employees on edge. He loved pitting his lieutenants in Tampa against his soldiers in New York, for instance. The baseball operations people in Tampa might acquire somebody Cashman didn't fully endorse, such as outfielder Gary Sheffield or infielder Tony Womack, but it would always be Cashman whom Steinbrenner would hold accountable. Finally, during the early dark days of that 2005 season, Cashman decided he had had enough of the scoldings.

"If this is really my team," he told Steinbrenner, "and I'm the only one fixing it, I'll fix it for the final time. That's it. At the end of the season I'm done. I've been telling you the storm clouds are coming."

Indeed, Cashman told Steinbrenner as his contract ran out after the season that he intended to leave because of the disorganization in the baseball operations hierarchy. Cashman wrote a "chain of command philosophy" memo to Steinbrenner, outlining exactly what the Yankees needed: clearly defined job descriptions and responsibilities for the baseball operations personnel, with the general manager holding top authority. Steinbrenner said he would institute those changes if Cashman agreed to return. Cashman decided to stay, now fully empowered to run the baseball operations and to keep the Tampa lieutenants in check.

While fixing the 2005 Yankees, Cashman introduced some youth. He promoted pitcher Chien-Ming Wang, who at the age of 25 gave the Yankees an 8-5 record, and second baseman Robinson Cano, who hit .297 at the age of 22. Cashman saw what was happening around baseball. His contemporaries and friends, such as Theo Epstein in Boston, Billy Beane in Oakland and Mark Shapiro in Cleveland, were using cutting-edge evaluation tools and processes to put together efficient rosters from top to bottom. Cashman wanted to join the information revolution, but he knew he couldn't join in if old-time baseball men in Tampa such as Billy Connors, Steinbrenner's trusted "pitching guru," could undo his carefully crafted plans with just one whisper in The Boss's ear about some broken-down veteran he liked. His new contract removed that problem.

The choice of the next pitching coach would immediately test Cashman's authority and philosophy. Cashman liked people with experience and he liked people with strong organizational skills with an understanding of statistical analysis, neither of which described Guidry. Cashman's idea of the modern pitching coach was someone such as Joe Kerrigan, the former Boston and Philadelphia pitching coach whom he hired in 2005 to be his special assistant. Kerrigan pored over scouting reports, computer printouts and videos to find any edge for the Yankees.

The Yankees, with Steinbrenner influencing Cashman, first tried to hire Leo Mazzone, who had plenty of experience and a proven track record with the Atlanta Braves, but who deployed an old-school philosophy. The Yankees were so close to a deal with Mazzone that when Torre called him one day, Mazzone said, "All right, I'll be with you. I'm looking forward to working with you."

"Good," said Torre, who knew Mazzone from when he managed the Braves.

The next day Mazzone signed with the Orioles, to work close to his hometown and with Baltimore manager Sam Perlozzo, a friend since childhood. Cashman then called up Torre.

"George wants to hire Guidry," Cashman said.

"That's fine with me," Torre said.

"George wants to talk to you about it."

Torre called Steinbrenner, who asked him, "What do you think of Guidry?"

"I trust him," Torre said. "It's going to take some time. He hasn't done it on an everyday basis. But he's very thorough, from the spring experiences I had with him."

Steinbrenner liked Guidry and he always liked

taking care of former Yankee greats. Cashman was a more difficult sell.

Said Torre, "Cash didn't want any part of it because Guidry had no experience. He likes people with experience. I understand that. I was sort of in a tough spot, because I know I had mentioned Guidry in passing when I had that meeting with George. I know Cash went to George about Guidry's inexperience, because I know Billy didn't like Guidry. George, I think, hired him because he remembered me saying it."

Torre had an idea to try to keep both Steinbrenner and Cashman happy.

"Cash," he said, "I know you're uncomfortable with this. So why don't you, with Guidry's lack of experience, bring Kerrigan on as the bullpen coach? Kerrigan will be right there to help Guidry with the administrative stuff."

Cashman signed off on the idea, though Torre knew Cashman still wasn't comfortable with an old-school guy like Guidry running his pitching staff. Guidry was one of the greatest lefthanded pitchers in Yankee history, an ace under manager Billy Martin on championship teams. He worked hard, got along with everyone, but looked at pitching development from a different perspective than Cashman. Guidry relied not so much on computers as he did personal experience, which he liked to share with his pitchers. He remembered, for instance, once in 1977 when he walked into the clubhouse during a game in the third inning and saw Hall of Famer Catfish Hunter, the starting pitcher in that game, sipping a beer.

"Cat, what are you doing?" Guidry asked.

"Gator, on a hot day like today I always drink a small beer while I'm pitching," Hunter said. "It helps me. I don't like Gatorade. Water bloats me. I come in and have a beer. Just during day games, not night games. It works for me."

Guidry figured if it worked for Hunter it could work for him. One day in 1978, on a hot Saturday afternoon, Guidry, who was pitching that day, sipped a beer in the clubhouse in the third inning. All of a sudden, Martin was standing in the doorway.

"What the hell are you doing?" the manager asked.

"I'm 11 and 0," Guidry replied. "What more do you want?"

Martin immediately calmed down.

"Go ahead," Martin said. "Take your time."

Said Guidry, "Every day game from that point on, when I'd come in after the third inning, Billy would go, 'Are you going to the lounge?' I'd say, 'Yeah.' And he'd say, 'I'll be right back.' I look back on everything we went through. Sometimes I think that's why we played so well. Because it was so much fun."

Cashman, though, was the kind of general manager who put his faith not in such folktales, but in cold, hard facts, such as pitch counts and statistical analysis, the kind of stuff at which Kerrigan excelled.

"The thing about Cash," Torre said, "was any time you talked to him about him being a numbers guy, he really had very little patience about it. He kept denying it. And he got very defensive about it."

When the 2006 Yankees spring training camp began, it was obvious that this was now Cashman's team. The first clues were the video cameras set up on tripods behind the home plates in the large bullpen area of the Legends Field complex. "We knew something was up in spring training when Cashman ordered every side session pitch filmed," said Borzello.

———

Torre also noticed that more and more people from the front office were trolling the clubhouse and coaches' dressing room. Cashman had surrounded himself with up-and-coming assistants who were raised more on statistical analysis than heavy, old-school scouting beliefs. They were young, smart and diligent, and were comfortable, even jazzed up, about discussing such things as players' VORPs— the acronym stat for something called value over replacement player—and in-house PlayStation tournaments.

They brought a new perspective to talent evaluation that, of course, no more solved the eternal
mysteries of baseball than the old-school scouting
methods had. Midway through 2007, for instance,
Cashman and his number crunchers zeroed in on
trading for Wilson Betemit, a switch-hitting infielder with the Los Angeles Dodgers. The word excitedly circulating around the hallways of Yankee
Stadium was that the Yankees had found "the next
David Ortiz"—not that Betemit fit Ortiz's profile as
a slugger, but that his numbers suggested he was an
undervalued gem who was on the cusp of a huge
breakout, like the one Ortiz had for Boston in
2003. The Yankees were dead wrong. Betemit,
plagued by extremely poor plate discipline and conditioning issues, was dreadful, posting on-base percentages of .278 and .289 with the Yankees over
that season and the next. On the other hand, the
new Yankee philosophy hit on such minor-league
free agent pitching finds as Brian Bruney, Jose
Veras, Darrell Rasner and Edwar Ramirez. Institut-
ing the new groupthink in 2006, however, was not
without internal strain.

"It got to the point where I was starting not to
trust people," Torre said of the 2006 spring training
camp. "There were so many other people Cash
wanted in the mix. I got very suspicious. There were
guys in the clubhouse and in the coaches' room that
weren't there before, like they were checking out
what was going on. Cash would say, 'We haven't

counted this guy's pitches!' There was always some information being sent back to Cash that helped him know everything that was going on rather than trusting what the baseball people were doing. And, of course, he was questioning Guidry. In spring training it looked like Cash was doing undercover work to check up on Guidry all the time."

———

A cultural clash was developing. Cashman, newly empowered, at last had the chance to run the team his way, and his way included a strong desire to hop aboard the information revolution. Torre saw numbers not as a guiding philosophy, but as one tool in a manager's toolbox, particularly when it came to culling information from batter-pitcher histories.

"Cash, once he was in charge, wanted to be as practical as possible," Torre said. "He put his trust in people he hired, like Billy Eppler. Billy was fine. I'd talk to him at batting practice behind the cage. I remember one time we were talking about Kyle Farnsworth. I was suspect about his ability to sustain any consistency. The thing Eppler came up with was, 'I think it's a good signing because of the money.' That's fine, but I'm trying to win games and put somebody in the setup position who's going to be consistent."

Torre and Cashman had been together for 11 years, the previous nine as the most successful manager–general manager combination in the game.

They had been through so much and, despite the difference in ages, had nurtured a deeply shared respect and a special kinship. If nothing else, both of them understand as well as anybody on the planet the joys and difficulties of working for George Steinbrenner, and that alone had the bonding powers of a six-month deployment on a nuclear submarine. But the 2006 spring training camp opened a professional, philosophical gap between them that would never entirely close. One day during that camp Torre met with Cashman in the manager's office.

"Cash, you've changed," Torre said.

"I have not," Cashman said.

"I accused him of looking for reasons to criticize Guidry," Torre said. "He had all his staff members around. He relied a lot less on opinions. He wanted documentation. That was more important."

After that, the two of them coolly kept their distance from one another for a few days.

"We had a falling-out in spring training," Torre said. "I basically challenged him. Then I apologized a few days later, because I really like Cash. I asked other people, 'Is this just me or has he changed?' It was his watch and he wanted to do it his way. I understand that. I would have liked to have him trust me. I was always a very loyal subject to him."

Torre had another key meeting with Cashman during the season in the general manager's office. "Cash, listen," Torre said. "I don't know how long we're going to be together. But do yourself a favor: never forget there is a heartbeat in this game."

After the 2006 season, the philosophical gap would become a chasm over what to do about one of the most important and beloved players in Yankees history. Torre's titanium-strong belief in the power of trust, the backbone of his entire managerial philosophy, would reach a critical showdown with Cashman's new-age practicality, the guiding principle of his newfound empowerment. Smack in the middle was one of the last vestiges of the championship years, an ever-graceful reminder of when trust and teamwork still mattered. At stake was the career and legacy of Bernie Williams.

12.

Broken Trust

Bernie Williams watched what would be the last game of his 16-year career from the bench, never making an appearance in an 8-3 clinching loss in Game 4 of the 2006 American League Division Series against the Detroit Tigers. The autopsy on the 2006 Yankees looked a lot like the postmortems of the previous two seasons. The Yankees fielded a spectacular lineup—they scored 930 runs, the most in baseball—but they could not hit in the clutch come October, particularly Alex Rodriguez. The pitching was again old, pedestrian—they were sixth in the league in ERA—and not nearly deep enough. With their season on the line in that Game 4, the Yankees gave the ball in that must-win situation to Jaret Wright, who would never win another big league game. Wright did not get out of the fourth inning, leaving the Yankees in a 4-0 hole from which they could not escape.

The Yankees went meekly in their second straight first-round exit since the Red Sox shifted the balance of power in that 2004 ALCS, though only after they stood halfway toward dismissing Detroit. The Yankees won Game 1 and held a 3-1 lead in the fifth inning of Game 2 with Mike Mussina on the mound at home. Mussina gave up single runs in the fifth, sixth and seventh and the game's greatest offense scored nothing more the rest of the game as the Yankees lost, 4-3. Detroit outscored the Yankees 17-3 over the last 23 innings of the series to send them home to yet another winter of anger and chaos.

The 2006 Yankees somehow managed not to get out of the first round despite employing the bats of Jeter, Rodriguez, Johnny Damon, Bobby Abreu, Gary Sheffield, Hideki Matsui, Jason Giambi, Jorge Posada and Robinson Cano, one of the deepest assemblages of premier hitters on one team. Or did they lose precisely because of that plethora? Torre, working around injuries and egos, struggled to find the combination of players that would click.

Damon, signed as a free agent when Boston showed lukewarm interest in keeping him, gave the lineup energy and surprising power. He hit a careerhigh 24 home runs. Cashman added Abreu in a deft midseason trade with Philadelphia after outfielders Sheffield and Matsui both went down with injuries that cost them most of the season. Williams picked up time at all three outfield positions, as did Melky Cabrera, and at designated hitter. Jason Giambi missed 23 games with his usual assortment of physical calamities, and split time between first base and designated hitter when he was in the lineup. Problem was, the Yankees entered October far from being a set team. Of those seven aforementioned hitters, two of them would be out of the lineup on any given day.

———

In late September, as Sheffield, who missed four months after undergoing wrist surgery, was getting ready to rejoin the team, Torre called the slugger into his office. The manager wanted to talk to Sheffield about the possibility of playing first base when he returned.

"Now that we have Abreu . . ." Torre said.

Sheffield stopped him.

"I already ordered my first baseman's mitt," Sheffield said.

"Perfect. I know you can do it."

Said Torre, "He was a team player. He finished a couple of games at third base for me, when we had to take guys out and move people around. He was willing to do anything. He'd even catch. 'I'll do anything,' he told me. He came in one day and brought in a VHS tape of when he caught in Little League.

THE YANKEE YEARS   503

He was a great teammate. He was just inconsistent with his moods."

Torre did try Sheffield at first base in the last week of the season. Torre wasn't sure that Giambi, who had his own wrist problem, could play the position.

"He looked fine," Torre said of Sheffield as a first baseman. "And then once we started the playoffs all of a sudden he regressed defensively. He started catching the ball awkwardly. And offensively, he didn't have enough time to get sharp. We forced it, but it's tough not to force it because of what you know he can bring to the table. But he wasn't the same guy. If he was the same offensive force, I would never have taken him out of a game for anybody. But at the time, I was looking for a little shot in the arm."

In Game 3 in Detroit, against lefthander Kenny Rogers, the two players Torre chose not to start were Sheffield and Cabrera. Torre started Giambi at first base and Williams at designated hitter, batting eighth. Williams was a .353 hitter against Rogers in 34 career at-bats. Sheffield was 1-for-8 in the series and batting .222 since he returned to the team September 22. Torre sought out Sheffield in the clubhouse before posting the lineup.

"I'm changing the lineup," Torre said. "I want to put Bernie in the lineup."

"Okay," Sheffield said.

A few minutes later, after Torre had walked down the hall to his office, Rodriguez poked his head into the manager's office.

"Can I talk to you?" said Rodriguez, who had batted sixth in Games 1 and 2 with almost no success and now was hitting fourth in Game 3.

"Sure."

"You know, when you left after talking to Gary, he started throwing stuff all over the place."

"Well, I can't help that. I told him. I didn't send anybody in to tell him. I told him. If he wanted to have an issue with me he could have had an issue."

"Don't worry. I'll handle it."

"Okay, thank you."

Said Torre, "That's more of Alex wanting to be the leader, to be Jeter, basically."

The Yankees were blown out, 6-0, as Rogers out-pitched a familiarly ineffective Randy Johnson, who gave up five runs in less than six innings, swelling his postseason ERA as a Yankee to 6.92. Rogers shut down the Yankees on five hits two outs into the eighth inning before relievers Joel Zumaya and Todd Jones gave them nothing more. Giambi and Williams went a combined 0-for-7. Rodriguez went 0-for-3 and was hit by a pitch, slipping deeper and deeper into a funk of near hitting-paralysis proportions. Rodriguez was 1-for-11 through the first three games of the series, was hitless in his previous 10 at-bats with four strikeouts, had batted with 10 runners on base and driven in none of them, and, as if unable to pull the trigger, had looked at 12 called strikes.

Another day brought another game of lineup roulette. Other than Jeter and Posada, Torre had nobody in this once formidable lineup who was swinging the bat well. This time, against right-hander Jeremy Bonderman in Game 4, Williams and Giambi were the odd men out, with Sheffield back at cleanup as the first baseman, and Cabrera hitting ninth as the designated hitter. The headline news to the lineup, however, was that Rodriguez was batting eighth. Torre did not tell Rodriguez about it before the lineup was posted in the clubhouse.

"At that point we were on our heels and I was just trying to get some energy," Torre said. "So I did it and I just posted it. And then the writers asked me in the pregame press conference about hitting him eighth. I said, 'You know it's sad that you guys didn't ask me this question, which would have been the better question: Why isn't Giambi playing against the righthander?' Nobody asked me that question. It was all about Alex.

"But Alex wasn't swinging worth a shit, and it was all about trying to put more energy people above him. It wasn't trying to purposefully piss him off. But knowing Alex, no matter what explanation I gave him, it was just going to be the eighth hole. I didn't know what I could tell him to appease him and still tell him the truth."

Rodriguez did not seek out Torre to ask about the lineup.

"No," Torre said. "That night he came to me on the tarmac, after we landed in New York, and he gave me a hug. That was it."

Rodriguez went 0-for-3 again. For the series, he batted .071, batted with 11 runners on base and drove in none of them, drew no walks, had no extra-base hits, and saw more than four pitches only twice in 15 plate appearances.

Jeter and Posada combined to bat .500 in the series. The rest of the team that had scored 930 runs in the regular season batted .173.

———

Soon after the Yankees' elimination, Steinbrenner released a statement through his public relations people, which had become nearly his sole means of public communication, to say, "Rest assured, we will go back to work immediately and try to right this sad failure and provide a championship for the Yankees, as is our goal every year."

The Yankees had won 97 games, drawn 4.2 million people to Yankee Stadium, made the playoffs for a 12th consecutive season, outscored every team in baseball by at least 60 runs, employed 36 past, current or future All-Stars . . . and their owner had winnowed it all down to a "sad failure."

Torre bore the brunt of the growing frustration in the organization. The playoff losses obliterated the story of the resolve of these flawed Yankee teams. The Yankees came from behind to make the playoffs in 2006 for the third time in four consecutive seasons. In 2004, they started 8-11 and began June in second place. In 2005, they started 11-19 and began July with a .500 record. In 2006, they trailed Boston for most of the first four months and started August in second place. In 2007 they started 21-29 and were a .500 team into the second half of the season. In every case Torre brought the team home to the playoffs. The collateral damage, however, was accumulating. The cost of playing from behind year after year was the constant organizational anxiety that covered the lengthy seasons. There was no margin for error, little room to breathe.

During the 2006 season, for instance, the Yankees suffered a blowout loss, 19-1, to the Cleveland Indians, Steinbrenner's hometown team, on the Fourth of July, Steinbrenner's birthday. The defeat left the Yankees in second place, four games behind the Red Sox. Steve Swindal, merrily enjoying the holiday on a boat, called up Cashman and began screaming at him. "I pay you and Joe all this money!" Swindal said as part of his rant.

Said Torre, "Cash got pissed and I got pissed. I talked to Steve the next day and I said, 'Steve, you have to understand: we're trying to win the game. And if we lose 2-1 or 18-6, there's no difference.'"

Three days later the Yankees were playing the

508 JOE TORRE AND TOM VERDUCCI

Devil Rays in St. Petersburg. Swindal walked into the Yankees clubhouse. The visiting manager's office is the first door on the left as you enter the clubhouse at Tropicana Field. As Swindal walked in, Torre motioned him into his office.

"Close the door," Torre said.

Swindal sat down.

"Let me tell you something," Torre said. "Either fire us, fire me, or trust what we do. If you think when we don't win it's because we're not paying attention, you've got another thing coming. That was ridiculous."

"Well," Swindal said with a nervous chuckle, "you know how I am."

"Yeah," Torre said. "And we'll work this through. But you hired us for a reason. You either believe in what we're doing or let us go."

The 2006 playoff loss to Detroit depleted further the goodwill account Torre had built in the Yankee organization, a reality made obvious the morning after Game 4.

———

Hours after the Yankees lost Game 4 to the Tigers, the back page of the New York **Daily News** the next morning featured a picture of Torre and declared in capital letters without the typical equivocation of a question mark, "OUTTA HERE!" The story said Steinbrenner was firing Torre and replacing him with Lou Piniella (though Piniella was deep in discussions to sign on as manager of the Cubs and had had no contact with Yankees officials). Reporters began staking out the front lawn of Torre's Westchester, New York, home. Steinbrenner and the rest of the Yankees' front office said nothing publicly about Torre's status for two days, letting the speculation continue ablaze, but they did conduct a high-level conference call that included Steinbrenner, Cashman, Torre, president Randy Levine, chief operating officer Lonn Trost and manager partner Steve Swindal. Several times the Yankees' decision makers brought up the idea that perhaps Torre had become "distracted" as the New York manager, even making reference to the charitable work he does for his foundation for victims of abuse by family members, the Safe at Home Foundation.

"I resented the fact that they claimed I was distracted by something," Torre said. "I told them, 'What suddenly happened in the postseason that distracted me that wasn't going on during the season when we won as many games as any team in baseball?'"

Indeed, the Yankees won 97 games, the most in the American League and tied with the New York Mets for the most in baseball. They scored more runs than anybody in baseball. They trounced Detroit in Game 1 of the best-of-five series, 8-4, and took a 3-1 lead into the fifth inning of Game 2 with veteran righthander Mike Mussina on the mound at Yankee Stadium. Apparently that's when the "distractions" must have manifested themselves, for the Yankees suddenly lost their grip on the series.

Ali, listening to her husband on the conference call, interjected in a stage whisper, "What are you defending yourself for? If they want to fire you, let them fire you. Simple as that."

Torre didn't hear much support from his bosses on the other end of the line. The Yankees had come to believe that anything short of a world championship was a failure. Of course, such thinking was possible only because of the four world championships they won in Torre's first five years on the job. No other team since 1953 has won four World Series titles in five years, a 53-year span that covers the advent of free agency, the beginning of expansion and the full integration of the major leagues. The credit in the bank from those titles had run out for Torre. If he was going to be judged harshly and almost entirely on two and a half games against the Tigers—23 innings in which Mussina, Randy Johnson and Jaret Wright got outpitched and the Yankees batted .163—well, that was the brutal truth of the job. The Yankees played every season as an "all-in" card game, and the manager had to understand the consequences if he didn't play a winning hand. Torre knew this reality. At the end of the conference call he stopped defending himself and his record and offered advice to George Steinbrenner.

"George, I always want to make you proud of

what I do," Torre said, "but if you feel in your heart you should make a change, then that's what you should do. I'm not begging for my job. I'm here to tell you that I'm going to work the same as I always have for you. I'm not going to do anything different. What am I going to do different? I can only be who I am. But if you're more comfortable making a change, then that's what you should do."

When the conference call ended, nothing had been decided. Steinbrenner needed to think about it. Torre hung up not knowing if he would manage the Yankees again. Another day passed. Still nothing. Torre was unable to take any questions from the media because he had no idea about his status. He did ask Jason Zillo, the Yankees' public relations director, if Zillo could do something about the reporters on his front lawn. Zillo promptly provided the lawn service, calling the news outlets to ask them to end the fruitless vigil.

On the next day the Yankees finally announced that Torre would meet with reporters at 1 p.m. at Yankee Stadium. For Torre, however, there was a slight hitch to the plans for a news conference: He still had no idea if he was going to manage the Yankees. He still had heard nothing from Steinbrenner. Torre was getting dressed to go to that news conference when he decided to do something about being left to twist in the wind. He called Cashman.

"Cash, have you heard anything yet?" Torre asked.

"No," Cashman replied. "I haven't heard anything."

"Do me a favor," Torre said.

"Sure, what's that, Joe?" Cashman said.

"Call them and tell them to fire me right now. If it takes them this long to make up their minds tell them to fucking find somebody else. I don't want to be here. This is ridiculous."

It was typical Torre. One of his strong suits for working for Steinbrenner was that from the moment he was hired he never needed the job badly enough to become Steinbrenner's lackey. Steinbrenner liked his managers and executives to be beholden to him (none were more so than "true Yankee" Billy Martin; and most deferentially called him "Mr. Steinbrenner"), but Torre saw the Yankee job as playing with house money. He called Steinbrenner "George."

But the "fire me" edict to Cashman was typical Torre, too, because it was such an emotional reaction. Ali often told him he took things too personally and reacted too emotionally, and this seemed to be yet another case.

Cashman argued to Torre to remain patient just a little while longer, and Torre eventually agreed. He could go to the press conference and simply answer questions to the best of his knowledge, of which he had very little when it came to his job status. Five minutes before the press conference was about to begin, Torre's phone rang. It was Stein-brenner.

"We want you to manage next year," The Boss said.

After being "fired" on the back page of the **Daily News,** after being told he was "distracted" while serving as the manager of the winningest team in the league, and after being placed in a limbo status for two days right up until five minutes before his press conference, Torre reacted to Steinbrenner's olive branch the best way he knew how: he politely thanked Steinbrenner.

———

It was the last meaningful conversation Torre would ever have with Steinbrenner. The change in the relationship had nothing to do with Torre's job status. It had everything to do with Steinbrenner's health. No one would tell Torre of any specific health issue afflicting Steinbrenner, but it was obvious to all in the Yankees family that Steinbrenner's physical and mental acuity were slipping quickly. Steinbrenner and Torre had spoken often over the years and developed a cordial, respectful relationship. Torre had a natural ease of dealing with Steinbrenner.

"It drove him nuts that it made sense when I talked to him," Torre said. "I remember one time I told him, 'George, we've got to talk about this.' He said, 'I don't want to talk about it because you'll talk me into it.' I forgot what the subject matter was. I laughed. He said, 'I don't want to talk to you about it because you'll put it in a way that makes it simple.' "

The banter and the conversations faded to almost nothing. About a month or so after Steinbrenner agreed to bring Torre back for the 2007 season—it was around Thanksgiving, 2006—Torre ran into Steinbrenner in Tampa after flying there on a private plane with his family. Steinbrenner, 76, was at the airport waiting for his grandchildren to fly in.

"Hi, pal," Steinbrenner said. Other than exchanging pleasantries, there was no conversation. Steinbrenner, as he had taken to doing regularly, was wearing dark glasses indoors. What struck Torre was that Steinbrenner's hand was shaking, and The Boss stuck his hand in his pocket to try to quell the tremors.

"He was okay," Torre remembered, "but you could see he didn't have the thunder he once had."

There was no diagnosis of which Torre was aware, but it had become obvious by 2007 that the old lion had reached his winter. Torre knew Steinbrenner had drifted away from the day-to-day operations and long-term planning. One day he ran into Steinbrenner in the parking lot of Legends Field as Steinbrenner was getting into his car. Torre was riding a golf cart. Steinbrenner walked over and put one foot on the golf cart and a hand on its roof to steady himself. What Torre noticed was that Steinbrenner's hand kept shaking on the roof of the cart. At about that time one of the Yankees star players also encountered Steinbrenner in the parking lot. Said the player after the meeting, "Honestly, I'm not even sure he knew who I was."

"I talk to him from time to time," Torre said one day in the 2007 spring training camp in the manager's office. "He doesn't show up down here anymore. He used to show up here every day. He loved it. But he can't sit there and talk to you anymore. And it's sad. No matter what you thought of him you never want to see anybody go that way, lose his spirit basically. You don't want to see it happen.

"I remember we were sitting on my couch together one day a few years ago and I said the same thing I would always tell him: 'You know, if you could just do me one favor. Just understand: I want to make you proud. I can't control the fact that people give me credit for what's happening. Because every time that happens I always credit you for bringing me here and getting the resources to do it. But don't blame me and don't get mad at me because of that, because I can't control that.'

"He said, 'Oh, I don't. I don't feel that way.' I knew better. And it kept us from being really as close as we could have been. Instead of him perceiving this as 'I got the right guy. I'm proud of that,' it's all about 'He's getting too much credit.' And because George likes to maintain control, and scare people, and I think he eliminated that with me. He couldn't control me and he couldn't scare me, and I think that frustrated him.

"I told him, 'I'd like to have a situation between the two of us where if you see something you don't like, you just call me. All right? Just call me. One thing I'll never lose sight of is you're The Boss. I'll always respect that. I never want to get to the point where I think I'm bigger than that, because that's not the case.'"

What Torre appreciated about Steinbrenner was that The Boss was always accessible. He was apt to come blustering into Torre's office at any time, call him on the telephone or summon him and his other baseball advisers to another emergency meeting in the thirdfloor executive boardroom of Legends Field. Torre liked knowing that Steinbrenner always was there and he knew where he stood with him.

But that was no longer true in 2007 due to Steinbrenner's health. One of his last true allies, Cashman, would move philosophically further away from him that winter, and Williams had everything to do with it.

———

Williams, 37, was a free agent who wanted to return to the only organization he had ever known. The 22-year-old kid who had reached the big leagues in

1991 with such a wide-eyed look that teammates derisively called him "Bambi"—their mistake was taking his naïveness for a competitive softness—had come to win four world championship rings, smash 2,336 hits, make five All-Star Games, win one batting title and earn $103 million. And after all of that he still gave forth that same youthful naïveness that charmed Yankees fans. Williams was one of their own. They had watched him grow up, deliver in the clutch and still remain humble, wide-eyed and sincere.

The beauty of Williams was that he hadn't changed much at all, wearing the same uniform and look of blissful earnestness. Before there was Manny being Manny, the catchphrase to excuse the childlike goofiness of Manny Ramirez, there was Bernie being Bernie. After the Yankees beat the Texas Rangers in the clinching Game 4 of the 1996 Division Series, Williams called up Torre in his hotel room.

"I've got a problem," Williams said.

"What's that?" Torre said, expecting the worst.

"My family flew out and it costs $500 to change the tickets to go back a day early. Do you know any-one at the airline?"

Williams was making $3 million in 1996.

"Stuff like that made him charming, it really did," Torre said. "Bernie Williams always expected the best. I'll always remember he made the last out of the 1997 Division Series, a fly ball to center field with a runner on second base, and I had to practically peel him off the steps leading to the clubhouse. I said, 'Bernie, it's not always going to turn out the way you want it to.' He was devastated."

Teammates delighted in Bernie being Bernie. One time he left Yankee Stadium after a night game and forgot his own child, who was playing video games. When he reached home he realized his oversight and called up Andy Pettitte and said, "Andy, can you bring him home?"

Another time, after the clinching game of a World Series, Williams drove home without his wife. Waleska Williams was left standing in the waiting room with trainer Steve Donahue.

On the last day of the 2005 season, the Yankees went to Fenway Park in Boston knowing that if they won the game they would open the Division Series at home against the Angels, and if they lost they would open against them on the road in Anaheim. Before the game Williams asked Torre, "Do you mind if I drive home with my wife after the game?" Said Torre, "Bernie, if we lose today we go to Anaheim." Replied Williams, "We do?"

Williams would call the Yankee Stadium clubhouse from his home in suburban Westchester at one o'clock in the afternoon and, like a Little Leaguer, say, "It's raining here. Are we playing tonight?"

He was known to be late reporting for work from time to time. Williams was late, for instance, for Game 6 of the 2001 World Series, and barely arrived in time after his taxi had to negotiate the heavy security measures and barricades set up around the ballpark.

There was another time when Torre walked up to Williams in the lunchroom of the visiting clubhouse in Tampa Bay. Williams was making a sandwich.

"How are you doing, Bernie?" Torre asked.

"I missed the bus. I'm sorry for being late," Williams said.

"Bernie," Torre said with a smile, "I didn't even know you were late. But thanks for offering it up. That sandwich is going to cost you $200."

Williams laughed.

Williams occupied a special place in Yankees history. He had played on a Yankees team that lost 91 games, in 1991, and he was there for the reconstruction and the run of a modern dynasty. Williams played in 2006 under a one-year deal for $1.5 million. He was a bargain at that rate, hitting .281 with 12 home runs and 61 runs batted in. He wasn't an everyday player anymore, not even a part-time center fielder, and he and Torre both knew that. Williams wanted to play another year as a bench player, occasionally starting in the outfield in the event of an injury or a needed day of rest for one of the main outfielders, Damon, Abreu, Cabrera and Matsui.

Soon after the Yankees lost the 2006 ALDS to Detroit, Cashman held a meeting with Torre and the coaching staff, in which they discussed whether Williams still had a role with the team for 2007. Cashman said that everyone in the room agreed that Williams was done. However, as the Yankees roster began to take shape over the winter, Torre came to believe that Williams re-emerged as their best option off the bench.

Torre knew that he could still be counted on to give a quality at-bat in a key spot, and who had the added benefit of being a switch-hitter, which causes difficult decisions to opposing managers when they try to match up their relief pitchers to gain platoon advantages. Over the previous two seasons, at ages 36 and 37, Williams hit .317 and .321 with runners in scoring position and two outs.

Torre told Cashman he wanted to bring back Williams on a similar deal that he had in 2006. Cashman wanted nothing to do with it. He had a better idea, he said. He pulled out some numbers. He started giving Torre pinch-hitting numbers and on-base percentage numbers for Josh Phelps and Doug Mientkiewicz. That was Cashman's plan: he could do better with a combination of Josh Phelps and Doug Mientkiewicz than bringing back Bernie Williams for one more year. Torre was astounded.

"Cash," Torre said, "Bernie Williams may not play much outfield because we don't have room in the outfield, but as a bench player, a switch-hitter, I know if I'm managing in the other dugout and I know they have Bernie Williams sitting there, it's going to affect who I bring in and how I manage the game. If you know the player Bernie was, and he's not that far removed from that, you know that the danger is still there."

Cashman stuck to the on-base percentage numbers.

"I can't fight that," Torre said. "For me and some of the other managers, is Mientkiewicz coming up to pinch-hit going to scare me like Bernie Williams does? Even though he's got a better on-base percentage?"

Cashman did not budge. He was also worried about the awkwardness of having to cut an icon like Williams if he showed he really was done. Torre said, "It was like talking to a brick wall. It never went anywhere."

The philosophical battle was no battle at all. Cashman's faith in numbers won out decisively over Torre's trust in his players. Cashman would not offer Williams a major league contract. He was open to the idea of letting Williams come to camp to try out with a minor league deal. Williams was too proud a Yankee for that. Torre tried multiple times to talk him into coming to camp as a non-roster invitee. Williams would have none of that scenario. The lack of a real major league offer told Williams all he needed to know: the Yankees had no more use for him.

"I talked to him about three or four times," Torre said, "and I kept trying to convince him to come down, and I did everything but promise him he was going to make the team. I couldn't do that. And I'm not even sure to this day what was going on in Bernie's head. I knew he was hurt by the fact that he was just dismissed. I just think that in Cash's mind, they were sort of stuck into paying him for so long, and paying him so much money, he felt he owed him nothing, which I'm not sure is the right way to look at things. And then Cash got upset with Bernie, was pissed off at something."

In January of 2008, Cashman unwittingly tipped his hand about how he felt about Williams in comments he made at a symposium at William Patterson College in New Jersey, an event Cashman did not figure was destined to hit the newspapers. Cashman took shots at Williams, saying he had a "terrible season" in 2005, that Torre played Williams in 2006 "ahead of guys who could help us win," and that Williams grew more involved in his music career "and that took away from his play."

The Mientkiewicz-Phelps Plan was, by most any measurement, a bust. Mientkiewicz broke his right wrist and played in only 72 games. (Williams played at least 119 games in his last 12 seasons after the strike-shortened 1994 season.) Phelps was waived in June after playing just 36 games. Combined, Mientkiewicz and Phelps batted .200 in all games coming off the bench, with five hits in 25 at-bats.

"I don't know how many times that year I would

look at Don Mattingly and say, 'This is a good spot for Bernie,'" Torre said. "You've got a pinch-hit opportunity coming up and they've got a lefty and righty warming up in the bullpen, and with Bernie you neutralize their choices."

The Yankees went to six World Series under Torre and Williams hit third or fourth in the lineup in every one of them. With his expressive eyes, fluid stroke and sprinter's body, Williams was not your typical middle-of-the-order slugger on championship teams. He never hit more than 30 home runs. He was, however, more than tough enough to hold down that kind of responsibility.

"Bernie was a son of a bitch; the pressure of the game never bothered him," Torre said. "It never bothered him. You know, you try to explain all that stuff, and unless you have a feel for what you're seeing, it's tough to rationalize with sheer numbers.

"I don't think Bernie cared about what it looked like on the field, as opposed to simply what it was. I think good players go on the field knowing there is a danger of being embarrassed and it doesn't bother them at all. Bernie never thought anything negative was going to happen until it happened."

For Torre, Cashman's dismissal of Williams was also, in part, a repudiation of the manager's trust and understanding of players. The hits to his standing as the secure manager of the New York Yankees were piling up: the sniping via the franchise's own network and the cold war with Steinbrenner in

2005, the virtual firing and subsequent twisting in the wind after the 2006 Division Series, and now this, the decision by Cashman to trust a belief in numbers rather than trust Torre's belief in Bernie Williams.

"The one that pissed me off more than anything was Bernie Williams, where my opinion was completely disregarded," Torre said. "I was beating a dead horse, and I'll never forget that."

———

The future of Joe Torre as manager of the New York Yankees was a last-minute addition to the menu at a March 9, 2007, benefit luncheon for the Boys and Girls Clubs of Tampa Bay at the Tampa Marriott Waterside Hotel. The Boys and Girls Clubs of Tampa had long been a favorite charity of George Steinbrenner, and you could find his name affixed to one of its buildings as proof of his generosity. Each spring training, Steinbrenner would make sure his staff and ballplayers joined him in supporting the Boys and Girls Clubs of Tampa Bay by attending the luncheon, which had grown to become one of its largest fund-raising events. Brian Cashman decided to use the 2007 luncheon, away from the prying eyes of the New York media, to address the thorny issue of what to do about Torre, which for the previous five months had grown cumbersomely into the elephant in the room nobody wanted to acknowledge. Torre's status beyond that 2007 season was unresolved.

Cashman approached Torre and asked him, "What do you want to do, Joe?"

Torre immediately recognized the opening. The general manager would not have asked the question if he didn't want Torre back. That qualified as a major development. Torre was on the last year of his contract, a status that carried more weight than his 11 consecutive seasons guiding the Yankees into the playoffs, four of which culminated with world championships. The impending end to the deal put him squarely in the crosshairs of his critics, some of whom happened to reside in his own organization. When Torre had left for spring training, his wife, Ali, sent him off with a kiss, a hug and this warning: "This is going to be your toughest year, because they're always going to refer to this being the last year of your contract."

Said Torre, "I guess I get naïve at times, but I didn't expect it was going to be tougher. That's because I thought you were always on the last year of your contract, no matter what it said. Even if you have a contract, there's always a threat you can be fired. But I never realized how right she really was."

Without a contract for 2008, Torre was a lame duck, made all the more wounded by what amounted to his mock dismissal after the 2006 season, which had played out like being put through every protocol of a firing squad—the blindfold, the cocking of the chambers, the ready, aim, fire! command—but for blanks being substituted for bullets.

The most important baseball operations decision in the 2007 spring training camp was what to do about Torre. Cashman opened the door to an extension when he approached Torre at the March 9 benefit. Cashman wasn't even sure if Torre had plans to manage beyond 2007. Torre didn't hesitate with a response. As difficult and painful as the fallout was from the 2006 Division Series loss, Torre had lost none of his enthusiasm for the job. He hated the interoffice sniping, the jockeying for credit and the assignment of blame, and he hated knowing not everybody in that front office fully supported him, but Torre loved managing people and ballgames as much as ever.

"I'd like to keep managing," Torre told Cashman. "I still enjoy it."

"Okay," Cashman said. "You're my guy. As long as I'm here, there's nobody I'd rather have managing this team than you. How long would you like to do this?"

Torre understood that the door to a contract extension suddenly was jarred open. He was wise enough not to even have broached the subject over the winter after very nearly being fired, but smart enough to know this was the opportunity to get it done. Torre had an idea.

"How long do you have on your deal?" Torre asked Cashman.

"Through next year."

"Okay. Just tie me to you. We'll have the same thing. Take it through next year so that we're on the same terms."

"That's fine with me," Cashman said.

Torre was making $7 million in 2007, the last year of his deal. A one-year extension would, if nothing else, remove his lame duck status and shrink the size of the bull's-eye on his back. It would minimize the speculation that at any moment he could be fired, a sword of Damocles that can drag down a team, not just the manager.

Torre took it as very good news that Cashman wanted to extend him, especially given Cashman's clout in the organization.

"When he said that, I'm thinking, It's just a formality," Torre said. "I thought it was a slam dunk. The general manager asks you how long you wanted to manage and I just assumed . . . of course, I shouldn't assume anything because he did say, 'I just want to know what to go to them with.'"

———

"Them." It was a new concept in the Steinbrenner regime. With Steinbrenner no longer robust enough to be The Boss, the absolute ruler with absolute power, the Yankees' power structure had devolved into a blurry one that still needed defining. Steinbrenner's sons, Hank and Hal, were in the loop but not yet fully vested in the daily operations of the club. Trost and Levine steered the business operations of the franchise, but contributed to baseball matters, too. One of Steinbrenner's sons-in-law, Felix Lopez, was growing increasingly interested in all aspects of the business of the New York Yankees, completing one of the most astounding rises in corporate American history. Lopez came to the Yankees' boardroom by way of landscaping. He met Jessica Steinbrenner, The Boss's daughter, while tending to her yard. He married The Boss's daughter and immediately became a baseball expert.

Another son-in-law, Steve Swindal, was the team's general partner and Steinbrenner's hand-picked successor. Steve Swindal had married The Boss's daughter Jennifer. He ran Bay Transportation Corporation, a marine towing company purchased by Steinbrenner's company American Shipbuilding. When the Yankees played in Miami against the Marlins in 1997, Steinbrenner asked him if he would like to become a general partner of the Yankees. Swindal loved the idea. He enjoyed the work while by and large tending to keep a low profile.

Then one day, June 15, 2005, to be exact, Swindal was sitting near George Steinbrenner at a press conference to announce the construction plans and financing for a new Yankee Stadium when Steinbrenner blurted out that Swindal, and not either of his own sons, would replace him someday as head of the Yankees. Most everyone in the room was surprised to hear Steinbrenner publicly anoint Swindal as his handpicked successor. One person was particularly surprised: Swindal himself. Steinbrenner never had told him he was his choice for running the team, never had discussed succession plans with him.

"It was news to me," Swindal said.

Steve Swindal was the man who would be king of one of the most valuable properties in professional sports, the New York Yankees, which had become an iconic global franchise worth about $2 billion when you folded in the YES network, the most successful regional sports network in the television industry.

Swindal's authority was soon to be completely wiped out by one of the most expensive drinking benders in the history of imbibing.

Only three weeks and one day prior to Cashman's meeting with Torre—it was Valentine's Day night and the second night of the Yankees' spring training camp—Swindal was driving his 2007 Mercedes in St. Petersburg at a little past two in the morning when he made a hard left turn at the intersection of Central Avenue and 31st Street, cutting off another car. The other vehicle had to brake abruptly to avoid a collision. The other vehicle just so happened to be a police cruiser driven by Officer Terri Nagel. At that moment at the corner of Central and 31st, the future operations of the New York Yankees also took an abrupt turn.

Nagel followed the Mercedes, which zoomed through the 35 mph zone at 61 mph. The officer pulled over the Mercedes some 18 blocks later. It was 2:12 a.m. Swindal failed a field sobriety test. He refused a Breathalyzer test. He was arrested for driving under the influence, taken to jail, booked at 4:26 a.m. and released at 9:53 a.m. His police mug shot was soon all over the Internet.

The Yankees actually released a statement that said, "Mr. Swindal apologizes profusely for this distraction during the Yankees' spring training." Distraction? Sure, driving under the influence is wrong because, well, you don't want it to distract from millionaires taking batting practice and fielding fungoes.

Despite the comically benign wording, Steve Swindal was soon to be finished with having anything to do with the New York Yankees. He just didn't know it quite yet. About four weeks later, Jennifer Swindal filed divorce papers in Hillsborough County Circuit Court's family law department, citing "irreconcilable differences" that led to the couple splitting on, yes, Valentine's Day. In the filing, Jennifer Swindal asked to keep the couple's $2.3 million home in Tampa's upscale Davis Island neighborhood. Swindal was out of the family, which meant he was out of the Yankees.

In between the arrest and the divorce, Swindal

continued to show up for work each day at Legends Field, the Yankees' grand but joyless spring training compound that was heavy on concrete, fencing and stern security officers. He and the Yankees kept up appearances while the lawyers started hammering out divorce papers and severance issues. Swindal remained in the loop on club issues, which meant Cashman would need to run his idea of a contract extension for Torre past both Swindal and Levine before presenting it to The Boss for approval. In times of better health for Steinbrenner, Cashman and Torre may have dealt directly with Steinbrenner, who then could have chosen to table the idea or give it a green light, perhaps handing it off to one of his lieutenants for negotiation. But with Steinbrenner's vitality in question, so was the usual power structure of the Yankees' front office. That's why Cashman told Torre he would need to run the idea of an extension past "them."

A couple of days passed without Cashman giving any word back to Torre about what he heard back from "them." Finally, Torre decided to ask Cashman what was going on. Torre had rented a home for spring training, and the owners wanted to know if he would be renting the place again in 2008.

"Cash, we just have to make a decision on this place we're renting here," Torre said. "Do you have any idea about a contract?"

"Well, I did talk to Swindal," Cashman offered.

"What did he say?"

"He said, 'How much is he going to want?'"
"Oh. Okay."

————

Swindal's response to Cashman was not an encouraging one for Torre. When Torre was hired after the 1995 season, the Yankees had not won a playoff series since 1981, the longest drought ever seen at Yankee Stadium since the joint was built back in 1923. They were drawing an average of 23,360 fans per game when Torre was hired, worse than 14 other franchises, including the Texas Rangers, Cincinnati Reds and Florida Marlins. But under Torre, the Yankees had made the playoffs every season and won 17 postseason series, including those four World Series, and the per-game attendance shot up 124 percent to a major league best 52,445. The Yankees were bankrolling gobs of money because of the demand for season tickets—nothing better for a club than having tickets sold with cash in hand months before the season even started— and the demand for season tickets was driven by the near certainty that every October the Yankees would be hosting playoff games. From 1996 through 2006 the Yankees played 59 postseason games at Yankee Stadium, two more than were played in the entire 94-year history to that point of Fenway Park in Boston.

"What drives season tickets is the expectation of postseason games," said a high-ranking business executive of a National League club. "And to make sure you get those postseason tickets that everybody wants, you have to get your season tickets. The opportunity to see postseason games is the big carrot."

Torre was at the helm during this period of staggering success and wealth for the Yankees. Yet when Cashman broached to Swindal the idea of simply adding one year to Torre's contract, Swindal reacted first not on the merit of the idea but on the bottom-line cost. Like a piece of bric-a-brac at a garage sale, Torre's value to the franchise was reduced to a pricing point. This was not a good sign for Torre. And it was about to get worse.

Cashman still needed to run the idea of an extension through Levine before it could get to Steinbrenner. He did so on March 13, which just happened to be the day after the Yankees lost an exhibition game the previous night to Boston, 7-5. Levine immediately told Cashman to forget about going to The Boss at the moment.

"I wouldn't go to The Boss with it right now," Levine told Cashman, according to what Cashman reported back to Torre. "Not after the team has lost a couple of games in a row. It's not a good time for this."

Torre was incredulous. Not a good time? Torre had won 1,079 games as manager of the Yankees (averaging 98 wins per year) and had won 21 World Series games. No man alive had won more than that. And now Levine was saying that just because the Yankees had lost two early spring exhibition games that they couldn't possibly broach the idea of an extension for Torre with Steinbrenner? How could it be possible that after 11 straight years in the postseason Torre's future was being judged on two meaningless spring training games? How could it be that his worthiness was tied to a game the night before that was so meaningless that the Yankees' lineup was packed with players that Steinbrenner himself would not have been able to identify if he ever happened to make one of his old, blustery sweeps through the clubhouse, the sweeps he had all but abandoned in his advancing age? How could it be that Torre's future employment was iced because of a loss with Todd Pratt at catcher, Alberto Gonzalez at shortstop, Chris Basak at third base, Josh Phelps at first base and Kevin Reese in right field? How could such a game possibly matter that much?

That was it for Torre. The Yankees had told him enough. The mock firing, the hand-wringing over the cost and now this, his extension considered unspeakable simply because of two spring training losses after 11 years on the job.

"Forget it," Torre told Cashman.

"What do you mean?" Cashman replied.

"Just forget it," Torre said. "Don't even bother asking anymore. I don't want any talk about an extension anymore. Just drop it. And if it does come up, tell them I'll wait until after the season to talk about it. Just forget it for now. I don't want to feel like I'm auditioning for this job. That's the last thing I want to do, to think about that while I'm doing my job. I can't do that.

"Listen, you guys either like what I do or you think somebody else can do it better. You're not going to hurt my feelings. That's reality."

Cashman nodded.

"I don't want you to have to think about it while you're doing your job," Cashman said. "Don't change anything. Just do what you do."

There. It was done. The trial balloon of an extension was shot to pieces before it ever got off the ground. The pitfalls of what Ali predicted would be the toughest year of her husband's life were officially put in place. Torre was a confirmed lame duck who, like it or not, was auditioning for the job he had held for 11 years. It was the beginning of the end.

13.

"We Have a Problem"

Every year Joe Torre would call a team meeting on the first day of spring training and make sure everyone knew what was expected of them: win the World Series. No other team in baseball began this way. The speech, of course, also would include the boilerplate stuff about being on time, hustling on the field and representing the Yankees franchise at all times with class and dignity. But Torre would make sure they also understood the expectations upon them. Twenty-nine other teams were hoping for a shot at the playoffs and taking their chances with the random nature of postseason baseball. The Yankees, having once pocketed four world championships in five years while winning an odds-defying 12 out of 13 postseason series, had come to believe not just that they should be playing every year in October, but also that they **should win the World Series.** They adopted the exception as their rule.

Each year that passed without the Yankees winning the World Series became a little more joyless, with the incremental successes and highlights of a long season—the kind of season that would have made 29 other franchises proud—lost to the disappointment of not having won at all. Torre got a glimpse of this emptiness at spring training in 2002 while signing autographs one day for a group of fans.

"Too bad about last year, Joe," one of them said. "You guys will do better this year."

The Yankees had lost the last game of the 2001 World Series on the last pitch of the last inning because of a broken-bat bloop hit, and yet the season was a failure. In 2007, you could multiply the disappointment by six, the number of seasons that had gone by without the Yankees winning the World Series. They were a more pedestrian 5-6 in postseason series in that time.

Torre decided he could no longer give his usual spring training speech. Baseball had changed too much. It had become too democratic. Ten different franchises had played in the six World Series since the Yankees last won one. Nobody talked about competitive balance problems anymore.

The Yankees themselves had changed too much. As Torre gathered his team in the clubhouse in

Tampa for his opening remarks, he saw around the room only four faces who had won a world championship in a Yankees uniform: Derek Jeter, Jorge Posada, Mariano Rivera and Andy Pettitte. Mostly, though, Torre was tired of hearing the Yankees' accomplishments diminished because the postseason wasn't breaking their way the way it did from 1996 through 2000. The 2006 Yankees had no reason to think they should have been world champions. Jaret Wright was their number four starter. Aaron Gueil and Andy Phillips got more at-bats than Hideki Matsui and Gary Sheffield, who missed chunks of the season with injuries. The Yankees were four games out of first place on the Fourth of July. But somehow the Yankees grinded out 97 wins, the most in the American League and tied with the Mets for the most wins in baseball. All of it, however, was flushed away with the Division Series loss to Detroit, starting from the moment midway through Game 2 when Mussina lost the lead at home. The season was an abject failure because of three days in October. Torre was nearly fired because of it.

Torre decided the speech this year would be different. The goal still was to win the World Series, but he no longer wanted his players to feel the pressure that they were expected to win it.

"Look, we're not going to worry about anybody else's perception," Torre told them. "Go out there and do the best that you can. Prepare yourselves the best that you can and give your very best effort. But don't get caught up in the perceptions and the expectations.

"Last year we won 97 games. Nobody won more games than us. I refuse to look at that as a failure. You can't always control the outcome. But what you can control is your preparation and how you play. Make sure you take care of preparation and effort. Get to the park every day ready to play and you basically earn where you wind up."

The Yankees had joined the other 29 teams, even if they were the last to admit it. The preponderance of players in the clubhouse had no idea what it was like to win a world championship in Yankee pinstripes, so how could they assume it was their manifest destiny? Besides, on the first day of spring training, Torre already had some problems on his hands. Three of his starting eight positional players, Bobby Abreu, Jason Giambi and Johnny Damon, had reported to camp out of shape. And it was about to get worse. Less than one week into workouts, general manager Brian Cashman walked into Torre's office and said, "We have a problem. Johnny's not sure if he wants to play baseball anymore."

Johnny Damon had reported to camp 15 pounds overweight, much of it carried in his midsection. All things considered, he much rather preferred riding his Jet-Ski on the lake right off his backyard in Orlando than getting ready for a baseball season. Damon hadn't bothered to work out that winter, partly, he said, because of a stress fracture in his foot that had not fully healed but also because he was burned out from baseball. For 11 consecutive years Damon had played in at least 145 games for four different teams without ever being placed on the disabled list. Even his off-seasons were frazzled. In 2001, for instance, he exercised his free agent rights and left Oakland to sign with the Red Sox.

In 2002 he divorced his wife, the mother of his two children, and lived the life of a hard-charging bachelor. Writing in his book, **Idiot,** about the 2002 season, Damon said, "If you're good-looking and a ballplayer, girls want a piece of you. For the rest of the season, I met some women, some good, some bad. I had some one-nighters that I had never gotten to experience before. It was fun. I ended up having to carry around a separate cell phone for the women to call me. I didn't want them to have my main number because my phone would have been ringing off the hook and it just got tiring."

One of the women he met that year, Michelle Mangan, would become his next wife. They were engaged in 2004. That previous off-season Damon suffered from serious migraines, blurred vision and postconcussion syndrome after a violent outfield collision with teammate Damian Jackson in the 2003 playoffs. It literally hurt him to shave, so he didn't, which is how Damon came to acquire the iconic, biblical, bearded, long-haired look from what became the 2004 world championship season of the Boston Red Sox. That winter, while also in demand for personal appearances and endorsements, he and Michelle were married.

The next off-season brought another divorce of sorts, as the Red Sox thanked him for his four years of service to the team, decided they already had benefited from the best years of his career, and sent him on his free-agent way. A disappointed Damon wound up signing a four-year contract with the Yankees for $52 million.

"Somehow I became a free agent and New York was the team that wanted me," he said. "The team I ran through walls for didn't even want me. And I was called everything in the book [for leaving]. I'm just a baseball player. If there was a team in Orlando, Florida, that's the team I would have had the biggest allegiance to. Unfortunately, there's not a baseball team there."

Damon gave the Yankees a typically solid season in 2006, including a career-high 24 home runs. As always, he played virtually every day, scored more than 100 runs for the ninth consecutive season, and provided a manic kind of energy and lightness of being that the more serious-minded Yankees sorely needed.

"I loved his personality," Torre said. "All the fun he had just before the game was great for the team.

He always checked with me, even if it was just to glance my way, before he did something stupid just for laughs before a game. He might pour water on himself or break a package of sunflower seeds . . . anything to relieve the tension. He was great."

It all caught up to Damon that winter. His life had been a nonstop string of catastrophes and triumphs . . . two rounds of free agency, divorce, marriage, concussion, the beard, the hair, the first Red Sox world championship in 86 years . . . so when the Tigers sent him and the Yankees home to the unusual quiet of that winter, Damon stopped thinking of himself as a baseball player and fell into the welcome comfort of being a stay-at-home dad. He played nearly every day with his 7-year-old twins from his first marriage, while Michelle gave birth in January to the couple's first child, a daughter.

"After the '06 season I had a broken bone in my foot," Damon said, "so every time I tried to do something physical, running or whatever, I couldn't. There was too much pain. So I didn't do much."

Torre said he didn't know Damon still had problems with his foot, but said, "I think it was all connected anyway, not knowing if he wanted to play. He never really got himself in shape for spring training. And if you think about the off-season in today's baseball, unlike when I played, guys use the off-season to get themselves into shape. Actually, into better shape than they were the previous season. They work all winter. But if he was in between about playing and not playing, he's not going to be committed to that kind of program.

"When he got to spring training and said he wasn't sure if he wanted to play, I'm sure that's not the first time it came up. I'm sure he was thinking about it all winter. So in having that thought process, he wasn't doing anything that was going to get himself ready for the season."

Damon admitted, "Every day in the off-season, I just . . . I didn't feel like getting ready for baseball. I was just having fun with the kids, playing on the lake every day. I felt unprepared to make that decision about playing."

Damon reported to Tampa for spring training, but his heart wasn't in it. Neither were his legs. His legs had helped make him a star, but being out of shape, Damon couldn't move or run the way he normally did with any kind of explosion.

"So every time I moved I felt brittle," he said. "And that's where all the leg issues started coming. And for me, that's part of the reason I'm playing baseball. That's why the scouts came out. Watch me run and do that kind of stuff. And when you're not able to do that and track down balls in center field and do that, you start thinking about quitting.

"I just couldn't see from my perspective going to the ballpark and preparing every day, mentally and physically. I had been doing it for a long time. I have three kids who don't get to see me at my best all the time because I'm constantly thinking about baseball. I'm constantly traveling, and my life off the field is so great that I needed a little bit of a break . . . I knew I still had some baseball in me. But once I started getting these nagging injuries I started thinking, I don't want to play this game just to be okay. [Former Royals infielder] Frank White told me one of the best things I heard when he was coaching the outfielders in Kansas City. He said, 'Don't just play the game to play. Try to leave a mark.' When I go out there and have a bad game, I feel bad for the fans wearing my jerseys in the stands because I want them to watch me and be impressed. And I didn't feel like I had that going for me."

The last straw was knowing that his father's birthday was coming up. Johnny couldn't remember the last time he was with Jimmy Damon on his birthday. Johnny was always playing baseball at spring training somewhere in February. He felt badly about not spending enough time with his father.

"I wanted to get back to him," Damon said. "I don't know how much time he has. I want to spend time with him. I mean, there was just so much going on. My older kids are getting older and bigger . . ."

On February 24 Damon told Cashman he was thinking seriously about quitting baseball. Cashman quickly arranged a meeting with Damon,

Torre and the team psychologist in Torre's office. Torre suggested they move somewhere else, knowing that any time reporters noticed the door to his office closed, a vigil would begin to see who would come out when the door opened. So the four of them moved the meeting to the trainers' room, in a back portion of the clubhouse not accessible to reporters.

"Johnny was apologetic, and I felt bad for him," Torre said. "Of course, Cashman's mind worked in a different way. It was more like, 'If you're going to retire, this is how much money we have to work with, this is what you're leaving on the table.' And we basically didn't try to talk him out of anything. We just said, 'Take what time you need.' And we're not going to lie to the media. We're just going to say you had to deal with some personal matters and whenever you come back, you come back."

Damon jumped in his car and drove home to Orlando. He played with his kids and took his father out to dinner to celebrate his birthday. Who knew how long he would stay away from baseball? A day? A week? Forever? His dinner with Jimmy actually convinced him he needed to get back to baseball, at least for the time being, anyway. Jimmy told him life after baseball would always be there for him, but for now baseball afforded him a national platform to affect people's lives. Damon, for instance, helps raise awareness and funds for the Wounded Warriors project, a charity that assists soldiers injured in battle to transition into civilian life. Being a baseball player, especially a **Yankee,** Jimmy told him, made his contribution to that kind of work much more impactful. On the third day of his sabbatical, Johnny Damon drove back to Tampa and became a baseball player again.

"I just found out the importance of going to play baseball again," Damon said. "What it came down to was coming back wasn't for me. It was for the Yankees. The Yankees were the reason I wanted to go play again. They showed faith in me and gave me a real nice contract.

"And there's a lot of fans out there who like what I do and a lot of charities out there I can help by being a ballplayer. I'm thinking about baseball now but I'm also thinking about life after baseball. There are so many people I can impact, and baseball gives me that avenue to do it."

It wasn't so simple, however. It would be months before Damon was fully vested in playing baseball again, months in which the Yankees' season staggered and swooned. At the same time, Abreu and Giambi were also out of shape and unproductive. On the same day Damon returned to camp, Abreu strained an oblique muscle while taking batting practice. Giambi hadn't done any running all winter, restricting his workouts to weight training and cardio machines. His legs, back and hips had pained him too much to do any running, the result, he would later discover, of having unusually high arches in his feet. The Yankees, quite literally, began the year in bad shape.

Torre had another issue to consider that spring: Should he bend his team rules to accommodate the possible signing of Roger Clemens? Clemens visited the Yankees at Legends Field on March 7, still coy about whether he was going to come out of "retirement" a third time or not. The Yankees understood, however, that bringing in Clemens meant allowing him the same privileges that the Houston Astros had granted him the previous three years. The Astros permitted Clemens to leave the team between his starts whenever he wished. So if Clemens wanted to watch his son, Koby, play minor league baseball or caddy for his wife, Debbie, at their local golf club championship, he was free to ditch his teammates. Clemens wasn't interested in giving up such a privilege to return to baseball.

Torre had allowed players to leave the team in the past, but only starting pitchers between starts and only then with workrelated issues, such as the medical treatments Kevin Brown needed for his back.

"I turned down a lot of regular players who wanted to go to graduations and things and I couldn't let them go," Torre said. "Wade Boggs asked me once and I told him no. You can't make a case for regular players."

Torre considered relief pitchers also as too necessary to allow them to take leaves of absence. Indeed, during that 2007 season, in June, closer Mariano Rivera asked Torre for permission to skip the Yankees' series in Colorado to attend his child's school graduation. Torre told him no, that the Yankees could not afford to let him go.

"I'm sorry," Rivera told Torre, "but I'm going to go whether I have permission or not."

"Listen," Torre said, "I can't stop you from going, but if it comes to the eighth or ninth inning and we have a lead and we need you and you're not there, what do I say to people? You tell me what I'm supposed to say. Say you're gone without permission? Do you want to deal with that kind of shit? I don't know what you want me to say, but I can't tell people I gave you permission when there are 24 other guys counting on you. I can't do that."

Rivera understood. He did not leave. And the Yankees were swept three games by the Rockies. Rivera wasn't needed at all.

As a starting pitcher, Clemens was different. He wasn't needed in the four games between starts. Still, Torre would have to decide if his disappearances would cause resentment or adversity within the team. At least Gary Sheffield and Randy Johnson, each traded after the 2006 season, were not still around. Torre figured both Sheffield and Johnson, both of whom were established stars given to moodiness, might have had trouble with the Yankees granting a privilege to Clemens that had not been extended to them. The Clemens Family Plan might have caused problems in a clubhouse with Sheffield and Johnson in it, Torre thought. "Cash felt the same way and it was for probably the same reasons," Torre said. To find out whether it still might cause resentment with the 2007 Yankees, Torre talked to some of his star players.

"Cashman told me in spring training we had a shot at Roger and this was going to be a part of his deal," Torre said. "It was part of the rules. If you wanted to get him it was part of the package. To be honest, when it was presented to me I first thought, I can't have that with this team. So when I got the heads-up then that he might be coming, I mentioned it to Jeter and Jason and Alex. I talked to them individually and casually, behind the batting cage. I said, 'I've got to know, is this going to bother anybody?' And everybody said, 'As long as he wins ballgames we don't give a shit about what he does.' No one had a problem with it.

"A lot of it depends on the makeup of your team. The comparison to me is when Richie Allen was coming from Philadelphia to the Cardinals when I was playing with the Cardinals. And we had stars like Bob Gibson and Lou Brock. Richie would show up late but we would protect his ass and nobody would know it. But then Richie was with the Dodgers and it was totally different. Richie would show up late there and players would be waiting for him to show up in the parking lot just so they could show up after him. So it depends on the makeup of your team. I just had a feeling that Roger wasn't going to be running home all the time and abusing the privilege. I said to Cash, 'I don't think it will be an issue, but we'll accept whatever it is.'

"My thinking is you have to see how it affects other people, and allow certain things because of that. I may be off base. That's just the way I feel, knowing the personality of a team, knowing what's real and what's made-up."

———

Of course, Clemens didn't know it yet, but he had far bigger problems than securing a season's worth of hall passes from the Yankees. Three months earlier, federal agents had raided the Long Island, New York, home of Kirk Radomski, a former Mets clubhouse attendant who for more than a decade had provided performance-enhancing drugs to baseball players. The agents discovered personal checks and phone records linked to Brian McNamee, the personal trainer of Clemens. It was only a matter of time before Clemens' career and his life would blow up into a complete mess.

The Yankees knew they would need Clemens, even with the righthander turning 45 that season. They went to spring training having committed two of the five spots in the starting rotation to Carl Pavano, who had not pitched in the big leagues since midway through the 2005 season because of a series of ailments, and Kei Igawa, a lefthander whom the Yankees acquired as a posted free agent from Japan at the cost of $46 million, including a $26 million posting fee that stunned everybody else in baseball.

Igawa inspired almost no confidence in his own clubhouse. Even before the Yankees were announced as having placed the winning bid in the posting process, an American League general manager, asked about how Igawa might fare in the major leagues, said, "He better stay out of the American League. Maybe if you put him in the NL West, with the pitcher batting and the bigger ballparks in that division, you might get by with him as a fourth or fifth starter. But he can't pitch in the American League. We had no interest in him."

The Yankees fell in love with Igawa, valuing him higher than anybody else. Not coincidentally, the Yankees turned in their bid on Igawa soon after losing the posting process for Diasuke Matsuzaka, another posted free agent from Japan. The Boston Red Sox blew away the field with a posting fee of $51.1 million for Matsuzaka, who was considered one of the best pitchers in the world. The Yankees had bid slightly more than $30 million for Matsuzaka. How was it possible that they could bid nearly the same amount for Igawa, who, though a strikeout champion in Japan, gave up too many home runs and walks, rarely broke 90 miles an hour with his fastball and did not own a single impressive out pitch? Well, they made sure they weren't going to go 0-for-2 in posting processes. Igawa was all theirs.

Meanwhile, free agent pitcher Ted Lilly was hoping the Yankees would sign him. Lilly had cried the day in 2002 when Cashman traded him to Oakland in a three-way deal in which the Yankees wound up with Jeff Weaver, who turned out to be the worst of the three pitchers traded. (Detroit obtained Jeremy Bonderman, who would help beat the Yankees on the Tigers' way to the 2006 pennant.) Lilly fit the profile of a classic Yankee contributor: a lefthanded pitcher who thrived in the pressure of New York and the AL East. He wanted to be a Yankee. Lilly had just won 15 games for the Toronto Blue Jays. He had no major arm issues.

Cashman didn't want Lilly. He preferred Igawa, though Igawa would cost the Yankees more money over four years ($46 million, including the $26 million posting fee) than what Lilly would cost on the free agent market ($40 million, with the Cubs winning his services). Cashman told Torre, "Igawa's as good as Lilly, and he won't cost us as much," because the posting fee did not count toward the Yankees' official payroll, thus rendering it tax-free money as far as their luxury tax bill was concerned.

"As soon as Cash said that—Igawa was as good as Lilly—that was good enough for me," Torre said.

Igawa was no sure thing, and even the Yankees

knew it. When the Yankees introduced Igawa at a news conference after his signing, Cashman did as much as he could to lower expectations for his $46 million man.

"We're trying to be very careful and respectful of the process, and not put too much on his shoulders," Cashman said then. "He seems like a tough kid and he's obviously pitched in front of big crowds for a very successful organization. At the same time, there's going to be a lot of new experiences for him here in the States and in this league. We'll have to wait and see what we get."

The Yankees had passed on Lilly as well as Gil Meche, another free agent, and traded Randy Johnson so they could commit two spots on their rotation to Pavano and Igawa. Worse, there was little insurance behind them, none of it proven. The Yankees had people such as Darrell Rasner, Matt DeSalvo, Jeff Karstens and Chase Wright behind them, all of them underwhelming. Phil Hughes was the crown jewel of the farm system, but he was only 20 years old. The Yankees had placed high-risk bets that Pavano could stay healthy and that Igawa could get major league hitters out, and it was apparent extremely quickly that both bets were losing propositions. In the case of Igawa, it took only one day to figure out he was a bust.

Bullpen catcher Mike Borzello was assigned to catch Igawa's first throwing session in spring training. Borzello was looking forward to it, especially after Billy Eppler, the assistant to Cashman, had raved about Igawa to Borzello.

"Did you catch Igawa yet?" Eppler asked excitedly.

"No," Borzello replied.

"Just wait," Eppler said. "He's got a nasty changeup. You'll see."

Igawa threw to Borzello at Legends Field. Borzello could not believe this was the same guy Eppler was talking about, the same guy to whom the Yankees gave $46 million, and the same guy the Yankees wanted instead of Lilly.

"I caught Kei Igawa," Borzello said. "It was awful. He maybe threw three strikes out of 25 pitches. The changeup was horrible. I was reaching all over the place for his pitches."

Eppler saw Borzello after the throwing session that day.

"So, what did you think of Igawa?" Eppler asked.

"The truth?" Borzello said.

"Yeah."

"He threw three strikes the whole time. His changeup goes about 40 feet. His slider is not a big league pitch. His command was terrible."

Eppler was stunned.

"I'll tell you this," Borzello continued. "I hope he's hurt, so there's an explanation for throwing like that."

"Oh, really?" Eppler said.

"Really," Borzello said. "He was terrible."

Igawa would never get any better.

"His command was a big problem," Torre said. "He could never throw two pitches in a row to the same spot, even in a bullpen session. He would miss and miss badly with his location consistently."

Borzello said the investment in a pitcher like Igawa caught the attention of the players in the clubhouse, who had once known the Yankees to be the big-game hunters of the pitching market, having acquired such talents as Jimmy Key, Orlando Hernandez, David Wells, David Cone and Clemens over the years.

"You're talking about a guy pitching for **the New York Yankees,**" Borzello said. "The New York Yankees always went after the premier guys. And after investing $200 million in payroll, why are you putting the ball in the hands of this kind of pitcher? It made no sense. But the Yankees kept making the same mistake. Pavano, [Jaret] Wright, Igawa . . . other organizations scrape up that kind of pitching. But the **Yankees?**"

These were the 2007 Yankees, the team on which Torre, in the last year of his contract, would be placing his managerial future. Forty percent of the rotation was assigned to Pavano, who couldn't stay healthy, and Igawa, who couldn't throw a strike. Pavano, because of injuries to the other starters, was the Yankees' Opening Day pitcher. The center fielder, Damon, wanted to quit. The right fielder, Abreu, was hurt and out of shape. The first baseman, Giambi, was too out of shape to play first-base anymore, so he had to be the designated hitter while the first-base position was an open casting call among Doug Mientkiewicz, Josh Phelps and Andy Phillips, none of whom could hit as a first baseman should. The biggest acquisition to come, Clemens, was turning 45 and had successfully lobbied for special treatment. Did this look like a team that should be expected to win the World Series? And did Torre have any loyalists left in the front office after being embarrassed in the public stocks after the 2006 Division Series?

In the clubhouse and on the field, these were no longer the Yankees as the baseball world knew them. They wore the same pinstripes, played in the same ballpark, claimed ownership to the same 26 World Series titles, but these Yankees were no longer the same Yankees who could regard the World Series as a virtual birthright. Most obvious of all, these were no longer George Steinbrenner's Yankees. The Boss had imposed his will and spirit upon the entire organization and the Yankees were the better and the worse for it all these years. Now there was a vacuum where there had been so much energy. For Torre, Steinbrenner's decline was another blow to the underpinnings of his management. Steinbrenner could be demanding and unreasonable, but Torre could always speak to him, and usually find the right words to keep The Boss from completely blowing a fuse. In 2007, the pipeline was cut. Torre knew it, especially when he would be leaving Legends Field in the early evening after a full day of work and see Steinbrenner only then coming to work himself. On the last day of spring training it was obvious that Steinbrenner was too frail to be The Boss.

Torre rode the elevator at Legends Field to the fourth floor to say goodbye to Steinbrenner. The Yankees were preparing to fly from Tampa to New York to begin the season in two days. The team would hold its annual Welcome Home dinner on the eve of the opener. Steinbrenner sat in the suite adjacent to his office. Hank Steinbrenner was there. Felix Lopez was there. Steinbrenner's wife, Joan, was there.

"Boss, I'm just here to say goodbye," Torre said.

"Okay," Steinbrenner said. "I'll see you tomorrow night."

Joan looked at Torre, and as they moved away from Steinbrenner and toward the door, she told him with a concerned look on her face, "I don't know how we're going to get him there."

They did get Steinbrenner to New York for the dinner, in what stood as a rare trip for him then. Torre saw Steinbrenner at the dinner and walked across the room to greet him. Steinbrenner was sitting with his family. He looked frail. He was wearing dark glasses in the ballroom. And even beneath those dark glasses, as Torre could see, Steinbrenner was crying. He was choked up, hit by another emotional jag, at what was supposed to be the birthplace of optimism and sunshine, Opening Day eve. As Steinbrenner dabbed at a melancholy tear, Torre knew life with the Yankees would never be the same for both of them.

———

The second game of the 2007 season was rained out, which was not a bad development for the Yankees. It kept them undefeated for one more day and postponed the hellish spring about to come their way. Alex Rodriguez peeled off his uniform and reassumed his proper East Side look: a green cable-knit sweater pulled over a black turtleneck, jeans and sneakers. His goal for the season was to be completely inoffensive, or, as third-base coach Larry Bowa constantly would remind him, "Vanilla." Rodriguez was off to a good start, the green sweater and a March interview with New York AM radio station WFAN notwithstanding. Rodriguez said on air that whether he stayed with the Yankees or used an opt-out clause in his contract to leave for another team after the season would be decided by whether New York fans accepted him or not. "It's a do-or-die situation," he said.

"He's night and day from where he was last year," Bowa said as the regular season began. "You could see it in him when spring training started. Everything he's doing is just natural. He's just letting his ability take over. I'm not going to use the word **relaxed,** because he's still intense. But there's a different look about him. He's not worried about everything that's going on around him. Vanilla. We use that word a lot when we talk. Simple. Keep it plain.

"I only had to get on him once. It was a couple of days after he went on WFAN. And I gave it to him pretty good. I told him, 'Why do you have to keep saying this stupid shit?'"

Bowa was an important part of Torre's management of the team. Players respected him because he had the substantial big league résumé few coaches have in the modern game. Bowa played 16 years in the major leagues, collected 2,191 hits, won two Gold Gloves at shortstop, finished as high as third in Most Valuable Player Award voting, was selected to five All-Star Games and won a world championship with the 1980 Phillies. His fiery temperament, colorful vocabulary and reactionary nature made him a volatile manager with the Padres and Phillies, but as a coach he established himself as one of the best in the business: a hardworking student of the game who, most importantly, kept players from getting too comfortable. His in-your-face manner was a nice complement to the relaxed style of Torre, and it seemed to be exactly what not only A-Rod needed, but also a young player like second baseman Robinson Cano, who knew he could be a good major leaguer strictly on his talent, but didn't know the work it would require to be a great major leaguer.

One day in April, talking about Cano, Bowa said, "He backhanded a ball the other day, an easy two-hopper he should have gotten in front of. He had a bad at-bat right before that. I'm convinced he took his at-bat out into the field with him. You have to stay on Robbie. Like out in Oakland. There was a relay and he just assumed Eric Chavez was going to stop at second base. He didn't. That's Robbie's fault. You have to assume the runner is going to continue, and then if you turn and see he's stopped, then you can relax. But he did the exact opposite. He just assumed Chavez wasn't going. That's a lazy mistake. I got on him pretty good about that.

"Just like today, too. He said to me, 'No ground balls. I'm just going to hit in the cage.'"

The Yankees that day offered only optional hitting in the indoor batting cage. There was no usual pregame hitting on the field, during which Bowa always made sure to hit Cano groundballs.

"And I tell him, 'No, you're not,'" Bowa said. "'You're not just going to the cage. You're going to get your ass out here and work. You're 23 years old, not some old veteran who needs a break.'

"See, the thing is you have to remind yourself that he's 23. You have to get on him, but then you ask yourself, who at the age of 23 has it all figured out? But you look at him and you see that he can be as good as he wants to be. As great as he wants to be. He's that talented. He glides into the ball, but unlike most guys who do that, he keeps his hands back. And then when he brings the bat through it stays through the strike zone for a very long time. He's like George Brett that way. He can be as great as he wants to be."

Cano, of course, took his groundballs that day. With Bowa riding him, Cano would hit .306 in 2007 with 97 runs batted in. Like Cano, Rodriguez knew Bowa was always there to push him. In spring training, for instance, Bowa berated Rodriguez for making soft, lazy throws to second base on the front end of double plays. "You're going to get your second baseman killed!" Bowa told him, and ordered Rodriguez to work on the throws early in the morning on a back field before most of his teammates had even showed up. The gruff Bowa was an important voice to someone like Rodriguez, who otherwise surrounded himself with a cadre of publicity agents and buddies who amounted to a back-slapping club.

"You know the big thing with these guys, they might not tell you they like it, but the real good players, they don't want to hear just that you agree with them," Bowa said. "I mean, if it happened once it happened ten times in two years with Alex: Alex would come up to me after making a mistake and say, 'Do you think I should have had that ball?'

And nine times out of ten he makes that play. And I said, 'Yeah, you've got to catch that ball.'

"After it happened four or five times I told him, 'Al, every time you come to me, you know you should have made the play or you wouldn't have come to me. I've seen you make mistakes on a line drive, backhand. You don't come to me because you know it's a tough play, but every play you think you should make you come to me. So I'm just going to reaffirm that I know you know you should have made that play.' And I think the players like when you're being honest. They might not like it at the time, but they like you to be up-front with them."

———

Rodriguez, however, already carried one of the highest capacities for work in baseball. The most important push he received from Bowa was not to work, but to keep himself out of trouble. Rodriguez made an obvious effort to do just that in 2007. The goal, as Bowa would say, was to prevent himself from "saying stupid shit." The Yankees had won nothing more than a Division Series matchup against Minnesota since they acquired Rodriguez, who had become, because of his talent, because of his industry-rattling $252 million contract that remained unsurpassed six years running, and because of his knack for calling attention to himself (not always for the better), the embodiment of Yankee failures. Much of it was unfair, of course, not unlike the prettiest girl in high school becoming an easy target for criticism. Torre knew that, and wanted Rodriguez to know he shouldn't fight it. One day in March, just before the Yankees were to play a spring training game, Torre pulled Rodriguez aside near the dugout.

"Look, a lot of what goes on with you is unfair," Torre told Rodriguez. "You're the story no matter what happens, if you get four hits or no hits, if we win or if we lose. I understand that. But you can't worry about that. What you've got to do is just play and not worry about what's going to happen. Just let it happen instead of worrying about the consequences."

Opening Day could not have begun much worse for A-Rod. He dropped the first ball hit to him, a foul pop-up. Batting cleanup—his first game since Torre batted him eighth in the Division Series–clinching defeat to Detroit—Rodriguez struck out with two runners on. It was only the first inning of the first game of the season and he was getting booed. But Rodriguez turned his day and the game around. With the game tied at 5, Rodriguez began the seventh inning with a single off Tampa Bay pitcher Brian Stokes. Running on his own, he stole second base and scored the tie-breaking run on a single by Jason Giambi. The stolen base reflected how Rodriguez had changed his body over the winter, dropping 15 pounds without losing strength and reducing his body fat from 18 percent to 10 percent, an astounding four-month transformation for someone turning 32 years old that summer.

Asked the next night, after the rainout, if he would have attempted a steal in the same situation the previous season, Rodriguez said, "Last year? No way. Because I would have been out by two feet. That wasn't part of my game.

"I knew I wanted to go early in the count. I waited one pitch. I wanted to see if he would slide step and just to get a look at him. But I wanted to be aggressive. The big thing is making sure you take the double play out of order. It's the situation, more so than the pitcher there."

Rodriguez is a unique talent, a guy who could break a game open with his power or win it with his legs or preserve it with his defense. But, because he lacked the pedigree that comes with a championship, and because he still seemed an awkward outsider trying to earn his pinstripes, he was regarded in his own clubhouse as not wholly reliable.

"The two guys on this team we can't afford to lose are Derek [Jeter] and Jorge [Posada]," one Yankee player said after that second-day rainout. "Pitching is still the name of the game, but if you're talking about guys who are out there every day, we need those two guys. There's nobody to replace them and what they mean to the team is so important. Alex isn't in that same category. He's important, too, but I think we could survive it if he got hurt."

2000 was the last championship year for Torre's Yankees, as they beat the Mets in the "Subway Series." A key play in the epic, 12-inning Game 1 was Derek Jeter's off-balance laser relay throw to Jorge Posada, which nailed Timo Perez at the plate and snuffed a Met rally.

Jeter, who was the MVP of the 2000 Series, celebrates the Yankees' third straight title with Torre.

JOE GIZA/REUTERS

The 2001 World Series was one of the best ever played, heightened by the emotional charge of the September 11th attacks.

V.J. LOVERO/SPORTS ILLUSTRATED/GETTY IMAGES

Scott Brosius's home run in the bottom of the 9th in Game 5 tied the score, and the Yankees went on to win—a night after Derek Jeter had won the game in the bottom of the 10th with a walk-off home run. But the Yankees lost in the 7th game on a very rare blown save by Mariano Rivera.

Torre did not fully endorse the Yankees' signing of Jason Giambi, a prodigious hitter with limited defensive skills. He put his objections in writing to Steinbrenner, so he couldn't be accused later of asking for Giambi if the acquisition did not work out.

Chuck Knoblauch was an All-Star second baseman and a key member of the Yankees' title teams from 1998-2000, but he developed a mysterious inability to throw to first base, an affliction that hastened his decline.

2003 featured a season-long battle with the Red Sox, peppered by a brawl during Game 3 of the ALC series that started when Pedro Martinez beaned role player Karim Garcia. In the dugout Martinez pointed to his head and then at Jorge Posada, infuriating Posada and the Yankees. In the melee, Martinez threw Don Zimmer to the ground. The bad feelings persisted, and when the Yankees won the pennant in one of the greatest Game 7's ever, the vindication was sweet. It was the last moment of grandeur for Torre's Yankees.

Andy Pettitte and Roger Clemens were the best of friends. When the Yankees let Pettitte leave after the 2003 season, many Yankee fans felt it was a terrible mistake. Clemens, who had retired with some fanfare, joined Pettitte with the Astros and took them to their first World Series in 2005. Later, when allegations that Clemens was a steroid user came out, Pettitte tearfully revealed that he had once used human growth hormone to recover from an injury. Pettitte returned to the Yankees in 2007 and pitched effectively.

The high-priced free agent pitcher Kevin Brown, whom Cashman brought in to anchor the rotation when Pettitte and Clemens left the team. Thiry-nine years old at the time the Yankees acquired him, Brown would distinguish himself by breaking his hand by punching a wall and spending several weeks on the disabled list, retreating to the clubhouse in the middle of a start and telling Torre he wanted to quit, and getting shellacked for 2 runs in the first inning of Game 7 of the 2004 American League Championship against the Red Sox.

The trade for Alex Rodriguez signalled a deep change in the culture of the Yankees. A-Rod was one of the greatest players in the history of the game, but his obsession with his own statistics, his strained relationship with Derek Jeter, his failure to perform in the clutch, and his penchant for creating media circuses did not endear him to his teammates, or the Yankee fans. Torre appreciated having someone of A-Rod's talents on the team (he did win two MVP Awards under Torre), but dealing with his complicated psyche and the clubhouse distractions he created became wearying.

The Yankees playoff run in 2007 ended in a cloud of bugs on a warm September night in Cleveland. Torre says the biggest mistake he ever made as Yankee manager was not pulling his team from the field.

Through it all, it was a job Torre loved. When the Yankees, no longer controlled by an ailing Steinbrenner, forced him out, an era ended.

Of course, Rodriguez was the primary source of righthanded power in a lefthand-dominant lineup and played terrific defense, so the Yankees could not come close to replacing his kind of value if he were hurt. Nonetheless, coming off his 1-for-14 performance in the postseason, and his sometimes awkward clubhouse manner, his perceived value on his own team was less than his actual value. It was a very strange circumstance for a superstar talent.

Fact is, these Yankees, whether they still belonged to Jeter, because of his captaincy or Swiss bank account of goodwill with Yankees fans, or to Rodriguez, because of his talent and knack for creating attention, were still looking to craft an identity in their postchampionship years. If the Yankees expected to win, it was only out of a perceived obligation to the past, not because they truly lived and breathed it. It took a repatriated Yankee such as Andy Pettitte to recognize that kind of important shift in the Yankee culture.

———

Pettitte won world championships in 1996, 1998, 1999 and 2000 with the Yankees. He left reluctantly after the lukewarm effort by the Yankees to keep him following the 2003 World Series loss to Florida to sign with his hometown Houston Astros. After three seasons in Houston, one of which included another World Series appearance for Pettitte, he jumped at the chance to come back to the

Yankees, having missed the energy and demands that come with playing in New York. It had nothing to do with the city itself. Pettitte almost never ventured into Manhattan. It had everything to do with the playing environment. The Yankees gave him back his old number, 46, his old locker (a spot along the right wall about halfway into the rectangular room), and his old default spot in the rotation, Pettitte being the classic number two starter. He was, in fact, scheduled to pitch that second game of the 2007 season before it was rained out. Sitting at his familiar locker after the game was called, Pettitte knew already that most everything else about the Yankees had changed in his three years away. These Yankees weren't sure who they were, didn't know if they were champions or not and didn't truly believe, the way the championship Yankee teams believed, that they **should** win.

"I have to be careful with how I say this," Pettitte said. "But in the years we were winning here, we expected to win. **Everybody.** And when we didn't win, it was devastating. I remember 2003, wanting to win so badly. It was personal for me because I hadn't pitched well in the 2001 World Series. And Josh Beckett just took it to us in the World Series and shut us down. We had a great year, but I remember thinking how the year was such a failure. It was such a bitter feeling. Bitter."

Just the memory of it pained Pettitte. He dropped his head and actually grimaced thinking about a four-year-old memory, especially that last night when Beckett beat Pettitte and the Yankees, 2–0, in what would be the last World Series game ever played at Yankee Stadium. Only seven men ever shut out the Yankees in a postseason game at Yankee Stadium, none since the Hall of Famer Warren Spahn did so back in 1958, and none struck out more batters than the nine Yankees Beckett fanned that night. Pettitte pitched courageously that night, allowing just one earned run over seven innings, but he was the losing pitcher nonetheless. He hated even thinking about it. He picked up his head and continued.

"And here's where I have to be careful," he said. "I think now we know how difficult it is to win. You have to be careful saying it because you don't want people to think you've lowered the expectations. The goal is still the same. But there's a different feeling now. It's a feeling that we know how difficult it is to win."

By losing, the Yankees came to know how difficult the winning really was. And maybe now they know that reality a little too well.

"Exactly," Pettitte said. "That doesn't mean we want to win any less, but the expectation that we **will** win? That's different now than it was before."

Jeter, meanwhile, remained wedded to the Yankees' old-school ways. He took losing hard and didn't tolerate those who did not. He still believed, despite the speech Torre gave in spring training about being proud of 97 wins, that the 2006 season was a failure.

"Maybe if it's a young team that never made the playoffs before they can say it wasn't a failure," Jeter said. "Not us. Not me. To me it's a failure if you don't accomplish what you set out to accomplish. Because you didn't reach the goal you set it's not a success."

But wasn't there a point, Jeter was asked, when even you realized that 2006 was a pretty good year, that the Yankees won as many games as anybody in baseball, even with many injuries and a slow start?

"No," he said. "Not at all."

That was the extent of his answer. It was as if the answer was so obvious that any explanation or expansion of it was superfluous. Twelve inches make a foot. There are 24 hours in a day. Any Yankees season that ends short of a World Series title is a failure. It was an immutable truth. Trouble is, as the Yankees' roster churned in the six years since they actually had a self-defined successful season, more and more of the Yankees didn't think like Jeter. Losing now was a property of baseball nature that applied as much to the Yankees as it did the 29 other franchises, especially in the first two months of the 2007 season.

———

The Yankees lost games with a frequency that ranked among the worst Yankees teams of all time.

They lost 29 of their first 50 games, a disaster that would have been far worse if not for the spectacular hitting of the newly buffed Rodriguez.

Only five other Yankees teams ever stumbled to a worse start, including only one in the past 93 years: the teams of 1905, 1912, 1913, 1914 and 1990. All of those teams finished with losing records in sixth place or worse. The 2007 Yankees had disaster written all over them.

After those 50 games, the Yankees' lefthanded hitting, which figured to be the backbone of the offense, was atrocious. Abreu was hitting .228, Damon was hitting .260 and Giambi was hitting .262. None of them were yet in proper game shape.

The back end of the rotation was hardly a surprise: it was as dreadfully unreliable as it had looked on paper. Igawa was so bad that after only six starts the Yankees demoted him and his 7.63 ERA all the way to the Class A Florida State League, essentially to have Steinbrenner's "gurus" of pitching, Nardi Contreras and Billy Connors, give him a beginner's tutorial on pitching. It was mind-boggling to think the Yankees could believe he was worth a $46 million investment and then decide after only six games he needed to learn how to pitch. And Pavano? He was the pitching version of why New York State enacted a lemon law to protect used car buyers. He lasted through spring training and exactly two regular season starts before he was done for the season with an elbow injury.

While the demises of Igawa and Pavano may have been predictable, Mussina, Chien-Ming Wang and rookie Phil Hughes also wound up on the disabled list (Hughes pulled a hamstring in the midst of throwing a no-hitter). The Yankees immediately were caught with a shortage of major league–caliber replacements. In just those first 50 games of the season, Torre was forced to use 11 different starting pitchers, seven of them being rookies and almost none of them with any significant future in the big leagues. One of them, Chase Wright, became the second pitcher in major league history to serve up four consecutive home runs, which he managed to do in his second big league game, in a span of just 10 pitches, in Boston against the Red Sox.

"Our problem right now is we have too many pitchers on the 15-day Pavano," Mussina said one day in April. "That's what it's officially called now. Did you know that? The Pavano. His body just shut down from actually pitching for six weeks. It's like when you get an organ transplant and your body rejects it. His body rejected pitching. It's not used to it."

Wins and decent pitching were so hard to come by that Torre quickly reneged on a plan he announced on the first day of spring training that Mariano Rivera would become a one-inning closer. Rivera was 37 years old, and Torre figured he could ease the physical burden on Rivera if he never asked him to get more than three outs, which is the way most managers were pampering their closers.

Rivera, though, sensed immediately that Torre's plan would be subject to change. Rivera was one of the most valuable weapons in baseball, a guy not only with dominating stuff, but also with a freakish efficiency—he rarely went deep into counts, let alone walked hitters—that enabled him to secure more outs than your typical closer. He was a manager's best friend, the go-to solution to a problem. In case of emergency, don't break glass; pitch Mariano.

"We'll see," a skeptical Rivera said in March of Torre's plan. "I've heard those kinds of things before, and then it doesn't happen. It doesn't matter to me. I pitch when they tell me to pitch and I'll be ready. But let's see."

Torre's plan lasted until April 21, when one of those typically wild games at Fenway Park against the Red Sox created one of those "in case of emergency" situations. The Yankees took a 6-2 lead into the eighth inning against the Red Sox when Torre had Mike Myers, his lefthanded specialist, pitch to David Ortiz, a lefthanded hitter. Ortiz ripped a double.

Then Torre tried his righthanded setup man, Luis Vizcaino, against the righthanded hitting Manny Ramirez. Vizcaino walked Ramirez. Vizcaino did get J. D. Drew to ground out, but then Mike Lowell rapped a single to drive in Ortiz. Now it was 6-3 with the tying run at the plate and one out. It was time for Torre to junk his plan and go to his best pitcher.

"I lied, what can I tell you?" Torre would say after the game. "I didn't plan on lying, but I did. As it turned out, he didn't pitch two innings."

Rivera blew the lead. Jason Varitek singled to drive in one run, Coco Crisp tripled to send home two more, and Alex Cora dumped a bloop single over the head of Jeter to account for the last run of what was a 7-6 Boston win.

———

For the Yankees, it was the start of seven consecutive losses, four of them to the Red Sox, including an 11-4 mugging at Yankee Stadium for loss number seven. It was April 27 and Torre was officially put on notice that his firing was imminent—well, if you consider newspaper leaks as the official form of Yankees front-office communication. "Joe in Jeopardy as Yanks Bomb," the **New York Post** declared the next morning. Wrote George King, "Yesterday, the word out of Tampa was that Steinbrenner 'was very displeased' about the way his high-price stable of talent is underachieving and was thinking about a change."

The story questioned whether Torre was to blame for the woeful pitching and inept hitting, going on to say, "If Steinbrenner and the voices he is listening to believe the answers are 'yes,' and if the

Yankees get swept this weekend by the Red Sox, it's not out of the realm of possibility that The Boss could make a change."

Translation: Torre's job was in the hands of starting pitchers Jeff Karstens and Chien-Ming Wang over the next 48 hours.

"It does bother me, the leaks," Torre said. "It's an insult. If you have a problem, come to me. Being with the Yankees this long, devoting myself to the organization . . . Somebody doesn't like what you do, then just tell me. Like in 2006, when I wasn't consulted at the end of the season. They left me hanging out there, and now I'm going to have a press conference and I don't know if I'm working or not. Then I have George calling me five or 10 minutes before my press conference and telling me I'm coming back, and then I'm even playing the role. 'Thanks a lot.'

"It's an insult because you think you deserve more than that. My wife tells me I'm overly sensitive and I said, 'You're probably right.' But there is a certain dignity to what you do.

"Again, as Ali pointed out, well, you know who you're working for. It's just the way they operate. And I didn't mind it when you win. And George still goes to the whip all the time. That's fine. You sort of grin at that and respect why he's successful and what he's made of. But there is a certain time you'd like people to trust what you do rather than question what you do."

Karstens, with his third major league win, and what would be his only victory of the season, saved Torre's job, pitching the Yankees to an improbable 3-1 win. The Yankees, though, reverted to form in the series finale, losing, 7-4. They had won one game in the previous 10 days.

Now it was time for Steinbrenner to weigh in, or at least the carefully managed version of Steinbrenner, rather than just the surreptitious whispers of "the voices he is listening to." Steinbrenner's publicity people had stopped allowing him to speak extemporaneously to the press, whether in person or on the telephone. He rarely made public appearances. It was a public relations risk to have Steinbrenner be heard or seen, if only because it would spark more debate about his health and the succession of power. The Boss would communicate with the media only through well-vetted statements released through the publicity firm, while officials from that firm or the Yankees front office continued to paint a picture of a robust Steinbrenner who, if you listened to them, was practically swimming the English Channel each morning and towing tractor trailers with his teeth in the afternoons. Truth was, when Torre would place calls to Steinbrenner, he no longer could get him at his office at Legends Field until four or five o'clock in the afternoon. Steinbrenner wasn't coming to his office until then.

"The season is still very young," the Steinbrenner statement said, "but up to now the results are clearly not acceptable to me or to Yankee fans. However, Brian Cashman, our general manager, Joe Torre, our manager, and our players all believe that they will turn this around quickly.

"I believe in them. I am here to support them in any way to help them accomplish this turnaround. It is time to put excuses and talk away. It is time to see if people are ready to step up and accept their responsibilities. It is time for all of them to show me and the fans what they are made of.

"Let's get going. Let's go out and win and bring a world championship back to New York. That's what I want."

It sounded like somebody doing his version of Steinbrenner, like one of those Hemingway writing contests for amateur authors, because, well, in times like this Steinbrenner would be expected to say **something,** wouldn't he? It included the typical veiled threats (Cashman and Torre having been the only ones named, were thus considered to have been placed on notice that any blame would fall to them) and the football halftime speech platitudes Steinbrenner believed could make baseball players play better. But it lacked the authentic from-the-gut fire and brimstone that made Steinbrenner such a fierce leader. Still, the statement was enough to fan more speculation that Torre's job was on the line.

"Every game we lost was a reference to getting fired," Torre said. "It was like it was imminent. That's the way people were talking. As much as you try not to read the paper, you have all your friends and relatives reading the paper. And you can't shut yourself off.

"It was just wearing me out having to answer all those questions. And I'd go in the clubhouse and I'd have players say to me, 'You all right? You all right?' Because of what was going on. And I hated that.

"You want everything nice. Win or lose, you want a clubhouse that's ready to compete, rather than having to sort of put stuff away first. And I was there 12 years. So there's a certain amount of respect that the players—even if they don't want you there as manager—that they feel they've got to show. It was just an uncomfortable time for me. The best part for me was the game. I didn't have to answer anything. I could just do what I knew how to do."

The games were not all that soothing for Torre. The Yankees had played only 23 games to the point when Steinbrenner issued his missive. They were 9-14 and had used nine different pitchers to start those 23 games. Five of those pitchers were rookies, and four of those had never before pitched in the big leagues, making the Yankees the first team since 1900 to use that many first-time pitchers that early in a season.

Cashman was trying to help, but the assistance he provided only served to underscore a subtle philosophical gap that was opening between him and Torre. Cashman would hand Torre lineup suggestions, almost always basing them on statistics such as on-base percentage. "Do what you want with it," Cashman said. In one lineup he suggested having Bobby Abreu bat leadoff and Jason Giambi bat second. Both were elite run producers, but Cashman's idea was to stack high on-base percentage hitters at the top of the lineup, whether or not they were traditional middle-of-the-order sluggers.

Torre generally disregarded the specific lineup ideas. Torre liked some numbers as a tool, not as a philosophy. He liked to know, for instance, how hitters and pitchers did over the long haul against righties and lefties. So Torre would politely thank Cashman for the suggestions and add a reminder for the general manager.

"Brian," Torre would say, "the numbers are good. But don't you ever forget the heartbeat."

Cashman did make one suggestion that Torre felt obligated to address immediately.

"Why don't you pitch Mike Myers against righthanded hitters?" Cashman said. "He's been getting groundballs from righthanders. If you have a big spot where you need a double play against a righthanded hitter, why don't you bring in Myers?"

Myers was a lefthanded pitcher whose sole purpose in his baseball life was to get out lefthanded hitters. He threw with a funky, slingshot sidearm delivery designed specifically to create difficulty for lefthanded hitters by increasing the angle from the release point of his throwing motion to home plate. The ball seemed to come sideways at lefthanded hitters. The delivery, though, granted righthanders a long look at the ball.

Over his career righthanders pounded Myers for a .300 batting average, but lefties hit only .219 against him. The 2007 season was an anomaly for Myers, one in which lefties actually hit better against him (.295) than did righthanders (.259). Cashman was putting his faith in the small sample of numbers early in the 2007 season, numbers compiled largely in low-leverage situations, not the late innings of close ballgames.

"Brian, the only time we're letting him pitch to righthanded hitters is when we have wiggle room," Torre said. "You have to look at the situations. He's not pitching to righthanded hitters with the game on the line."

The Yankees were a mess. Steinbrenner really did have reason to be worried. His team was in full-blown turmoil, and it was not just because of the injuries.

———

Damon, the leadoff hitter who once injected the Yankees with a goofy kind of energy, had become a drag on the team with his leg injuries and lackluster attitude. Once Damon made the decision to return to the Yankees after spring training, he still needed to get his legs in shape, but he was too far behind schedule for that to happen in time for the start of the season. Sure enough, on Opening Day no less, Damon was drifting back on a fly ball by Elijah Dukes of the Tampa Bay Devil Rays, a fly ball that would be a home run, when he felt a grabbing sensation in his calf.

"I actually felt ready to go," Damon said, "and then Opening Day, in 30-degree weather—why we play in New York then and not in Tampa I don't know—on Elijah Dukes' home run I felt my calf go. I was like, **You've got to be shittin' me.** I kept playing through it. I couldn't get to balls. The team was losing because I couldn't get to balls. It was brutal. I kept trying to do something, but my legs wouldn't let me."

For two months Damon would brood over the condition of his legs, never getting the spark back in his desire to play baseball. There were days when he said he could not play and days he played when he did not seem enthused to be doing so. Back and forth it would go: Is he in the lineup or not? Does he want to play or not? Teammates grew frustrated. It didn't help, either, that Damon moped most of the time around the clubhouse. There was no more of that pregame joking in the clubhouse and the dugout.

Damon presented Torre with a multifaceted problem. There was the problem of putting together a lineup with the day-to-day nature of Damon's leg problems. There was the problem of Damon's lack of production when he was in the lineup. And there was the problem of Damon's teammates, especially the old-guard Yankees, angry about Damon's lack of commitment. Torre spoke privately with Damon from time to time, and came away thinking Damon was in the same place he was when he walked away from the team in spring training: he was still waffling on whether or not he wanted to play baseball—not exactly the kind of guy a sinking team needs as its leadoff hitter and would-be catalyst.

In one of their private meetings, Torre told Damon, "The kind of player you've been your whole life is the player who goes out there and fully commits himself. You're not that kind of person now. It's easy to see that."

Damon agreed with Torre.

"I'm not sure I want to do this," Damon told him.

Damon's teammates grew so frustrated with him that several spoke to Torre out of concern that he was hurting the team. One of them visited Torre one day in the manager's office and was near tears talking about Damon.

"Let's get rid of him," the player said. "Guys can't stand him."

Torre told him, "I understand the way you feel, and I am disappointed, too, and all of that stuff, but we've got to find a way to make it work instead of just walking away from it. We just have to. And you're going to have to help me find a way to get this thing straightened out.

"The easiest thing in the world—I mean, not that you could actually do it—is just get rid of him. You can't do that. **We** can't do that. So let's figure out a way to make this thing work.

"Listen, we've always had somebody here from time to time that we had to deal with, somebody we weren't crazy about. But we're doing badly right now, so that's why it may feel different. The bottom line is he's a part of this team. And as long as he is a part of the team it's up to all of us to find a way to make this work. Let's just do whatever we can to help him and move on."

Damon continued to frustrate his teammates. Damon was hitting .229 with one home run when the Yankees, stumbling badly at 9-14, and fresh off having had Steinbrenner put them on notice, went to Texas for a three-game series against the Rangers. Torre decided a meeting was in order, a meeting in which it was just as important for the players to talk as it was for Torre to talk. The Yankees assembled in the trainers' room of the visiting clubhouse of the Ballpark in Arlington.

"To get through something like this, you need each other," Torre told them. "I don't care what you think of each other, whether you like the guy next to you or whether you don't, but you need each other. We only have one thing that we're trying to accomplish and you can't do it alone.

"When you go up there to the plate or you go out to that mound, you have to know that guys have your back. If you don't do the job, you have to understand that somebody else will do it for you.

"You can't control the result all the time. You just have to be prepared every day and play your ass off. And . . . it has to be important to you."

Much of the old guard spoke. Jeter spoke. Pettitte spoke. Rivera spoke. They spoke about getting everybody on the same page, fully invested with some urgency. They spoke about the importance of relying on each other. Nobody mentioned Damon by name. Then, to Torre's surprise, Damon got up to speak. He basically repeated the same message, straight from the "This is what we need to do" speech archive. He concluded by saying, "I wish I could have helped you. I was hurt. Now **I** need to help."

The words had no effect on his teammates. Damon may have meant well, but he was in no position, they thought, to be rallying the troops when he was the one most in need of being rallied. Torre was surprised to hear Damon speak.

Damon did improve his game slightly after that, but it was still subjected to fits and starts that vexed Torre. On May 15, with the Yankees in Chicago to play the White Sox, Torre knew he had to speak with Damon yet again. A storm was coming. Heavy, ominous clouds gathered over U.S. Cellular Field as the Yankees conducted an optional early hitting workout.

"We were fine in Texas and even at home after

that," Torre said at the time, "but we're missing that spark. We're just missing that put-away attitude. We're playing well enough but we're not getting the job done. And I've got two guys who are trying to decide whether they want to play or not."

The spark they missed most was the one Damon was supposed to provide. Giambi, too, was a problem. His foot, like Damon's legs, was a daily issue that seemed to drag down his resolve. As if on cue, the clouds over U.S. Cellular Field opened up with a deluge, sending the Yankees scurrying for cover in the clubhouse. Torre found Damon and Giambi there and told each of them he wanted to see them in the weight training room.

"There's one thing I need to know from you guys," Torre said to them. "I need to know if you guys are ready to play. Because we're at a point where we really need to win games, and you guys are very important to us. But you're only really important to us if your heart's in it. So let me know: Do you want to play baseball or not?"

Damon and Giambi both said the right things. They would give Torre whatever they had.

"In the past," Giambi said, "he's asked us a ton to play hurt, and Johnny and I would play to the extent that we probably shouldn't have been out there. But we would do anything for Joe. I think Joe was trying to get across the point of, 'If you guys are really that beat up, just be honest with us, because we're losing and if it's not there let me know, instead of, "Yeah, we're fine, Joe."' He was looking to mix and match players to win.

"I told him, 'I'm beat up. I'm giving you everything I've got. If you don't think it's enough, then go with somebody else. But I'm giving you everything I've got.' It was to the point where I blew out. I tore my foot in half I don't think much longer after that."

Meanwhile, Torre had to find a way to get Abreu untracked as well. His suspicion with Abreu was perhaps that he was trying too hard.

"He's a good soldier," Torre said at the time. "He's just putting a lot of pressure on himself because he feels like he's letting everybody down. He's not the best physical specimen in the world, but he's a good hitter. He's physically fine, but right now he's fighting himself more than anything."

A few days earlier, Torre had met with Abreu and bench coach Don Mattingly to try to pull Abreu out of his funk.

"I'm fine," Abreu told them.

"No you're not," Torre shot back. "You're not fine. I know what you want and I know that you work at it and go after it. But let's try to figure out what's going on here."

Said Torre, "I just wanted to make sure that the possibility of being a free agent wasn't a part of it, and I think he convinced me that it wasn't. The responsibility of letting people down was more of an imposing thing than anything else."

Meanwhile, hitting coach Kevin Long was also trying to get Abreu untracked. Long decided he needed to go back to the fundamentals of his swing, so he pulled out a batting tee. Abreu told Long something that completely surprised the hitting coach: Abreu had never before worked with a tee.

"You'll try anything to get a guy going," Long said, "but basically when a guy's in a slump you're working on his head. He's stepping in the bucket now, but even when he's hot he'll do that. It's how he hits. But he lost all confidence on his ability to hit and we're working on getting some confidence back."

Abreu was 33 years old. Damon was 33. Giambi was 37. Mussina, who was on the disabled list, was 38. Eight of the 12 most-used regular players that season and three of the four most-used starting pitchers that season were 33 or older. Maybe, just maybe, these Yankees just had too many miles on them. Torre was asked about that possibility as he sat in the U.S. Cellular Field dugout in Chicago.

"No, I don't think so," he said. "They may be worn down but I don't feel they're old. I think it's more of a case of how hard it is to put up with things on a regular basis. Last year we certainly had our share of problems and Melky Cabrera came up and gave us a shot of energy, no question. Two years ago it was Robinson Cano and Wang. Grinding every day in New York, especially when you have to answer for it every day, sometimes I think it wears people down. I don't think it's age."

The Yankees were rained out that night in Chicago, forcing a doubleheader the next day. Damon managed one hit in five at-bats while striking out a career-tying three times in a 5-3 loss to Chicago. Torre started the 22-year-old Cabrera in center field in the second game instead of Damon. Cabrera hit a home run in an 8-1 New York victory. So Torre put Cabrera in the lineup the next day, too, keeping Damon on the bench. Cabrera went hitless and the Yankees lost, 4-1.

Damon showed some life in his legs and bat after that benching, spraying nine hits over his next six games. Not coincidentally, the Yankees played better, too. They did lose two out of three to the Mets at Shea Stadium, but Torre liked the way the Yankees played. They were showing real energy for the first time, having better at-bats, posting rallies when they were behind instead of giving in to deficits. Indeed, when the Yankees hosted Boston after the series at Shea, Torre called a team meeting to let his team know it finally was acquiring a grinder's personality.

"Congratulations, guys," he told them. "You've got that personality now. You can fight. Now that you see you have it, you're stuck with it. Let's go."

The manager wanted his players to know, after they had proved they could play with such vigor, that he would expect this personality as a rule, not an exception.

Torre scanned the room, routinely making eye contact with players as he talked as a way to fully engage them in the message and to read their body language to see if they were buying into it. Just as Torre happening to lock on to the gaze of Damon, he said, "No matter what you might have going on at home or off the field, the time you spend here has to continue to be focused on giving everything you have to the team."

Torre had not meant to catch Damon's eyes at that moment, but he immediately considered the eye contact to be a happy stroke of synchronicity. The truth was that the message applied as much to the hobbled, confused Yankees center fielder as anybody in the room.

Meanwhile, behind the press releases, the real Steinbrenner, not the propped-up one issuing statements through a PR firm, wasn't showing the old fire and brimstone to Torre, either. Before the middle game of the series against the Mets, Cashman was in Torre's office when the general manager's cell phone rang. It was Steinbrenner. The call was a mistake. Steinbrenner had just spoken with Cashman a while earlier, but he had redialed by mistake. Torre saw it as an opportunity and asked to speak to The Boss. Torre liked calling Steinbrenner every couple of weeks or so, just to keep the communication going, tell him how much he appreciated his support, but the conversations were becoming increasingly shorter and generic. Torre and Steinbrenner would be on the phone only for about 30 seconds. This was another one of them.

"You're my guy," Steinbrenner told Torre. "Keep your chin up."

"Thanks, George," Torre said. "We're doing our best to make you proud."

That was about it. Meanwhile, during these rough days, Cashman was throwing himself in front of Torre as a human shield, trying to hold off the fire of Steinbrenner and, more accurately, Steinbrenner's lieutenants who had strongly considered firing Torre after the previous season and again in April and in May.

"Joe's not the problem," Cashman would tell Steinbrenner. "If you need to fire anybody, fire me, not Joe."

The Yankees took two out of three from Boston. They had something to build on. But nothing good was sustainable in those first 50 games, and the inconsistency was reflected mostly in Damon. Every time Damon's game began to percolate just so, he suddenly would appear brittle and disengaged again. May 25 was one of those frequent bad days for Damon. Before the game, while closing in on 2,000 hits, Damon sounded oddly subdued about the possibility of playing long enough to have a shot at 3,000 hits.

"It's not out of the question," he said, "but right

now I don't know if this is what I want to be doing when I'm 37, 38, 39—playing baseball. I don't know about that."

In the game that night, against the Los Angeles Angels, Damon virtually embarrassed himself with his play. He went hitless in three at-bats, dropped a sinking line drive, could not run down two fly balls that should have been outs, and finally asked Torre to take him out of the game. Several of his teammates took notice when Damon asked out and were not happy about it. Here the Yankees had dug themselves a two-month hole to start the season, leaving them with little margin for error, and Damon was pulling himself from the game.

"Just a bad day at the office," Damon told reporters after the game. "I don't know what happened. The last few days I felt like the Fountain of Youth was injected in me. And then this happens."

Damon was asked if he was better off going on the disabled list than continuing to play like that.

"I don't know," he said. "I'll let them decide what's best for the team."

On paper, the Yankees looked formidable. With 45-year-old Roger Clemens signing on to make another comeback, their roster included one of the greatest starting pitchers of all time (Clemens), the greatest relief pitcher of all time (Rivera), one of the greatest infielders of all time (Rodriguez) and one of the greatest offensive shortstops of all time (Jeter). They had five of the nine highest paid players in baseball (Giambi, Rodriguez, Jeter, Clemens and Abreu) and the highest paid manager in the game.

In reality, the Yankees were a wreck. Damon was hurt and at times disinterested to the point of angering his teammates. Giambi was hurt. Abreu had no confidence. Igawa was taking remedial pitching lessons. Pavano was hurt. Somebody named Tyler Clippard and somebody named Matt DeSalvo made up 40 percent of the rotation. So-called voices in Tampa were putting Torre's job on the line on almost a series-by-series basis. Steinbrenner wasn't showing up for work until late in the afternoon while an unpredictable scramble ensued to see how the enormous power vacuum would be filled.

The Yankees were 21-29, off to the fifth-worst start in the history of the franchise, to put them 14½ games behind the first-place Red Sox and 8½ games out of the wild card spot—with **seven** teams in front of them. Only three teams had ever been that far out of the wild card that deep into the season and still made it to the postseason. It was as if Torre ran an automobile repair shop and the lot was overrun with beaters and clunkers that needed his daily attention, oil leaking and transmissions dropping everywhere.

Where do you begin to save the season and save your job? Torre began in Toronto. He began with one more meeting. He began with the kick-ass meeting to end all kick-ass meetings.

14.

The Last Race

Another city. Another day. Another crisis. Another meeting. This is how the first one-third of the schedule went by for the 2007 Yankees.

They were in Toronto to finish May, their second straight horrible month. For weeks Torre had tried to prompt his team into playing with urgency, with an understanding and a trust for one another, but the results did not come. Worse, in the preceding days his coaches began to alert him that some players were actually becoming less focused, not more so, amid the heap of losses that piled up. Guys were showing up late for stretching, maybe skipping some extra pregame work . . . cutting some corners at a time when the Yankees needed to take nothing for granted.

"I think they took a lot of things for granted

because the Yankees won before and they thought things would happen automatically, just kick in," Bowa said. "Just some little things that were happening . . . I don't know, they weren't New York Yankee–style things.

"They're little things, like being late for stretching, but then they keep adding up. And the guys who were late were not just utility players. I mean, they were guys that were star players.

"You know, when you start losing games, you see a lot of shit happening and guys say, 'Why bother?' That's how the game has changed. Because when I used to play, when you were losing, that's when you did everything by the book. When you're losing and not playing up to your capabilities you want to be as quiet as possible and toe the line, whatever the manager wants. It's when you're winning that you might try to pull some shit. Now, it's in fact the other way around."

There was something about this team that concerned Torre. Maybe it was unfair to compare it to his championship teams, but that was the frame of reference with which he worked. In a room filled with grinders such as Paul O'Neill, Tino Martinez and Scott Brosius the lapses in concentration and effort over the long season never lingered. Those teams responded quickly to the inevitable lags in energy or focus.

"Those teams, all they needed was a little poke, a little reminder, and they responded," Torre said.

This was a very different team. Most of the players in the room had never won anything. Many didn't know **how** to win. There was a noticeable lack of effort, to do what it took to win.

"Yeah. You could just sense that," Mussina said. "You could just feel that everyone was getting used to losing. People were getting used to just playing, and win or lose it didn't matter."

This team didn't need just a poke or a nudge. This one needed a kick in the ass. Several kicks.

The Yankees took extra hitting at 2:30 p.m. in Toronto, which is their custom upon their first trip of the season into a ballpark. A short time after it ended, Torre called a team meeting to be held in the visiting clubhouse of the Rogers Centre.

"My angry meeting," Torre said. "That was the first time in my years with the Yankees where I felt there weren't enough guys who really gave a shit. I had that meeting and I was just angry.

"We were just terrible at the time. We played badly and it didn't look like it bothered them."

Torre lit into his players for how they were playing, but he did so in a calm, measured voice.

"Let's stop this shit right now," he said.

From now on, he said, the Yankees would start taking infield practice, the kind of old-school pregame work that had long disappeared as a staple of the game. Guys would be fined if they were even a minute late for stretching. Everyone would have to be all in, heart and soul. He talked about responsibility and focus.

"And," he warned them, "it's too late to keep saying it's early."

The change would have to come immediately.

And then Bowa spoke.

"Guys, you're playing for the best manager you could possibly play for," Bowa told the players. "He never rips you. He sticks up for you whether you're right or wrong. He gives you the benefit of the doubt on anything. He tells you the night before whether you're playing or resting the next day. I think you're fucking taking advantage of this guy.

"You go somewhere else? You're not going to see a manager like this. This is a once-in-a-lifetime opportunity for your career. Don't fucking abuse it. Don't fucking take it for granted because this is a manager that comes along every 25, 30 years. You guys, you have no idea how fucking good you have it playing for this guy."

The players were taken aback by the in-your-face intensity of both Torre and Bowa in the meeting. Maybe that kind of anger is what they had come to expect from the spring-loaded Bowa. But Torre? Many of them had never seen him so angry. It made an impression.

"There was real emotion," Mussina said. "I think that got everybody's attention. There was really a feeling we got from Joe and the staff that there was real concern. Maybe not anguish, but just real . . . emotion. Almost like, 'If you're going to get this turned around you better start real soon.' Like it was getting too late. I think everybody picked up on the emotion."

When Torre, Bowa and the rest of the staff left the room, the players remained. They decided to reinforce the message with their own meeting. Pettitte spoke. Jeter spoke.

"There are times when you can be too comfortable," Jeter said. "And that's not always a good thing. I think sometimes people think if they play for this organization, if they play for this team, it's just going to automatically win. You know what I mean? I'm not saying anybody in particular. Sometimes that can be the mindset and you get caught up in that. 'Ahh, if we don't win today we'll just get 'em tomorrow. You know, we're the Yankees. We'll be in the playoffs. Winning just happens.'

"But the meeting was a wakeup call for us. I've said a lot of things over the years. People always assume I don't. People always assume. They make that assumption. 'Jeter's not vocal.' Let me ask you a hypothetical situation. Say I pulled Mo over. First of all, I'm not going to do it with a camera on me. I think people that do that probably know the camera is on them. Say I pull Mo aside, and say I just yell at Mo all day long. For an hour. Is he going to tell you? He's not going to tell you. I'm not going to tell you. But then I always hear, 'Well, he's not vocal.' Yeah. Okay. I talk to everybody. But I don't do it when there is a camera around."

Jeter's words caught the attention of the players.

"You know, it's one thing to hear something from the manager and staff," Mussina said, "and it's another thing to hear it player-to-player. Not that the manager doesn't have an impact, but it's like hearing from your parents as opposed to hearing it from your peers. It has a very different impact.

"Basically, what was said was to make sure each guy was doing absolutely everything he could to be prepared and to play to the best of his ability. When you win it's because you pay attention to all the details and do all the work. You take nothing for granted. But it's real easy to get used to losing. You fall behind in the beginning of a game and it's like, 'Okay, another loss. We'll go get 'em tomorrow.' It's easy to give in to that feeling and to get used to losing. That's what the players were concerned about. To make sure we weren't falling into that mindset by making sure we did everything we could to be a winning team. No individuals were called out, but there's a way to deliver a message to people without having to call them out."

Said Jason Giambi, "Joe just wanted us to play harder. No matter how good your team is, every once in a while you have to put people in check. I think he did that. We kind of sorted it out and talked. The biggest thing, too, is everybody started to come back from their injuries, and I think that's what got the ball rolling, too."

Meetings, even players-only meetings, tend be fairly routine, full of platitudes and posturing, not unlike a political convention. But these meetings were different. There was an edge to what people were saying. Players were openly questioning the attitudes of other players, if not by name.

"Guys were saying stuff to other guys that maybe they didn't want to hear," Borzello said, "and they didn't want Joe there to stop it because Joe would have, that's how heated it got. Guys were questioning who wanted to play and who didn't, injuries that some people didn't feel were real, stuff like that."

The two meetings lasted nearly an hour. The Yankees missed virtually their entire batting practice. They had been challenged by Torre, scolded by Bowa and put on notice by Pettitte and Jeter. This either was going to be the turning point to their season or verification that this group of Yankees just didn't give a damn.

"I started thinking about myself," Mussina said. "I got to the point where some of the players were speaking where I wasn't listening. I mean, I knew guys were getting fired up, and I knew basically they were telling us that we were abusing all the privileges we were given. The trust of us doing what we had to do to be ready to play—and to go out and play the game the way we were capable of playing—was being lost. That trust was being lost.

"What each player should do is they should be looking at themselves saying, 'Am I involved in this? Am I one of these people?'

"But some guys sit there and they don't even listen to it. They don't think anybody is ever talking about them. But I was actually at that point where I was just sitting there thinking, Is this me? Whether I was or I wasn't . . . I mean, I had been hurt for half the time up to that point anyway, and then I was on the DL with a hamstring thing for half of the period before this meeting. But I still wondered if I was doing all that I could or should be doing. And the meeting made a difference, ultimately."

———

There was just one problem with the timing of the meeting: the Yankees were starting rookie Matt DeSalvo on the mound that night. DeSalvo was a decent enough pitcher, and actually contributed a couple of good games, but he essentially was an unproven placeholder for Roger Clemens, or, more accurately given all the injuries, a placeholder for a placeholder for a placeholder for Clemens. He was not the kind of proven pitcher you want to consolidate a kick-ass meeting about getting the season turned around immediately. DeSalvo was gone before the fifth inning ended. The Yankees lost, 7-2.

At least the Yankees had Pettitte, a member of their old guard, and one of their few reliable pitchers they were starting those days, taking the ball in the next game. Turns out, that was a problem, too.

"Tightest I've ever seen this team," Torre said. "They played like they felt they had to win the game because Andy was pitching. And it showed."

The Yankees lost again, 3-2, dropping their record to 21-29 after 50 games. Then a funny thing happened after the game: the bus ride back to the hotel turned into a comedy club on wheels. Guys were laughing and joking, not because they didn't care that they lost, but because they were just . . . well, just goofy. The tension had broken, like a cloudburst in a heat wave. The Yankees knew they had played a good, clean game, coming back from two one-run deficits, with Pettitte pitching into the eighth inning, before losing on a sacrifice fly in that inning. It was as if they fully understood Torre's mantra about how you can't always control the result but you can control your effort. The Yankees had given a focused effort with urgency. They had lost the game, but they had found themselves. They were the Yankees again, and they seemed to know that on the bus ride back to the hotel. The next day they demolished the Blue Jays, 10-5. They were on their way.

"I just felt like they got it," Bowa said. "You hear Joe use that word **urgency.** 'You need a sense of urgency.' I really felt that after that airing out and then the guys talking, there was that sense of urgency every time they took the field. I really felt it.

You could see how the players responded. The way they took batting practice. The way they focused in meetings when we're going over pitchers. I just felt like they were more attentive. And they knew we had a long road to get to the playoffs because of where we were."

The Yankees, of course, couldn't get out of Toronto and on track without Rodriguez managing to create a controversy. Running toward third base on what was a routine pop-up to third baseman Howie Clark, Rodriguez yelled something at Clark in an attempt to distract him. It worked. Clark dropped the ball, extending the inning. The Blue Jays were enraged. Like most observers, they regarded it as a play that, while possibly within the rules, smacked of a bush league maneuver. Mussina, Rodriguez's teammate, even referred to it as "unsportsmanlike." Torre told reporters that Rodriguez probably wished he had not done it, especially considering the ill will it stirred. Torre's response to the writers' questions came out like this in the next day's tabloids: "Torre to A-Rod: Shut Up."

"Alex took a hit in that thing," Torre said, "and my feeling was, and I mentioned it to him, that if he was the one under the pop-up and somebody did it to him, and he let it drop, he would be the one criticized. It is true.

"I told the media he would probably think twice about doing it again. And that's when they put in the paper that I told him to shut up. I never did that.

I told him, 'You're getting this reaction, Alex. What are you going to do? You're trying to win a game.'

"He was excited. He was swinging the bat really well. He went by the guy at third base. You know he does shit all the time during the game when he's going good. I didn't think it was a bush play. He plays hard. Maybe it was unnecessary, but you certainly didn't expect the guy to miss the ball. I thought they overreacted. And I thought it was horseshit the way they reacted. They waited until they got back to their ballpark to get even. They come into Yankee Stadium and . . . nothing. Nothing happens. Then they come back home, and they threw a ball behind him. And that's when Rocket got thrown out of the game. He's pitching a hell of a game, then he gets thrown out protecting Alex, and we had to scratch by our ass to win the game. Roger was floating along really well. Of course, when he was ejected he told me he thought that was his last inning, anyway. I said, 'You could have waited for two outs.' He did it to the leadoff guy. But Roger was a lot like Alex in a lot of ways. Kind of in their own world."

On the day of the last game in Toronto, Torre decided to check in with Steinbrenner. He liked calling him after losses. It was a way to help calm Steinbrenner's anxieties.

"I'm excited about the young pitching," Torre

told him. "With all the money this organization has spent over the years, it's good to see the young pitching. This is huge. You've got young pitching with substance to it. It's great. It's going to save you a lot of money, George."

"Yeah, buddy. Good luck," Steinbrenner said. He wasn't much of a conversationalist anymore. The Yankees were traveling to Boston to play the Red Sox the next day, which Torre mentioned to Steinbrenner.

"We've got the Red Sox next and we'll get 'em," Torre said.

"Yeah, you've got to beat those guys," Steinbrenner said. "You get 'em."

And just like that the conversation was over.

"He would sort of echo, or mimic what you were saying," Torre said. "And that would be the extent of the conversation. I talked to him and he would get me off the phone in 30 seconds. That was it. He really wouldn't be in touch with what was happening."

Torre, in fact, would make sure he would jog Steinbrenner's memory. For instance, a little more than a week later, after Torre won his 2,000th career game as manager, he called Steinbrenner to thank him for the gift the Yankees gave him in recognition of the milestone, a sterling plate. Torre made sure to name the specific gift because he wasn't sure if Steinbrenner would recall it or not.

"Oh, okay. You deserve it," Steinbrenner said.

If Steinbrenner wasn't the conversationalist he was once, the divide-and-conquer leadership philosophy he engrained in the Yankee organization still ran strong. As the Yankees arrived in Boston, word reached Torre that somebody on the staff was going to be fired, probably bullpen coach Joe Kerrigan, if the Yankees lost the series there. The "voices" in Tampa needed some blood spilled to send a message that the losing would not be tolerated, or even to send a message to Torre that his job security was growing thinner by the day.

Kerrigan was a Cashman hire and ally, and a rather odd, iconoclastic personality. He kept copious charts and statistics, ran half the pregame pitchers' meetings with pitching coach Ron Guidry, broke down miles of videotapes to try to decode the habits of opposing hitters, and believed that immutable truths about the game could be found in his numbers. Cashman, of course, liked that analytical side of him. Kerrigan's people skills, however, were not his strong suit. He had confrontations with players in just about every stop of his baseball life, including Philadelphia, Boston and the Yankees, where he had angry, ugly exchanges with Carl Pavano and Jason Giambi. Pavano wanted to fight Kerrigan when they had a shouting match at the hotel bar in Boston. The confrontation with Giambi happened in a restaurant bar.

"I called him in, in Texas," Torre said of Kerrigan, "and told him, 'First of all, you shouldn't be sitting with players out at night. And secondly, if you can't control your emotions, then you can't go out yourself.' Then he just stopped coming to dinners. I would invite him to join me and others on the staff to dinners, and he just stopped coming."

Torre liked Kerrigan's work ethic and saw him as a good complement to Guidry, who was the old-school-style pitching coach. But Torre wasn't sure he could trust Kerrigan. He knew Kerrigan was connected to the front office by way of Cashman, and word reached Torre that Kerrigan was having private conversations with Cashman about the team and Torre. One staff member even said Cashman had telephoned Kerrigan during a game. Torre wanted to find out if the rumors were true, if Cashman had a pipeline behind his back to Torre's own staff, so he confronted Cashman about it.

"I remember asking Cash point-blank if he has conversations with Kerrigan," Torre said, "and he said, 'No.'"

A short time later, one of Torre's staff members told him that he and a couple of other staff members were riding in a car with Kerrigan when Kerrigan's cell phone rang. "Hi, Cash," Kerrigan said into the phone, and the two of them proceeded to chat at length. Torre felt wounded, not so much because he thought Kerrigan might be keeping a secret pipeline to the general manager, but more because Cashman had denied such an arrangement to Torre.

In bad times, Kerrigan turned out to be expendable. He didn't have the Yankee pedigree that Guidry and Mattingly did, and his confrontations with Pavano and Giambi had caused concern about his abrasiveness anyway. The Yankees split the first two games in Boston. Kerrigan was going to be fired if they lost the series finale. At that moment, an unlikely ally stepped in and fought for Kerrigan to keep his job: Torre. The manager called Cashman.

"You can't fire him," Torre said. "We're going horseshit. I would fire him at the end of the year, but this is not the time to do it. Because then it's going to look like he's the cause of our problems, and that's not right."

Cashman took Torre's plea under advisement. That night, the Yankees blew a 4-0 lead to Boston and fell behind, 5-4, entering the eighth inning. But they rallied for a run in the eighth and won the game in the ninth on a home run by Rodriguez off Red Sox closer Jonathan Papelbon. Kerrigan was safe. And the Yankees had won only their third road series of the year.

———

The Yankees continued to play with the focus and energy they had summoned from the Toronto meeting. They went to Chicago and took three out of four. Back home, they swept the Pirates— with Clemens, rusty as an old oil derrick, back in pinstripes pitching again—swept the Diamondbacks and took two out of three from the Mets. The 13-3 run put them two games above .500. Damon and Abreu were at last rounding into shape, body and mind.

Said Mussina at the time, "The difference now is we have more than three guys giving good at-bats. It's eight or nine, and the team is feeding off of that. The pitchers know this team can come back and the hitters know it doesn't fall on one guy to get it done. We're in a real good place right now."

Cano, the young second baseman prone to lapses in concentration, provided a good example of the players' rededication. Cano had been Bowa's pet project, an arrangement the coach made clear in spring training when he sat down with the second baseman.

"Robby, if you want to be the best player that you can be, you need to come out here and work every day," Bowa told him. "I know you're a natural hitter. I know you can hit .300. But you've got to do everything. And I'm going to be honest with you. I'm not going to tell you what you want to hear. You know, you get lazy out there on double plays. You let the ball get real deep. And I'm going to let you know that's not how you make the double play.

"For the most part, you're real good at what you do. Then all of a sudden you get into these little spells where you'll go, 'Oh, I've got it,' and then—boom!—you get into bad habits. So here's what we're going to do. Every time we have an off day the next day we're coming out to the field early to do extra work."

Cano stayed true to Bowa's plan. Then, in June, Bowa decided that Cano had been so good about his work and staying focused that he decided to cut him some slack. Bowa called off the mandatory extra workouts for him. A week later, Cano sought out Bowa.

"Hey, I want to go back to working early after every off day," Cano said.

Bowa smiled.

"Great," the coach said.

The Yankees had a new vibe. They reached the All-Star break 43-43. They had a pulse. Torre held a quick meeting before the first game after the break. It was nothing more than a reminder to keep playing hard, to continue to be mentally sharp every day. When he was done, Torre asked, "Anybody have any questions?"

Nobody had a question, but Derek Jeter wanted to say something. Over the years, and especially after Jeter was named captain, Torre would sometimes use Jeter as a messenger. He might give him a heads-up about a team meeting so he could be ready with a contribution. "I might want you to say something," Torre might tell him. Torre knew the peer-to-peer delivery system among ballplayers is a powerful one, especially when it is Jeter.

"I'd push him and he'd do it," Torre said, "but when he spoke it was always, 'We,' never 'You' or

'I.' 'We're doing this.' After he became captain he did more of that. It wouldn't be a rah-rah thing. He would be critical, without calling people out. He'd say something like, 'We can't **not** run a ball out.' He may have been aiming the message at an individual, but he would be critical in his remarks without picking on any one person. He was good that way.

"With Alex, I'd ask Alex to say something and he never wanted to say anything. Never wanted to say anything."

In that post-All-Star break meeting, Torre had not prompted Jeter to say anything, so even the manager was curious to hear what the captain would say.

"Starting today," Jeter said, "every game is a play-off game. That's how we have to treat every game: like it's a playoff game."

Jeter's words got everybody's attention. Jeter, like Torre, was faithful to the belief that everything was going to work out fine in time. He had no time or energy to waste on negative thoughts. But here the Yankees were in the middle of July and Jeter, Captain Cool, was pressing the accelerator.

"Even in him you could see that he was concerned," Bowa said. "When Jeet talks, because he really doesn't talk all that much, he gets their attention."

The Yankees began not just beating teams but demolishing them with an offensive might of historic proportions. They won 12 of their first 16 games coming out of the All-Star break while scoring a whopping 151 runs. Only two other teams in franchise history ever scored 150 runs in any 16-game span, and those teams did so way back in 1930 and 1939. Finally, after months in which Torre had pushed and poked and yelled at them, the Yankees were totally invested in the entire process of winning baseball games: the preparation, the intensity, the focus, the ferocious **will** to win. They cared.

———

The Yankees were rolling. But there was a problem. Torre could not enjoy it. He knew from his mock firing after the previous season, from the sniping in April and May and from the Yankees having no contractual obligation to him beyond 2007 that his job status was a major issue in the organization. Torre knew working for Steinbrenner meant your job was always in jeopardy, no matter the length of the contract, but this was different. He felt some of the "voices" talking to Steinbrenner didn't fully support him. What bothered him just as much, however, was knowing that his players and coaches knew he was hanging by a string. Torre always worked to keep the clubhouse "uncluttered," the way he called it, so that the players and staff could occupy themselves only with the diligence that winning baseball required. If the newspapers were full of leaks and whispers about his job, that noise was bound to create conversation and speculation that could only detract from that diligence.

"I was trying, really trying to always be that same guy for them," Torre said, "even though what I was going through was uncomfortable. It was certainly difficult going to the park in 2007, knowing shit had been in the paper and on the radio. And you walk in the clubhouse and you go in the coach's room, and there's this dead silence in there, because they don't know what to say to me. And you go in the training room with the players, and unless I start kidding about it, nobody really knows what to say. It was a very uncomfortable time."

Some players noticed a change in Torre. He seemed tired. Worn.

"What Joe always tried to do a good job of was no matter what was going on, keep the matter from affecting the clubhouse," Giambi said. "Really, every year for his last three years Joe's head was on the block. Basically every year he had to like fight for his job. 'Well, Joe's gone!' Then something incredible happened, and then they couldn't fire him, because we would come from 15 games down to win and get in the postseason.

"In '07, for us, it was mostly a situation where we felt bad for him. For a human being to go through that it would have to be tough. I mean, he acted like it wasn't, but it had to be wearing on him. I mean, I noticed a difference probably between my first three years and my last three years here. Just because, I think when you have to go through that all the time it's tough. He handles himself with class and dignity, but . . .

"It had to be wearing him down. It had to be something on his mind all the time. I felt he was a little more tired. Does that make sense? He felt more tired. I mean, you could kind of see it. I'd even ask Jeet sometimes. 'Jeet, is he doing okay?' And Jeet would go, 'Yeah, he probably has a lot on his mind.' And I just think that's what I noticed."

Other players, though, did not notice a change in Torre.

"It didn't seem like it was ever there," Mussina said of Torre's job status being a clubhouse issue. "He never portrayed it as being there. I think we all read the papers and understood what was going on, and we knew it, and people were talking to us about it. But it never leaked into the everyday stuff.

"Joe has a great ability, and he had a great ability **in New York.** He has a great ability to diffuse things so they don't leak into his clubhouse, so they don't get to the players, so they don't become distractions. That's one of his best qualities."

Maybe as the Yankees began to win over the summer the victories bought Torre a little more time, but it didn't change the reality that he was living in the crosshairs of people who wanted him gone, and probably anything short of a World Series championship would not have been enough. What was debilitating for him was knowing they no longer trusted him, and yet he was the same man who had helped bring home those six pennants and four world championships.

"Cashman has a problem telling people things," said Borzello, the bullpen catcher. "He would say comments about Joe, like he did this or he did that in a game, and he'd be telling people who he must have known know and like Joe. What, he didn't think Joe would hear it from them? But Cash operated that way all the time. It was a big problem. And then we would all talk about it and say, 'Doesn't he realize we're all a family down here?'

"The team pretty much knew if we didn't get to the World Series he wasn't coming back, and there was no denying it. It wasn't so much that's what we were told. The silence said enough. There would be rumors out there or stuff in the papers about Joe's job being on the line, and nobody in the front office would deny it or say anything about it. The silence said it all. Joe never brought it up in the clubhouse. But we started to believe that Joe was gone."

Said Torre, "I asked Donnie [Mattingly] about it, about not enjoying it. And he said the same thing: he didn't enjoy it. Even after winning games, we wouldn't enjoy it. I was drained.

"The questions came hot and heavy. A lot of it was because we started so badly. I find that when people talk about what they want to talk about— and it was about me getting fired—they don't want to consider the reasons why we may have started so badly. It's all about the bottom line and it's all about what's going to be the fallout from it—not about how many guys we had hurt. We had Abreu on the disabled list most of the spring. We had Johnny Damon who stumbled out of the gate. You had pitchers on the DL.

"But that wasn't the back page. People want to get the meat and potatoes: I'm on the last year of a contract. And the media knew whoever was leaking the information. I just felt like it was coming at me from a lot of different directions, and I was uncomfortable with it.

"You'd like to think if you work for somebody for a certain period of time that there'd be a time where they'd trust you somewhat. And I never got that. Even when we were winning I never got that. That bothered me."

The Yankees won like nobody else after that kick-ass meeting in Toronto and that 21-29 start. They played .652 baseball over the final four months, the best record in baseball. It took much more than the usual little poke or nudge he would give his championship teams, but Torre had found a way to get this team to respond, even after the fifth-worst start to a season in franchise history. As the Yankees clobbered opponents and passed one team after another in the wild card race, Yankee Stadium buzzed that summer with the familiar electricity about the possibilities of another October. Life was good again in the Bronx.

Except in the manager's office at Yankee Stadium.

One day during the summer, even while the Yankees were winning with uncanny regularity, the only kind of regularity that could overcome a 21-29 beginning, Torre looked around his office and saw the accumulations of a successful 12-year-run. The trophies, the pictures, the baseballs . . . the small remnants of achievement, the little reminders of the awesome power of trust. Even with the wins coming apace, Torre knew what was coming for him. He turned to his personal assistant, Chris Romanello.

"Chris," Torre said, "why don't you start packing some things up."

———

The game on Friday night, July 20, 2007, was a particularly ugly one for the Yankees, providing a harsh reminder that as far back as they had come from that 21-29 start, they still had a long, rough road to October. By the fifth inning in front of 53,953 peeved fans at Yankee Stadium, the Yankees trailed the Tampa Bay Devil Rays, 9-0, thanks to abysmal pitching from Mike Mussina, who looked more and more as if his career was headed to its finish, and Edwar Ramirez, an independent league find by the Yankees whose career looked as if it might never get started.

Mussina allowed six earned runs in 4⅔ innings, falling to 4-7 on the season. Torre brought in Ramirez to stem the damage, but the carnage grew so bad as to be almost painful to watch. Ramirez threw 19 pitches. Seventeen of them were balls. One of the two pitches that wasn't a ball was hit for a grand slam. This is what the first five batters did against Ramirez: walk, walk, grand slam, walk, walk. Yankees pitchers walked 10 batters in a game for the first time in six years.

Edwin Jackson, a righthanded pitcher for Tampa Bay who entered the game with a 1-9 record, befuddled the Yankees hitters, allowing no runs over six innings. The lefthanded trio of Damon, Abreu and Matsui went 1-for-14. Another lefty, Giambi, wasn't even in the lineup.

The defeat dropped the Yankees to 49-46, their worst record after 95 games in 16 years. Twenty-six other Yankees team were 49-46 or worse after 95 games. None of them made the playoffs.

All things considered, it was a good night to be in New Britain, Connecticut, instead of the Bronx. That is exactly where you could find all of the most important decision makers in the Yankees baseball operations department. Indeed, it was a beautiful evening at New Britain Stadium, home of the Rock Cats, the Minnesota Twins' Double-A affiliate: temperature in the low 70s, low humidity, a nice breeze. It was a good night to dream. Into the 6,000-seat ballpark walked the who's who of Yankees brass: general manager Brian Cashman, stats guru and assistant general manager Billy Eppler, head of player development Mark Newman, pitching guru Nardi

Contreras (the Yankees, naturally, did not hire mere experts; they unearthed the gurus of their profession) and special adviser Reggie Jackson. They did not come for the comfort of the evening, nor for the $6.50 burritos or the $5.50 Sam Adams Cherry Wheat drafts.

They came to see the future.

The Rock Cats were playing the Trenton Thunder, the Yankees' Double-A affiliate, who were starting a beefy 21-year-old righthanded pitcher named Joba Chamberlain. Cashman, Eppler, Newman, Contreras and Jackson wanted to see if Chamberlain was ready to help the Yankees in their uphill climb. The single biggest reason that the Yankees dynasty had devolved into just another franchise scrambling to even get into the playoffs as a wild card was because Cashman and his gurus had made mistake after mistake after mistake when it came to evaluating pitchers, both on the major league and amateur sides.

Kevin Brown, Randy Johnson, Jaret Wright, Jeff Weaver, Steve Karsay, Esteban Loaiza, Kyle Farnsworth, Jose Contreras, Javier Vazquez, Kei Igawa, Carl Pavano, Roger Clemens (the 44-year-old version) . . . None of those 12 pitchers, all brought in from outside the organization, pitched three consecutive seasons with the Yankees. None. It was a losing pattern that defied enormous odds. The Yankees would typically overvalue a pitcher, bringing him in when he was either at the end of his career or not a fit for New York, then dump the pitcher to move on to the next mistake. The balance sheet on those 12 investments was ugly:

Record: 125-105 (including 3-7 in the
postseason)
Cost*: $255 million
Cost per win: $2.04 million

*Does not include prospects surrendered in trades

Cashman was in New Britain because he had a pretty good inkling that flushing $255 million on pitching mistakes did not exactly make for good business practice. The Yankees put themselves in the position of dumping all that money on the wrong pitchers because they couldn't develop any decent pitchers of their own. They **had** to scramble to find available veteran pitchers because their system was producing nothing. And, because the revenue-sharing system and new revenue streams put more money in the pockets of smaller revenue teams, the pool of available veteran pitchers for the Yankees to wave their money at was drying up. In another era, the Yankees might have cherry-picked elite pitchers in their prime from organizations that could no longer afford them, in the same way they had plucked David Cone from the Blue Jays in 1995 and Mussina from the Orioles after playing out his contract in 2000. Instead, the Blue Jays locked up Roy Halladay, the Indians locked up CC Sabathia, the Brewers locked up Ben Sheets, the Astros locked up Roy Oswalt and the Twins locked up Johan Santana—all small-revenue teams who suddenly had the cash to keep their ace pitchers off the trade and free agent markets. The kicker for the Yankees was that under the revenue-sharing system they were financing some of the newfound solvency of those teams.

For the next decade after bringing Andy Pettitte to the big leagues in 1995, the Yankees did not use even one homegrown pitcher of any consequence with the exception of Ramiro Mendoza, and though he had value as a middle reliever, Mendoza was neither a starter nor a closer, the premium slots for a pitcher. So each year the Yankees had to fill spots in their staff by trading for or buying somebody else's problems.

Cashman recognized the downward spiral such desperation created, so in 2006 he began to prioritize the signing and development of young pitchers. His strategy began with flexing the Yankees' financial muscle in the amateur market, even if it meant spitting in the face of the commissioner's unofficial "slotting" system, in which teams could conspire to hold down signing bonuses by keeping to established ceilings based on the draft position of the player. The Yankees didn't play by those rules because, well, because money wasn't a problem for them. This meant the Yankees would even buy up the amateur medical risks, throwing big money at pitchers with high ceilings that scared off most clubs because of the possibility they were break-downs waiting to happen. Most clubs could not afford to take the financial risk of handing out a huge signing bonus for a first-round talent with arm trouble. The Yankees could do so because if the player never made it to the big leagues they were out only some pocket change. It would change nothing about how they did business.

If the pitcher defied the medical reports, they had themselves a potential homegrown ace. That's exactly how the Yankees wound up with Alan Horne, who had reconstructive elbow surgery in college after Cleveland picked him in the first round out of high school; Andrew Brackman, who went straight from the draft to the operating room to have Tommy John surgery; and the burly kid who brought the Yankees' brass to New Britain on July 20, 2007, Joba Chamberlain, whose shaky medical reports regarding his arm, knee and weight (he weighed as much as 290 pounds at the University of Nebraska) scared off most teams before the Yankees took him with the 41st overall pick of the 2006 draft.

Cashman and the Yankees finally got religion when it came to young pitching, and their faith mostly was tied up in three righthanders: Phil Hughes, Ian Kennedy and Chamberlain. It was Cashman's hope that these were the bedrocks of the next Yankee dynasty or, in the very least, three reasons to keep him from blowing another $255 million.

"The message that I've got for everybody," Cashman told the **Hartford Courant** while in New Britain, "is that if you pitch to the point where it forces us to look at guys that are not Roger Clemens, I want that."

The Yankees rotation at that moment consisted of three guys past their prime—Pettitte, 35, Mussina, 38, and Clemens, 44—and two international free agents—Wang, 27, and Igawa, 27. Chamberlain pitched poorly with the Yankees' brass looking at him in New Britain. He gave up seven runs on nine hits in less than five innings. Still, the Yankees liked what they saw: a fastball that was clocked in the upper-90-mph range and a violent slider. His changeup and curveball were major-league quality as well. Cashman called Torre from New Britain and said, "You'll love him. He's better than Hughes."

"That," Torre said, "got my attention."

The Yankees immediately put Chamberlain on the fast track to the Bronx. Four days after the Yankees executives saw him in New Britain, Chamberlain was in Triple-A, and just seven days after that, Chamberlain was in the big leagues. The only catch was that Chamberlain was not permitted to start. Indeed, Cashman and Contreras sent Chamberlain to Torre with instructions on how he could be used, a mandate that came to be known as the "Joba Rules."

The Yankees would no longer allow Chamberlain to start because they were concerned about piling up too many innings after throwing 88⅓ innings in the minors, or only one less than he had thrown in 2006 at Nebraska. The rules were that Chamberlain would have to pitch out of the bullpen, he was not to be used to close games, he was not to be used on consecutive days and he would get one day of rest for every inning he pitched in an outing. The media perceived the Joba Rules as a slap at Torre. The conventional wisdom was that the Yankees didn't trust Torre to handle Chamberlain with care, so they had to give him instructions about how to use him. Torre, however, had no problem with the rules.

"No, I really didn't," he said. "Unless I'm very naïve. I mean, I know it was written about and I was asked about it, but unless I was just naïve to it, I never took it as anything more than protecting the kid. And Nardi's the one I called. I never talked to Cashman about it. I called Nardi on a regular basis.

"And the other fact is I didn't think there was anything wrong with the rules or talking about the rules. It's like a guy with an injury. Why look to hide something?"

Chamberlain was an immediate sensation. He was a character straight out of a cornball 1950s Hollywood casting job: a country kid in the big city with a fastball that could reach 100 miles an hour and a tendency to celebrate strikeouts with a howl and a fist pump. Yankees fans loved his act. So did Torre. With Chamberlain in front of Rivera, the Yankees had their best late-inning lockdown combination since the tag team of Rivera and Wetteland in 1996. Chamberlain would pitch in 19 games for the Yankees and they would win 17 of them. He allowed only one earned run. With runners in scoring position, he was perfect: nobody got a hit off him. He struck out 34 of the 91 hitters he faced. He was as close to unhittable as anybody had seen in a long time—a 21-year-old kid who was in college the previous year, mind you, a kid who had never seen big league hitters before.

———

Chamberlain's arrival had the effect of making Kyle Farnsworth rather useless in any meaningful situation, which bothered Yankees fans not at all. Cashman was ecstatic to have signed Farnsworth as a free agent after the 2005 season to a three-year, $17 million deal. Farnsworth essentially replaced Tom Gordon, who signed as a free agent with Philadelphia. Farnsworth threw hard and owned a nasty, if misbehaving slider, but the knock on Farnsworth was that he wilted in the big spots. Indeed, only two months before the Yankees gave him $17 million, the Braves were six outs away from sending their Division Series against Houston to a fifth and deciding game when Atlanta manager Bobby Cox gave the ball to Farnsworth. Atlanta was leading, 6-1. Farnsworth gave up a grand slam in the eighth and a solo home run in the ninth to cough up the lead. Houston won in the 18th inning, sending the Braves home.

In the Yankees' 2006 spring training camp, Eppler could not contain his enthusiasm over the Farnsworth addition.

"Farnsworth is really going to help us," Eppler told Borzello, the bullpen catcher. "He's got one of the best sliders in the game."

"Yeah, sure. Great," an unimpressed Borzello said. "His slider **is** great, except maybe only one out of every seven is great."

Farnsworth did flash nasty stuff. Opposing hitters batted .242 against him in his two years pitching for Torre—as long as there were no runners in scoring position. With runners in scoring position, Farnsworth wasn't as tough to hit. They batted .272 against him in those spots.

The other curious glitch in the Yankees' $17 million reliever was that Farnsworth was built like an NFL tight end and somehow he was one of their more brittle pitchers, mostly due to a balky back that might go out on him while warming in the bullpen. It was Torre's understanding that the Yankees did not want him to use Farnsworth two days in a row. In two years under Torre, Farnsworth made only 20 of his 136 appearances without rest, and he was generally poor in those situations, posting a 5.60 ERA in those rare times when Torre did use him on back-to-back days.

"I was told we shouldn't use him two days in a row," Torre said, "Billy Eppler and Cash, I mean . . . that was their baby when they brought him on."

The arrangement created a problem for Torre. By trying to avoid using him on back-to-back days, Torre could not give Farnsworth tuneup work in games that appeared to be already decided. If Torre did throw him into such games, he would not have Farnsworth available the next day in a game where he might be needed to set up Rivera. It was a catch-22. The problem, however, was that Farnsworth didn't know he came with his own set of instructions. He was also a highly emotional sort. (On May 19 at Shea Stadium, for instance, Torre found Farnsworth on the floor in the corner of the tiny, run-down trainers' room in the visiting clubhouse, crying. Farnsworth was hurt because his teammates disapproved of comments he made to the media that Clemens was getting special treatment from the Yankees.)

On July 29 in Baltimore, Torre brought Farnsworth in to pitch the eighth inning with a 10-4 lead. He promptly gave up two runs, inflating his ERA to 4.57. Farnsworth had pitched only once in the previous seven days, and he was angry about his lack of work. He popped off to the press after the game, saying, "I didn't come here to sit the bench."

"Farnsworth," Torre said, "was a good kid. Just a

little emotional, that's all. I don't think he was trying to show me up. He was just upset, that's all."

Torre arranged for a meeting with Farnsworth
and invited Cashman, too. Farnsworth said he
wanted to be traded.

"Listen," Torre said. "It's tough for me to bring
you in in a game we're way ahead or way behind just
to get you an inning, knowing I can't use you the
next day. Because I don't know if I'll need you the
next day in a close game."

"What are you guys talking about?" Farnsworth
said. He had no idea about the ban on him pitching
back-to-back days. "I want to pitch."

"Fine," Torre said. "I'll make sure you don't go
more than three days in a row without pitching,
whatever the score, and then we'll take our chances."

Said Torre, "He seemed perfectly satisfied with
that. And I think he was satisfied with my reason-
ing, as opposed to thinking I had something against
him, I guess. That was the end of the whole scene.
Then once Joba came on the scene, well, he basically took a backseat. That was that."

Farnsworth finished the season with a 4.80 ERA
while allowing 89 baserunners in 60 innings. The
next spring he blamed Torre for his lousy season.

"It's tough when you do lose the confidence
from your manager to maybe prepare yourself, day
in and day out when you have no clue about anything," Farnsworth told reporters. "It happened a
few times last year."

With Chamberlain in front of Rivera rather than Farnsworth, the Yankees were almost impossible to beat when they held a late lead. The Yankees played 50 games after Chamberlain joined the team. The team that began the year 21-29 in its first 50 games went 32-18 in its final 50. The only hitch to the run was the pitching of Mussina, who was so bad, giving up 19 runs in 9⅔ innings over three starts, that on August 29 Torre decided to pull him from the rotation in favor of Ian Kennedy. Mussina was sitting in the tiny office of clubhouse manager Rob Cucuzza that day when Torre walked in.

"I'm going to have Kennedy start in your spot," Torre told Mussina after he heard the Yankee organization had already informed Kennedy of the change. "This doesn't mean you're out of the rotation."

"Well, it sure sounds like that's what it is to me," Mussina replied.

Said Mussina, "And he was gone in like 45 seconds."

Mussina was hurt. Being taken out of the rotation was bad enough—the only game he ever pitched in relief was that 2003 ALCS Game 7 gem—but being dropped in 45 seconds chapped him. The next day he marched into Torre's office.

"You would never have done that to Mo, or Derek, or anybody else," Mussina said. "And I've been here for seven years. I deserve more than that."

"You're right," Torre said.

Said Mussina, "I should have been in his office and there should have been more discussion. Ultimately, when you let all the negative stuff settle out, I agreed with him. I probably needed a break. I was fried and pitching terribly. And I got back in there like 10 days later or whatever and I pitched better. The guy's made a lot of right decisions.

"It ended up being the right thing to do. It got me away from it for a while, and then when I came back I was better, and my head was better, which is most of the battle.

"When you have a manager that completely trusts you to do your job, you can't ask for any more than that as a player. Even when he took me out of the rotation, and even though it wasn't done the way I think it should have been done, a couple days later I'm like, 'You know what? I probably should have come out of the rotation even though I didn't like it.' And I didn't like the way he did it, but it's okay."

———

Mussina became a reliable pitcher when he returned to the rotation in September. On September 25, the Yankees arrived in Tampa with a chance to clinch the wild card. They held a 5½-game lead over Detroit with six games to play. The Yankees took a 5-0 lead into the sixth inning that night, but Edwar Ramirez and Brian Bruney coughed up six runs in that inning alone. The Yankees eventually lost, 7-6, on a 10th inning home run by Dioner Navarro off Jeff Karstens.

The next day Torre was summoned to a meeting in the Legends Field conference room with Steinbrenner—or more accurately, the family members who had assumed the daily operations of the franchise from The Boss. There was nothing unusual about the need for a meeting. Whenever the Yankees played Tampa Bay the manager usually was obligated to make an appearance at the team headquarters in Tampa. Torre wasn't sure if his job status would be discussed, though, true to his spring training vow, he preferred not to talk about it, anyway. Torre expected Steinbrenner, his sons, Hank and Hal, and son-in-law Felix Lopez to be at the meeting. When Torre walked into the room he saw that all of them were there except Hank. Steinbrenner didn't bother to say hello, as is his usual custom. He believes in the dramatic element of **in medias res** when it comes to his telephone calls and meetings.

"What happened last night?" was how Steinbrenner "greeted" Torre.

"Don't worry, Boss," Torre said. "We'll get 'em tonight."

It was classic Torre: smooth, familiar and, above all, disarming and reassuring to the man he called by his nickname or his first name, not by the deferential "Mr. Steinbrenner."

This was not classic Steinbrenner, however. He

didn't say much at all. He sat there, slightly slouched, and kept his dark glasses on in the indoor room. At one point he got up to make himself a sandwich. He contributed almost nothing to the meeting. It was obvious to Torre that Steinbrenner's reign as everyone knew it was over, which meant he would no longer be able to deal directly with Steinbrenner when it came time to talk about his future with the team.

"It was sad," Torre said. "As much as you might have been confrontational with him at times or hated what he did, you hate to see that. It was sad. Because now you knew it: the other guys were running the team. A few years before he would say, 'I'm going to back out of this and let other people take over. Let the young elephants into the tent.' But that was never going to be the case.

"It's not quite the same when Don Corleone was shot and was recovering and was sitting in the garden. At least he was talking to his son in a very lucid way, explaining what was going to happen. I don't think George had those capabilities. And when you talked to anybody in the organization, Steve Swindal being one, when he was in good graces, you'd ask, 'What's wrong with him?' And they'd say, 'Nothing. We don't know.' I believed him when he told me that."

As Steinbrenner occupied himself with his sandwich, the rest of them talked about how happy everyone was with the young pitching. In addition to Chamberlain, Phil Hughes and Ian Kennedy were throwing well for the Yankees.

"Kennedy . . . ," mused Lopez. "That's a great name for marketing. Better than **Rodriguez.**"

The Yankees, they believed, looked like a dangerous postseason team again. The lineup was formidable—the Yankees wound up scoring more runs than any Yankee team in 70 years—the bullpen was dominating with Chamberlain and Rivera at the back end, and the rotation appeared decent enough with Chien-Ming Wang, Andy Pettitte, a hobbled but game Roger Clemens (he was nursing yet another injury to his legs) and Mussina, who seemed be back on track after a mostly miserable summer.

"Nobody wants to play the Yankees in the playoffs," Hal crowed.

"I like to think we intimidate people," Torre said, "but it depends on which team you're talking about."

It was a cheery enough lunch meeting. The Yankees were headed to the playoffs for the 12th consecutive season under Torre. The food was good. And nobody brought up the question of whether Torre, even after bringing the team back from 21-29 to easily win a postseason spot, would continue to manage the club.

"My situation never came up," Torre said. "I didn't ask or anything. Basically I felt like Cash was on my side and I'd leave it to him to ultimately present it."

That night, true to the promise Torre gave Steinbrenner, the Yankees beat Tampa Bay, 12-4, to clinch a postseason berth. Steinbrenner watched the game from a luxury box at Tropicana Field. The final out had the familiar patina of the good old days: Steinbrenner watching, Rivera pitching, Posada catching, Jeter, who had homered in the game, at shortstop and Torre in the dugout. The Yankees, beset by injuries and a malaise that put them in that 21-29 hole, unloosed a wild celebration in the Tropicana Field visiting clubhouse. This was the 29th time that Torre's Yankees earned the privilege of spraying champagne over themselves amid the triumph of clinching a playoff spot or winning a postseason series. But this one was different from all the others. This road to October, Jeter told reporters, "has definitely been the hardest one." Torre obviously felt the same way. He called the team together for a toast in the middle of the clubhouse, and as he began he could not help but think about all the team had been through that season and all that he had been through. When he began to speak he could hardly get the words out.

"I'm proud of each and every one of you guys," Torre said.

He was tearing up. He continued as best he could.

632 JOE TORRE AND TOM VERDUCCI

"This one," he said, his voice cracking, "means a lot to me . . ."

He was choking up. He wanted to continue, to tell his players how important this postseason berth meant to him, but he could not speak. All he could do was bow his head and try to gather himself. No words would come. There was a brief, awkward silence in the room as the ballplayers waited to see if Torre could pull himself together. And then an old friend stepped in to save him from the emotions and the awkwardness. Jeter, who had taken part in all 29 of these parties, reached over and pulled the hat off Torre's head and dumped a bottle of champagne on his manager. The room erupted in a big cheer, and the celebration started anew in full force.

Twenty-nine times Torre helped bring the Yankees to this kind of celebration. Twenty-nine times, including at least once every year for 12 consecutive seasons. Twenty-nine times, and yet this one, at the end of a long, painful season, was unlike all the others.

There would never be another.

15.

Attack of the Midges

M ajor league managers hate the best-of-five-games format of the Division Series. The inferior team has a better chance to beat the superior team in a shorter series than what the best-of-seven League Championship Series and World Series offer; the smaller the sample, the more havoc that chance can create. Moreover, managers must decide between using three starting pitchers or four, especially if a loss in Game 1 creates the palpable urgency of having to win three out of the next four games. Torre's 2007 Yankees, the 94-win American League wild card entrant, drew the Cleveland Indians, the 96-win AL Central champions, in this best-of-five-game anxiety attack.

The Indians owned the home-field advantage, which meant they would host the first two games, a comforting arrangement for a young team that had not played a playoff game since 2001, had lost all six games it had played against the Yankees that season and had scored 157 fewer runs than New York, or almost a full run fewer per game.

"We have to focus on not playing the Yankees, but playing our best, the best baseball we can play," is how Indians general manager Mark Shapiro remembered his thinking going into that series. "Talent-wise, I think we stack up. But there's a reality to playing in Yankee Stadium. There's a reality to how it affected our team prior to that, and those names. Imposing names."

Most every postseason, Torre would give a motivational speech to his players on the eve of the opening game. This time, as he did with modifying his usual spring training speech at the start of the season, Torre would choose a different tack. His team had grinded so hard just to get to the playoffs—coming back from a losing record 95 games into the season—that Torre felt a different touch was needed than the usual football locker room machismo. Actually, it was a conversation with New England Patriots coach Bill Belichick that convinced Torre to keep the mood light. Belichick's Patriots were Torre's Yankees of the NFL, routinely playing to higher expectations than every other franchise. The Patriots were being heavily criticized at the time for what was being called Spygate, the team's illegal use of recording devices to tape the coaching signals of opponents. Belichick told Torre that in those difficult, tense times his instinct was that his team needed to laugh and stay loose, so he brought a comedian into the New England locker room. Torre liked the idea. He called his good friend and Yankees fan, Billy Crystal.

"Can you put a bit together for us that I can show the guys?" Torre asked him.

Crystal agreed, and he quizzed Torre for some information about the players that he could use in his monologue, which he taped, burned to a DVD and sent to Torre in Cleveland. On the workout day before Game 1, Torre gathered his team in the visiting clubhouse at Jacobs Field and popped in the DVD. Suddenly a pornographic scene began playing on the monitor. There was nervous laughter. What sort of mistake was this? Had somebody mixed up the DVDs? No. A close-up of Crystal suddenly replaced the pornography.

"Now that I've got your attention . . ." Crystal said.

He then launched into a 12-minute comedy segment in which, with the help of fellow comedian Robin Williams, he poked fun at Jorge Posada, Alex Rodriguez, Derek Jeter, Melky Cabrera and others. The players loved it. Crystal turned serious at the end of his bit. He implored the Yankees to make sure they played with an effort that would leave them no regrets. He talked about how lucky they were to have this opportunity and their health.

"And there is someone we should all pray for," Crystal said, "because he has not been blessed with the same great health. So before you go out there, when you hit your knees, say a prayer . . . for Carl Pavano!"

The room erupted in laughter.

"Cashman didn't think it was very funny," Torre said. "Cash would have liked a motivational video. I've been in the postseason so often that I can't see the point in bringing up the expectations. You don't need to remind guys. I think I got to the point, whether it was because of my own situation and being criticized, or whether I felt there was a lot of tension in the playoffs anyway based on the expectations, we should keep it light and airy."

———

Torre's most serious decision heading into the Division Series was how to deploy his starting pitchers. Chien-Ming Wang was the unquestioned leader of the staff, having won 19 games for a second straight season, and an obvious choice to start Game 1. He was not your typical ace, though. Wang was a groundball specialist who did not strike out many batters and, like a parent with a two-year-old at Sunday service, was at the mercy of the unpredictable behavior of his power sinker. Andy Pettitte, Torre's traditional Game 2 security blanket, also was a lock, though he did pitch poorly in September. Roger Clemens would get a start, if only because of his reputation and because of all the money the Yankees were paying him. But Clemens wasn't the warrior the Yankees had known from his first round with the team. He was a rusted battleship. Clemens was 45 years old and had not pitched since September 16 because of a hamstring injury.

Torre's toughest decision was what to do about Game 4. He thought about giving the start to Mike Mussina, who had salvaged something from his awful season by posting a 3.49 ERA in September, and who had beaten the Indians in August in a strong start in which he pitched into the eighth inning. If Torre started Mussina, then he could use Pettitte again on normal rest in Game 5. Under that scenario, Torre would have given the ball in four out of five games to veteran pitchers 35 and older.

"I was thinking about Mussina in Game 4," Torre said. "I thought maybe somebody with breaking stuff, somebody who could change speeds, would be efficient against the Indians. But he really hadn't pitched much and you had to wonder about how sharp he was going to be."

Torre decided to ask Cashman for his preference, "though I already had an idea of where he was going," Torre said. "He said he liked Wang on short rest in Game 4 instead of Mussina. He said if you go with Mussina, then you've got Pettitte for Game 5 and Wang doesn't go a second time."

Wang was the Yankees' best starting pitcher. He also was 10-4 with a 2.75 ERA at Yankee Stadium, where Game 4 would be played. Cashman had no problem making sure Wang pitched two of the first four games, even if the second one would carry the risk of pitching him on only three days of rest instead of the normal four. Torre agreed with him. Wang had pitched on three days of rest only once in his 80 major league starts, and that had gone badly, losing 7-2 to Boston without getting out of the fifth inning back in 2005.

As it turned out, Wang was awful even fully rested for Game 1. In what was one of the worst pitching performances in postseason history, Wang, who couldn't get his power sinker to stay down on its best behavior, was shellacked for a postseason record-tying eight earned runs in less than five innings of what was a 12-3 Cleveland rout. Only six pitchers previously had allowed eight earned runs in a postseason start, and none of them had allowed as many as the 14 base runners that Wang did. It was a classic example of the dark side of living with Wang as your ace. If his sinker wasn't acting properly, he had nowhere else to go to get people out with any consistency. He had nothing to make hitters swing and miss.

With just one defeat, the Yankees had come to fully understand the danger of a five-game series. One defeat essentially threw them in a must-win situation in the other team's ballpark. Were they to lose Game 2, they would have to win three consecutive games to win the series. What they needed was for Pettitte to deliver a lead to their lockdown late-game specialists, Chamberlain and Rivera. Pettitte did exactly that, though barely so in a taut pitching duel with Fausto Carmona, Cleveland's 23-year-old 19-game winner. Pettitte handed a 1-0 lead in the seventh inning to Chamberlain, who stranded the two runners Pettitte had left for him. The Yankees felt good about bringing the series back to New York tied, and why not? They had never lost a game that season when they entrusted a lead to Chamberlain. He went back out for the eighth, with Rivera behind him to pick up the final three outs. Everything was coming together straight off the Yankees' blueprint for winning. Torre was six routine outs away from the first of the seven wins he would need to win the pennant and return the Yankees to the World Series, which most observers considered the minimum requirement for him to ensure he would be back as manager in 2008.

And then suddenly all hell broke loose, or at least the two-winged version of it. It took at that exact moment a convergence of bizarre forces that had nothing to do with baseball—rather, they were ecological, meteorological and entomological—to put the Torre Era on the brink of its extinction.

———

The perfect swarm.

Midges, thousands upon thousands of the buggers, suddenly swarmed around the pitching mound, many of them flying into Chamberlain's eyes, nose, ears, face and neck, with many of those sticking to the wet skin of the heavily perspiring pitcher. He couldn't concentrate. He had trouble even seeing home plate through the cloud of bugs. A trainer came running out with an aerosol can of bug spray and showered him with the insecticide, but that didn't help at all. The midge infestation actually seemed worse. What the hell was going on?

The answer went all the way back to the 1950s and 1960s. Lake Erie was so polluted in those days that midges, or mayflies as some people called them, disappeared. These midges are harmless creatures except for the annoyance they engender. They don't bite or carry disease. They begin in a larval state on the bottom of lakes, streams and standing water. With enough clean, oxygen-rich sediment, they emerge from the water as adults that fly off to swarm and, while doing so, to mate. Lake Erie, however, used to be too polluted for the midges to prosper. But after a major cleanup effort, the midges began returning to the Cleveland area in the mid-1990s. People near the western basin of Lake Erie came to regard them as a regular warm-weather nuisance. The midges typically would swarm three times a year, only for a day or two each time, and usually toward artificial light sources in the 45 minutes after dusk during days in May or June when warm weather set off their activity. Theirs was a 24-

to 72-hour lifespan. In that short time adult midges would leave the water, swarm, breed and die.

In 2007, the first week of October happened to be unusually warm in Cleveland. It felt like spring—apparently to the midges, as well. The unusual heat (it was 81 degrees when Game 2 began at five o'clock) tricked the midges into a fourth active cycle. They left the water—likely Lake Erie or the Cuyahoga River, another waterway that had been cleaned up—saw the bright lights of Jacobs Field and headed straight to the ballpark. Only because of the odd starting time, made to accommodate the telecast of the Angels–Red Sox Division Series game in prime time to follow, did the Indians and Yankees happen to be playing the eighth inning smack in the middle of peak swarming time for midges: the 45-minute window after dusk.

So after an uninterrupted 12-year run, the Torre Era was about to come undone for good by an incredible series of events: a major cleanup of Rust Belt waterways, a freakish autumnal heat wave and an odd starting time to a playoff game.

Oh, and one more thing: the mistake of using bug spray to try to ward off the bugs.

A Cleveland insect specialist, an Indians fan, happened to be watching the game on television when he saw Yankees trainer Gene Monahan spraying down Chamberlain. The bug expert quickly reached for the phone and called the Indians' front office.

"For God's sake," he said, "tell your guys down on the field, whatever they do, **don't** use bug spray. It's useless against these bugs. It actually makes it worse because they will be attracted to the moisture on the skin."

Chamberlain, glistening from the spray and his heavy sweat, was a midge magnet. The television pictures resembled a teen horror flick. Watching in Boston, Red Sox officials were shocked that play continued. "I can't believe they're playing in that," one of them remarked.

This wasn't just some meaningless August game. This was a playoff game, a game the Yankees and their manager all but had to win. A 1-0 game in the eighth inning. And their pitcher was trying to pitch while slathered in a sticky stew of sweat, insecticide and bugs while a swarm of more midges probed every uncovered orifice of his body. It was quickly evident how badly Chamberlain was compromised. He walked the leadoff batter, Grady Sizemore, on four pitches. Chamberlain had faced 91 batters during the season and only twice even went so far as a 3-and-0 count.

It grew worse. His next pitch sailed past Posada for a wild pitch, sending Sizemore to second. The Indians now had the tying run in scoring position and they had yet to even take a swing. The Yankees, however, were swinging wildly. Derek Jeter and Alex Rodriguez, New York's $43 million left side of the infield, were constantly waving their gloves and throwing hands at the little midges. Fighting for their playoff lives, the most expensive team in baseball had devolved into a vaudeville act.

Chamberlain looked into the Yankees dugout at Torre and said, "I can't see!"

Torre started toward the mound but stopped. He was worried about being charged with a trip to the mound, though he could have appealed to the umpires to consider it an unofficial visit, as is the case when possible injuries are involved, because of the extraordinary circumstances.

"Geno!" Torre said.

He called for Monahan, the trainer, to check on Chamberlain.

Said Torre, "For some reason I stopped because I was thinking about a trip, and I didn't want to make a trip, even though this was something extraordinary. I just didn't realize how extraordinary it was. I sent the trainer out."

Monahan raced out to the mound—armed with more bug spray.

Torre didn't know how bad the situation was because the midges inexplicably kept their swarming activities to the middle of the diamond. There was almost no problem in the Yankees dugout, where Torre sat, or down the right-field line, where umpire Bruce Froemming, the crew chief working the final postseason of his career, enjoyed a comfortable, bug-free view. So Torre made no appeal to the umpires to stop the game the way they would when rain is heavy enough to compromise playing conditions. It was a moment he would later identify as his one regret in 12 years as the Yankees manager.

"I see Jeter out there at shortstop, just waving," Torre said, "but it was never one of these things like Joba was going through. So my feeling is if I had gone out there, and could've called the umpire out and said, 'You can't pitch in this' . . . well, I'm not sure if it would've gotten me anywhere, but I may have been convincing enough to at least call a time-out for a time, like a rain delay of some kind."

Torre was under the impression that another round of bug spray helped Chamberlain, though it did not.

"It looked like it was okay," Torre said. "It looked like something you could deal with. I'm not saying it disappeared, but it looked like something that was less than what it actually was. But I think Joba just got rattled, which is understandable."

Chamberlain managed to get his next pitch over the plate. Cleveland second baseman Asdrubal Cabrera bunted it, sending Sizemore to third on the sacrifice. Travis Hafner, the Indians' designated hitter, ripped Chamberlain's next pitch on a line, but first baseman Doug Mietkiewicz caught it. Somehow Chamberlain was one out away from escaping this sticky mess. He needed only to retire catcher Victor Martinez to turn over the lead and the final three outs to Rivera. Chamberlain, however, let loose yet another wild pitch, and Sizemore came barreling home to tie the game. Chamberlain had thrown 343 pitches in the major leagues and only one of them had been a wild pitch. Now, completely bugged, he had thrown two in a span of 10 pitches.

The Yankees had lost a lead with Chamberlain on the mound for the first time, and done so in a manner bizarre enough to make Stephen King envious: one walk, one bunt, two wild pitches and one million midges. During the entire rally neither the baseball nor the midges ever left the infield. Chamberlain hit Martinez with a pitch and walked Ryan Garko before he finally ended the nightmare by striking out Jhonny Peralta.

———

The Yankees still had hope. After all, Carmona, the Cleveland pitcher who had allowed only two hits over eight innings, would have to deal with the midges himself in the top of the ninth inning while facing the top of the prodigious Yankees lineup.

"I was standing there coaching third base," Bowa said, "and the next thing I knew it was the return of these bugs. I said, 'What the fuck are these?' And the third baseman said, 'Oh, they come out every now and then.' I mean, I could hardly see. And they're all over your skin. They weren't biting or anything. It was just a nuisance. Hindsight being 20/20, we should have said, 'Everyone get off the field.' It would have been like a downpour, where you say, 'We can't play in these conditions.'"

Something very strange happened, though. Carmona pulled his cap down a little lower and threw the baseball as if the midges around him and on his face and neck did not exist. He gave the appearance of a man in a crisp suit walking down the street in a rainstorm, oblivious to the extreme conditions. Behind him, the Cleveland infielders gave none of the burlesque histrionics seen from Jeter and Rodriguez. The swarm had not minimized, but the Indians gave the appearance otherwise.

"I thought there were clearly differences to how the two teams were reacting to it," general manager Mark Shapiro said. "But our year had been one to give our team multiple valid excuses. Snowouts, home games on the road, home games in Milwaukee, no off days in forever . . . our guys just never gave in to it, which was an affirmation to what tough players they are. You talk about tough players and a team approach, that's what we hope to build here as a culture. It's less about feel good things, less about objective things, and it is the manager that can help implement that culture in a clubhouse."

Carmona would have to face the best Yankees hitters in the ninth inning of a tie game in the playoffs with insects surrounding him and sticking to him. What happened next was a triumph of the Cleveland Indians organizational intellect. As much as any other, this one inning would confirm exactly how a middle-market team erased the competitive advantage the Yankees enjoyed in their championship seasons over the rest of baseball, and the Indians had done so with a payroll that amounted to less than one-third of what the Yankees were spending on players.

———

The postmodern general manager prototype, Shapiro, in his wrinkle-free crisp khakis and sports shirt, sits at his sleek desk in front of his computer, navigating through his team's propriety and copyrighted software program, DiamondView, the program so valuable that the Arizona Diamondbacks once only half jokingly were asked to consider trading it for Carlos Quentin, their top power-hitting prospect. Not even a server to be named later could have convinced Cleveland's general manager to give up the computational brains of the organization. Shapiro looks as if he might well be running a private hedge fund or operating a technology startup from his office above Progressive Field in Cleveland.

Fueled by bottled water and energy bars, Shapiro spends every day searching for any ground, everywhere from the sandlots of the Dominican Republic to the kudzu-like blogosphere, for any incremental edge that will make the Indians better and more efficient than they were and, in turn, bring them closer to cutting into the huge advantage the Yankees enjoyed because of their revenues.

Shapiro, Princeton-educated, the son of a powerful sports agent, a history major who played collegiate football but not a day of professional baseball, was exactly the kind of hands-on, business-savvy chief executive that has become necessary for teams to cut into the Yankees' advantage. The general manager genus that existed when the Yankees were winning championships was marked by men who would make baseball decisions by the seat of their pants—or perhaps a barstool—and knew little about the business side of the organization. These were baseball men, and proud of it, whose responsibility rested almost entirely with player acquisition. They sought or kept almost no business intellect.

"At some point ownership decided with all the dollars at stake they wanted to talk with someone—not all ownership—that they had a comfort level with from a business standpoint," said Shapiro. "That doesn't diminish the human side of the game. It doesn't diminish the necessity for baseball acumen or scouting to play a role in decision making. But at the top a lot of ownerships decided they wanted someone that had a combination of skill sets, instead of just being one of evaluation, of just picking 25 players. That's the delineation here. The job shifted, from picking 25 guys to building and running an organization. A CEO of a baseball organization."

In 2002, Shapiro's second year as general manager, the Indians spent $24 million on player development and scouting, more than all but two teams in baseball and a 50 percent increase in their R&D from three years earlier. They obtained 22 prospects from outside the organization that year alone, including Sizemore, Phillips, Lee, Travis Hafner, Coco Crisp and Ben Broussard, all of them soon to be bona fide big leaguers. The Indians knew that the currency of information was gaining in value around baseball. If ballclubs could not match the Yankees' resources, which allowed New York a wide margin of error, those teams could use intellect—specifically, the gathering and analysis of information—to operate more efficiently.

Shapiro made some mistakes early in his tenure, but learned from those while building an organization that was at the cutting edge of the information age that was just dawning in baseball. For Shapiro, it wasn't just about getting information; it was also about using it wisely and efficiently.

"Somewhere along the line we realized you have so much information that we were spending approximately 50 percent of our time assembling it and 50 percent of our time analyzing it," Shapiro said. "That's when we created DiamondView, and DiamondView really evolved where now we spend 10 percent of the time assembling the information and 90 percent of the time evaluating it."

The Indians created DiamondView in the spring of 2000, though it began as a rather simple venture. Shapiro wanted an easy way to track and rank the major league and minor league players in every organization as a way to identify players the Indians might pursue in trades. DiamondView originally relied only on the reports from Cleveland scouts to grade the players. Over the years, however, DiamondView has grown into a complex, vast program to compile, store and analyze all kinds of information. For example, every morning at 6:45 DiamondView electronically collects game information, injury reports and transactions on the nearly 6,000 players in professional baseball and updates the profiles on those players.

"For any player . . . ," Shapiro explained. "So you pull up, say, Jared Weaver of the Angels. It's got your basic biographical facts, the history of all the reports on him, going all the way back to his time as an amateur in college. You can actually pull up one of those reports and look at it . . . here's our scouting director's report on him. He was obviously a little bit light. Our area scout was more accurate. So that's the actual report on him. Again, it's a question of what's available to us here . . . There are journal entries, which could be anything from **Baseball America** articles to a spring training look to blog reports, to the 16PF test—a psychological test in college—and we actually have our own psychological test in there also . . . Now these are newspaper articles that might contain something interesting toward building a biographical background on the guy . . . physical attributes . . . when he hit different top prospect lists. . . . Now this happens to be a guy who we haven't had any trade discussions on, but I'll show you a guy that we have."

Every conversation with player agents about players is also logged into DiamondView. "When we talk about a guy, we have a history of every agent's conversation," Shapiro said, "like when a guy's a free agent. Every conversation. So you have a history and start to learn who's lying and who's not lying. You can say, 'Okay, we know this agency. They lie. They told us this was out there.' We have it. We recorded the conversation afterward, just in notes. And there's a clear pattern here. It's good information.

"So it's not a question of having the information. Every organization has it. It's a question of having it accessible quickly. I think there are at least 15 teams that have a lot of objective analysis, their own proprietary smart guys, mathematicians, smart guys turning out stats . . . How much they factor in decisions and how much they weigh it, how they use it, I'm not sure. But how accessible is it? How many teams have everything together: stats, scouting reports, video, contractual information, the history, college stuff . . . I don't think very many have that all together in one place."

The Indians, of course, also have their own proprietary information, such as the psychological tests, which they give to every player in their system. They also try to give it to amateur players that they scout, though resistance to the test from agents and colleges often forces the club to approach the players about it in summer leagues, such as the Cape Cod League.

"Now you start to get into what kind of things we do that are creative," Shapiro said. "Stats, objective analysis . . . There's a lot of unique, proprietary information. Very unique. It's all mixed in here."

The Oakland Athletics found an inefficiency to exploit almost a decade ago with an emphasis on on-base percentage while the rest of baseball remained focused on batting average. The Indians exploited an inefficiency by using DiamondView to quickly collect and analyze the flood of information pouring into the game. Like marine recovery teams searching for buried treasure in the vastness of the oceans, smart ballclubs constantly are looking for the next inefficiency to exploit.

———

With Carmona on the mound in Game 2 of the 2007 ALDS was every incremental improvement by Cleveland—advanced medical and prehabilitation systems, proprietary software, statistical analysis, biomechanics, sports psychology, a holistic approach to player development, a redefining of the general manager as a CEO, and more money to invest in those developments because of revenue sharing and central fund distributions from revenue streams that didn't exist when the Yankees were winning championships.

All of that happened while the Yankees, in a relative sense, slept. The Yankees' response to the growth of revenue and intellect around the game had been to keep patching the roster with expensive veterans, regardless of what they may bring to the clubhouse culture. A barren farm system had given them little room to consider much else.

The Indians signed Fausto Carmona as a free agent out of Santo Domingo, Dominican Republic, on December 28, 2000, three weeks after he celebrated his seventeenth birthday. He was a tall, skinny kid—six-foot-three and only 160 pounds—with an 83-mph fastball. The Indians gave him a signing bonus of $10,000.

"It wasn't brilliant scouting," Shapiro admitted.

Carmona was nothing special. Every year the Indians, like most teams, would sign about 15 of these raw, mostly underweight kids from Latin America, the same way somebody might buy 15 lottery tickets. The investment was a pittance to major league teams—$150,000 for 15 players—but the potential payoff was enormous if even one of those fliers made it to the big leagues.

If anyone wondered why professional baseball was acquiring a more Latin American presence, the decisions by the Indians on amateur players in 2000 provided one clue. Teams like the Indians knew Latin America offered a much bigger bang for the player development buck than the stateside high school and college kids who went through the First-Year Player Draft. The Indians spent a combined $2.25 million just on their first two picks of the draft, Corey Smith, a high school shortstop from

New Jersey taken 26th overall, and Derek Thompson, a lefthanded high school pitcher from Florida selected 37th overall. Neither of them ever played a day in the big leagues for Cleveland. For a fraction of the money they burned on those two top picks— less than 7 percent—the Indians could sign **15 players** out of Latin America, including a future 19-game winner who would finish fourth in the American League Cy Young Award voting.

"You don't sign anyone for $10,000 anymore," Shapiro said. "Now it's 50. The new $10,000 is $50,000."

The Indians kept Carmona in his home country for his first professional season, assigning him to the Dominican Summer League. The next year he reported to Cleveland's minor league camp in Winter Haven, Florida, where the education of a pitcher truly began. The Indians provided English classes for Carmona and other young Latin players. (They have since added the equivalent of secondary school education programs for such players. The players attend these schools in the Dominican in the off-season to earn the equivalent of a General Education Degree.) They provided nutritional and dental assistance. (Carmona had significant dental issues that compromised his eating habits, not an uncommon trait from a part of the world where good, affordable dental care is not readily available.) A nutritionist provided educational seminars for the Latin American players and even escorted them on field trips to local grocery stores to teach them how to shop and what to buy.

The Indians assigned Carmona to Burlington, where he pitched well and showed exceptional control for a teenager. The next year they sent him to Lake County in Class A ball. "That's when he jumped up," Shapiro said. Carmona went 17-4 with a 2.06 ERA. This was 2003, when **Moneyball** began to change the vocabulary of scouting and player development, so at first blush Carmona's numbers might have been met with some skepticism because he was not a big strikeout pitcher, a preferred trait among the statistical analysts. But Shapiro saw the value in his entire statistical profile rather than one column.

"You look at the strikeouts to innings pitched," Shapiro said, referring to Carmon's pedestrian 5.04 strikeouts per nine innings in 2003. "But he had few walks and was an extreme groundball pitcher. Pure objective analysis? Some people would devalue him to some extent because his strikeouts were not that great. But the walks were still low and the groundball to flyball rate was so high."

Carmona continued to improve and grow. He impressed his coaches with his work ethic. Even after clocking in his usual six innings or so of work, Carmona, rather than retreating to the training room for the usual ice therapy for a pitcher's arm, would run or bike for another 15 minutes. The Indians' attention to prehabilitation also helped his development. Indians trainers found that Carmona had a slight sway in his back, which would likely compromise his back and shoulder health over time, so they assigned him specific exercises to improve his core strength and posture. By 2006 Cleveland decided that Carmona, now 22 and about 220 pounds, and throwing his fastball 95 miles per hour, was ready for the big leagues.

Carmona initially had disastrous results. Pitching mostly out of the bullpen, Carmona went 1-10, becoming only the eighth pitcher since 1901 to post a winning percentage worse than .100 in his first big league season.

The worst of it for Carmona was when the Indians, desperate for late-inning help, decided to try him as a closer in the middle of the season. Carmona blew ninth-inning leads in three straight appearances, losing each one of them on a walkoff extra-base hit, twice in Boston to the Red Sox and once in Detroit to the Tigers. It was the sort of nightmare that can ruin a career, especially for a rookie. What was happening to him? The Indians again put their holistic approach to work to find an answer. They looked for an objective reason why Carmona was getting hit so hard and they found it: a study of the digital video files of his outings revealed that his sinker had straightened out. And why had it straightened out? The same reason why the Indians wanted to try him as a closer in the first place: they knew he was wired to be a fierce competitor. In this case, given the high leverage created by a ninth-inning lead, Carmona was victimized by trying too hard to succeed. The harder he tried, the more his release point dropped, and the more his release point dropped, the less sink he generated on his pitches.

"His strength worked against him," said Shapiro. "So we didn't try to scrap everything. We just said, 'Hey, you need to recognize when your mental condition works against you, when you're delivery breaks down, and what happens in your delivery.'"

After Carmona's bullpen meltdowns, the Indians sent the rookie righthander to Triple-A Buffalo to start games, not finish them. They called him back to Cleveland as a starter, then sent him to the Dominican Winter League to start some more, the better to develop the greater stamina needed by a starting pitcher after spending most of 2006 in the bullpen. In 2007, in the seventh year of Carmona's holistic development—mental, physical, hell, even dental—the Indians' little $10,000 investment had become a workhorse major league starter. Carmona threw 215 innings. He finished second in the league in wins (19) and second in ERA (3.06). Trying to hit his power sinker was like trying to hit a bowling ball. Nobody threw more double-play grounders (32). He had, by far, the best groundball-to-flyball ratio in the league (3.28). The Indians had themselves a young pitching star.

The Indians had won the lottery.

When the kid from Santo Domingo took the ball for the ninth inning of Game 2 against New York— the game tied, the midges swirling madly, the Yankees sending Johnny Damon, Derek Jeter and Bobby Abreu to the plate, with Alex Rodriguez waiting in case any of them reached base—Carmona's task would test every bit of that holistic development. No Cleveland pitcher this young ever had thrown nine innings in a postseason game. No starting pitcher had lasted nine innings against this formidable Yankees lineup all year. Carmona pulled his cap down a little lower, ignored the midges and went to work with the calm purposefulness of a diamond cutter.

Damon grounded out. Jeter struck out. Abreu reached first base on an infield single, to shortstop, then promptly swiped second base on the next pitch. The must-have game for the Yankees had come down to this: Rodriguez, the most expensive player in baseball, against Carmona, the erstwhile $10,000 kid, with the potential winning run at second base. Rodriguez, for all of his 156 runs batted in during the regular season, was in need of some serious holistic postseason help himself. He was 0-for-5 in the series (without getting the ball out of the infield) and had four hits in his previous 49 postseason at-bats with the Yankees, including 27 consecutive at-bats without a hit on the road.

Rodriguez did see nine pitches, but it ended badly for him. Carmona, with his 113th of the night, buzzed a ferocious sinker under the hands of a swinging Rodriguez for strike three.

When Carmona marched into the Cleveland dugout, Indians trainers were amazed at what they saw: his face and neck were covered with hundreds of midges. Not once had he taken a peeved swat at any of them. It was as if they were never there.

The midges left a short time later, their 45-minute window to wreak havoc on the Yankees and help close the curtain on the Torre Era having expired. Rivera did provide two shutout innings, but as soon as Torre had to go to anybody else in the bullpen, and in this case it was Luis Vizcaino, the game was over. Vizcaino walked the leadoff hitter of the 11th inning, the preamble to an eventual game-winning single by Travis Hafner.

———

The Yankees were one game away from elimination. The same could be said for Torre. Steinbrenner made sure the world knew it, too. On the morning of Game 3, Steinbrenner, out of nowhere, was quoted in the **Bergen Record** explaining that Torre was gone with one more loss.

"His job is on the line," Steinbrenner said. "I think we're paying him a lot of money. He's the highest-paid manager in baseball, so I don't think we'd take him back if we didn't win this series."

The bluster would have been normal procedure from Steinbrenner 10, even five, years earlier. But in 2007? It was shocking. Steinbrenner's handlers had kept him away from the press all year. He communicated with the media only through carefully worded statements from his public relations representative. When writer Franz Lidz, assigned by **Portfolio** magazine to write a piece on the Yankees' owner, breached the protective wall around Steinbrenner by visiting him that summer unannounced at his Tampa home, the description that emerged of The Boss was a pathetic one. Steinbrenner was portrayed as barely lucid, mumbling and repeating himself. Steinbrenner was well enough to make only three games in New York all year before this series. And now, with his team on the brink of elimination, he had suddenly found the old gusto?

Ian O'Connor, a columnist for the **Bergen Record,** had called Steinbrenner at his place in the Regency Hotel. It was a play taken from an old Yankees beat writer playbook: call Steinbrenner when the team is playing poorly and you just might get yourself a headline if The Boss decides to pop off. In the 1980s the beat writers used to call Steinbrenner "Mr. Tunes," because getting outrageous quotes from him was as easy as dropping a quarter into a jukebox and making your selection. Many of the quotes were as familiar as hit records, straight from the Steinbrenner catalog. But this was 2007, and Steinbrenner's declining health had rendered him little more than a figurehead who was barely seen or heard from. Indeed, not more than a week later the Yankees would announce that Steinbrenner officially was no longer actively running the team, but would serve as a kind of patriarch to the operations.

There was no answer on Steinbrenner's phone. O'Connor kept calling. No answer. Another call. Then suddenly, Steinbrenner picked up the phone. He answered questions. O'Connor decided that Steinbrenner sounded lucid enough for the quotes to have merit. He had his headline. It was big news. Torre found out about Steinbrenner's win-or-be-gone edict on his drive into Yankee Stadium for Game 3. He always did hate having his job security become a public issue around his players, but now it had become **the** issue. At his scheduled pregame news conference, Torre took 13 questions. Nine of them were about his job status and Steinbrenner's comments.

"You don't always get used to it," Torre said in response to one question about his reaction to Steinbrenner's comments, "but you understand if you want to work here, and certainly there's a great deal of upside to working here, that you understand that there are certain things you have to deal with. You know, that's pretty much where I am."

Cashman sought out Torre behind the batting cage during batting practice.

"I'm sorry," Cashman said. "I had nothing to do with it."

"I'm pissed about the timing of it," Torre said. "We don't need this."

Said Torre, "At that point I knew I wasn't coming back, even if we won."

———

All things considered, Torre did a fairly good job concealing his hurt and disappointment. The urgency of the Yankees' plight demanded his attention. It was up to Roger Clemens to save the franchise and the manager. Clemens was 45 years old, had not pitched in 20 days and, with his body betraying him, was staring at the possibility that this finally could be the last game he pitched in the big leagues—especially considering at that moment the two tons of dirt on him sitting on the desk of baseball's independent steroids investigator, George Mitchell. Even if the Yankees somehow managed to survive that game, the decision by Torre and Cashman to have Wang pitch two of the first four games looked far more suspect now that the Indians had hammered Wang in Game 1.

As the Yankees took batting practice before Game 3, Mussina walked over to Wang in the Yankee Stadium outfield.

"Can you pitch tomorrow?" Mussina asked him.

"No, **you** pitch tomorrow," Wang said.

"I didn't ask you that," Mussina said. "I said **can** you pitch tomorrow."

"Uh, yeah, I'm okay," Wang said.

Said Mussina, "He really didn't give me an answer. He was just kind of confused about the question. And then, 15 minutes later, they told him that he was going to pitch the next day. On three days of rest. I knew he was getting worn down. It was a long year. He had thrown a lot of innings. I knew he was worn down.

"The point is I know Joe would have been scrutinized to death if he had pitched me in Game 4 and I got beat. I still think I would have given us the best chance to win that day because I was rested. Wang wasn't. Wang had been beat up. I had had success against the Indians and it was a home game. Whether that would have made a difference or not in that game, I don't know. Just personally, I felt good about facing them."

To even get to a Game 4 the Yankees needed to survive a start from Clemens, who was a physical wreck, with hamstring and elbow woes, but who basically called his own shots. There was a game September 3 against Seattle, for instance, when Torre thought Clemens might consider not making the start because of his elbow trouble. Torre had Mussina standing by as an emergency starter. He left it up to Clemens.

"Roger insisted he could pitch," Torre said. "I must have asked him 10 times. I said, 'You know, you don't have to pitch this game.' And I know he's bullshitting me because he's bullshitting himself. He has this meeting with himself and he convinces himself that he can do this. He wills himself. So in getting that same point across to me, I'm still looking at this from the more rational side, so I'm still a little skeptical.

"It's like David Cone. You go to David Cone and ask him, 'Can you get this guy out?' And he goes, 'Yeah, I'll get him out.' He may have to pull a gun to do it, but whichever way he has to do it, he'll get him out. It gets to a point with certain guys, guys you've been around and trust, you know when they make that commitment they're going to do it. It may not be pretty, but they're going to get it done. So with Roger, you want to give him the responsibility, but you're sitting there thinking, I don't know why I let him do this. Then again, if I didn't let him do it, I'd be sitting there thinking, I wonder if he could have done it? It's one of those things where you second-guess yourself but you know there was no other way to do it."

In that September 3 game, Clemens lasted only four innings before the elbow pain forced him out. He gave up five runs and the Yankees lost to the Mariners, 7-1. Now Torre was rolling the dice on a creaky Clemens again, only this time with their season and the manager's job riding on it.

"There was no hesitation," Torre said.

Clemens never made it out of the third inning against the Indians. He needed to throw 59 pitches just to get seven outs. His hamstring fairly groaned in protestation when he tried to field a soft groundball near the mound in the second inning. His body was giving out. After that episode he told Torre, "Skip, I'll give you a signal if I can't do it."

Of course, a failing Clemens, still too proud, never gave the signal. He was laboring obviously when, already down 2-0, he walked the leadoff batter of the third inning. Torre told catcher Jorge Posada to talk to Clemens.

"Let me get this guy," Clemens said, referring to the next batter, Victor Martinez. Somehow, Clemens struck out Martinez. But Posada looked into the dugout at Torre and shook his head, signaling that Clemens was done. It was the last batter Clemens would ever face. Torre removed Clemens, replacing him with Phil Hughes, who would allow the third run to score. Clemens walked off for the final time, limping. He walked down the dugout steps gingerly, needing to hold a handrail to steady himself. His great career was over.

"It was pretty obvious he had to come out," Torre said. "You could tell just by watching him that he couldn't get the ball to do what he wanted it to do. He wasn't locating it. He always talks when he comes into the dugout, and he was talking that night about not being able to get the ball to behave the way it's supposed to.

"When you look back you say, 'Well, it was his age. What are you going to do?' The body just doesn't heal as quickly as you would want it to or used to. But no second thoughts. When you get to

the postseason a lot of it is emotions. It sort of over-
rides ability a lot of times."

Down 3-0, the Yankees rallied to win the game,
8-4. Hughes pitched 3⅔ innings of shutout ball.
The offense awoke. Still, the front office wasn't
happy about Torre using Chamberlain for two innings. The Yankees were leading 5-3 heading into
their at-bat in the sixth inning when Chamberlain
began throwing with the instructions that he would
pitch the seventh to protect the two-run lead. The
Yankees tacked on three runs in their at-bat. Chamberlain was already warming by then, so the best
course of action was to get him in the game, rather
than sit him down and risk having to get him up
again if Cleveland threatened. Chamberlain cruised
through the seventh inning in order on 16 pitches.

Now Torre had a choice: Did he pull Chamberlain to keep him strong for Game 4? If he did that,
then he would have given the eighth inning of a
must-win game to Kyle Farnsworth. And if Farnsworth wobbled even just a bit, Torre would have
to send Rivera into the game in the eighth inning,
which would limit his availability for Game 4. Torre
was not prepared to take that kind of gamble,
not with Farnsworth, especially not in an elimination game.

"I was trying to do whatever I could to stay away
from Mariano to have him for two innings the next
day," Torre said. "Chamberlain got through the seventh with the low pitch count. Now my choice is to

go with someone else in the eighth, but if I don't get a clean inning, then I've got to get Mariano up, which was the one thing I was trying to avoid. I guess I never really had enough trust in everybody else down there to think that getting three outs in that spot is so simple."

Chamberlain stumbled in the eighth. He gave up a run while needing 22 pitches to get through it. Rivera breezed through the ninth inning in order, needing only 10 pitches. Torre's plan had worked. He won the game and got to a Game 4 with his best pitcher, Rivera, fresh and available for two innings. Chamberlain, freed from the "Joba Rules," still could come back with one inning. If the Yankees could win the first six innings of Game 4, Torre felt Chamberlain and Rivera, barring another biblical-like plague, could get the final nine outs to bring the Yankees to a Game 5, when each would be re-freshed by a day of rest from an off day after Game 4. Some members of the front office, though, saw that Chamberlain had thrown 38 pitches in an 8-4 game and shook their heads.

Once again, after the game, Torre was forced to talk about his job status.

"The only thing I try to do," Torre said at his press conference, "is allow my players to roll the dice out there and play, because every time we go to postseason there's nothing that's going to satisfy anybody unless you win the World Series. And that's very difficult. Those are very difficult situations for the players to play under. I understand the requirements here, but the players are human beings, and it's not machinery here. Even though they get paid a lot of money, it's still blood that runs through their veins. And my job is to try to get them to be the players they are by, you know, allowing them to understand that the best effort you can give is all you can do."

His words seemed for the consumption of Cashman, Steinbrenner and Steinbrenner's cabinet as much as for the assembled media in front of him. It had been another long day in a long season: the shocking Steinbrenner win-or-be-gone mandate, which was more proof his bosses no longer trusted him, the focus on his job security, the sight of Clemens hobbling off the mound for what this time really did look like the end to his career . . . to the very end, even victory exacted a toll.

It was the 1,249th win with the Yankees for Torre, including postseason play, over 12 seasons. It would be the last.

———

The last game of the Torre Era began with a wish, a sort of last request, which seemed fitting because Torre delivered it in the maze of narrow hallways in the basement of Yankee Stadium, which at times like these had the feel of catacombs winding darkly toward the gallows. Torre was walking to his usual pregame news conference before Game 4 with

Phyllis Merhige, senior vice president of club relations for Major League Baseball.

"I hope we win the World Series this year," Torre told her, "so I can tell them they can shove this job up their ass."

There was no hiding the hurt. Three years of growing distrust from his employers had culminated with Steinbrenner taking a shot at him out of the blue, and with his team down to its last breath, no less. Torre didn't know O'Connor was telling people he had kept dialing Steinbrenner on his own accord in search of a story. "It sounded like somebody set it up," Torre said, referencing people close to Steinbrenner, "especially knowing where George was at that time with his health. People couldn't get to George all year. It looked like it had other fingerprints on it. Of course, I was probably gun-shy at that point, anyway.

"I said what I said before Game 4 because I didn't want to come back with that whole attitude of distrust in place. It was all stuff that seemed contrived. I can't stand living like that, where people are looking for ways to trick you. If you don't want somebody around, just tell them."

The end held little drama. It was 87 degrees when the game began, the hottest October 3 in the recorded history of New York. Wang, pitching on short rest, was even worse than he was in Game 1. The first batter hit a home run. The third batter singled and the fifth batter singled, accounting for a

2-0 Cleveland lead. In the second inning, the lead-off batter singled and so did the next batter. Wang hit the next batter with a pitch. Torre had seen enough. Wang had faced nine batters and retired only three of them. He left the bases loaded for Mike Mussina, who allowed two of those runners to score before pitching out of the inning. Wang, already tagged for a playoff-record-tying eight earned runs in Game 1, became only the 10th starting pitcher in postseason history to lose an elimination game while failing to get more than three outs.

The gamble to pitch Wang twice in four games blew up on Torre and Cashman. Mussina, who had wanted the ball and who had described Wang as worn down heading into that start, pitched decently in relief, allowing two runs over 4⅔ innings.

"They stayed off pitches that other teams swing at," Torre said about how the Indians battered Wang. "I think he maybe tried too hard, tried to do too much."

Said Bowa, "You could have the greatest manager in the world, but if your ace gets rocked in two playoff games and it's best out of five, you're in trouble. You're in deep shit. That's what happened. Now, I still say that if we win that one game, the Joba game with the bugs, we beat them."

The Yankees had an early chance to recover from Wang's miserable start. They put runners at first and second with one out in the first inning, whereupon Alex Rodriguez whiffed on three pitches from soft-tossing journeyman pitcher Paul Byrd. Rodriguez did hit a home run later—with nobody on base in the seventh inning and the Yankees losing 6-2.

The Yankees batted .228 in the series. They did hit seven home runs, but six of them came with nobody on base. Abreu, Jeter, Giambi and Rodriguez, four of the nine highest-paid players in the game, batted a combined .238. Rodriguez was, again, particularly dreadful, especially in the big spots, failing to drive in a single run but for his cosmetic solo home run in Game 4.

The team with the $61 million payroll dominated the team with the $190 million payroll. The team with 13 past and future All-Stars crushed the team with 26 past and future All-Stars. Was it a fluke, another casualty of the randomness of a short series? No. It was an affirmation that the rest of baseball, fortified by increased revenues and smarter business practices, had chipped away at the competitive advantage the Yankees had enjoyed because of resources alone, and the Indians were at the front of that wave.

Cleveland, for instance, cut the gap on the Yankees with their attention to detail on medical and health issues. In 2007, the Indians lost only 324 player days to the disabled list—the fewest in the league and second fewest in baseball—while paying a total of just $4.3 million to players who were physically unable to play. Over the previous three seasons, the Indians ranked number one in baseball in fewest days lost to the disabled list. They were the best at keeping their players on the field, a huge factor for lower-payroll teams who could not afford the depth to withstand injuries.

The Yankees, meanwhile, were abysmal when it came to age and injuries. They flushed away $22.22 million on players who couldn't play, or almost 12 percent of their bloated payroll. They lost 1,081 player days to the disabled list, more than three times as many down days as had the Indians. Over the previous three seasons, the Yankees ranked 23rd in baseball in days lost to the disabled list, a trend that would continue in 2008.

The 2007 Division Series was the continuation of a downward spiral for the Yankees. The more they tried to recapture the magic of the dynasty, the more money they spent on acquiring players from outside the organization, most of whom did not bring a winning pedigree. And the more they focused on patching holes with veterans from winter to winter, the more they lost sight of the importance of a farm system. And the more they needed those veterans, particularly when it came to pitching, the fewer good options were available, as the rest of baseball, armed with new revenues and new intelligence to help evaluate player value, held on to their prime assets rather than lose them to big spenders such as the Yankees.

That new paradigm was particularly evident in

October when the Yankees no longer had any power pitchers in their prime to match up against the better teams in the league. In their dynasty the Yankees could match up their number four starter, be it a young Andy Pettitte or Orlando Hernandez or David Cone or Roger Clemens, against an opponent's number one starter and still feel good about the matchup. No matter how their rotation fell, the Yankees never were disadvantaged. But in their downward spiral the Yankees kept sending to the mound broken-down pitchers or pitchers who could not throw the ball past hitters with any consistency.

In Torre's final 17 postseason games, his starters were 2-8 with a 6.36 ERA while averaging only 4⅔ innings and three strikeouts per start. In the last six games in which the Yankees faced playoff elimination, Torre's starting pitchers were a broken-down Kevin Brown, seven-game-winner Shawn Chacon, a broken-down Mike Mussina, a broken-down Jaret Wright, a broken-down Roger Clemens and sinker-ball specialist Chien-Ming Wang on short rest.

The demise of the Yankees was a thick stew of multiple ingredients, but the main one, the one that gave it its most distinctive flavor, was the inability to develop or acquire starting pitchers with prime stuff that could make hitters swing and miss. Strikeouts are a quick and easy barometer of the quality of a pitcher's stuff. The most damning statistic to quickly explain what happened to the Yankees is that in the seven years after the Yankees last won the World Series, their starting pitchers, without exception, were worse every year at striking out batters than they had been the year before (while generally throwing fewer and fewer innings, shifting more of the workload to the bullpen). Every year without fail they suffered through a diminution of pure stuff. They were a franchise leaking oil. Here is the steady plummet in their starting pitchers' strikeouts:

NEW YORK YANKEES STARTING PITCHERS (2001–07)

YEAR	W-L	ERA	IP	SO/9 IP
2001	64-48	4.34	974.1	7.79
2002	79-41	4.34	1024.2	7.32
2003	83-42	4.02	1066	6.91
2004	70-46	4.82	942.1	6.55
2005	70-51	4.59	965.1	6.11
2006	74-42	4.54	933.2	5.84
2007	65-47	4.57	921	5.61

"You need that dominant number one starter," Jason Giambi said. "That's what you need, especially in a short series. You need to change the tide. Quick. Because if you're down, even 0-2, if you have that big guy to come back and win that big one, now it's up for grabs.

"You need guys who can strike guys out. You need big punchouts. You're not going to play those

9-8 games anymore in the postseason. You need to win 3-2, 2-1, and be able to match up against the other team's big guys. You need big outs, big punch-outs. Guy on second base, two outs. You can't have the ball put in play, where it's putting pressure on you every inning. You need to get out of that inning sometimes without having to make a play.

"And really, in that regard, we had a role reversal with the Red Sox. Until they got Schilling to go with Pedro, we could beat them. Then once they got that extra power guy, that's what kind of turned the table for them. Then they went and got Beckett. That's where they turned the tide on us."

From 2001 through 2007, the best young strike-out pitchers never reached the free agent market to become available to the Yankees, such as Mark Prior, Kerry Wood, Johan Santana, Jake Peavy, Carlos Zambrano, CC Sabathia and Brandon Webb. The swap of Ted Lilly, a gutsy strikeout pitcher if not an ace, for Jeff Weaver, a sinkerballer with questionable makeup, was a criticalmistake. And when the Yankees did acquire a hard thrower in his prime, Javier Vazquez, they somehow saw the worst of him and punted him after just one year.

What made their search for a power pitcher all the more desperate was that their draft and player development system went bankrupt when it came to homegrown pitchers. In the 13 drafts in between taking Andy Pettitte in 1990 and Phil Hughes in 2004, the Yankees drafted 397 pitchers. Not one of

them made a significant contribution to the Yankees' rotation. Not one. No sleeper pick came
through. No top pick panned out. No middle-
round pick developed that one pitch or made that
key adjustment to be a good starting pitcher for the
Yankees. The odds were staggering that the Yankees
could not hit on **somebody,** even by dumb luck,
but that's what happened. With more resources to
plow into scouting and development than every
other franchise, the Yankees went 0-for-397 over
more than a decade of pitching bankruptcy.

With each year the Yankees spiraled further
downward from their last World Series championship, the more frustration and distrust bubbled from
within the organization, with the manager taking
the brunt of it. And while all of this was happening, the team's most dynamic asset, George Steinbrenner, was fading into a sad personal twilight,
physically unable to provide leadership when the
franchise most needed it. "Lead, Follow or Get
the Hell Out of the Way" read the sign that for
three decades sat on his desk at Yankee Stadium. The
charismatic man could no longer lead or follow, so
he was consigned to getting the hell out of the way,
which created an enormous void and, at best, un-
certainty in the power structure of the team.

With their advantage in resources, the Yankees
would be virtually unbeatable if they ran a clean,
efficient and self-sustaining organization. When
other teams smelled chaos there, however, they

knew they had a chance. The Yankees had rivals and enemies throughout baseball, but their greatest threat came from within.

"We're counting on there being dysfunction in other places that have greater resources," said Shapiro, the Indians' general manager. "And is that going to make the difference? No. But it's a hundred different little things that together hopefully will."

———

By Game 4 of the American League Division Series, the Indians had turned "a hundred different little things" into an advantage over the Yankees. They had the better team, and it was there for all to see on that weirdly warm night at Yankee Stadium. With one out in the top of the eighth inning, only six outs left in his tenure as Yankees manager, Joe Torre walked to the mound to make his last pitching change, removing Jose Veras and bringing in Mariano Rivera for the last time. As Torre walked off the mound toward the dugout, something spontaneous and touching happened. The crowd started chanting his name in the way that had become the official Yankee Stadium salute, the way the fans chanted for Paul O'Neill at the end of World Series Game 5, knowing how it would be O'Neill's last game at The Stadium. **Joe Tor-re! Joe Tor-re! Joe Tor-re!**

In the back row of the press box, a Yankees official, one of the voices who had Steinbrenner's ear, heard the outpouring of support for Torre from

Yankees fans, and, with a stunned look, could muster only two words: "Holy shit." This was not good for the voices. They didn't like the fact that Torre was liked.

It was 11:38 p.m. when the end came. Jorge Posada swung and missed at a pitch from Cleveland closer Joe Borowski for the final out of a 6-4 Yankees loss. It was the last pitch of the last postseason game ever played at Yankee Stadium.

Borzello, the bullpen catcher who had been there through the entire Torre Era, took that long walk from the bullpen, across that great big outfield, across the infield and toward the Yankees dugout on the first base side. He made sure he looked up and gazed around the cathedral one last time.

"I knew this was it," Borzello said. "I knew Joe wasn't coming back. And then I saw Paul O'Neill, who was standing there by the dugout, working for the YES network, and he goes, 'Tough series, Borzy.' I looked at him and I realized how much things had changed. And I almost wanted to cry."

As the Yankees trudged into the clubhouse, Torre called them together one last time under his command. He spoke briefly, with little emotion, and never addressed his own situation.

"Guys, sometimes you can try your best, give it everything that you can, and it's just not supposed to happen," Torre said. "We just weren't good enough. I'm proud of what you did. You dug yourselves out of a hole and learned what it takes to be a team."

Torre made his way through the catacombs to the interview room for one last news conference. Of course, he was asked what he thought would happen to him next.

"This has been a great 12 years," he said. "Whatever the hell happens from here on out, I mean, I'll look back on these 12 years with great, great pleasure, based on the fact that I'm a kid who had never been to the World Series, other than watching my brother play in the '50s, and paying for tickets otherwise. To have been in six World Series and going to postseason, I can tell you one thing, it never gets old. It never gets old. It's exciting. The 12 years just felt like they were 10 minutes long, to be honest with you."

The news conference was being broadcast on the stadium monitors. Torre's coaching staff was gathered in his office, standing there in front of the television, listening to the manager say his goodbyes. They knew he was gone.

When he left the news conference he returned to the clubhouse, where players were speaking in whispers, trading hugs and handshakes. The room had the pall of a funeral. Cashman walked into Torre's office. They had been together for 12 years, but they were strangers in that room. Cashman couldn't find the right words. It was as if they were standing on the same train platform, and Cashman knew Torre was on the next train out of town but that he was staying.

"He looked uncomfortable," Torre said. "He didn't know what to say. He later admitted to me that he was uncomfortable. I don't even know what he said."

One by one, most of the players stopped by to say thanks or goodbye to Torre. Pettitte . . . Clemens . . . Jeter . . . Mussina. . . . Chamberlain . . . Chamberlain was crying when he came in to say goodbye to Torre.

Asked if he assumed Torre would not be back, Mussina said, "Oh, yes. Those of us that are older, we knew they weren't treating him very well. I talked to him. It was only about 15 seconds. Everybody was talking to him, especially the guys that had been with him for a long time." Ever the optimist, Jeter thought his manager still was coming back in 2008.

Rodriguez never did come by to see his manager. (He would be named the Most Valuable Player one month later, prompting a congratulatory message from Torre. Rodriguez never called him back.) Rodriguez was one of the last players to emerge from the back rooms of the clubhouse to make himself available to the media. He was already showered and dressed when he stood at his locker and answered questions without any emotion.

"At the end of the day my job is to help the team

win a championship," Rodriguez said. "I have failed at that. Whatever blame you want to put on me is fair."

Rodriguez had the contractual right to opt out of his contract. The Yankees had declared very publicly on more than one occasion that should he elect to tear up his contract and seek a new one through free agency, they would not so much as negotiate with him. One Yankees official said no less than an hour after the Game 4 loss that they figured it would take $300 million to get Rodriguez signed to a new deal, and they already had developed a backup plan: trade for pitcher Johan Santana of the Twins. The Yankees could take **half** of the money it would have taken to keep A-Rod and give it to Santana, the lefthanded ace, who at 28 years old and as a three-time strikeout champion who had whiffed more than one batter per inning over the length of his career, was exactly the kind of pitcher the Yankees had needed for years. Rodriguez left Yankee Stadium that night not knowing if he would wear the Yankees uniform ever again.

Torre was much more certain. He showered, dressed and left his office and the clubhouse believing this would be the final time he would do so as manager of the New York Yankees. He did not look back.

16.

The End

"Do you want me to manage?"

Joe Torre began the meeting with that simple question. They were sitting in the Legends Field office of George Steinbrenner. There was a time, and as recently as only 24 months earlier, when Torre could look The Boss in the eye and propose that question and he would get an answer that would let him know exactly where he stood. But Steinbrenner wasn't The Boss anymore; he was the aging patriarch of a seven-man tribunal. His family members and front office lieutenants went through the exercise of playing to tradition and formality, anyway. Steinbrenner sat at his desk and the others sat at the table that ran lengthwise away from his desk. There was Torre, of course, and Steinbrenner's two sons, Hank and Hal, his son-in-law, Felix

Lopez, team president Randy Levine, chief operating officer Lonn Trost, and general manager Brian Cashman, who sat behind Torre's right shoulder.

On October 18, 2007, ten days after the Yankees lost the Division Series to Cleveland, ten days of public waiting for Steinbrenner to follow through on his Game 3 warning that Torre would not be back in the wake of defeat, the question Torre proposed was now the domain of the seven other people in the room. Steinbrenner sat slumped in his chair with dark glasses covering most of his face. Occasionally he would take them off, put them back on, take them off, put them back on . . . He contributed virtually nothing to the meeting except for occasionally simply repeating the last sentence of what someone in the room had just said.

The strange, sad element to the setting was that the men were surrounded by old reminders of Steinbrenner's vitality and iron will to win. Steinbrenner always had envisioned himself as a cross between a Hemingway character and a military leader, a man's man who gave no quarter, who boasted of bringing a football mentality to baseball, and the room reflected his pride in such obstinence. On a table behind him there was a picture of him as a halfback on the 1951 Williams College football team, reaching for a pass while a defensive back from Ball State elbows him in the back. Steinbrenner liked to tell people that he did not catch the ball, that the Ball State defensive back "knocked me

684 JOE TORRE AND TOM VERDUCCI

flat on my ass." The man, he wanted you to know, could take a hit.

There was a picture of the horse Comanche. Why Comanche? Steinbrenner liked the idea that the horse was the only survivor of Custer's last stand. He admired survivors. There was also a picture of General George S. Patton, given to him by a member of Patton's staff. It was not your typical military portrait. Patton is seen pissing into the Rhine. There was a picture of his grandfather, George M. Steinbrennner the first, who married a girl from Germany and who started the Kinsman Shipping line of freighters, which carried ore and grain over the Great Lakes.

Of course, there were the aphorisms with which Steinbrenner literally liked to surround himself. Some of them were captured in frames and some of them were kept under the glass top of his desk.

"The measure of a man is the way he bears up under misfortune. Plutarch."

"And do not go where the path may lead. Go instead where there is no path and leave a trail. Ralph Waldo Emerson."

"You can't lead the cavalry if you can't sit in the saddle."

"The speed of the leader determines the rate of the pack."

And his favorite:

"I am wounded but I am not slain. I shall lay me

down and rest a while and then I will rise and fight again. Anonymous."

Times were different now. For Steinbrenner, it was time to rest, not time to fight. This was his office, but it was not his meeting. It was not his decision alone, anymore.

The meeting was Torre's idea. Hank, Hal, Felix, Levine, Trost and Cashman had kicked around the idea of what to do about Torre for the better part of a week. Do they offer him another contract and, if so, for how long and for how much money? Do they even want him back at all? While they deliberated, Torre told Cashman he wanted to meet with the group face-to-face. It wasn't much different from how he managed: you look somebody in the eye and rely on direct honesty, rather than leaks and secondhand information. The six Yankee lieutenants thought it was a good idea. By then they had decided that they would offer Torre nothing more than one guaranteed year.

The day before the meeting, as the two sides finalized arrangements for the meeting, Cashman broke the news to Torre that he probably would not do any better than a one-year offer.

"They only want to give you one year," Cashman told him over the phone.

"What about a second year?" Torre asked.

"I don't think they're going to offer you that."

"Cash, I have an idea. What about a two-year

contract? It doesn't even really matter what the money is. Two years, and if I get fired in the first year, the second year is guaranteed. But if I get fired after the first year, I don't get the full amount of the second year, just a buyout. The money doesn't matter. I mean, as long as it's not just something ridiculous. It's not about the money. It's the second year."

Torre had just gone through the toughest year of his career, what with the leaks, the sniping, the constant talk about getting fired, and the feeling that people within his own organization were rooting against him. He was worn-out by all of that. There was no way he was going to go through another season like that. And there was one scenario that would have set the table for exactly that kind of season all over again: working under a one-year contract. That scenario would stamp him a lame duck all over again, with the leaks and sniping and managerial death watch starting up again upon the first three-game losing streak in April.

All Torre wanted was to manage one more season in relative calm, and the second year on a contract would help provide that kind of stability. The second year was nothing but an insurance policy. He planned to retire after that one season, anyway.

"I couldn't do it on a one-year deal," Torre said. "I couldn't go through what was the worst year of my professional life all over again. I couldn't put my family through it again. I couldn't put my coaches through that again. All I wanted was one year where nobody is questioning me about how you're going to lose your job."

———

On October 18, Torre, Cashman and Trost boarded a private jet in Westchester, New York, for the flight to Tampa. He had told his coaches that he wasn't sure what was going to happen.

"I knew at the time I thought it was going to be 60/40 that he wouldn't come back," third-base coach Larry Bowa said. "You know, Joe kept everything pretty quiet. He said, 'I'll get in touch with you guys.' Selfishly, I wanted him to come back because I loved coaching there, but he had to do what he had to do. Coming back on a one-year deal would not be fair to him or the players, because he would have been gone quickly. No question.

"For a guy with what he's done for the city and that team, that's the one thing I thought was very unfair. I don't think he was treated the right way. I mean, I think Joe earned the right to go out on his own, and he should have earned the right to open that new stadium. At least they should have said, 'Okay, this year we'll give you, and for the new stadium you have an option if you want to stay or not, or go upstairs and be an adviser.' I really thought that was going to happen because of what Joe meant to the city, the players that played there and to the organization. And it didn't happen like that. It turned out to be an ugly ending."

On the plane ride to Tampa, Cashman repeated his warning to Torre about the length of the contract, again choosing a pronoun carefully as if to distance himself from what was about to go down.

"I don't think they're going to go to more than one year," Cashman said. "What are you going to do then?"

"I don't know," Torre said. "I don't know what I'm going to do. I'm just going to go in there."

Torre was putting his faith in the power of personal communication, anticipating that a face-to-face meeting with the lieutenants would bring about an honest negotiation. He held out hope that there was a way to manage the Yankees in 2008 without his head in a noose from the first day of spring training. The first thing he needed to know was if they really wanted him in the first place.

"Do you want me to manage?"

Levine and Hal told him that yes, they wanted him back, and it was a unanimous decision by everyone in the room. Hal said they had decided on an offer: a one-year contract at $5 million, a 33 percent pay cut from his 2007 salary. Hal told him, "I want you to manage because you're good with young players." Torre wondered why, if that were the case, they were offering only one year.

If the Yankees reached the postseason, Torre would get another $1 million. He would get another $1 million if the Yankees reached the League Championship Series and another $1 million if they reached the World Series. Levine classified the bonus money as "incentives," implying at the meeting and later to reporters that Torre needed to be motivated. "It's important to motivate people," Levine would later tell reporters, "as most people in everyday life have to be, based on performance."

Motivate? The 2007 Yankees had come back from the sixthworst 50-game start in franchise history to make the playoffs. They had used 14 different starting pitchers—no Yankees team except the wartime 1946 team ever needed more—and yet they still won 94 games. They roared back from a losing record as late as July 7 to play .675 baseball down the stretch (52-25). Three-fifths of their original rotation was a disaster—Kei Igawa and Carl Pavano combined for three wins, and Mike Mussina endured the worst season of his career—and yet they won the third-most games in all of baseball.

Did Torre help accomplish all of that and then suddenly lose his motivation during, of all times, the playoffs? Or did the Yankees' exit have something to do with their ace throwing two of the worst games in postseason history and a freakish attack of Lake Erie midges?

Torre would later tell reporters he considered the incentives "an insult." In doing so, he was not referring to the idea of incentives or the money itself, but rather to the thinking of the Yankees executives that he needed such a carrot to be "motivated."

"I don't need motivation to do what I do," he

told the Yankees executives at the meeting. "You have to understand that."

Said Torre, "I've always had a $1 million bonus for winning the World Series. In fact, in my last contract, when we put it together, Steve Swindal and myself, we had different stages, if you win-win-win. That's the way it was when I took over initially, even in my first year, that you got so much for getting to different levels. I said then, 'Let's admit it: the only thing that's worthwhile is the World Series. The only bonus I want you to put in there is the World Series.'"

———

As much as Torre was bothered by the idea that he needed incentives to be motivated, what really stopped him was the term of the contract. Sure, maybe the seven executives in the room did want him back, but they wanted him back only in the exact compromised position in which he had managed the 2007 season: with a noose around his neck and a trapdoor below his feet. They wanted him to manage the Yankees only from an exposed position.

There was no way Torre was coming back under those conditions again, not when he knew it meant being put in the crosshairs of being fired and undermined from Day One. The seven executives, meanwhile, would consider no other arrangement but that one.

"Going back to the first question I asked—'Do

you want me to manage?'—the answer they gave me really wasn't honest," Torre said. "They said they wanted me to manage. If they wanted me to manage, we would have found a way to get it done. And that was never the case. Because there was never any movement. Negotiation is something that takes place between two sides. That didn't happen. It was, 'Either take it or leave it.' And my feeling was that only because I was here so long that they felt they were obligated to make an offer."

Torre calmly tried to make a case for himself. For instance, he pointed out that over the course of his tenure attendance at Yankee Stadium had skyrocketed 90 percent. The Yankees ranked in the middle of the pack in attendance in Torre's first year, in 1996—seventh of 14 teams, with 2.2 million fans. In 2007 the Yankees ranked first with 4.2 million fans. He talked about ad revenues he brought to the Yankees himself, from companies that wanted to be associated with one of the most successful managers in modern history. Under Torre, of course, the Yankees were a postseason guarantee: a perfect 12-for-12 in postseason appearances with pennants in half of those years and world championships in a third of them. The promise of October baseball helped drive season ticket sales and offered another month of revenues when most ballparks were dark. And even when Torre's teams did not win the World Series in the seven-year "drought," the Yankees were far and away the best team in baseball. In that

2001–2007 "drought," the Yankees were at least 37 wins better than every other team in baseball.

None of it meant anything to the seven other people in the room, not, anyway, in terms of even considering a second year.

"The reason I went there to Tampa," Torre said, "is I wanted to see somebody face-to-face, and I wanted to see if any of these points I brought up made any sense. I mean, where the attendance was when I first got there and where it was now, the revenues they've made since then . . . maybe all this stuff would somehow negate some of the fact that they felt I was overpaid and overstayed. Overpaid and overstayed. And then nobody had the guts to just say, 'Get out.' That was the worst part."

There would be no negotiations. When Cashman was asked later by reporters why the Yankees refused to negotiate, he said, "It's just complicated, given the dollars."

But dollars had nothing to do with it. Torre would even tell reporters later that the $5 million salary was "generous." He wasn't asking to negotiate dollars. He was asking to negotiate one year of some security and peace. The Yankees would have none of it, and when the seven executives made it clear to him that theirs was a take-it-or-leave-it offer, Torre understood the greatest pillar of his management style had been destroyed: the trust was gone. He knew his employers did not trust him. For a man who made trust the single most important ingredient of championship teams—trust among team-mates, trust from those players in the honesty and integrity of the manager and staff—he could not continue without it. It became an easy decision: he told the seven executives he could not accept their offer.

"Yeah, I was leaving a lot of money on the table," Torre said, "but I didn't give a shit because I knew what I went through the year before, sitting behind that desk every day and dreading coming to the ballpark. It would have been the same thing.

"I mean, if I could go right from my house to the dugout, it would have been wonderful. But that other shit I had to put up with, I didn't want any more of that, and there was no price tag I could put on that. I couldn't do it for all the money in the world for one year like that. And really, I only wanted to manage one more year, but I wanted to manage that one year in peace."

So that was it. The 12-year Torre Era had come to a nonnegotiable end. Torre's run as manager of the New York Yankees ended with a meeting that took little more than 10 minutes. As Torre got up from his seat in Steinbrenner's office, Hal Steinbrenner said to him, "The door's always open. You can always work for the YES network!"

Torre was too stunned to speak, caught between bemusement and anger. Did The Boss's son really just dangle the consolation of working for the Yankees-run regional television network after the

Yankees refused to negotiate with the second-winningest manager in franchise history? Wow, Torre thought. They really don't get it.

Torre shook the hands of everybody in the room, starting with George. The old man took his dark glasses off and said, "Good luck, Joe."

"Thanks again, Boss," Torre said.

Felix was the only one who walked out of the room with Torre toward the elevators in the reception area of the third-floor offices. But then Cashman appeared.

"Joe, Lonn and I won't be flying back with you," Cashman said. "We'll be staying here."

Seeing Cashman suddenly reminded Torre of something: that two-year proposal he made to Cashman over the phone in advance of the meeting, the one with the buyout in it. The offer never had been discussed in Steinbrenner's office. Torre figured Cashman already had presented it to the other executives, and he was curious as to what happened to the proposal.

"Cash," Torre said, "they had no interest in that buyout proposal, the one I gave you over the phone?"

Cashman looked at Torre oddly, as if this was something new.

"Uh, I really didn't understand it," Cashman said. "Remind me, what was it again?"

"Two-year contract, whatever the number. If they fire me during the first year, they pay me both years. If they fire me after the first year, they pay me some reduced amount we can talk about."

"I'll see."

Cashman walked back into Steinbrenner's office. Torre was incredulous.

"I'm thinking, Well, shit! He never told them!" Torre said.

They had spent 12 years together, Cashman first as the assistant to general manager Bob Watson and then as the general manager of three consecutive world championship teams with Torre as the manager. Torre had presented Cashman with the lineup card from the clinching game of the 1998 World Series, the one in which those Yankees established themselves as one of the greatest teams of all time with a record 125 wins, postseason included. Torre and Cashman had shared dinners and champagne and laughs and arguments. Twelve years. It was an eternity in baseball for an executive and a manager to work together for that long.

But at the moment when Torre was searching for some way to save his job, and when he turned to Cashman in his moment of need, Cashman did not so much as pass on to his bosses a proposal from Torre—a simple one, too, one that was not at all difficult to understand. Twelve years together, and it ends like this.

Come to think of it, Torre thought, Cashman had said **nothing** during the entire meeting. Cashman was the general manager who had convinced

Steinbrenner after the 2005 season to put in writing that he would have control over all baseball operations. The manager is a fairly important part of baseball operations. And when the future employment of the manager was being discussed, how was it that the empowered general manager had nothing at all to say?

"Cash was sitting right over my right shoulder," Torre said, "and never uttered a sound the whole meeting." Cashman, for his part, said simply, "It was Joe's meeting."

Only much later did Torre start to put the picture together of what had happened to his working relationship with Cashman. The personal fallout they had in 2006 spring training, Cashman's conversion to the religion of statistics, his disregard for bringing back Bernie Williams, his submission of odd lineup suggestions based on stats, his lack of regard for Ron Guidry as a pitching coach, his detachment from the responsibility "they" were making on an offer to Torre, his failure to offer any comment or support in the meeting to decide Torre's future, his failure to personally relay to the Steinbrenners Torre's proposal to find a way to reach an agreement . . .

Where could Torre find support in the end? Steve Swindal, thanks to one DUI charge, had been run out of the organization and the Steinbrenner family. George Steinbrenner was not fit enough to deal directly with Torre himself. And now Cashman had retreated to silence with Torre's job on the line. The allies of Joe Torre had dwindled to zero.

"I thought Cash was an ally, I really did," Torre said. "You know, we had some differences on coaches, and the usefulness of the coaches. I know he didn't think much of Guidry. And Zimmer. You know, Zimmer could not trust Cash, and I disagreed with Zimmer vehemently for the longest time. Then, you know, you start thinking about things . . . I have a—I don't want to say it's a weakness, but I like to believe that I want to trust people. And I do trust people until I'm proven wrong. And it's not going to keep me from trusting somebody else tomorrow because it's the only way I can do my job—is to be that guy."

Torre still held out faint hope that the two-year proposal could be the pathway to an agreement. He waited by the elevators.

"It was a last-ditch effort by me to remind them, 'Does this make any sense for us to get together?'" Torre said. "There weren't any cross words. I didn't say things to them in anger or anything. It was more like, 'If that's the way you want it, that's the way it is.' It was just trying to move a little bit and give them an offer that maybe they could live with. I just wanted to make sure before I did walk away from this thing that I gave them every opportunity to keep me."

Not more than 30 seconds after Cashman left Torre at the reception area, Cashman came walking back to him. It took less than a minute for the Steinbrenners, Levine and Trost to wholly reject the idea.

"No, they have no interest in doing that," Cashman told Torre.

No interest. Rejected in less than a minute. That was it. It was done. The Torre Era officially was finished. He stepped into the elevator and pushed the button for the ground floor. A strong feeling washed over him.

"Relief," Torre said. "A feeling of relief." The relief came from knowing it was a very easy decision. He flew back home alone.

Acknowledgments

Joe Torre

My heartfelt gratitude to George Steinbrenner for giving me the opportunity to accomplish something very special with his Yankees.

Arthur Richmond for suggesting to The Boss that he hire me.

A family of loving all-stars: my son, Michael, and his family; my daughters, Cristina and Lauren; my late brother, Rocco, and his dear wife, Rose; my mentor, brother Frank; my sisters, Rae and Sister Marguerite; my grandchildren, Kendra, Dylan, Talisa and Reed; all my nieces and nephews; my really cool late father-in-law, Big Ed Wolterman; and my equally cool mother-in-law, Lucille; plus Ali's 15 siblings and their children.

Joe Ponte, my best man and dear friend.

Katie, my very special sister-in-law.

C2 Matt Borzello, my childhood buddy, for being there, and here, and there, and here . . .

Joe Platania and Arthur Sando, my devoted friends, who are the Oscar and Felix of my life.

Billy Crystal, the former Yankee, for his enduring friendship.

Don Zimmer and Mel Stottlemyre, for being the greatest bookends any manager could ever have. I wouldn't have been able to do it without them.

Drs. Bill Catalona and Howard Scher, for getting me through some tough times.

Dal Maxvill, for getting me back in the game.

Chris Romanello, my assistant, for trying to keep me organized.

Maury Gostfrand, for continuing to be my go-to guy.

John Wooden, for teaching us all the principles of coaching.

George Kissell, for teaching me more about baseball than anyone.

Sonny, a treasured family friend.

My players and staff members, without whom it would not have been possible.

The fans, both those who cursed and those who cheered.

And, for everyone I forgot, thanks for understanding.

Tom Verducci

This book is many years and many opportunities in the making. The year of 1993, for instance, and the opportunity given me then by Mark Mulvoy of **Sports Illustrated** are most definitely embedded in these pages. Everyone needs someone to believe in them, and Mark believed in me. He hired me in 1993 to work at **Sports Illustrated,** which was and still is the most evolved form of sports writing to be found. Like a kid getting a roster spot on the 1998 Yankees, I learned and grew from being in the company of the very best, including all-stars such as Gary Smith, Jack McCallum, Rick Reilly and Richard Hoffer. Bill Colson, Mark's successor, was no less an important source of support for me.

Education and the importance of teamwork never stop. I am fortunate enough today to work for a wise and kind man named Terry McDonell, who understood the rigors of this project and generously afforded me the breathing room to confront them. I am indebted to his graciousness. Likewise, Chris Stone at **SI** was and remains the writer's best friend: a trusted editor who respects the difficulty and the art of telling stories with words. This book would not be possible without his counsel and understanding.

Heartfelt thanks, too, must be sent to David Bauer, Mike Bevans, Larry Burke, Paul Fichtenbaum, Rob Fleder, Dick Friedman, Damian Slat-

porters at **SI** whose influences are part of these
pages. The reporting in this book often reflects and
draws on my reporting and writing at **SI** in the
years of the Torre Era. Steroids and the Yankees
consumed many of my assignments at the magazine
in those years. Thanks, too, to Nate Gordon for not
just putting up with me pestering him for photos
while he was traveling the world, but also for coming through in the clutch.

I must also express my extreme gratitude for the
existence of websites such as baseball-reference.com
and retrosheet.org. Like cell phones, remote con-
trols and titanium drivers, I don't know how we
ever existed without them.

Special thanks go to the Yankee players themselves. The Yankees' clubhouse can be perceived as a
tightly closed society, but when you begin to understand the Yankees as people and not just ballplayers,
you start to understand who they are and catch
glimpses of their soul. I was fortunate enough to see
the kindness in almost all of them, though those
who went above and beyond a baseline of cooperation deserve special mention, including David
Cone, Johnny Damon, Jason Giambi, Derek Jeter,
Mike Mussina, Andy Pettitte, Jorge Posada and
Mariano Rivera.

Similarly, I have found the general managers,
owners and executives of major league teams to be
extraordinarily eager to discuss the sport we love,

and special thanks from that group must be accorded to Billy Beane, Theo Epstein, Bud Selig and Mark Shapiro.

The people who are most responsible for bringing this book to life were the ones I knew were there for me every day. David Black, my literary agent, believed in me long before I believed in myself. Every writer should be so lucky as to have a confidante like David in his corner, and not just because he knows the most fabulous places to eat lunch in New York. Bill Thomas, my editor at Doubleday, kept a cool head and sharp wit while up against an unforgiving production schedule and cruel economic times for the publishing industry and beyond. His enthusiasm for the project, especially as the pages came in, meant the world to me.

Of course, extra special thanks to Joe Torre. He gave this project far more than his name. He gave it his sincere care and attention, and for that I am extremely grateful. Above all, I thank him, as you should, for his unblinking honesty. What may be the last dynasty in baseball, and one of the most eventful eras in baseball history, has been illuminated by the honesty of a man who saw it all up close. Best of all, he knows only one way to share it: by telling the truth. He neither ran from the truth nor attempted to so much as bend it.

Finally, and most of all, I am thankful for the love and support from my wife, Kirsten, and our sons, Adam and Ben. I am incomplete without them, and having to give this book the time and attention it required often left me missing them. Kirsten, Adam and Ben, I am forever grateful for your understanding, but most of all, for your love.

Index

and downward spiral of
Yankees, 673
and evaluation of Yankee
pitchers, 616
and fans, 472
injuries/medical
treatments of, 300,
426, 428, 547
meltdown, 449, 472–474
and Mussina, 404, 448,
451
and pitching as central to
Yankees, 404–405
as quitting in middle of
game, 472–474
salary for, 100, 126
and Stottlemyre, 428
teammates relationship
with, 371, 451
temper and disposition
of, 388
Torre comments about,
428–429, 449–451,
474
and 2004 ALCS, 455,
461, 471
and 2004 games, 371,
426, 449–451
and 2005 games, 371
Wells compared with,
404
and Yankee culture, 371,
404, 426–427

and Yankee pitching
rotation, 404
Yankee signing of, 388
Burkett, John, 313, 319–
320, 328–329
Bush, George W., 223,
307
Bush, Homer, 74, 99

Cabrera, Melky, 502, 503,
505, 519, 585–586,
635
Cabrera, Orlando, 110,
264, 423, 424, 437
Cairo, Miguel, 413, 441,
442, 444
Caminiti, Ken, 166–167,
168–169
Cano, Robinson, 264,
476, 491, 501, 560,
561, 586, 606, 607
Canseco, Jose, 135, 136,
154
Canyon of Heroes, Yankee
parades in, 207
Carmona, Fausto, 639,
645, 646, 652, 653,
654, 655-658, 659
Cashman, Brian "Cash"
and Abreu signing,
501
and "abyss" of Yankees,
463, 471

Vazquez, Javier, 388, 451,
463, 616, 675
Vazquez, Juan, 403, 404,
426, 430, 448–449,
452, 455, 470, 479
Vizcaino, Luis, 191, 192,
571, 659

Wakefield, Tim, 308, 309,
337, 338, 417, 431,
457
the walk, 94
Walker, Todd, 288, 289,
313, 321–322
Wang, Chien-Ming, 265,
491, 570, 573, 586,
620, 630, 636, 637–
638, 662–663, 669,
670, 673
Watson, Bob, 3, 7, 8, 9,
60, 180–181
Weaver, Jeff, 72, 252–253,
305, 344, 345, 387–
388, 470, 479, 552,
616, 675
Wells, David "Boomer"
as Blue Jay, 99
book by, 151, 295–296,
304
brawls involving, 317
Brown compared with,
429
and Cashman, 99

and Clemens deal, 99,
101–102
and Cone, 69–71, 73, 91
and fans, 89, 101
fine for, 305
injuries/surgery of, 376
and Jeter, 56
leaves Yankees, 375, 405
as lying to Torre, 292–
293, 294
and media, 69, 305
Mussina comments
about, 295–296
and 1998 games, 69–70,
73, 74, 88–89, 91
and O'Neill, 56
Padres signing of, 403
perfect game of, 71, 101,
107, 125
popularity of, 101
quitting by, 304
rejoins Yankees, 291–292
and Rivera trade to
Tigers, 95
salary for, 403
and **Sports Illustrated**
cover, 305
as starting pitcher, 74
and Steinbrenner, 296–
298
and steroids/HGH, 151
talent of, 107, 295
Torre anger at, 69–70

About the Authors

Joe Torre played for the Braves, the Cardinals, and the Mets before managing all three teams. From 1996 to 2007, Torre managed the New York Yankees. He is currently the manager for the Los Angeles Dodgers.

Tom Verducci is the senior baseball writer for **Sports Illustrated** and SportsIllustrated.com. He coauthored Joe Torre's first book, **Chasing the Dream,** and has also published an anthology of his work from **Sports Illustrated,** titled **Inside Baseball: The Best of Tom Verducci.**